Stochastic Drawdowns

Modern Trends in Financial Engineering

ISSN: 2424-8371

Series Editor

Tim Leung *(University of Washington, USA)*

Editorial Board

Farid AitSahlia *(University of Florida, USA)*
Kiseop Lee *(Purdue University, USA)*
Tim Leung *(University of Washington, USA)*
Kazutoshi Yamazaki *(Kansai University, Japan)*
Masahiko Egami *(Kyoto University, Japan)*
Olympia Hadjiliadis *(City University of New York — Hunter College, USA)*
Liming Feng *(University of Illinois-Urbana Champaign, USA)*
Matt Lorig *(University of Washington, USA)*

This new book series, Modern Trends in Financial Engineering, publishes monographs on important contemporary topics in theory and practice of Financial Engineering. The series' objective is to provide cutting-edge mathematical tools and practical financial insights for both academics and professionals in Financial Engineering. The modern trends are motivated by recent market phenomena, new regulations, as well as new financial products and trading/risk management strategies. The series will serve as a convenient medium for researchers, including professors, graduate students, and practitioners, to track the frontier research and latest advances in the field of Financial Engineering.

Published

Vol. 2 *Stochastic Drawdowns*
by Hongzhong Zhang

Vol. 1 *Optimal Mean Reversion Trading:*
Mathematical Analysis and Practical Applications
by Tim Leung and Xin Li

Forthcoming

Employee Stock Options: Exercise Timing, Hedging, and Valuation
by Tim Leung

More information on this series can also be found at http://www.worldscientific.com/series/mtfe

Modern Trends in Financial Engineering | Volume 2

Stochastic Drawdowns

Hongzhong Zhang
Columbia University, USA

World Scientific

NEW JERSEY · LONDON · SINGAPORE · BEIJING · SHANGHAI · HONG KONG · TAIPEI · CHENNAI · TOKYO

Published by

World Scientific Publishing Co. Pte. Ltd.
5 Toh Tuck Link, Singapore 596224
USA office: 27 Warren Street, Suite 401-402, Hackensack, NJ 07601
UK office: 57 Shelton Street, Covent Garden, London WC2H 9HE

Library of Congress Cataloging-in-Publication Data
Names: Zhang, Hongzhong, 1981– author.
Title: Stochastic drawdowns / Hongzhong Zhang (Columbia University, USA).
Description: New Jersey : World Scientific, [2018] | Series: Modern trends in financial engineering ;
 Volume 2 | Includes bibliographical references and index.
Identifiers: LCCN 2017053364 | ISBN 9789813141636 (hc : alk. paper)
Subjects: LCSH: Finance--Mathematical models.
Classification: LCC HG106 .Z43 2018 | DDC 332.01/51923--dc23
LC record available at https://lccn.loc.gov/2017053364

British Library Cataloguing-in-Publication Data
A catalogue record for this book is available from the British Library.

Copyright © 2018 by World Scientific Publishing Co. Pte. Ltd.

All rights reserved. This book, or parts thereof, may not be reproduced in any form or by any means, electronic or mechanical, including photocopying, recording or any information storage and retrieval system now known or to be invented, without written permission from the publisher.

For photocopying of material in this volume, please pay a copying fee through the Copyright Clearance Center, Inc., 222 Rosewood Drive, Danvers, MA 01923, USA. In this case permission to photocopy is not required from the publisher.

For any available supplementary material, please visit
http://www.worldscientific.com/worldscibooks/10.1142/10078#t=suppl

Desk Editors: V. Vishnu Mohan/Sylvia Koh

Typeset by Stallion Press
Email: enquiries@stallionpress.com

Printed in Singapore

To my family.

Preface

I was introduced to the subject of drawdown in 2009, when the S&P 500 lost 50% of its value since the outset of the US financial crisis in 2007. I was wondering if stochastic models could be used to provide comprehensive quantitative characterizations of the market crisis such as its magnitude, speed or durations, so that one could make effective risk assessments or design financial and insurance products in order to hedge against such risks in the future. Over the years, researches on stochastic modeling of drawdown have been developed by many scholars working on financial engineering, mathematical finance, and applied probability. This book is a subset of these advances that I have been involved in.

This book provides a systematic study on the probabilistic characteristics of drawdowns and their applications in hedging, insurance, and optimal trading. Using a first passage time approach, we mathematically investigate various aspects of drawdowns, which include the drawdown risk in finite time-horizons, the speed of market crashes/drawdowns, the frequency of drawdowns, the occupation time (time in distress), and the duration of drawdowns. Moreover, a number of applications of drawdowns in financial risk management, insurance and algorithmic trading are also discussed, such as schemes on hedging and synthesizing of maximum drawdown insurances, (cancellable) drawdown insurance contracts and their fair premiums, as well as optimal trading under drawdown-type constraints called trailing stops.

The purpose of this book is twofold. In the first place, we present analytical tools and results for rigorously analyzing drawdowns to graduate students, advanced undergraduate students, and researchers in financial engineering, mathematical finance, and applied probability, so as to stimulate new researches on drawdowns that are both mathematically interesting and practically important. In the second place, we offer risk management and algorithmic trading practitioners a variety of tractable drawdown measures for assessing risk, and a number of mathematically justified quantitative strategies for optimal trading and execution amid drawdown risks.

I would like to express my gratitude to several people who have helped make this book possible. The research conducted in collaboration with Peter Carr, David Landriault, Bin Li, Olympia Hadjiliadis and Tim Leung has contributed significantly to various chapters of the book. I have also benefited from valuable remarks and suggestions by Zhenyu Cui, Martin Forde, Andreas Kyprianou, Thomas Mikosch, Ryozo Miura, Zbigniew Palmowski, Jim Pitman, Libor Pospisil, Philip Protter, Neofytos Rodosthenous, Johannes Ruf and T. Shi.

Last, but certainly not least, I would like to express my special thanks to Rochelle Kronzek and Yulin Jiang of World Scientific for their assistance in finishing this book project.

Hongzhong Zhang

About the Author

Hongzhong Zhang is an Associate Research Scientist at Industrial Engineering and Operations Research Department of Columbia University. Prior to that, he was Assistant Professor at Statistics Department. He graduated from the PhD program in Mathematics Department at City University of New York in 2010. His research focuses on the broad area of applied probability with applications in engineering, finance and insurance. He is especially interested in study of drawdowns and their applications in financial engineering, actuarial sciences, and sequential change-point detection. His research has been published in journals such as *Annals of Applied Probability, Bernoulli, IEEE Transactions on Information Theory, International Journal of Theoretical and Applied Finance, Mathematics of Operations Research*, and *SIAM Journal on Control and Optimization/Financial Mathematics*.

Contents

Preface   vii

About the Author   ix

1. Introduction   1
   - 1.1 Chapter Outline 4
   - 1.2 Related Studies 8
   - 1.3 Notation 12

Part I   Drawdown Measures   15

2. Drawdowns Preceding Drawups in a Finite Time-Horizon   17
   - 2.1 Random Walk Model 18
   - 2.2 Brownian Motion with Drift Model 24
   - 2.3 One-Dimensional Linear Diffusion Model 28
     - 2.3.1 Analytical results 29
     - 2.3.2 Example: Brownian motion with drift 34
   - 2.4 Applications 35
   - 2.5 Concluding Remarks 38
   - 2.6 Proof of Lemmas 39

3. Drawdowns and the Speed of Market Crashes   41
   - 3.1 Mathematical Formulation and Analytical Results 43
   - 3.2 Progressive Enlargement of Filtrations by g_a 44
   - 3.3 Proof of the Main Results 46

	3.4	Applications	52
		3.4.1 Brownian motion with drift	53
		3.4.2 The CEV model	54
	3.5	Concluding Remarks	56
	3.6	Proof of Lemmas	56
4.	Frequency of Drawdowns in a Brownian Motion Model		59
	4.1	Preliminaries	61
	4.2	Sequences of Drawdown Times	63
		4.2.1 Drawdown times with recovery	63
		4.2.2 Drawdown times without recovery	66
	4.3	Numerical Results	74
	4.4	Insurance of Frequent Relative Drawdowns	74
	4.5	Concluding Remarks	78
	4.6	Proof of Lemmas	79
5.	Occupation Times Related to Drawdowns		81
	5.1	Definition of Occupation Times	83
	5.2	Analytical Results	84
		5.2.1 Occupation time below a level until the first exit time	84
		5.2.2 Occupation time below a level until the first passage of drawdown	85
		5.2.3 Occupation time of the drawdown process until the first passage of drawdown	86
		5.2.4 Occupation time of the drawup process until the first passage of drawdown	89
		5.2.5 Occupation time of the drawdown process at an independent exponential time	90
	5.3	Examples	91
		5.3.1 Brownian motion with drift	91
		5.3.2 Three-dimensional Bessel process (BES(3))	92
	5.4	Applications	93
		5.4.1 Probabilities regarding drawdowns and defaults	93
		5.4.2 Option pricing for the drawdown process	94
	5.5	Concluding Remarks	96
	5.6	Proof of Lemmas	96

6.	Duration of Drawdowns under Lévy Models		99
	6.1 Preliminaries		101
	6.1.1 Spectrally negative Lévy processes and scale functions		101
	6.1.2 The ascending ladder process of general Lévy processes		104
	6.2 Magnitude of Drawdowns Revisited		106
	6.3 Asymptotics of Magnitude of Drawdowns		107
	6.3.1 Spectrally negative Lévy processes		108
	6.3.2 A class of Lévy models with two-sided jumps		110
	6.4 Duration of Drawdowns		112
	6.4.1 Bounded variation case		114
	6.4.2 Unbounded variation case		118
	6.5 Examples		122
	6.6 Concluding Remarks		125
	6.7 Proof of Lemmas and the Extended Continuity Theorem		125

Part II Applications of Drawdown 131

7.	Maximum Drawdown Insurance Using Options		133
	7.1 Setup and Replicating Instruments		136
	7.2 Static Hedging of the K-drawdown Preceding a K-drawup with One-Touch Knockouts		139
	7.3 Semi-static Hedging of the Maximum Drawdown with One-Touch Knockouts		141
	7.4 Semi-static Replication with One-Touches		143
	7.4.1 Hedging the maximum drawdown		145
	7.4.2 Hedging the K-drawdown preceding a K-drawup		146
	7.5 Semi-static Replication with Path-Independent Options		148
	7.5.1 Hedging the maximum drawdown		150
	7.5.2 Hedging the K-drawdown preceding a K-drawup		151
	7.6 Static Hedging of the K-relative Drawdown Preceding a K-relative Drawup with One-Touch Knockouts		152

xiv   Contents

	7.7	Semi-static Replication with One-Touches in Geometric Models	153
		7.7.1 Hedging the maximum relative drawdown	155
		7.7.2 Hedging the K-relative drawdown preceding a K-relative drawup	159
	7.8	Semi-static Replication with Path-Independent Options in Geometric Models	162
		7.8.1 Hedging the maximum relative drawdown	164
		7.8.2 Hedging the K-relative drawdown preceding a K-relative drawup	165
	7.9	Poisson Jump Processes	167
		7.9.1 Arithmetic case	167
		7.9.2 Geometric case	169
	7.10	Concluding Remarks	172
	7.11	Proof for GBM	172
8.	Fair Premiums of Drawdown Insurances	175
	8.1	Model for Drawdown Insurance	176
		8.1.1 Drawdown insurance and fair premium	178
	8.2	Cancellable Drawdown Insurance	180
		8.2.1 Contract value decomposition	181
		8.2.2 Optimal cancellation strategy	182
	8.3	Incorporating Drawup Contingency	187
		8.3.1 The finite maturity case	187
		8.3.2 Perpetual case	189
	8.4	Drawdown Insurance on a Defaultable Stock	191
	8.5	Concluding Remarks	197
	8.6	Proof of Lemmas	197
9.	Optimal Trading with a Trailing Stop	203
	9.1	Model Formulation	204
		9.1.1 Standing assumption	207
	9.2	Optimal Trading with a Fixed Stop-Loss	208
		9.2.1 Optimal liquidation subject to a stop-loss exit	209
	9.3	Optimal Trading with a Trailing Stop	210
		9.3.1 Optimal liquidation	210
		9.3.2 Optimal acquisition with a trailing stop	214

9.4	Case Study: Trading with a Trailing Stop under the Exponential OU Model .	216
	9.4.1 Value function and optimal strategy	217
	9.4.2 Sensitivity analysis	220
9.5	Concluding Remarks	222

Appendix. Briefly on One-Dimensional Linear Diffusions   225

Bibliography   229

Index   239

Chapter 1

Introduction

Financial turmoils are most often marked with series of sharp falls in asset prices triggered by certain market events, with the recent examples of the S&P downgrade of US debt, and default speculations of European countries. Many individual and institutional investors are wary of large market drawdowns as they not only lead to portfolio losses and liquidity shocks, but also indicate potential imminent recessions. As is well known, hedge fund managers are typically compensated based on the fund's outperformance over the last record maximum, or the high-water mark. As such, drawdown events can directly affect the manager's income. Also, a major drawdown may also trigger a surge in fund redemption by investors, and lead to the manager's job termination. Hence, fund managers have strong incentive to seek insurance against drawdowns (see, e.g., Burghardt et al. (2003)).

Formally, the drawdown is defined as the difference between the present value X_t of a portfolio or asset and its running maximum $\overline{X}_t := \sup_{s \in [0,t]} X_s$. That is,

$$D_t := \overline{X}_t - X_t, \quad \forall t \geq 0. \tag{1.1}$$

Drawdowns provide a dynamic measure of risk in that they measure the drop of a stock price, index or value of a portfolio from its running maximum. They thus provide portfolio managers and commodity trading advisers a tool with which to assess the downside risk taken by a mutual fund during a given economic cycle. On the other hand, the maximum drawdown, which is defined as the running maximum of the drawdown process,

$$\overline{D}_t := \sup_{s \in [0,t]} D_t, \tag{1.2}$$

records the worst performance that could have happened in the past, and serves as an overall performance measure of the holding during a given period. To visualize the drawdown and the maximum drawdown processes, we illustrate in Figure 1.1 their sample paths for the S&P 500 index from January 3, 2000 to December 31, 2015.

Naturally, a prerequisite for controlling drawdown risks properly in practice is to understand them thoroughly. One popular probabilistic approach in study drawdowns is through probabilistic studies of the first passage time of the drawdown process, namely, for a given threshold $a > 0$, the stopping time defined as

$$\tau_D^+(a) := \inf\{t > 0 : D_t > a\}. \tag{1.3}$$

Probabilistic characterizations of $\tau_D^+(a)$ and other related quantities can provide investors information about drawdown risks from different angles. For instance, by $\{\tau_D^+(a) < T\} = \{\overline{D}_T > a\}$, one gets the distribution of the maximum drawdown $\overline{D}_T$ from the distribution of $\tau_D^+(a)$, and hence, the maximum drawdown or the downward momentum during an investment horizon can be assessed through relevant formulas for $\tau_D^+(a)$; by studying excursions of the underlying process below its maximum until $\tau_D^+(a)$, one obtains a measurement for the speed at which a large drawdown occurs.

On the other hand, protective means against a large drawdown of the underlying can be introduced by using the first passage time $\tau_D^+(a)$ as the indicator for the drawdown events. For instance, a portfolio manager who suffers from the loss of income due to large positive realizations of maximum drawdown may be interested in a contract that pays the holder $1 at the maturity if the maximum drawdown exceeds a pre-specified level. Such a contract can be considered as a digital options that pays either one dollar or zero at the maturity T, depending on whether the event $\{\tau_D^+(a) < T\}$ occurs or not.

Drawdown and its first passage time also play a meaningful role in trading practices to control/limit risks. In particular, a popular trade order called *trailing stops*, which is widely used by proprietary traders and retail investors to provide downside protection for an existing position, is to liquidate when the value of the existing position drops from its running maximum for more than a pre-specified percentage. While a trailing stop always limits the drawdown of the existing position capped, it is non-trivial to determine whether the investor can improve her expected payout from the trade by liquidating earlier. This motivates the investigation of the optimal

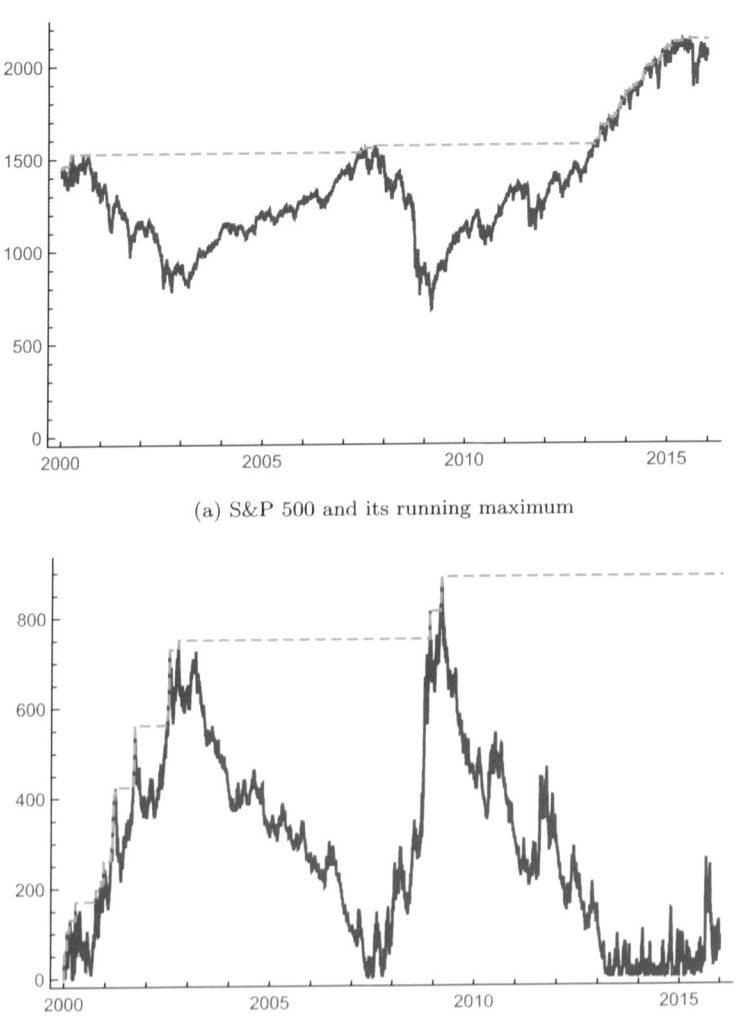

Fig. 1.1. (a) Plots of S&P 500 index (black) and its running maximum (gray dashed) from January 3, 2000 to December 31, 2015. (b) Plots of the drawdown process (black) and the maximum drawdown process (gray dashed) of S&P 500 index during the same period. These plots reveal that the market has experienced two major cycles in this period. Moreover, while it took about 7.5 years for the market to fully recover in the first cycle, it only took 5.5 years in the second cycle.

liquidation prior a trailing stop, and optimal timing for setup the position with a trailing stop.

In this book, we take the aforementioned first passage time approach to study drawdowns and address some practically important applications of drawdowns in financial engineering. Specifically, in Part I of the book, we study probabilistic properties of drawdowns in five aspects, namely, the finite time-horizon property, the speed, the frequency, the occupation times, and the durations, of drawdowns. Through Laplace transforms, we provide rigorous mathematical analysis and calculations for these quantities under diffusion models and Lévy models. In Part II of the book, we focus on applications in drawdowns, including replication of maximum drawdown options, fair evaluation of drawdown insurances, and optimal trading with a trailing stop. The objective of the book is to offer both researchers from academia and practitioners an overview of the state-of-art probabilistic research on drawdowns and a better understanding of the hedging and optimal trading amid challenges arise from drawdown risks.

1.1. Chapter Outline

We begin our journey to the subject of drawdown in Chapter 2, where we determine the probability that a drawdown of a units precedes a drawup of b units in a finite time-horizon. Formally, the drawup of a stochastic process $X.$ is defined as

$$U_t := X_t - \underline{X}_t, \quad \forall t \geq 0, \tag{1.4}$$

where $\underline{X}_t := \inf_{s \in [0,t]} X_s$ denotes the running minimum of $X..$ Thus, this probability assesses the relative strength of downside risk (drawdown) compared to upward momentum (drawup) over a finite time-horizon. To determine this probability, we first consider the simple case with equal-sized drawdown/drawup (i.e., $a = b$), and derive analytic formulas of this probability by drawing connections to the first exit problems under a simple random walk model and a Brownian motion with drift model. For the general case, we randomize the time-horizon with an independent exponential random variable — a technique known as Canadization, and reduce the probability of interest to the Laplace transform of the first passage time of the drawdown when it precedes a drawup. Using a classical approximation argument as in Lehoczky (1977), we derive analytical formulas for this Laplace transform under general linear diffusion models. Finally, we use Laplace inversion to evaluate the drawdown preceding drawup probability and the conditional density of the maximum relative drawup given a drawdown event, under a geometric Brownian motion (GBM) model.

Apart from the finite time-horizon properties of drawdowns and drawups, the issue of how fast a market crash occurred is also of vital importance to investors and portfolio or hedge fund managers. This motivates us to study the joint distribution of the drawdown and the speed at which it is realized in Chapter 3. In particular, we measure the *speed of market crash* by the time elapsed between the first passage time of the drawdown to level $a > 0$, $\tau_D^+(a)$, and the last reset time of the running maximum prior to that drawdown, $g_a := \sup\{t < \tau_D^+(a) : X_t = \overline{X}_t\}$. The analysis involves studying of the last reset time of maximum g_a, for which we make use of the technique of progressive enlargement of filtration and path decomposition at the random time g_a. By deriving the joint Laplace transform of g_a and $\tau_D^+(a)$, we provide the analytical basis for the pricing of financial claims based on the drawdown and its speed, which can be used to hedge against dramatic market crashes.

While sustaining downside risk can be appropriately characterized using the drawdown process and its first passage time, economic turmoil and volatile market fluctuations are better described by quantities containing more path-wise information, such as the frequency of drawdowns. In Chapter 4, we directly address the problem on the *frequency of drawdowns* by determining the probability distributions of two sequences of drawdown first passage times, depending on whether the maximum is revisited between these first passage times. These stopping times characterize the fluctuations of the underlying through consecutive drawdowns. We illustrate how our analytical formulas can be used for evaluating options written on the number of drawdowns in a given time-horizon.

The amount of time when the underlying price is in distress can characterize investment risks from a different angle. In Chapter 5, we propose to study a number of *occupation times* that are related to the drawdowns and drawups of a linear diffusion process. To that end, we derive analytical formulas for the Laplace transform of the occupation time of the underlying below a fixed threshold y upon leaving a given finite interval. We then use Lehoczky's approximation technique and progressive enlargement of filtration to extend these results to occupation times of the drawdown or drawup process. In special cases of drifted Brownian motion and three-dimensional Bessel process, our results imply that the occupation time of the drawdown process has the same distribution as the first passage time of the drawdown process. We also demonstrate how our analytical results can be used for computing probabilities of drawdown events under Omega default models, and for evaluation of Parisian-like or α-quantile options written on the drawdowns.

An alternative way to model the time under distress for an asset price is through the length of excursions from its running maximum process, namely, the amount of time it takes for the asset price to revisit the previous peak. Such quantities are of interest to investors who are more concerned about the *duration of drawdown* than the actual magnitude of drawdowns experienced. In Chapter 6, we study the duration of drawdown for a wide class of Lévy models, by deriving the distribution of a Parisian time of the drawdown process. Given a time threshold b, this Parisian time is defined as the first time when the underlying is continuously below the running maximum for more than b units of time. Our analysis makes use of renewal equations, weak convergence, asymptotics of the magnitude of drawdowns, and some recent work on the asymptotic analysis of the running maximum of Lévy process. We illustrate how our results can be applied to popular models including Brownian motion with drift, spectrally negative α-stable process, spectrally negative Gamma process, and Kou's jump diffusion.

Chapters 7–9 are dedicated to applications of drawdown and maximum drawdown in hedging, insurance and trading, respectively. As the building blocks for more sophisticated options on drawdown or maximum drawdown, in Chapter 7 we study two types of digital options written on them, namely, the digital call on drawdown preceding a drawup, and the digital call on maximum drawdown. Such options are of interest to an asset manager who knows in advance that her portfolio risk is being evaluated wholly or in part by the portfolio's maximum drawdown or drawdowns. To determine the fair value of these digital options, we aim to develop self-financing replicating portfolios with the least possible time instances in which trading/rebalance is involved. Using results in Chapter 2, we develop a static model-free replication of the former digital option with one-touch knockouts. By using reflection principle and the expansion of the Canadized option price, we also develop semi-static replication strategies for both digital options with gradually more liquid instruments such as one-touches or path-independent options. We demonstrate that these strategies are valid for models such as Black model, geometric Brownian motion (GBM) model and models obtained from their continuous time-changes.

Our study on drawdown insurance in Chapter 8 approaches the protection against drawdowns differently. In particular, we derive the fair premium for a drawdown insurance that delivers a fixed compensation upon an drawdown event. In order to provide the investor with more flexibility in managing the path-dependent drawdown risk, we also incorporate the right to terminate the contract early. We formulate an optimal stopping problem that aims to maximize the early termination premium. By using the principle of smooth pasting, we solve the associated variational inequality and identify the optimal cancellation strategy as a first passage time of the drawdown process, which subsequently determines the fair premium of the contract. Moreover, we expand our analysis of drawdown insurance contracts by incorporating a drawup contingency, and the default risk of the underlying — a feature absent in other related studies on drawdown, and studying their impacts to the fair premium.

Trailing stops are a popular trade order widely used by proprietary traders and retail investors to provide downside protection for an existing position. A trailing stop is triggered when the prevailing price of an asset falls below a stochastic floor, which is often a percentage of the running maximum. In contrast, a limit sell order can be considered as a selling order that is triggered when the asset price reaches some target. Whether an asset holder should passively wait until a trailing stop is triggered or sell the asset more aggressively with a limit sell order is a question that remains open. In Chapter 9, we address this question by deriving the optimal trading strategy when a trailing stop is imposed. We develop an analytical tractable framework with linear diffusion models, and identify the early exercising premium that an asset holder can get by trading aggressively. Our approach is to first derive some key technical results by solving an auxiliary optimal trading problem with a fixed stop-loss level. Then, we study the optimal exit strategy for selling the asset no later than the trailing stop, and prove that the early exercising premium is maximized when a limit sell order is placed in conjunction with the trailing stop. In order words, an asset holder should only trade passively if the key price target is not reached; otherwise, an immediate sell is optimal and better than waiting for the trailing stop. Different from the variational inequality approach we used in Chapter 8, our solution method is to demonstrate that a proposed stopping rule yields strictly positive "time value", then prove that the optimal continuation region cannot be larger than the one in the proposed stopping rule. Moreover, we also study the optimal entrance strategy for purchasing this asset and setting up the trailing stop. Using an exponential Ornstein–Uhlenbeck (OU) model, we numerically demonstrate our optimal trading strategy, and show that the optimal entrance region is of the form $(0, A)$, while the optimal exit region is (B, ∞) for $0 < A < B < \infty$.

1.2. Related Studies

In the applied probability literature, there has been a long history for studies on the magnitude and the first passage time of drawdown process. The Laplace transform of the first passage time of drawdown process was derived in Taylor (1975) under Brownian motion and subsequently in Lehoczky (1977) under a general linear diffusion process. Recently, this result has been extended to general time-homogeneous Markov process with jumps in Landriault et al. (2017b). Probabilistic properties of drawdowns under Brownian motions have been studied in Douady et al. (2000) and Graversen and Shiryaev (2000). Hu et al. (2015) computed the exact value of a negative moment of the maximum drawdown of the standard Brownian meander. Magdon-Ismail and Atiya (2004) and Magdon-Ismail et al. (2004) determined the distribution of the maximum drawdown of a Brownian motion with drift model, based on which they described another time-adjusted measure of performance based known as the Calmar ratio. An overview of drawdown-based performance measures and existing techniques for analysis of market crashes related to the drawdown and maximum drawdown can be found in Schuhmacher and Eling (2011) and Sornette (2003).

In Chapter 2, we study the probability that a drawdown precedes a drawup in a finite time-horizon. This chapter is based on Zhang and Hadjiliadis (2010) and part of Zhang (2015). The work extends the results in Hadjiliadis and Večeř (2006) and Pospisil et al. (2009) from a perpetual setting to a finite investment horizon. Relatedly, the joint distribution of the maximum drawdown and the maximum drawup of a drifted Brownian motion in an exponentially distributed time-horizon is studied in Salminen and Vallois (2007). The joint Laplace transform of the running maximum, the running minimum, and the earlier of the first passage times of the drawdown and drawup, is derived in Gapeev and Rodosthenous (2016a) under a diffusion-type model with path-dependent coefficients. The statistical modeling of drawdowns and drawups is also of practical importance, and we refer to the recent studies (Johansen, 2003; Leal and Mendes, 2005; Rebonato and Gaspari, 2006; Goldberg and Mahmoud, 2017), among others.

In Chapters 3 and 4, we respectively study the speed of market crash and the frequency of drawdowns. The work in Chapter 3 is based on Zhang and Hadjiliadis (2012a), where we derive the joint law of the last reset time of the maximum and the first passage time of the drawdown process. In our derivation we use the method of progressive enlargement of filtration developed in Jeulin and Yor (1978) and Jeulin (1980). A similar analysis using the excursion theory of spectrally negative Lévy models can be found in Mijatović and Pistorius (2012), who derived a sextuple formula for the joint Laplace transform of the first passage, the last passage times, the running maximum, the running minimum, and the overshoot of drawdown. Recently, Egami and Oryu (2015) and Ben-Salah *et al.* (2015) demonstrated the value of the speed of market crash in bank regulation and in insurance, respectively. In Chapter 4, we study the frequency of drawdowns under a drifted Brownian motion model. This chapter is based on Landriault *et al.* (2015b), where we determine the probability distributions for two sequences of drawdown first passage times. An extension of the work in Chapters 3 and 4 is done in Cui and Nguyen (2017), where the authors derived the joint Laplace transforms of the first passage time and the speed of market crash for a sequence of consecutive drawdowns.

The work on occupation times in Chapter 5 is based on part of Zhang (2015). Some classical results of occupation time for general linear diffusion processes using the Feynman–Kac representation and excursion theory can be found in Pitman and Yor (1999, 2003). Cai *et al.* (2010) provided Laplace transform-based analytical solution to pricing problems of various occupation time related derivatives under Kou's double exponential jump diffusion model. Landriault *et al.* (2011) and Loeffen *et al.* (2014) derived the Laplace transform for the occupation time before the first passage time or the first exit time under a spectrally negative Lévy model. These results are generalized to refracted Lévy models in Kyprianou *et al.* (2014). For recent studies on occupation time under diffusion models, we refer to Li and Zhou (2013) and Forde *et al.* (2013). Compared with the early work, our results in Chapter 5 specifically focus on occupation times that are related to the drawdown or the drawup process of a general linear diffusion process. An alternative formulation of the temporal dimension of drawdown risks using axiomatic approaches is done in Mahmoud (2017).

In mathematical finance, there has been an research interest in the excursion length of the underlying asset, through the study of Parisian barrier options, see the celebrated work of Chesney *et al.* (1995, 1997). Chesney and Gauthier (2006) considered the pricing of American-style Parisian option. Thereafter, the concept of Parisian time was adopted by insurance mathematics. Czarna and Palmowski (2011) and Loeffen *et al.* (2013) worked with a spectrally negative Lévy process to obtain representations of the so-called Parisian ruin probability that happens when surplus process stays below zero longer than a fixed amount of time. As an extension of the prior work, in Chapter 6 we derive the Laplace transform for the

Parisian time for the drawdown process, which is the first time the drawdown of the underlying stays above zero long than a fixed amount of time. This work is based on Landriault et al. (2017a). In contrast to early work, our method of solution is based on a perturbation approach that origins from Lehoczky (1977) and is further developed in Dassios and Wu (2010), Landriault et al. (2011), Li and Zhou (2013), Loeffen et al. (2013), Zhang (2015), and our formulas for the Laplace transform the drawdown Parisian time are valid when positive jumps are present. For recent advances on study of drawdown with Lévy models, we refer to Landriault et al. (2015a), Baurdoux et al. (2017) and Avram et al. (2017).

In Chapters 7, we propose and replicate financial contracts that insure against a drawdown or the maximum drawdown. This chapter is based on Carr et al. (2011). In existing literature related to this topic, Večeř (2006, 2007) studied through simulation the returns of calls and puts written on the underlying asset's maximum drawdown, and discuss dynamic trading strategies to hedge against a drawdown associated with a single asset or index; Pospisil and Večeř (2010) applied PDE methods to investigate the sensitivities of portfolio values and hedging strategies with respect to drawdowns and drawups; Cheridito et al. (2012) took a probabilistic approach, and used properties of processes of class (Σ) to derive a dynamic hedging strategy of a perpetual option with drawdown triggers. In contrast to these approaches, our work in Chapter 7 focuses on synthesizing a number of finite maturity European-style digital derivative contracts on drawdowns with portfolios of market-traded barrier options and vanilla options. Our method requires portfolio rebalances only when either the running maximum or the running minimum of the underlying changes, and they apply to a GBM time-changed by an independent stochastic volatility model. This is closely related to static and semi-static replications as studied in Breeden and Litzenberger (1978), Bowie and Carr (1994), Carr and Chou (1997), Carr and Madan (2001), Carr et al. (1998), Derman et al. (1994) and Sbuelz (2005).

In Chapter 8, we study the valuation of a number of insurance contracts against drawdown events. This chapter is based on Zhang et al. (2013). Specifically, we derive the fair premium for insuring a number of drawdown events, with both finite and infinite maturities, as well as new provisions like drawup contingency, early termination. In particular, the early termination option leads to the analysis of a new optimal stopping problem, which is similar to the surrender right that arise in many common insurance products such as equity-indexed annuities (see, e.g., Cheung and Yang (2005), Moore (2009) and Moore and Young (2005)), and the step-up, step-down and cancellation right in credit default swaps (see, e.g., Leung and Yamazaki (2013)). Furthermore, we incorporate the underlying's default risk into our analysis. Similar equity models with defaults have been considered, for example, in Merton (1976) and more recently in Kovalov and Linetsky (2006), among others.

In Chapter 9 we study an optimal trading problem with a trailing stop. Despite being commonly used by practitioners, trailing stops have been scarcely studied in the mathematical finance literature. We trace back to Glynn and Iglehart (1995), who studied the expected discounted reward at a trailing stop under a discrete-time random walk or a GBM model, and found that it would be optimal to never use the trailing stop if the stock followed a GBM with a positive drift. In contrast, our study is conducted in a more general linear diffusion framework, and provides concrete illustrative example on how to the use of a trailing stop will affect the optimal timing to sell an asset under the exponential Ornstein–Uhlenbeck model. In a random walk model, Warburton and Zhang (2006) performed a probabilistic analysis of a variant of trailing stop. Yin *et al.* (2010) implemented a stochastic approximation scheme to determine the optimal percentage trailing stop level that maximizes the expected discounted simple return from liquidation. The recent study by Imkeller and Rogers (2014) compared the performance of a number of trading rules with fixed and trailing stops under an arithmetic Brownian motion model. Compared to these works, we tackle the trading problem in Chapter 9 from an optimal stopping perspective, and rigorously derive the optimal trading strategy. These results are based on Leung and Zhang (2017). Mathematically, we introduce a new optimal double stopping problem subject to a stopping time constraint induced by the trailing stop. Our method of solution applies to a general linear diffusion framework, and our analytical results are amenable to computation of the value function and optimal timing strategies.

Our list of topics on drawdown is not exclusive. There are a number of notable directions of research on drawdowns (drawups) that have not been covered in this book. For instance, risk management of drawdowns and portfolio optimization with drawdown constraints have gained increased attention among practitioners, see, for example, Grossman and Zhou (1993), Cvitanić and Karatzas (1995), Chekhlov *et al.* (2005), Elie and Touzi (2008), Carraro *et al.* (2012), Cherny and Obłój (2013) and Sekine (2013); the optimal stopping problems associated with the maximum are closely related to the first passage times of the drawdown process, see, for example, Shepp and Shiryaev (1993), Peskir (1998), Meilijson (2003), Asmussen et al. (2004), Avram et al. (2004), Ott (2013), Gapeev and Rodosthenous (2014, 2016b), Rodosthenous and Zervos (2017) and Egami and Oryu (2017); the drawup of the log-likelihood process has demonstrated some optimality in detecting an abrupt change-point in quickest detection problems, see, for example, Shiryaev (1996), Poor and Hadjiliadis (2008), Hadjiliadis et al. (2009), Zhang and Hadjiliadis (2012b) and Zhang et al. (2014, 2015); minimizing the drawdown probability has also become a new direction in insurance mathematics, see, for example, Angoshtari et al. (2015), Chen et al. (2015) and Angoshtari et al. (2016a,b).

1.3. Notation

Before we close this chapter, we provide a list of symbols that are used throughout the book, as a quick reference for readers.

$\mathbb{Z}$ Integers
$\mathbb{N}$ Natural numbers
$\mathbb{N}_0 = \mathbb{N} \cup \{0\}$
$\mathbb{R}$ Real numbers
$\mathbb{R}_{>0} = \{x \in \mathbb{R} : x > 0\}$
$\mathbb{R}_{\geq 0} = \{x \in \mathbb{R} : x \geq 0\}$
$\mathbb{C}$ Complex numbers
$\mathbb{H}_{\geq 0} = \{s \in \mathbb{C} : \Re(s) \geq 0\}$ Complex numbers with non-negative real part
$\mathbf{1}_E$ The indicator function for event E
$a \vee b = \max\{a, b\}$
$a \wedge b = \min\{a, b\}$
$\lfloor x \rfloor = \max\{n \in \mathbb{Z} : n \leq x\}$
$\lceil x \rceil = \min\{n \in \mathbb{Z} : n \geq x\}$
$\mathbf{e}_q$ Exponential variable with mean $1/q > 0$
$\tau_X^{\pm}(x) = \inf\{t > 0 : X_t \gtrless x\}$
$\overline{X}$. The running maximum of process X.
$\underline{X}$. The running minimum of process X.
$\mathbb{E}_x$ Expectation given $\{X_0 = x\}$
$\mathbb{E}_{x,\overline{x}}$ Expectation given $\{(X_0, \overline{X}_0) = (x, \overline{x})\}$
$\mathbb{E}_{x,\overline{x},\underline{x}}$ Expectation given $\{(X_0, \overline{X}_0, \underline{X}_0) = (x, \overline{x}, \underline{x})\}$
$\mathbb{P}_x$ Probability given $\{X_0 = x\}$
$\mathcal{I}_q$ Laplace inversion in variable q
$C^k(A)$ Functions with continuous kth derivatives on set A
$s(\cdot)$ A scale function of a linear diffusion

$\phi_q^\pm(\cdot)$ An increasing/decreasing positive eigenfunction of a linear diffusion process, see the Appendix

$W_q(\cdot,\cdot), W_{q,1}(\cdot,\cdot), W_{q,2}(\cdot,\cdot)$ Functions defined in (A.6) and (A.9), associated with a linear diffusion

$W_q(\cdot)$ The q-scale function of a spectrally negative Lévy process

Moreover, we follow the convention that $\inf \emptyset = \infty$ and $\sup \emptyset = 0$ throughout the book.

Part I
Drawdown Measures

Chapter 2

Drawdowns Preceding Drawups in a Finite Time-Horizon

In this chapter, we determine the probability that a drawdown of a units precedes a drawup of b units in a finite time-horizon T. The drawdown is defined as the drop of the present value from the running maximum, while the drawup is defined as the increase of the present value over the running minimum. To determine this probability, we begin by considering the case with $a = b$, and derive analytical formulas for this probability under a simple random walk model and a Brownian motion with drift model. By randomizing the time-horizon with an independent exponential random variable, we extend the solution techniques to treat the problem as $a \neq b$ under a general time-homogenous linear diffusion model.

Drawdowns provide a dynamic measure of risk in that they measure the drop of a stock price, index or value of a portfolio from its running maximum. They thus provide portfolio managers a tool to assess the risk taken by a mutual fund during a given economic cycle, i.e., a peak followed by a trough followed by a peak. The fact that they are reset to 0 every time a cycle of a peak and a trough followed by a peak is completed, renders them unbiased with respect to time, contrary to the maximum drawdown which is a measure that is non-decreasing with respect to time and thus has an increasing bias (see Figure 1.1).

Drawdowns also provide investors a measure of "relative regret", while drawups can be perceived as measures of "relative satisfaction" since the drawup of a portfolio gives the maximum profit that can be realized if the investor chooses to liquidate now. Thus the first time of a drawdown or a drawup of certain units may signal the instant at which an investor chooses to adjust her investment position depending on her perception of future moves of the market and her risk aversion. The probability computed in this chapter can then be understood as the likelihood that the investor who makes decisions based on the relative change in her wealth will exit on a drawdown (or a drawup) of her wealth, given a finite investment horizon. One can view this problem as an extension of the classical gambler's ruin problem (see, e.g., Ross (2008)), in which an investor with a finite time-horizon makes decisions based on the relative wealth process.

The results in this chapter extend those of Hadjiliadis (2005) in discrete time, and the results of Hadjiliadis and Večeř (2006) and Pospisil et al. (2009) in continuous time. In contrast to this chapter, Hadjiliadis (2005), Hadjiliadis and Večeř (2006) and Pospisil et al. (2009) formulate the drawdown preceding drawup probability with an infinite time-horizon and the main solution technique is martingale approach. However, we cannot obtain from these work the information about when the drawdown actually occurs. Yet, such information is crucial to many applications in practice.

The rest of the chapter is structured as follows. In Section 2.1, we derive the probability of a drawdown preceding a drawup in a finite time-horizon under a simple random walk model. In Section 2.2, we derive an infinite series formula for this probability under a Brownian motion with drift model. In Section 2.3, we randomize the time-horizon with an independent exponential random variable, and extend previous results to a general linear diffusion model by deriving the Laplace transform of the first passage time of the drawdown of a units when it precedes any drawup of b units. A numerical example with a geometric Brownian motion (GBM) model is presented in Section 2.4, where we determine the conditional density of the maximum relative drawup before a drawdown event in a finite time-horizon. We conclude this chapter in Section 2.5. Proofs of lemmas can be found in Section 2.6.

2.1. Random Walk Model

We begin our study of drawdown and drawup using the simplest stochastic process — a simple random walk model with parameter $p \in (0,1)$. That is,

$$X_n = \sum_{i=1}^{n} Z_i, \ X_0 = 0, \qquad (2.1)$$

where Z_i's are independent, identically distributed (henceforth i.i.d.) with distribution

$$Z_i = \begin{cases} 1 & \text{with probability } p, \\ -1 & \text{with probability } q \equiv 1 - p. \end{cases}$$

Denoting the running maximum and minimum of $X.$ by $\overline{X}_n = \max_{0 \le k \le n} X_k$ and $\underline{X}_n = \min_{0 \le k \le n} X_k$, then the drawdown and drawup processes are then defined respectively as

$$D_n = \overline{X}_n - X_n, \quad U_n = X_n - \underline{X}_n, \quad \forall n \in \mathbb{N}_0.$$

For any fixed $a, b \in \mathbb{N}$, we define the first passage time of $D.$ and $U.$ respectively as

$$\tau_D^+(a) = \min\{n \ge 1 : D_n \ge a\},$$
$$\tau_U^+(b) = \min\{n \ge 1 : U_n \ge b\}.$$

In the next theorem, we compute the probability that a drawdown of a units precedes a drawup of equal size in a finite time-horizon T, where $T > a$.

Theorem 2.1. *For any $a, T \in \mathbb{N}$ such that $T > a$, we have*

(1) *for $a = 1$,*

$$\mathbb{P}(\tau_D^+(a) < \tau_U^+(a) \wedge T) = q;$$

(2) *for $a = 2$,*

$$\mathbb{P}(\tau_D^+(a) < \tau_U^+(a) \wedge T) = q^2 \underbrace{(1 + p + (qp) + p(qp) + \cdots)}_{(T-1)\text{-terms}};$$

(3) *for $a \ge 3$,*

$$\mathbb{P}(\tau_D^+(a) < \tau_U^+(a) \wedge T)$$
$$= q^a \left(1 + \sum_{L=a+2}^{T} \sum_{i=1}^{a} \sum_{k=0}^{L-a-1} c_{i,1}^{a,L-a-k-1} \cdot c_{1,a-2}^{a-1,a+k-3} \cdot q^{\frac{L-a-i}{2}} p^{\frac{L-a+i-2}{2}} \right),$$

where for $m, k, i, j \in \mathbb{N}_0$,

$$c_{i,j}^{m,k} = \frac{2^{k+1}}{m+1} \sum_{\iota=1}^{m} \left(\cos\frac{\pi\iota}{m+1}\right)^k \sin\frac{i\pi\iota}{m+1} \sin\frac{j\pi\iota}{m+1}.$$

In order to proceed with the proof of this theorem, we will need to make use of two preliminary lemmas. In the first lemma, we compute the n-step transition probability for the random walk X. in (2.1), which is killed at exiting from a negative strip.

Lemma 2.1. *For $u, v, A, n \in \mathbb{N}$ and $0 \leq u, v \leq A$, we have*

$$\mathbb{P}_{-u}(-X_n = v, 0 \leq -X_k \leq A, \forall k \leq n) = c_{u+1,v+1}^{A+1,n} \cdot q^{\frac{n-u+v}{2}} p^{\frac{n+u-v}{2}},$$

where $c_{u+1,v+1}^{A+1,n}$ is defined in Theorem 2.1.

In the second lemma we compute the probability that a random walk X., reaches a specific level $-v$ in n steps while its maximum is exactly at level $B - v$ and its minimum stays above $-(v+1)$. We denote this probability by $g(n, v; B)$.

Lemma 2.2. *For $B, n \in \mathbb{N}$ with $B \leq n$, and $v = -1, 0, \ldots, B$, define*

$$g(n, v; B) := \mathbb{P}(X_n = -v, \underline{X}_n \geq -(v+1), \overline{X}_n = B - v). \quad (2.2)$$

Then

$$g(n, v; B) = \sum_{k=0}^{n-B} c_{B-v+1,1}^{B+2,n-B-k} \cdot c_{1,B}^{B+1,B+k-1} \cdot q^{\frac{n+v}{2}} p^{\frac{n-v}{2}}, \quad (2.3)$$

with coefficient $c_{i,j}^{m,k}$ defined in Theorem 2.1.

We can now proceed to the proof of Theorem 2.1.

Proof of Theorem 2.1. The cases that $a = 1$ and $a = 2$ can be easily proved. We now fix an $a \geq 3$, then

$$\mathbb{P}(\tau_D^+(a) < \tau_U^+(a) \wedge (a+1)) = q^a.$$

In order to establish the formula when $a \geq 3$, it suffices to calculate for any $a, T \in \mathbb{N}$ and $T > a + 1 \geq 4$ that

$$\Delta(T; a, p) := \mathbb{P}(\tau_D^+(a) < \tau_U^+(a) \wedge T) - \mathbb{P}(\tau_D^+(a) < \tau_U^+(a) \wedge (T-1))$$
$$= \mathbb{P}(\tau_D^+(a) = T - 1, \overline{U}_{T-1} \leq a - 1), \quad (2.4)$$

where $\overline{U}_n = \max_{0 \leq k \leq n} U_k$.

We begin by examining the properties of all paths that are included in the event considered in (2.4).

(1) For all such paths,
$$-X_{T-1} \in \{1, 2, \ldots, a\},$$
for otherwise, the drawup process attains a units before the drawdown process does so, or the range is less than a at time $T - 1$.

(2) Let us assume $-X_{T-1} = x \in \{1, 2, \ldots, a\}$, then
$$\overline{X}_{T-1} = a - x.$$

(3) Assume $-X_{T-1} = x \in \{1, 2, \ldots, a\}$, then
$$X_{T-2} = 1 - x, X_{T-3} = 2 - x, \underline{X}_{T-3} \geq 1 - x.$$

This is because the drawdown (which precedes the drawup) is achieved by a downward move of the random walk X.; moreover, the lowest position of the random walk before $T - 1$ can be at least $1 - x$.

(4) The last two increments Z_{T-1}, Z_T must be -1 in order to establish a new minimum at time T.

By the Chapman–Kolmogorov equation, these properties give rise to the following representation

$$\Delta(T; a, p) = p^2 \cdot \sum_{v=-1}^{a-2} g(T - 3, v; a - 2). \tag{2.5}$$

Using Lemma 2.2, the result follows. This completes the proof of Theorem 2.1. □

In the case that an investor is not restricted by a finite time-horizon, the probability that her wealth makes a drawdown of a units before a drawup of equal size is summarized in the following corollary. However, this result cannot be easily obtained from Theorem 2.1 by taking the limit as $T \to \infty$, because of the threefold summation. A more direct, martingale approach is applied in Hadjiliadis (2005) to treat the perpetual case, which yields the closed-form formula in the following corollary.

Corollary 2.1. *In the case of an infinite time-horizon we have*
$$\mathbb{P}(\tau_D^+(a) < \tau_U^+(a)) = \frac{(\frac{q}{p})^{a+1} - (a+1)(\frac{q}{p}) + a}{[1 - (\frac{q}{p})^a][(\frac{p}{q})^{a+1} - 1]} \quad \text{if } p \neq \frac{1}{2}.$$
And the case of $p = \frac{1}{2}$ is obtained in the limit of the above as p tends to $\frac{1}{2}$.

The next corollary draws a connection of our result to the range process which is defined to be the difference of the running maximum and the running minimum.

Corollary 2.2. Let $R_n = \overline{X}_n - \underline{X}_n$ be the range process of a random walk with parameter p. Then for $a, T \in \mathbb{N}$ with $T > a$, we have

(1) for $a = 2$,

$$\mathbb{P}(R_{T-1} \geq 2) = q^2 \underbrace{(1 + p + pq + \ldots +)}_{(T-2)\text{-terms}} + p^2 \underbrace{(1 + q + pq + \ldots)}_{(T-2)\text{-terms}};$$

(2) for $a \geq 3$,

$$\mathbb{P}(R_{T-1} \geq a) = q^a + p^a$$

$$+ \sum_{L=a+2}^{T} \sum_{i=1}^{a} \sum_{k=0}^{L-a-1} \left\{ c_{i,1}^{a,L-a-k-1} \cdot c_{1,a-2}^{a-1,a+k-3} \right.$$

$$\left. \times (pq)^{\frac{L-2}{2}} \left[q \left(\frac{q}{p}\right)^{\frac{a-i}{2}} + p \left(\frac{p}{q}\right)^{\frac{a-i}{2}} \right] \right\}.$$

Proof. We observe that

$$\mathbb{P}(R_{T-1} \geq a) = \mathbb{P}(\tau_D^+(a) < \tau_U^+(a) \wedge T) + \mathbb{P}(\tau_U^+(a) < \tau_D^+(a) \wedge T), \quad (2.6)$$

where the first term of the right-hand side is given in Theorem 2.1. To determine the second term, we notice that the drawdown of $-X$., $\max_{0 \leq k \leq n}(-X_k) - (-X_n) = X_n - \min_{0 \leq k \leq n} X_k$, is the same as the drawup of X.; while the drawup of $-X$., $(-X_n) - \min_{0 \leq k \leq n}(-X_k) = \max_{0 \leq k \leq n} X_k - X_n$, is the drawdown of X.. Since $-X$. is a simple random walk with parameter $q = 1 - p$, we can obtain an analytical expression of the second term in (2.6) by switching p with q. □

Remark 2.1. In the case of a symmetric random walk (i.e., $p = \frac{1}{2}$) we notice that we can write

$$\mathbb{P}(\tau_D^+(a) < \tau_U^+(a) \wedge T) = \frac{1}{2}\mathbb{P}(\tau_R^+(a) < T), \quad (2.7)$$

where $\tau_R^+(a) = \inf\{n \geq 1 : R_n \geq a\}$ is the first passage time of the range process R.. It is now easy to deduce that as $T \to \infty$ (2.7) reduces to

$\frac{1}{2}$ as expected. Finally, the case of a symmetric random walk ($p = \frac{1}{2}$) is summarized in the following corollary for any pre-specified time-horizon T.

Corollary 2.3. *Let $a, T \in \mathbb{N}$ with $T > a$. For the symmetric random walk the probability that a drawdown of a units precedes a drawup of equal size in finite time-horizon T is given by*

(1) *for $a = 1$,*

$$\mathbb{P}(\tau_D^+(1) < \tau_U^+(1) \wedge T) = \frac{1}{2};$$

(2) *for $a = 2$,*

$$\mathbb{P}(\tau_D^+(2) < \tau_U^+(2) \wedge T) = \frac{1}{2} - \frac{1}{2^T};$$

(3) *for $a \geq 3$,*

$$\mathbb{P}(\tau_D^+(a) < \tau_U^+(a) \wedge T)$$
$$= \frac{1}{2^a} + \frac{1}{2} \sum_{L=a+2}^{T} \frac{1}{2^{L-2}} \sum_{i=1}^{a} \sum_{k=0}^{L-a-1} c_{i,1}^{a,L-a-k-1} \cdot c_{1,a-2}^{a-1,a+k-3},$$

where for $c_{i,j}^{m,k}$ is defined in Theorem 2.1.

In Table 2.1 we calculate the probability $\mathbb{P}(\tau_D^+(a) < \tau_U^+(a) \wedge T)$ for specific values of the parameters p, a, and T. We notice that the entries in Table 2.1 decrease across columns, reflecting the fact that as p increases, a drop in X. is more likely to occur than an rise, so the probability of a drawdown preceding a drawup of equal size also decreases. On the other hand, as the threshold a increases, this probability typically decreases, due to the diminishing likelihood for the random walk to have a large drawdown (or drawup) with a finite number of steps. However, in the case that $p = 0.55$ this probability experiences a slight increase from $a = 1$ to $a = 2$, because a slightly larger a in this case makes the requirement on drawdown and

Table 2.1. The probability studied in Theorem 2.1 for $T = 30$.

a	$p = 0.45$	$p = 0.5$	$p = 0.55$
5	0.5338	0.4001	0.2646
10	0.1603	0.0792	0.0321
15	0.0159	0.0047	0.0010

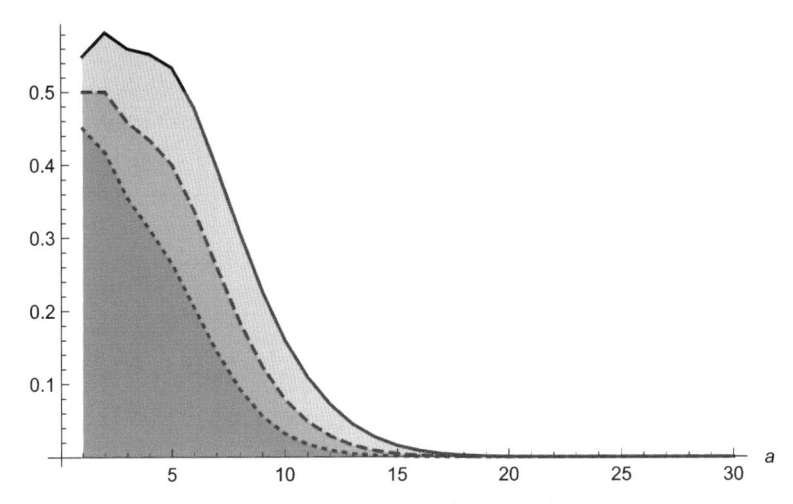

Fig. 2.1. A graph of the mapping $a \mapsto \mathbb{P}(\tau_D^+(a) < \tau_U^+(a) \wedge T)$ for $T = 30$, and $p = 0.45$ (solid), or $p = 0.5$ (dashed), or $p = 0.55$ (dotted).

drawup less binding. This reflects a tradeoff, as we increase a, between the drawdown (and drawup) being rare events and the drawdown preceding drawup condition becoming less binding. This is seen in Figure 2.1.

Next, we proceed to the study of drawdowns and drawup under a Brownian with drift motions.

2.2. Brownian Motion with Drift Model

In this section, we consider the case of a Brownian motion with drift coefficient $\mu \in \mathbb{R}$ and diffusion coefficient $\sigma > 0$:

$$\mathrm{d}X_t = \mu \mathrm{d}t + \sigma \mathrm{d}W_t, \quad X_0 = 0, \tag{2.8}$$

where $\{W_t\}_{t \geq 0}$ is a standard Brownian motion. Similar as the simple random walk model, we denote by $\overline{X}_t = \sup_{s \in [0,t]} X_s$ and $\underline{X}_t = \inf_{s \in [0,t]} X_s$ respectively the running maximum and minimum processes of $X.$, and define the drawdown and the drawup processes as

$$D_t = \overline{X}_t - X_t, \quad U_t = X_t - \underline{X}_t, \quad \forall t \geq 0.$$

The first passage times of $D.$ and $U.$ from below are respectively denoted as

$$\tau_D^+(a) = \inf\{t > 0 : D_t > a\},$$
$$\tau_U^+(b) = \inf\{t > 0 : U_t > b\},$$

for any $a, b > 0$. The first passage time of $X.$ is denote by $\tau_X^{\pm}(x)$:

$$\tau_X^{\pm}(x) = \inf\{t > 0 : X_t \gtrless x\}, \quad \forall x \in \mathbb{R}.$$

In the following theorem, we compute the probability that a drawdown of a units precedes a drawup of equal sizes in a pre-specified finite time-horizon $T > 0$.

Theorem 2.2. *We have*

$$\mathbb{P}(\tau_D^+(a) < \tau_U^+(a) \wedge T)$$

$$= \frac{e^{-2\delta a} + 2\delta a - 1}{e^{-2\delta a} + e^{2\delta a} - 2} - \sum_{n=1}^{\infty} \frac{2n^2\pi^2}{C_n^2} e^{-\frac{\sigma^2 C_n}{2a^2} T} (A_n + B_n T),$$

where[1]

$$A_n := (1 - (-1)^n e^{-\delta a}) \left(1 - \frac{4\delta^2 a^2}{C_n}\right) + (-1)^n \delta a e^{-\delta a}, \tag{2.9}$$

$$B_n := (1 - (-1)^n e^{-\delta a}) \frac{n^2\pi^2\sigma^2}{a^2}, \quad C_n := n^2\pi^2 + \delta^2 a^2, \quad \delta := \frac{\mu}{\sigma^2}. \tag{2.10}$$

The proof of the above theorem makes use of the following propositions.

Proposition 2.1. *For $t > 0$ and $-a \leq x < 0$, we have*

$$\mathbb{P}(\tau_D^+(a) \in dt, \tau_U^+(a) > t, X_t \in dx) = g(t, x) \, dt \, dx,$$

where

$$g(t, x) = \frac{\sigma^2}{a^5} \sum_{n=1}^{\infty} n\pi e^{\delta x - \frac{\sigma^2 C_n}{2a^2} t}$$

$$\times \left\{ n\pi a x \cos\left(\frac{n\pi x}{a}\right) - (n^2\pi^2\sigma^2 t - 2a^2) \sin\left(\frac{n\pi x}{a}\right) \right\},$$

with δ and $C_n, n \in \mathbb{N}$ defined as above.

Proof. Similar as in the proof of Theorem 2.1, we observe that for any $x \in (-a, 0)$,

$$\{\tau_D^+(a) \in dt, \tau_U^+(a) > t, X_t \in dx\} = \{\tau_X^-(x) \in dt, \overline{X}_t \in x + da\},$$

---

[1] In the risk theory literature, the constant 2δ is known as the *adjustment coefficient*.

from which we obtain

$$g(t,x) = \frac{\partial}{\partial a} \frac{\mathbb{P}(\tau_X^-(x) \in \mathrm{d}t, \overline{X}_t \leq a+x)}{\mathrm{d}t}. \qquad (2.11)$$

Moreover, the density $\mathbb{P}(\tau_X^-(x) \in \mathrm{d}t, \overline{X}_t \leq a+x)/\mathrm{d}t$ appears in Anderson (1960, Theorem 5.1). In particular, using the expression for $\mathrm{d}P_2(t)/\mathrm{d}t$ there with parameters $\gamma_1 = (x+a)/\sigma, \gamma_2 = x/\sigma$ and $\delta_1 = \delta_2 = -\mu/\sigma$, we obtain

$$\begin{aligned} q(t,x,x+a) &:= \frac{\mathbb{P}(\tau_X^-(x) \in \mathrm{d}t, \overline{X}_t \leq a+x)}{\mathrm{d}t} \\ &= \frac{1}{\sigma t^{\frac{3}{2}}} e^{\delta x - \frac{\sigma^2 \delta^2}{2} t} \sum_{k=-\infty}^{\infty} (2ka - x) \phi\left(\frac{2ka - x}{\sigma \sqrt{t}}\right) \\ &= -\frac{\sigma^2}{a^2} e^{\delta x - \frac{\sigma^2 \delta^2}{2} t} \sum_{n=1}^{\infty} (n\pi) e^{-\frac{n^2 \pi^2 \sigma^2}{2 a^2} t} \sin\left(\frac{n\pi x}{a}\right), \qquad (2.12) \end{aligned}$$

where $\phi(x) = \frac{1}{\sqrt{2\pi}} e^{-\frac{x^2}{2}}$ is the standard normal probability density, and the last line is due to Fourier transform of the above infinite sum in x. □

In the case that an investor is not restricted by a finite time-horizon, the probability that her wealth makes a drawdown of a units before a drawup of equal size in the model of (2.8) is derived by using a martingale arguments (Hadjiliadis and Večeř, 2006).

Proposition 2.2. *In the case of an infinite time-horizon, we have*

$$\mathbb{P}(\tau_D^+(a) < \tau_U^+(a)) = \frac{e^{-2\delta a} + 2\delta a - 1}{e^{-2\delta a} + e^{2\delta a} - 2}.$$

We can now proceed to the proof of Theorem 2.2.

Proof of Theorem 2.2. We use Proposition 2.1 to obtain

$$\begin{aligned} &\mathbb{P}(\tau_D^+(a) < \tau_U^+(a) \wedge T) \\ &= \mathbb{P}(\tau_D^+(a) < \tau_U^+(a)) - \mathbb{P}(T \leq \tau_D^+(a) < \tau_U^+(a)) \\ &= \mathbb{P}(\tau_D^+(a) < \tau_U^+(a)) - \int_T^{\infty} \int_{-a}^{0} \mathbb{P}(\tau_D^+(a) \in \mathrm{d}t, \tau_U^+(a) > t, X_t \in \mathrm{d}x) \\ &= \mathbb{P}(\tau_D^+(a) < \tau_U^+(a)) - \int_T^{\infty} \mathrm{d}t \int_{-a}^{0} g(t,x)\,\mathrm{d}x. \qquad (2.13) \end{aligned}$$

Applying Propositions 2.1 and 2.2 yields the results. This completes the proof of Theorem 2.2. □

The case of a Brownian motion without a drift is summarized in the following corollary.

Corollary 2.4.

$$\mathbb{P}(\tau_D^+(a) < \tau_U^+(a) \wedge T) = \frac{1}{2} - \sum_{n\geq 1, odd} \frac{4}{n^2\pi^2} e^{-\frac{n^2\pi^2\sigma^2}{2a^2}T} \cdot \left(1 + \frac{n^2\pi^2\sigma^2}{a^2}T\right).$$

As expected, the above expression converges to $\frac{1}{2}$ as $T \to \infty$.

As the counterpart of Corollary 2.2, the next corollary draws a connection of our result to the range process of a Brownian motion.

Corollary 2.5. Let $R_t := \overline{X}_t - \underline{X}_t$ be the range process of $X.$ in (2.8). Then

$$\mathbb{P}(R_T < a) = \sum_{n=1}^{\infty} \frac{4n^2\pi^2}{C_n^2} e^{-\frac{\sigma^2 C_n}{2a^2}T}(\tilde{A}_n + \tilde{B}_n T),$$

where

$$\tilde{A}_n := (1 - (-1)^n \cosh(\delta a))\left(1 - \frac{4\delta^2 a^2}{C_n}\right) - (-1)^n \delta a \sinh(\delta a), \quad (2.14)$$

$$\tilde{B}_n := (1 - (-1)^n \cosh(\delta a))\frac{n^2\pi^2\sigma^2}{a^2}. \quad (2.15)$$

Proof. Define the first passage time of range process $R.$ by

$$\tau_R^+(a) = \inf\{t \geq 0 : R_t > a\},$$

then it is easily seen that

$$\tau_R^+(a) = \tau_D^+(a) \wedge \tau_U^+(a).$$

That is, the range increases over a as a result of either a drawdown or a drawup. Therefore, we have

$$\mathbb{P}(R_T < a) = \mathbb{P}(\tau_R^+(a) \geq T) = 1 - \mathbb{P}(\tau_R^+(a) < T)$$
$$= 1 - \mathbb{P}(\tau_D^+(a) < \tau_U^+(a) \wedge T) - \mathbb{P}(\tau_U^+(a) < \tau_D^+(a) \wedge T)$$
$$= 1 - \mathbb{P}(\tau_D^+(a) < \tau_U^+(a) \wedge T) - \tilde{\mathbb{P}}(\tau_D^+(a) < \tau_U^+(a) \wedge T),$$

where $\tilde{\mathbb{P}}$ is a probability measure under which the law of $X.$ is the same as that of $-X.$ under the original measure $\mathbb{P}$. The last equality in the above is due to reflection: the drawdown (respectively, drawup) of $X.$ is the same as the drawup (respectively, drawdown) of the $-X.$. The result then follows from applying Theorem 2.2 to $X.$ and $-X.$. □

The result in Corollary 2.5 is also seen in Tanré and Vallois (2007, Proposition 4.4).

We now proceed to treat the general case with $a \neq b$ under a one-dimensional time-homogenous linear diffusion model.

2.3. One-Dimensional Linear Diffusion Model

In a filtered probability space $(\Omega, \mathbb{F}, \mathcal{F}, \mathbb{P})$ with filtration $\mathbb{F} = \{\mathcal{F}_t\}_{t \geq 0}$, we consider a linear diffusion $X.$ on $I \equiv (l, r)$, whose evolution is governed by the stochastic differential equation

$$dX_t = \mu(X_t)dt + \sigma(X_t)dW_t, \quad X_0 = x \in I, \qquad (2.16)$$

where $\{W_t\}_{t \geq 0}$ is a standard Brownian motion with respect to $\mathbb{F}$, and $(\mu(\cdot), \sigma(\cdot))$ is a pair of real-valued functions that satisfy (A.2) and (A.3) in the Appendix. We assume that the boundaries of I are either natural or entrance-not-exit (see, e.g., Itô and McKean (1965, p. 108)).

Let us introduce the running maximum and minimum processes of $X.$ respectively by $\overline{X}_t = \sup_{s \in [0,t]} X_s$ and $\underline{X}_t = \inf_{s \in [0,t]} X_s$. Then the drawdown and drawup processes of $X.$ are defined respectively as

$$D_t = \overline{X}_t - X_t \quad U_t = X_t - \underline{X}_t, \quad \forall t \geq 0.$$

We consider the first passage time of the drawdown and the drawup processes:

$$\tau_D^+(a) = \inf\{t > 0 : D_t > a\},$$
$$\tau_U^+(b) = \inf\{t > 0 : U_t > b\},$$

for any $a, b < 0$. The first passage time of $X.$ is denote by $\tau_X^\pm(x)$:

$$\tau_X^\pm(x) = \inf\{t > 0 : X_t \gtrless x\}, \quad \forall x \in I.$$

For preliminaries on linear diffusion and definitions of the scale function $s(\cdot)$ and other related functions used in this section, please refer to the Appendix.

2.3.1. *Analytical results*

We now derive the probability that $\tau_D^+(a)$ precedes $\tau_U^+(b)$ in a finite time interval $[0, t]$ for any $t > 0$, $a, b > 0$ under a general linear diffusion. A key step to accomplish this is to randomize the time-horizon t with an independent exponential random variable, a technique known as Canadization in literature (see, e.g., Carr and Madan (1999)). This is equivalent to deriving the Laplace transform of the mapping $t \mapsto \mathbb{P}_x(\tau_D^+(a) < \tau_U^+(b) \wedge t)$ for all $t \in \mathbb{R}_{>0}$. In particular, for any x, a such that $x - a \in I$, we will calculate

$$\mathbb{P}_x(\tau_D^+(a) < \tau_U^+(b) \wedge \mathbf{e}_q) = q \int_0^\infty e^{-qt} \mathbb{P}_x(\tau_D^+(a) < \tau_U^+(b) \wedge t) \, dt.$$

2.3.1.1. *The case of* $a \geq b > 0$

Theorem 2.3. *On the event* $\{\tau_D^+(a) < \tau_U^+(b) \wedge \mathbf{e}_q\}$, *we have* $\tau_D^+(a) < \tau_U^+(b)$ *and* $X_{\tau_D^+(b)} \in (x - b, x)$. *Moreover,*

$$\mathbb{P}_x(\tau_D^+(a) < \tau_U^+(b) \wedge \mathbf{e}_q)$$
$$= \int_{x-b}^x \frac{s'(u+b) W_q(x, u)}{W_q^2(u+b, u)} \exp\left(\int_{u+b-a}^u W_{q,1}(v, v+b) dv\right) du. \quad (2.17)$$

On the event $\{\tau_U^+(a) < \tau_D^+(b) \wedge \mathbf{e}_q\}$, *we have* $\tau_U^+(b) < \tau_D^+(b)$ *and* $X_{\tau_U^+(b)} \in (x, x+b)$. *Moreover,*

$$\mathbb{P}_x(\tau_U^+(a) < \tau_D^+(b) \wedge \mathbf{e}_q)$$
$$= \int_x^{x+b} \frac{s'(u-b) W_q(u, x)}{W_q^2(u, u-b)} \exp\left(-\int_u^{u+a-b} W_{q,1}(v, v-b) dv\right) du.$$
$$(2.18)$$

Proof. First, it is easily seen that for $t > 0$, and $u \in (x - b, x)$,

$$\{\tau_D^+(b) \in dt, X_t \in du, \tau_U^+(b) > t\} = \{\tau_u \in dt, \overline{X}_t \in b + du\}, \quad \mathbb{P}_x\text{-a.s.}$$

It follows from integration by parts that,

$$\mathbb{P}_x(\tau_D^+(b) < \tau_U^+(b) \wedge \mathbf{e}_q, X_{\tau_D^+(b)} \in du)$$
$$= \int_0^\infty q e^{-qt} \mathbb{P}_x(\tau_D^+(b) < \tau_U^+(b) \wedge t, X_{\tau_D^+(b)} \in du) \, dt$$
$$= \int_0^\infty e^{-qt} \mathbb{P}_x(\tau_D^+(b) \in dt, X_t \in du, \tau_U^+(b) > t).$$

On the other hand, we observe the fact that $\tau_D^+(b) \wedge \tau_U^+(b) = \inf\{t \geq 0 : \overline{X}_t - \underline{X}_t > b\}$, $\mathbb{P}_x$-a.s., is the first range time. Following the proof of Proposition 2.1, we have

$$\mathbb{P}_x(\tau_D^+(b) \in \mathrm{d}t, X_t \in \mathrm{d}u, \tau_U^+(b) > t)$$
$$= \frac{\partial}{\partial b}\mathbb{P}_x(\tau_X^-(u) \in \mathrm{d}t, \tau_X^+(u+b) > t)\,\mathrm{d}u.$$

From Lemmas A.2 and A.1 in the Appendix, we obtain (2.17) for the case $a = b$.

If $a > b$, then any path in the event $\{\tau_D^+(a) < \tau_U^+(b) \wedge \mathbf{e}_q\}$ can be decomposed into two fragments: $\{X_t\}_{0 \leq t \leq \tau_D^+(b)}$ and $\{X_t\}_{\tau_D^+(b) \leq t \leq \tau_D^+(a)}$. Conditioning on $\{X_{\tau_D^+(b)} = u\}$, the second fragment is a process starting at u, and decreasing to $u+b-a$ before the drawup of b units. Formally, using Markov shifting operator $(X_t \circ \theta_s = X_{t+s})$, we have

$$\tau_D^+(a) = \tau_D^+(b) + \tau_X^-(u - a + b) \circ \theta_{\tau_D^+(b)}, \quad \forall u \in (x-b, x).$$

Using strong Markov property and memoryless of $\mathbf{e}_q$, we have

$$\mathbb{P}_x(\tau_D^+(a) < \tau_U^+(b) \wedge \mathbf{e}_q, X_{\tau_D^+(a)} \in b - a + \mathrm{d}u)$$
$$= \mathbb{P}_x(\tau_D^+(b) < \tau_U^+(b) \wedge \mathbf{e}_q, X_{\tau_D^+(b)} \in \mathrm{d}u)$$
$$\times \mathbb{P}_u(\tau_X^-(u-a+b) < \tau_U^+(b) \wedge \mathbf{e}_q).$$

Now (2.17) follows from Proposition 2.3 below. Equation (2.18) can be proved using a similar argument. □

Proposition 2.3. *For $x, y \in I$, let $m = x \vee y$ and $n = x \wedge y$. Then we have*

$$\mathbb{P}_m(\tau_X^-(n) < \tau_U^+(b) \wedge \mathbf{e}_q) = \exp\left(\int_n^m W_{q,1}(v, v+b)\,\mathrm{d}v\right), \quad (2.19)$$

$$\mathbb{P}_n(\tau_X^+(m) < \tau_D^+(a) \wedge \mathbf{e}_q) = \exp\left(-\int_n^m W_{q,1}(v, v-a)\,\mathrm{d}v\right). \quad (2.20)$$

Proof. First we notice that

$$\mathbb{P}_m(\tau_X^-(n) < \tau_U^+(b) \wedge \mathbf{e}_q) = \mathbb{E}_m(\mathrm{e}^{-q\tau_X^-(n)}; \tau_X^-(n) < \tau_U^+(b)).$$

To compute the above expectation on the right-hand side, we follow the idea of Lehoczky (1977), and partition the interval $[n, m]$ into N equal length subintervals with length $\epsilon = \frac{m-n}{N}$. In particular, using the fact that $\mathbb{P}_m(\tau_X^-(m) = 0) = 1$ and continuity of $X.$, we have $\mathbb{P}_m$-a.s. that,

$$e^{-q\sum_{i=0}^{N-1}(\tau_X^-(m-(i+1)\epsilon)-\tau_X^-(m-i\epsilon))} \mathbf{1}_{\{\tau_X^-(m-(j+1)\epsilon) < \tau_X^+(m-j\epsilon+b),\, \forall 0 \le j \le N-1\}}$$

$$\to e^{-q\tau_X^-(n)} \mathbf{1}_{\{\tau_X^-(n) < \tau_U^+(b)\}},$$

as $N \to \infty$. Applying the Lebesgue dominated convergence theorem, the strong Markov property and continuity of X, we obtain that

$$\mathbb{E}_m(e^{-q\tau_X^-(n)} \mathbf{1}_{\{\tau_X^-(n) < \tau_U^+(b)\}})$$

$$= \lim_{N \to \infty} \prod_{i=0}^{N-1} \mathbb{E}_{m-i\epsilon}(e^{-q\tau_X^-(m-(i+1)\epsilon)} \mathbf{1}_{\{\tau_X^-(m-(i+1)\epsilon) < \tau_X^+(m-i\epsilon+b)\}}).$$

To compute the above limit, we use Lemma A.1 in the Appendix to obtain that

$$\mathbb{E}_m(e^{-q\tau_X^-(n)}; \tau_X^-(n) < \tau_U^+(b))$$

$$= \lim_{N \to \infty} \prod_{i=0}^{N-1} \frac{W_q(m - i\epsilon, m - i\epsilon + b)}{W_q(m - (i+1)\epsilon, m - i\epsilon + b)}$$

$$= \exp\left(\lim_{N \to \infty} \left[\sum_{i=0}^{N-1} W_{q,1}(m - (i+1)\epsilon, m - i\epsilon + b) \cdot \epsilon + O(\epsilon)\right]\right)$$

$$= \exp\left(\int_n^m W_{q,1}(v, v + b)\, dv\right),$$

which completes the proof of (2.19). Equation (2.20) can be proved using a similar argument. □

As $q \downarrow 0$, using Lemma A.2 in the Appendix we obtain the result with an infinite time-horizon in Pospisil et al. (2009, Theorem 4.2).

Corollary 2.6. *For any $a \ge b > 0$, we have*

$$\mathbb{P}_x(\tau_D^+(a) < \tau_U^+(b), \tau_D^+(a) < \infty)$$

$$= \int_{x-a}^x \frac{s'(u+b)(s(x) - s(u))}{(s(u+b) - s(u))^2} \exp\left(\int_{u+b-a}^u \frac{-s'(v)\, dv}{s(v+b) - s(v)}\right) du,$$

$$\mathbb{P}_x(\tau_U^+(a) < \tau_D^+(b), \tau_U^+(a) < \infty)$$

$$= \int_x^{x+b} \frac{s'(u-b)(s(u) - s(x))}{(s(u) - s(u-b))^2} \exp\left(-\int_u^{u+a-b} \frac{s'(v)\, dv}{s(v) - s(v-b)}\right) du.$$

2.3.1.2. *The case of $b > a > 0$*

To obtain the result for general $b > a$, we notice the $\mathbb{P}_x$-a.s. identity

$$\{\tau_D^+(a) < \tau_U^+(b) \wedge \mathbf{e}_q\} = \{\tau_D^+(a) < \mathbf{e}_q, \overline{U}_{\tau_D^+(a)} < b\}, \quad \forall b > a > 0,$$

where $\overline{U}_{\tau_D^+(a)}$ is the maximum drawup at $\tau_D^+(a)$. Thus, we can write

$$\mathbb{P}_x(\tau_D^+(a) < \tau_U^+(b) \wedge \mathbf{e}_q)$$
$$= \mathbb{P}_x(\tau_D^+(a) < \mathbf{e}_q, \overline{U}_{\tau_D^+(a)} < a) + \mathbb{P}_x(\tau_D^+(a) < \mathbf{e}_q, \overline{U}_{\tau_D^+(a)} \in [a,b))$$
$$= \mathbb{P}_x(\tau_D^+(a) < \tau_U^+(a) \wedge \mathbf{e}_q) + \int_a^b \mathbb{P}_x(\tau_D^+(a) < \mathbf{e}_q, \overline{U}_{\tau_D^+(a)} \in \mathrm{d}z).$$
(2.21)

The density appearing in (2.21) is derived in the following result.

Proposition 2.4. *For any $b > a > 0$, on the event $\{\tau_U^+(b) < \tau_D^+(a) < \mathbf{e}_q\}$, $X_{\tau_U^+(b)} \in (x+b-a, x+b)$. Moreover,*

$$\mathbb{P}_x(\tau_U^+(b) < \tau_D^+(a) < \mathbf{e}_q)$$
$$= \int_x^{x+a} \frac{s'(u-a)W_q(u,x)}{W_q^2(u,u-a)}$$
$$\times \int_{u+b-a}^\infty \frac{s'(v)}{W_q(v,v-a)} e^{-\int_u^v W_{q,1}(w,w-a)dw} \, \mathrm{d}v\mathrm{d}u.$$

Hence, for any $b > a$, we have

$$\frac{\mathbb{P}_x(\tau_D^+(a) < \mathbf{e}_q, \overline{U}_{\tau_D^+(a)} \in \mathrm{d}b)}{\mathrm{d}b}$$
$$= \int_x^{x+a} \frac{s'(u-a)W_q(u,x)}{W_q^2(u,u-a)}$$
$$\times \frac{s'(u+b-a)}{W_q(u+b-a, u+b)} e^{-\int_u^{u+b-a} W_{q,1}(w,w-a)dw} \, \mathrm{d}u.$$

Proof. Notice that the event $\{\tau_U^+(b) < \tau_D^+(a) < \mathbf{e}_q\} = \{\tau_U^+(b) < \tau_D^+(a) \wedge \mathbf{e}_q\} \cap \{\tau_D^+(a) < \mathbf{e}_q\}$, $\mathbb{P}_x$-a.s. Using the strong Markov property of X. and memoryless property of $\mathbf{e}_q$, we have

$$\mathbb{P}_x(\tau_U^+(b) < \tau_D^+(a) < \mathbf{e}_q, X_{\tau_U^+(b)} \in b - a + du)$$
$$= \mathbb{P}_x(\tau_U^+(b) < \tau_D^+(a) \wedge \mathbf{e}_q, X_{\tau_U^+(b)} \in b - a + du)$$
$$\times \mathbb{P}_{u+b-a}(\tau_D^+(a) < \mathbf{e}_q).$$

The result follows from Theorem 2.3 and Proposition 2.5 below. □

Proposition 2.5 (Equation (4) of Lehoczky (1977)).

$$\mathbb{P}_x(\tau_D^+(a) < \mathbf{e}_q) = \mathbb{E}_x(e^{-q\tau_D^+(a)} \mathbf{1}_{\{\tau_D^+(a) < \infty\}})$$
$$= \int_x^r \frac{s'(u)}{W_q(u, u-a)} \exp\left(-\int_x^u W_{q,1}(v, v-a) \, dv\right) du.$$

Now by using (2.21) and Proposition 2.4, we obtain the following theorem.

Theorem 2.4. *For any $b > a > 0$, we have*

$$\mathbb{P}_x(\tau_D^+(a) < \tau_U^+(b) \wedge \mathbf{e}_q)$$
$$= \int_{x-a}^x \frac{s'(u+a)W_q(x,u)}{W_q^2(u+a,u)} du + \int_x^{x+a} \frac{s'(u-a)W_q(u,x)}{W_q^2(u,u-a)}$$
$$\times \int_a^b \frac{s'(u+z-a)e^{-\int_u^{u+z-a} W_{q,1}(w,w-a)dw}}{W_q(u+z-a,u+z)} dz du.$$

As $q \downarrow 0$, using Lemma A.2 we obtain from Theorem 2.4 the result with an infinite time-horizon in Pospisil *et al.* (2009, Theorem 4.1).

Corollary 2.7. *For any $b > a > 0$, we have*

$$\mathbb{P}_x(\tau_D^+(a) < \tau_U^+(b), \tau_D^+(a) < \infty)$$
$$= \int_{x-a}^x \frac{s'(u+a)(s(x)-s(u))}{(s(u+a)-s(u))^2} du + \int_x^{x+a} \frac{s'(u-a)(s(u)-s(x))}{(s(u)-s(u-a))^2}$$
$$\times \int_a^b \frac{s'(u+z-a)e^{\int_u^{u+z-a} \frac{-s'(w)dw}{s(w)-s(w-a)}}}{s(u+z-a)-s(u+z)} dv du.$$

2.3.2. Example: Brownian motion with drift

In this section we derive explicit formulas for probability $\mathbb{P}_x(\tau_D^+(a) < \tau_U^+(b) \wedge \mathbf{e}_q)$ under a Brownian motion with drift, which will provide analytical results for cases of $a \neq b$ that are not considered in Section 2.2. Specifically, consider a Brownian motion with drift $\mu \in \mathbb{R}$ and diffusion coefficient $\sigma > 0$:

$$dX_t = \mu\, dt + \sigma dB_t, \quad X_0 = x \in I \equiv \mathbb{R}.$$

For any $q > 0$, let us denote

$$\delta := \frac{\mu}{\sigma^2}, \quad \gamma := \sqrt{\delta^2 + \frac{2q}{\sigma^2}}.$$

Then the increasing and the decreasing eigenfunctions of X. can be chosen as (see, e.g., Borodin and Salminen (2002, p. 295))

$$\phi_q^+(x) = e^{(\gamma-\delta)x}, \quad \phi_q^-(x) = e^{-(\gamma+\delta)x}. \tag{2.22}$$

Fix the scale function $s(x) = \frac{1}{\delta}(1 - e^{-2\delta x})$ if $\mu \neq 0$ and $s(x) = 2x$ if $\mu = 0$, we have that $w_q = \gamma$, and

$$W_q(x,y) = 2e^{-\delta(x+y)}\frac{\sinh(\gamma(x-y))}{\gamma}, \quad W_{q,1}(x,y) = \gamma\coth(\gamma(x-y)) - \delta.$$

From Theorems 2.3 and 2.4 we have the following corollary.

Corollary 2.8. *If $a \geq b > 0$, then*

$$\mathbb{P}_x(\tau_D^+(a) < \tau_U^+(b) \wedge \mathbf{e}_q)$$
$$= \frac{\sigma^2\gamma}{2q}\left(\frac{e^{-\delta b}(\gamma\coth(\gamma b) + \delta)}{\sinh(\gamma b)} - \frac{\gamma}{\sinh^2(\gamma b)}\right)e^{-(a-b)(\delta+\gamma\coth(\gamma b))}.$$

If $b > a > 0$, then

$$\mathbb{P}_x(\tau_D^+(a) < \tau_U^+(b) \wedge \mathbf{e}_q)$$
$$= \frac{1 - \frac{\sigma^2\gamma}{2q}\left(\frac{e^{\delta a}(\gamma\coth(\gamma a) - \delta)}{\sinh(\gamma a)} - \frac{\gamma}{\sinh^2(\gamma a)}\right)e^{(a-b)(-\delta+\gamma\coth(\gamma a))}}{\gamma\cosh(\gamma a) - \delta\sinh(\gamma a)}\gamma e^{-\delta a}.$$

2.4. Applications

Consider the case of a stock with GBM model:

$$dS_t = \mu S_t dt + \sigma S_t dW_t, \quad S_0 = 1. \tag{2.23}$$

Using Corollary 2.8, we are in a position to address the following question:

"What is the probability that this stock would drop by $(100 \times \alpha)\%$ from its maximum before it rises $(100 \times \beta)\%$ over its minimum a pre-specified time-horizon T?"

A different form of the above question is:

"What is the joint probability distribution of the instant when the stock drops by $(100 \times \alpha)\%$ from its maximum and the maximum possible simple return before that instant?"

Apparently, answers to these two related questions will provide useful economic insights towards the market status by evaluating the likelihood of experiencing a large drawdown before realizing a substantial recovery, in a given finite investment horizon.

Formally, let us denote by $\overline{S}_t = \sup_{s \in [0,t]} S_s$ and $\underline{S}_t = \inf_{s \in [0,t]} S_s$. the running maximum and minimum prices, respectively. We consider the first time when the stock price S drops from $\overline{S}$ by $(100 \times \alpha)\%$ for some $\alpha \in (0,1)$:

$$\varrho_D^+(\alpha) := \inf\{t > 0 : \overline{S}_t - S_t > \alpha \overline{S}_t\} \equiv \inf\{t > 0 : S_t < (1-\alpha)\overline{S}_t\},$$

as well as the first time when S rises over $\underline{S}$ by $(100 \times \beta)\%$ for some $\beta \in (0, \infty)$:

$$\varrho_U^+(\beta) := \inf\{t > 0 : S_t - \underline{S}_t > \beta \underline{S}_t\} \equiv \inf\{t > 0 : S_t > (1+\beta)\underline{S}_t\}.$$

In other words, $\varrho_D^+(\alpha)$ is the first time when the percentage drawdown of S exceeds α, and $\varrho_U^+(\beta)$ is a first passage time for the percentage drawup process $(S_t - \underline{S}_t)/\underline{S}_t$, which gives the maximum possible simple return if selling the stock at time t:

$$\sup_{s \in [0,t]} \frac{S_t - S_s}{S_s} = \frac{S_t - \overline{S}_t}{\overline{S}_t}.$$

For a measure of drawdown risks in a finite time-horizon $T > 0$, we propose a quantity that incorporates both the percentage drawdown for the bearish strength and the percentage drawup for the bullish strength. Namely,

$$\mathbb{P}(\varrho_D^+(\alpha) < \varrho_U^+(\beta) \wedge T). \tag{2.24}$$

This quantity also gives the joint distribution of the stopping time $\varrho_D^+(\alpha)$ and the maximum possible profit by $\varrho_D^+(\alpha)$: $\sup_{t\in[0,\varrho_D^+(\alpha)]}(S_t - \underline{S}_t)/\underline{S}_t$, thanks to the identities that

$$\frac{1}{\mathrm{d}\beta}\mathbb{P}(\varrho_D^+(\alpha) < T, \sup_{t\in[0,\varrho_D^+(\alpha)]}(S_t - \underline{S}_t)/\underline{S}_t \in \mathrm{d}\beta)$$

$$= \frac{\partial}{\partial\beta}\mathbb{P}(\varrho_D^+(\alpha) < T, \sup_{t\in[0,\varrho_D^+(\alpha)]}(S_t - \underline{S}_t)/\underline{S}_t < \beta)$$

$$= \frac{\partial}{\partial\beta}\mathbb{P}(\varrho_D^+(\alpha) < \varrho_U^+(\beta) \wedge T). \tag{2.25}$$

To calculate the probability in (2.24), we use Itô's lemma to obtain that

$$\mathrm{d}\log S_t = \nu \mathrm{d}t + \sigma \mathrm{d}W_t, \quad \log S_0 = 0,$$

where $\nu = \mu - \frac{1}{2}\sigma^2$ represents the drift of the logarithm stock price. Then the stopping times $\varrho_D^+(\alpha)$ and $\varrho_U^+(\beta)$ are the same as the first passage times of the drawdown and the drawup of $\log S$ at levels $-\log(1-\alpha)$ and $\log(1+\beta)$, respectively. More specially, denoting by $\tau_D^+(-\log(1-\alpha))$ and $\tau_U^+(\log(1+\beta))$ the latter two first passage times, then for any $T > 0$,

$$\mathbb{P}(\varrho_D^+(\alpha) < \varrho_U^+(\beta) \wedge T) = \mathbb{P}(\tau_D^+(-\log(1-\alpha)) < \tau_U^+(\log(1+\beta)) \wedge T),$$

where the right-hand side is given in Theorem 2.2 if $(1-\alpha)(1+\beta) = 1$, and in Corollary 2.8 in general cases via Laplace inversion.

In Figure 2.2 we plot the probability in (2.24) for specific values of the yearly logarithmic return ν and volatility σ. We fix the time-horizon to $T = 1$ year and set $\alpha = 0.2$. To evaluate this probability, we implement the fixed-Talbot method (Abate and Valkó, 2004) to numerically invert the Laplace transform

$$\int_0^\infty \mathbb{P}(\tau_D^+(a) < \tau_U^+(b) \wedge t)\mathrm{e}^{-qt}\mathrm{d}t = \frac{1}{q}\mathbb{P}(\tau_D^+(a) < \tau_U^+(b) \wedge \mathbf{e}_q),$$

with $a = -\log(1-\alpha)$ and $b = \log(1+\beta)$.

From Figure 2.2, we find that the probability $\mathbb{P}(\varrho_D^+(\alpha) < \varrho_U^+(\beta) \wedge T)$ decreases with the annualized logarithm return ν and increases with the volatility σ, suggesting that this quantity is an effective indicator for the strength of ν and σ. In all cases, the probability increases with β, and as β increases, the value of the probability converges to the limit $\mathbb{P}(\varrho_D^+(\alpha) < T)$, which only measures the maximum percentage drawdown of S by time T.

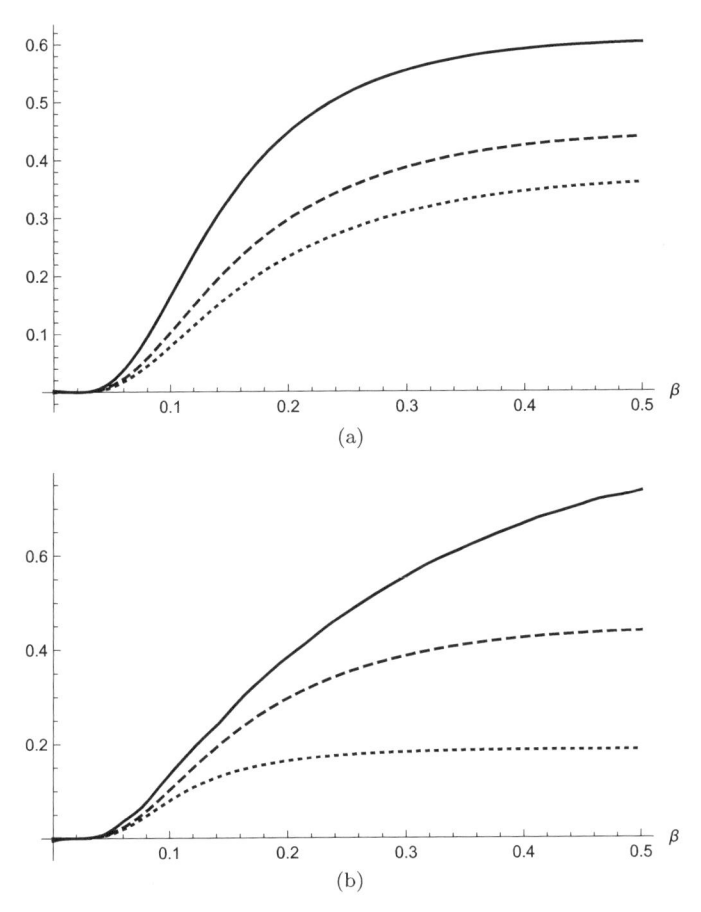

Fig. 2.2. Plot of the probability in (2.24) as a function of β. Here we set $T = 1$ year and $\alpha = 0.2$. (a) we set $\sigma = 0.2$ and $\nu = -0.05$ (solid), or $\nu = 0.05$ (dashed), or $\nu = 0.1$ (dotted). (b) we set $\nu = 0.05$ and $\sigma = 0.3$ (solid), or $\sigma = 0.2$ (dashed), or $\sigma = 0.15$ (dotted).

As seen in (2.25), we can obtain the conditional density of the maximum possible profit at $\varrho_D^+(\alpha)$ given $\{\varrho_D^+(\alpha) < T\}$:

$$\frac{1}{\mathrm{d}\beta}\mathbb{P}\left(\sup_{t\in[0,\varrho_D^+(\alpha)]}(S_t - \underline{S}_t)/\underline{S}_t \in \mathrm{d}\beta | \varrho_D^+(\alpha) < T\right)$$

$$= \frac{1}{(1+\beta)\mathbb{P}(\varrho_D^+(\alpha) < \infty)} \frac{\partial}{\partial b}\bigg|_{a=-\log(1-\alpha), b=\log(1+\beta)}$$

$$\times \mathbb{P}(\tau_D^+(a) < \tau_U^+(b) \wedge T), \qquad (2.26)$$

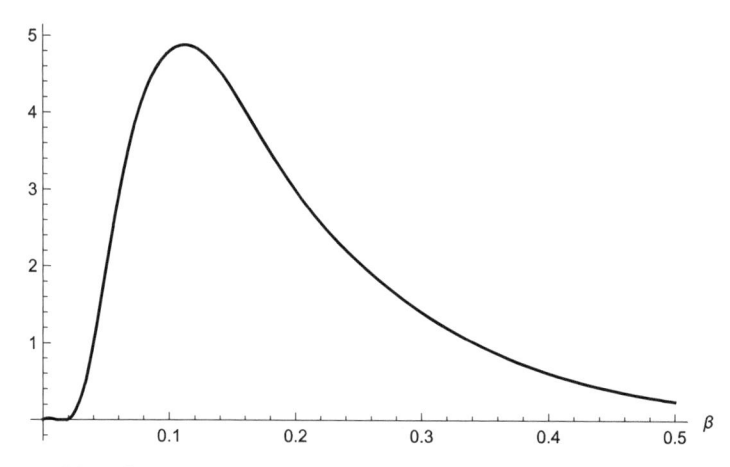

Fig. 2.3. Plot of the conditional probability density of the maximum percentage drawdown given that $\tau_D^+(\alpha) < T$, which is given in (2.26). Here we set $T = 1$ year and $\alpha = 0.2$, $\nu = 0.1$ and $\sigma = 0.2$.

where the derivative in the second line can be interpreted as the slope of tangent lines of the curves in Figure 2.2. Using again the fixed-Talbot method, we numerically obtain this density shown in Figure 2.3.

One can use the above conditional distribution of the maximum percentage drawdown at $\varrho_D^+(\alpha)$ to define value-at-risk type risk measures using the quantiles of this distribution. Furthermore, the expectation under this probability distribution gives the expected maximum profit[2] before a trailing stop, if the trailing stop is triggered by the time-horizon $T > 0$. See Chapter 9 for more discussions on the relationship between trailing stop and drawdowns.

2.5. Concluding Remarks

In this chapter, we study the probability that a drawdown of a units precedes a drawup of b units in a finite time-horizon, under random walks, Brownian motion with drift, and general linear diffusion models. In the case that $a = b$, we make use of existing results on Toeplitz matrix and

---

[2]Notice that this maximum profit can never to attained because that requires the investor's ability to spot the moment when the underlying is at a "turning point" in real-time. However, such turning points can never be identified by a stopping time. See Chapter 3 for how one can handle such random times with progressive enlargement of filtration.

Brownian motion exit times to derive series expansions for this probability under random walk models and Brownian motion with drift. By using Canadization, we obtain results for the general cases of $a \neq b$ under a general linear diffusion model. Finally, we apply these results to GBM to numerically evaluate this probability and the conditional probability density of maximum relative drawup given a drawdown event.

2.6. Proof of Lemmas

Proof of Lemma 2.1. Consider a random walk that is obtained from $-X.$ with killing upon entering either $[A, \infty)$ or $(-\infty, 0]$, then the one-step transition matrix of this killed process on $[0, A]$ is given by the Toeplitz matrix M_{A+1} generated by column vector c and row vector r:

$$c = (\underbrace{0, p, 0, \ldots, 0}_{A+1}) \quad r = (\underbrace{0, q, 0, \ldots, 0}_{A+1}).$$

The n-step transition matrix is the nth power of that matrix. Therefore, the probability under consideration is the $(u+1, v+1)$-th entry of this n-step transition matrix. By Salkuyeh (2006, Theorem 2.3), the result follows. □

Proof of Lemma 2.2. By the strong Markov property of $X.$, we have

$$g(n, -1; B) = p \cdot g(n-1, 0; B), \tag{2.27}$$

$$g(n, B; B) = q \cdot g(n-1, B-1; B) + q \cdot g(n-1, B-1; B-1), \tag{2.28}$$

and for $-1 < v < B$ that,

$$g(n, v; B) = q \cdot g(n-1, v-1; B) + p \cdot g(n-1, v+1; B). \tag{2.29}$$

To see why (2.28) holds, we observe that $g(n, B; B)$ is the probability of an event that only includes paths on which the process $-X.$ remains nonnegative. Equation (2.28) represents the decomposition of these paths into the ones on which the process stays strictly positive after the first upward step, and the ones on which it does not. Equation (2.29) follows by conditioning on the first step being up or down respectively.

Equations (2.27), (2.28), and (2.29) can be summarized in vector form as

$$G_n^{(B)} = M_{B+2} \cdot G_{n-1}^{(B)} + Y_{n-1}^{(B)}, \tag{2.30}$$

where M_{B+2} is the one-step transition matrix of a simple random walk killed on exiting $[-1, B+1]$ as appeared in the proof of Lemma 2.1, $G_n^{(B)}$ and $Y_n^{(B)}$ are the $(B+2) \times 1$ vectors

$$G_n^{(B)} = (g(n, B; B), g(n, B-1; B), \ldots, g(n, -1; B))^\mathsf{T},$$

and

$$Y_n^{(B)} = (p \cdot g(n, B-1; B-1), 0, \ldots, 0)^\mathsf{T},$$

respectively, while

$$G_B^{(B)} = Y_{B-1}^{(B)} = (p^B, 0, \ldots, 0)^\mathsf{T}.$$

We can now use (2.30) recursively to obtain

$$G_n^{(B)} = [M_{B+2}]^{n-B} \cdot G_B^{(B)} + \sum_{k=0}^{n-B-1} [M_{B+2}]^{n-B-k-1} \cdot Y_{B+k}^{(B)}$$

$$= \sum_{k=0}^{n-B} [M_{B+2}]^{n-B-k} \cdot Y_{B+k-1}^{(B)}. \qquad (2.31)$$

Equation (2.3) now follows from (2.31) Salkuyeh (2006, Theorem 2.3), and Lemma 2.1. □

Chapter 3

Drawdowns and the Speed of Market Crashes

In this chapter, we derive the joint Laplace transform of the last reset time of the maximum of a stochastic process prior to a drawdown event, the speed of market crash, and the maximum of the process under a general time-homogenous linear diffusion model. The drawdown event of an asset occurs at the first time when its drawdown process reaches a pre-specified level $a > 0$, which is denoted by $\tau_D^+(a)$. The speed of a market crash, $\mathcal{S}_a$, which measures how fast the process drops a units below its running maximum, is defined as the difference between $\tau_D^+(a)$ and the last reset time of the maximum prior to it, $g_a := \sup\{t < \tau_D^+(a) : X_t = \overline{X}_t\}$. Namely, $\mathcal{S}_a = \tau_D^+(a) - g_a$.

A key step in our analysis is to establish the conditional independence of sample paths before and after the random time g_a, given the location of the process X_{g_a}. After separately establishing the existence and uniqueness properties of the stochastic differential equations that govern the evolution of these two conditional independent components, we derive analytical formulas for the Laplace transforms of the random time g_a and of the speed of market crash $\mathcal{S}_a$ conditional on X_{g_a}. Using the law of X_{g_a}, we then combine these results to derive the joint Laplace transform for the triplet $(g_a, \mathcal{S}_a, X_{g_a})$. Finally, we discuss applications of our results in the pricing of insurance claims based on the drawdown and its speed under a Brownian motion with drift model and a constant elasticity of variance (CEV) model (see, e.g., Jeanblanc et al. (2009)).

Our results extend the work of Taylor (1975), Lehoczky (1977) and Nikeghbali (2006) from which it is possible to extract the Laplace transform of the random variable X_{g_a} under a Brownian motion with drift model and general linear diffusions. In our derivation of the Laplace transform of g_a, we use the method of progressive enlargement of filtration developed in Jeulin and Yor (1978) and Jeulin (1980). A good reference in English on this topic can be found in Protter (2003, Section VI.3). In Tanré and Vallois (2007), this method is used to derive the last reset time of the extreme values of a Brownian motion with drift before the range process reaches a given level. Kardaras (2015) uses this technique to show the effective use of randomized stopping times in studying the distributional properties of optional processes up to random times. However, none of these works are concerned with random times related to the drawdown or the drawdown itself.

The most important reason for the popularity of the drawdowns in financial risk management is due to the fact that they provide a dynamic measure of risk. It is also conceivable that a portfolio or hedge fund manager may want to insure against such market crashes as measured by large realizations of the drawdown. Yet, the issue of how fast a market crash occurred is of vital importance to investors and portfolio or hedge fund managers. This is because a slow transition from the maximum-to-date to a drop of a pre-specified level (i.e., a drawdown) is far easier to absorb or react to than a dramatic one. Therefore, the speed at which a drawdown is realized is a very relevant quantity in the description of a market crash. This is precisely the motivation of our work which for the first time studies quantities related to the joint distribution of the drawdown and the speed at which it is realized. Our work thus provides the analytical basis for the pricing of insurance claims based on the drawdown and its speed and which can be used to hedge against dramatic market crashes.

The rest of the chapter is structured as follows. In Section 3.1, we begin by the mathematical formulation of our problem and provide the main result, which is an analytical formula of the joint Laplace transform of X_{g_a}, g_a and $\mathcal{S}_a$. In Section 3.2, we review some useful results on progressive enlargement of filtrations and establish preliminary results. Section 3.3 is devoted to the proof of the main result with these preliminary results and the path decomposition of X. at the random time g_a. As applications, in Section 3.4 we propose and price a novel drawdown insurance using Canadization. We provide an analytical formula for the Canadized claim price in the special cases of a Brownian motion with drift and a constant elasticity of variance (CEV) model. We finally conclude with some closing remarks in Section 3.5. Proofs of lemmas can be found in Section 3.6.

For preliminaries on linear diffusion and definitions of the scale function $s(\cdot)$ and other related functions used in this chapter, please refer to the Appendix.

3.1. Mathematical Formulation and Analytical Results

In a filtered probability space $(\Omega, \mathbb{F}, \mathcal{F}, \mathbb{P})$ with filtration $\mathbb{F} = \{\mathcal{F}_t\}_{t\geq 0}$, let $X_. = \{X_t\}_{t\geq 0}$ be a one-dimensional time-homogenous linear diffusion on interval $I \equiv (l, r) \subset \mathbb{R}$ on this probability space:

$$\mathrm{d}X_t = \mu(X_t)\mathrm{d}t + \sigma(X_t)\mathrm{d}W_t, \quad X_0 = x \in I. \tag{3.1}$$

where $\{W_t\}_{t\geq 0}$ is a standard Brownian motion with respect to $\mathbb{F}$, $(\mu(\cdot), \sigma(\cdot))$ is a pair of real-valued functions that satisfy (A.2) and (A.3) in the Appendix. We assume that the boundaries of I are either natural or entrance-not-exit.

The first passage time of $X_.$ is denote by $\tau_X^{\pm}(x)$:

$$\tau_X^{\pm}(x) = \inf\{t > 0 : X_t \gtrless x\}, \quad \forall x \in I.$$

We denote the running maximum of $X_.$ by $\overline{X}_t = \sup_{s \in [0,t]} X_s$. The drawdown process of $X_.$, which is denoted by $D_.$, is defined as the drop of X_t from its running maximum $\overline{X}_t$:

$$D_t = \overline{X}_t - X_t, \quad \forall t \geq 0.$$

For any fixed $a > 0$ such that $x - a \in I$, we denote the first passage time of the drawdown process $D_.$ at level a. That is,

$$\tau_D^+(a) = \inf\{t > 0 : D_t > a\}. \tag{3.2}$$

The last reset time of the maximum $\overline{X}_.$ before the stopping time $\tau_D^+(a)$ is denoted by g_a. That is,

$$g_a := \sup\{t < \tau_D^+(a) : \overline{X}_t = X_t\}. \tag{3.3}$$

Notice that g_a is defined as a "last passage" time, which means that g_a is not a stopping time so cannot be identified with an real-time algorithm. By the above definition, we see that $X_t < \overline{X}_t$ for $t \in [g_a, \tau_D^+(a)]$, and $X_{\tau_D^+(a)} = \overline{X}_{\tau_D^+(a)} - a$. Thus, the process $X_.$ is experiencing a crash during the period $[g_a, \tau_D^+(a)]$. We will call the time elapsed between g_a and $\tau_D^+(a)$

the speed of market crash, which we denote by $\mathcal{S}_a$:

$$\mathcal{S}_a := \tau_D^+(a) - g_a. \tag{3.4}$$

The probability distribution of the random variable $X_{g_a} = \overline{X}_{\tau_D^+(a)}$ is well studied (see, e.g., Lehoczky (1977) and Nikeghbali (2006)). However, the fact that g_a is not a stopping time makes it difficult to analyze the random time itself. The main contribution of this chapter is the derivation of an analytical formula for the joint Laplace transform of random variables g_a, $\mathcal{S}_a$ and X_{g_a}. In particular, we have the following result.

Theorem 3.1. *Let $q, p, \rho > 0$ be positive numbers. Then, for the diffusion in (3.1), we have*

$$\mathbb{E}_x(\exp(-qg_a - p\mathcal{S}_a - \rho X_{g_a}))$$
$$= \int_x^r \frac{e^{-\rho m} s'(m)}{W_p(m, m-a)} \exp\left(-\int_x^m W_{q,1}(u, u-a) du\right) dm, \quad \forall x \in I, \tag{3.5}$$

where the scale function of X., $s(\cdot)$, and functions $W_q(\cdot, \cdot)$, $W_{q,1}(\cdot, \cdot)$ are defined as in the Appendix.

It is worth pointing out that, by letting $\alpha = p = q > 0$ in (3.5), we obtain Lehoczky's joint Laplace transform of $\tau_D^+(a)$ and X_{g_a}.

Corollary 3.1. *Let $q, \rho > 0$. Then we have*

$$\mathbb{E}_x(\exp(-q\tau_D^+(a) - \rho X_{g_a}))$$
$$= \int_x^r \frac{e^{-\rho m} s'(m)}{W_q(m, m-a)} \exp\left(-\int_x^m W_{q,1}(u, u-a) du\right) dm, \quad \forall x \in I.$$

In the next section, we will use the method of progressive enlargement of filtration to study g_a, $\mathcal{S}_a$, as well as the path decomposition of X. before and after the random time g_a. To this end, we prove our main result in (3.5).

3.2. Progressive Enlargement of Filtrations by g_a

In this section, we prove the main result through optional projection and path decomposition. More specifically, we consider the optional projection of the random process $\mathbf{1}_{\{g_a > t\}}$ on the natural filtration $\mathbb{F}$,

$$Y_t^g := \mathbb{P}_x(g_a > t | \mathcal{F}_t). \qquad (3.6)$$

The fact that $\mathbf{1}_{\{g_a > t\}}$ is non-increasing implies that the process $Y^g = \{Y_t^g\}_{t \geq 0}$ is a supermartingale, so a decomposition of the Doob–Meyer type exists. That is,

$$Y_t^g = M_t^g + A_t^g, \qquad (3.7)$$

where $\{M_t^g\}_{t \geq 0}$ is a local martingale and $\{A_t^g\}_{t \geq 0}$ is a predictable non-increasing process. Using the scale function for linear diffusions, it is convenient to derive analytical formulas for Y^g, M^g and A^g. In particular, we have the following lemma.

Lemma 3.1. *Let s be a scale function of the process in (3.1). Then*

$$Y_t^g = \frac{s(X_t) - s(\overline{X}_t - a)}{s(\overline{X}_t) - s(\overline{X}_t - a)} \mathbf{1}_{\{t < \tau_D^+(a)\}}, \qquad (3.8)$$

$$M_t^g = 1 + \int_0^{t \wedge \tau_D^+(a)} \frac{s'(X_u) \sigma(X_u) dW_u}{s(\overline{X}_u) - s(\overline{X}_u - a)}, \qquad (3.9)$$

$$A_t^g = \int_0^{t \wedge \tau_D^+(a)} \frac{-s'(\overline{X}_u) d\overline{X}_u}{s(\overline{X}_u) - s(\overline{X}_u - a)}. \qquad (3.10)$$

The random time g_a is an honest time. This is because, on the event $\{g_a \leq t\}$, one has $g_a = \sup\{s \leq t : X_{s \wedge \tau_D^+(a)} = \overline{X}_{t \wedge \tau_D^+(a)}\}$, which is $\mathcal{F}_t$-measurable.[1] To enlarge the filtration in order to make g_a a stopping time, we consider the progressive enlargement of filtration

$$\mathcal{F}_t^g := \mathcal{F}_t \vee \sigma\{g_a \wedge t\}, \quad \forall t \geq 0. \qquad (3.11)$$

Under the enlarged filtration $\mathbb{F}^g := \{\mathcal{F}_t^g\}_{t \geq 0}$, a square integrable $\mathbb{F}$-martingale is a semimartingale since g_a is an honest time. In particular, we have the following lemma.

Lemma 3.2 (Theorem VI.18 of Protter (2003)). *Let $\{N_t\}_{t \geq 0}$ be a square integrable $\mathbb{F}$-martingale. Then it is a $\mathbb{F}^g$-semimartingale. Moreover,*

---
[1] See Protter (2003, p. 373).

N_t has a Doob–Meyer decomposition

$$N_t = \left(N_t - \int_0^{t \wedge g_a} \frac{1}{Y_s^g} \mathrm{d}\langle N, M^g \rangle_s + \mathbf{1}_{\{t \geq g_a\}} \int_{g_a}^t \frac{1}{1-Y_s^g} \mathrm{d}\langle N, M^g \rangle_s \right)$$
$$+ \left(\int_0^{t \wedge g_a} \frac{1}{Y_s^g} \mathrm{d}\langle N, M^g \rangle_s - \mathbf{1}_{\{t \geq g_a\}} \int_{g_a}^t \frac{1}{1-Y_s^g} \mathrm{d}\langle N, M^g \rangle_s \right).$$
(3.12)

Here the first line of the right-hand side is an $\mathbb{F}^g$-martingale, and the second line of the right-hand side is a process with finite variation.

3.3. Proof of the Main Results

As a result of Lemma 3.2, the driving Brownian motion of a diffusion process is now a semimartingale. Using Lévy's characterization of Brownian motion (see, e.g., Revuz and Yor (1999, Theorem IV.3.6)), we can see that the martingale part of this semimartingale is in fact a standard $\mathbb{F}^g$-Brownian motion. This will enable us to separately study the law of the diffusion path in (3.1) during the period $[0, g_a]$ and the period $[g_a, \tau_D^+(a)]$, by conditioning on the event $\{X_{g_a} = m\}$.

In particular, we can establish the following result.

Proposition 3.1. *Conditionally on $X_{g_a} = m$, $\{X_t\}_{t \in [0, g_a]}$ is a process with the same law as the unique non-explosive weak solution of the following stochastic differential equation, stopped at the first passage time of a level m, $\tau_Z^+(m)$:*

$$\mathrm{d}Z_t = \left(\mu(Z_t) + \frac{s'(Z_t)\sigma^2(Z_t)}{s(Z_t) - s(\overline{Z}_t - a)} \right) \mathrm{d}t + \sigma(Z_t) \mathrm{d}\widetilde{W}_t, \quad Z_0 = \overline{Z}_0 = x,$$
(3.13)

where $\{\widetilde{W}_t\}_{t \geq 0}$ is a standard $\mathbb{F}^g$-Brownian motion.

Proof. Using (3.12) we know that for any $t \in [0, g_a]$, the process defined as

$$\widetilde{W}_t = W_t - \int_0^t \frac{s'(X_u)\sigma(X_u)\mathrm{d}u}{s(X_u) - s(\overline{X}_u - a)}$$

is a standard $\mathbb{F}^g$-Brownian motion. Therefore, for any $t \in [0, g_a]$, we have

$$\begin{aligned}
\mathrm{d}X_t &= \mu(X_t)\mathrm{d}t + \sigma(X_t)\mathrm{d}\widetilde{W}_t + \frac{s'(X_t)\sigma^2(X_t)\mathrm{d}t}{s(X_t) - s(\overline{X}_t - a)} \\
&= \left(\mu(X_t) + \frac{s'(X_t)\sigma^2(X_t)}{s(X_t) - s(\overline{X}_t - a)}\right)\mathrm{d}t + \sigma(X_t)\mathrm{d}\widetilde{W}_t.
\end{aligned}$$

To finish the proof, we need to show that the stochastic differential equation in (3.13) admits a unique weak solution. To that end, for any x such that $x, x - a \in I$, we choose a scale function $s(\cdot)$ such that $s(z) > 0$ for all $z > x - a$. Consider function for any (z, m) such that $r > m \geq z > m - a > l$ and $z \geq x$:

$$H(z, m) := \frac{-s(z)}{s(z) - s(m - a)} \exp\left(-\int_\kappa^m \frac{s'(u - a)\mathrm{d}u}{s(u) - s(u - a)}\right),$$

where $\kappa \in (l, x)$ is a fixed constant. Then it is straightforward to verify that $\frac{\partial}{\partial m} H(z, m)|_{z=m} = 0$, and

$$\frac{1}{2}\sigma^2(z)\frac{\partial^2}{\partial z^2}H(z, m) + \left(\mu(z) + \frac{s'(z)\sigma^2(z)}{s(z) - s(m - z)}\right)\frac{\partial}{\partial z}H(z, m) = 0.$$

Hence, if $\{Z_t\}_{t \geq 0}$ is a solution to (3.13) such that $Z_0 = x' \geq x$ and $\overline{Z}_0 = m' \in [x', x' + a)$, then for any $\epsilon > 0$ sufficiently small, by applying the optional sampling theorem (see, e.g., Karatzas and Shreve (1991, p. 19–20)) to bounded martingale $\{H(Z_t, \overline{Z}_t)\}_{t \in [0, \tau_Z^+(m), \tau_Z^-(m - a + \epsilon)]}$, we obtain

$$\mathbb{P}_{x', m'}(\tau_Z^+(m) < \tau_Z^-(m - a + \epsilon)) = \frac{H(x', m') - H(m' - a + \epsilon, m')}{H(m', m') - H(m' - a + \epsilon, m')}.$$

Taking the limit of the above as $\epsilon \downarrow 0$ we obtain that $\mathbb{P}_{x', m'}(\tau_Z^+(m) < \tau_Z^-(m - a)) = 1$. Hence, for any solution to (3.13) such that $\overline{Z}_0 - Z_0 < a$, we will have $\overline{Z}_t - Z_t < a$ for all $t \geq 0$.

In the sequel we prove the existence and uniqueness of the solution to (3.13) by using the method of removal of drift (see, e.g., Karatzas and Shreve (1991, p. 339)). We notice that $H_z(z, m) := \frac{\partial}{\partial z} H(z, m)$ satisfies

$$H_z(z, m) = \frac{s'(z)s(m - a)}{(s(z) - s(m - a))^2} \exp\left(-\int_\kappa^m \frac{s'(u - a)\mathrm{d}u}{s(u) - s(u - a)}\right) > 0.$$

It follows that, for a fixed $m \geq x$, $H(\cdot, m)$ is strictly increasing over interval $(m - a, m]$, and function $h(m) := H(m, m)$ is also strictly increasing over $[x, \infty)$ since $h'(m) = H_z(m, m) > 0$. Denoting $h^{-1}(\cdot)$ the inverse of $h(\cdot)$, and $H^{-1}(\cdot, m)$ is the inverse of $H(\cdot, m)$, i.e., $h(h^{-1}(m)) = m$ and $H(H^{-1}(z, m), m) = z$.

Suppose $\{Z_t\}_{t \geq 0}$ is a solution to (3.13) such that $Z_0 = \overline{Z}_0 = x$, and consider the bi-variate process $(Y_t, \widetilde{Y}_t) := (H(Z_t, \overline{Z}_t), h(\overline{Z}_t))$. Notice that, for any $t > 0$, the running maximum of Y. is given by

$$\overline{Y}_t = \sup_{s \in [0,t]} H(Z_s, \overline{Z}_s) = \sup_{s \in [0,t]} H(\overline{Z}_s, \overline{Z}_s) = \sup_{s \in [0,t]} h(\overline{Z}_s) = h(\overline{Z}_t) = \widetilde{Y}_t,$$

where we used the monotonicity of $H(\cdot, \overline{Z}_s)$ in the second equality, and the monotonicity of $h(\cdot)$ in the fourth equality. Hence, $\widetilde{Y}.$ is the same as the running maximum $\overline{Y}..$. Thus, we have $\overline{Z}_t = h^{-1}(\overline{Y}_t)$ and $Z_t = H^{-1}(Y_t, h^{-1}(\overline{Y}_t))$. Using Itô's lemma we obtain that

$$\begin{aligned} dY_t &= H_z(Z_t, \overline{Z}_t)\sigma(Z_t)d\widetilde{W}_t \\ &= H_z(H^{-1}(Y_t, h^{-1}(\overline{Y}_t)), h^{-1}(\overline{Y}_t))\sigma(h^{-1}(\overline{Y}_t))d\widetilde{W}_t \\ &= \tilde{\sigma}(Y_t, \overline{Y}_t)d\widetilde{W}_t, \quad Y_0 = \overline{Y}_0 = h(x). \end{aligned} \quad (3.14)$$

Conversely, because $\tilde{\sigma}^2(y, \bar{y}) > 0$ for all $\bar{y} \geq h(m)$ and $y \in (H(h^{-1}(\bar{y}) - a, h^{-1}(\bar{y})), \bar{y}]$, we can follow the proof of Theorem 2.1 in Forde et al. (2013) to prove that (3.14) has a unique non-explosive weak solution until $Y_t = H(h^{-1}(\overline{Y}_t) - a, h^{-1}(\overline{Y}_t))$. Define $Z_t := H^{-1}(Y_t, h^{-1}(\overline{Y}_t))$ and $\widetilde{Z}_t := h^{-1}(\overline{Y}_t)$. Then by similar argument as above, we know that $\overline{Z}. \equiv \widetilde{Z}..$. Moreover, $(Z., \overline{Z}.)$ solves (3.13) and is the unique non-explosive weak solution such that $Z_0 = \overline{Z}_0 = x$, up until the moment when $\overline{Z}_t - Z_t = a$. From previous discussion, we know that $\overline{Z}_t - Z_t = a$ will never happen. This concludes the proof of Proposition 3.1. □

A consequence of Proposition 3.1 is that the Laplace transform of the random time g_a conditional on $\{X_{g_a} = m\}$ is the same as the Laplace transform of the stopping time $\tau_Z^+(m)$. More specifically, we have the following proposition.

Proposition 3.2. *Conditionally on $X_{g_a} = m$, the Laplace transform of the random time g_a is given by*

$$\mathbb{E}_x(e^{-q g_a} | X_{g_a} = m) = \exp\left(\int_m^x \left(\frac{-s'(u)}{s(u) - s(u-a)} + W_{q,1}(u, u-a)\right) du\right).$$

Proof. We apply the Feynman–Kac formula (see, e.g., Karatzas and Shreve (1991, p. 366)) to the diffusion in (3.13). In particular, we need to find a locally bounded function of (z, m) on $\{z, m \in I, m \geq z, m - z < a\}$ satisfying the following partial differential equation for any given $\lambda > 0$:

$$\frac{1}{2}\sigma^2(z)\frac{\partial^2 f}{\partial z^2} + \left(\mu(z) + \frac{s'(z)\sigma^2(z)}{s(z) - s(m-a)}\right)\frac{\partial f}{\partial z} = \lambda f(z, m), \quad (3.15)$$

$$\left.\frac{\partial f}{\partial m}\right|_{m=z} = 0. \quad (3.16)$$

To this end, consider

$$f(z, m) = \exp\left(\int_\kappa^{m \vee \kappa} \left(\frac{-s'(u)}{s(u) - s(u-a)} + W_{q,1}(u, u-a)\right)du\right)$$

$$\times \frac{W_q(z, m-a)}{W_q(m, m-a)} \frac{s(m) - s(m-a)}{s(z) - s(m-a)}, \quad (3.17)$$

where $\kappa \in I$ is a fixed constant. Then it is straightforward to verify that $f(\cdot, \cdot)$ is a locally bounded function that solves (3.15) and (3.16). Thus, we can express the conditional Laplace transforms of g_a as

$$\mathbb{E}_x(e^{-qg_a}|X_{g_a} = m) = \mathbb{E}_x(e^{-q\tau_Z^+(m)}) = \frac{f(x, x)}{f(m, m)}, \quad (3.18)$$

This completes the proof. □

On the other hand, the Brownian path during the drawdown, $[g_a, \tau_D^+(a)]$, can be similarly described by conditioning on $\{X_{g_a} = m\}$. In particular, we give the law of $\{m - X_{t+g_a}\}_{t \in [0, S_a]}$.

Proposition 3.3. *Conditionally on $X_{g_a} = m$, the law of $\{m - X_{t+g_a}\}_{t \in [0, S_a]}$ is the same as the unique strictly positive weak solution of the following stochastic differential equation, stopped at the first passage time to level a, $\tau_J^+(a)$:*

$$dJ_t = \left(-\mu(m - J_t) + \frac{s'(m - J_t)\sigma^2(m - J_t)}{s(m) - s(m - J_t)}\right)dt - \sigma(m - J_t)d\widetilde{W}_t, \quad (3.19)$$

where $J_0 = 0$, $\{\widetilde{W}_t\}_{t \geq 0}$ is a standard $\{\mathcal{F}_{g_a+t}^g\}$-Brownian motion. Moreover, the processes $\{X_t\}_{t \in [0, g_a]}$ and $\{X_t\}_{t \in [g_a, \tau_D^+(a)]}$ are independent.

Proof. Using (3.12) we know that for any $t \in [0, \mathcal{S}_a]$, the process defined as

$$\widetilde{W}_{t+g_a} = W_{t+g_a} - W_{g_a} + \int_{g_a}^{t+g_a} \frac{s'(X_u)\sigma(X_u)}{s(m) - s(X_u)} du \qquad (3.20)$$

is a $\{\mathcal{F}_{t+g_a}^g\}_{t \geq 0}$-standard Brownian motion. Therefore, for any $t \in [g_a, \tau_D^+(a)]$, we have

$$dX_t = \mu(X_t)dt + \sigma(X_t)d\widetilde{W}_t - \frac{s'(X_t)\sigma^2(X_t)}{s(m) - s(X_t)}dt$$

$$= \left(\mu(X_t) - \frac{s'(X_t)\sigma^2(X_t)}{s(m) - s(X_t)}\right)dt + \sigma(X_t)d\widetilde{W}_t.$$

Since $\{\widetilde{W}_{t+g_a}\}_{t \geq 0}$ is independent of $\mathcal{F}_{g_a}^g$, $\{\widetilde{W}_{t+g_a}\}_{t \geq 0}$ is independent of X_{g_a} and $\{X_t\}_{t \in [0, g_a]}$. To prove the existence and uniqueness of a weak solution to (3.19) with initial condition $J_0 = 0$, we first use discussions in Karatzas and Shreve (1991, p. 329–353) to conclude (3.19) admits a unique positive weak solution on $I' \equiv (0, m-l)$ for any initial condition $J_0 \in I'$. To prove that J_0 can be taken as 0, we need to prove that 0 is an entrance boundary. To that end, we choose a scale function of $X_{\cdot}$, $s(\cdot)$, such that $s(x) < 0$ for all $x \in (l, m]$. Then it is straightforward to verify that a scale function of $J_{\cdot}$ can be chosen as

$$\tilde{S}(x) := \frac{s(m-x)}{s(m) - s(m-x)}, \quad \forall x \in I',$$

which is negative on I', and its derivative is

$$\tilde{S}'(x) = \frac{-s(m)s'(m-x)}{(s(m) - s(m-x))^2} > 0, \quad \forall x \in I'.$$

Consider the integral for the test of entrance (see, e.g., Borodin and Salminen (2002, p. 14)):

$$\int_0^z \frac{2(\tilde{S}(z) - \tilde{S}(y))dy}{\tilde{S}'(y)\sigma^2(m-y)} < 2\int_0^z \frac{\tilde{S}(y)}{\tilde{S}'(y)} \frac{dy}{\sigma^2(m-y)}$$

$$= -2\int_0^z \frac{s(m-y)(s(m) - s(m-y))}{s(m)s'(m-y)} \frac{dy}{\sigma^2(m-y)}$$

$$\leq \sup_{y \in [0,z]} \left|\frac{2s(m-y)(s(m) - s(m-y))}{s(m)s'(m-y)}\right| \int_{m-z}^m \frac{du}{\sigma^2(u)},$$

which is finite when $z > 0$ is sufficiently small, thanks to (A.3). Thus, 0 is an entrance boundary. Because $\tilde{S}(0+) = -\infty$ and $\tilde{S}((m-l)-) < \infty$, we

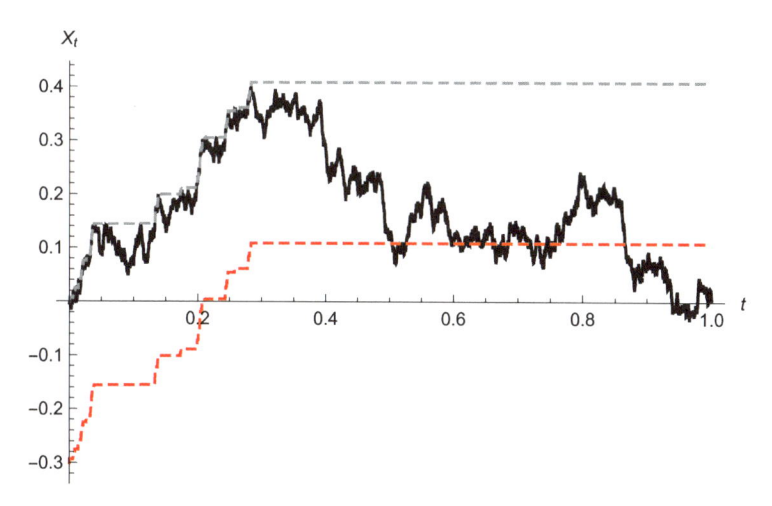

Fig. 3.1. Sample paths of a Brownian motion with drift (black), its running maximum $\overline{X}.$ (gray dashed), and the moving boundary $\overline{X}. - a$ (red dashed), simulated using (3.13) and (3.19) given $X_{g_a} = 0.4$. Here we set $\mu(\cdot) = 0.05$, $\sigma(\cdot) = 0.2$, $X_0 = 0$ and $a = 0.3$.

can use the same argument as in the proof of Proposition 3.2 to prove that 0 is inaccessible after time 0, hence 0 is an entrance-not-exit boundary, and (3.19) has a unique strictly positive weak solution with initial condition $J_0 = 0$. □

Remark 3.1. Propositions 3.1 and 3.3 effectively give a simulation scheme for generating sample paths given $X_{g_a} = \overline{X}_{\tau_D^+(a)}$. See Figure 3.1 for an illustration with Brownian motion.

As a consequence of Proposition 3.3, the Laplace transform of the random variable $\mathcal{S}_a$ can be derived by solving for the Laplace transform of the stopping time $\tau_J^+(a)$. Therefore we have the following proposition.

Proposition 3.4. *Conditionally on $X_{g_a} = m$, the Laplace transform of the random variable $\mathcal{S}_a$ is given by*

$$\mathbb{E}_x(e^{-q\mathcal{S}_a}|X_{g_a} = m) = \frac{s(m) - s(m-a)}{W_q(m, m-a)}. \tag{3.21}$$

Proof. We apply the Feynman–Kac formula to the process in (3.19) and search for a locally bounded function on $(0, m-a)$ which satisfies the following partial differential equation for any given $z > 0$:

$$\frac{1}{2}\sigma^2(m-z)\frac{\partial^2 f}{\partial z^2} + \left(-\mu(m-z) + \frac{s'(m-z)\sigma^2(m-z)}{s(m) - s(m-z)}\right)\frac{\partial f}{\partial z} = qf(z). \quad (3.22)$$

Let us consider a function defined as

$$f(z) = \frac{W_q(m, m-z)}{s(m) - s(m-z)}. \quad (3.23)$$

Then it is straightforward to verify that $f(\cdot)$ is a locally bounded function that solves (3.22). In terms of this solution, we can express the conditional Laplace transform of $\mathcal{S}_a$ as:

$$\mathbb{E}_x(e^{-q\mathcal{S}_a}|X_{g_a} = m) = \mathbb{E}_x(e^{-q\tau_J^+(a)}) = \frac{f(0)}{f(a)}, \quad (3.24)$$

which gives (3.21). □

Finally, using the independence of path before and after the random time g_a, as well as individual Laplace transforms of g_a and $\mathcal{S}_a$ given X_{g_a}, we are able to compute their joint Laplace transform in (3.5) from (3.18) and (3.24). In particular, we have the following lemma.

Lemma 3.3 (Equation (3) of Lehoczky (1977)). *For the random variable $\overline{X}_{\tau_D^+(a)} = X_{g_a}$, we have*

$$\mathbb{P}_x(\overline{X}_{\tau_D^+(a)} > m) = \mathbb{P}_x(\tau_X^+(m) < \tau_D^+(a))$$

$$= \exp\left(-\int_x^m \frac{s'(u)}{s(u) - s(u-a)}du\right), \quad \forall m > x.$$

By applying the results in Proposition 3.2, Proposition 3.4, and Lemma 3.3, we obtain our main result in (3.5).

3.4. Applications

In this section we propose and price an innovative claim which can be used as a mean of insurance against market crashes. More specifically, let X. denote the underlying process. We consider a perpetual barrier claim with a pre-specified knockout barrier $B > X_0 = x$ and a pre-specified strike $T > 0$. This claim will pay one dollar at $\tau_D^+(a)$ if and only if the underlying has not been knocked out by time $\tau_D^+(a)$, and the speed of market crash of the underlying is smaller than the strike T. In the case $\tau_D^+(a) = \infty$, the claim is regarded as delivering zero payoff.

In the presence of no arbitrage, no transaction cost, and a constant risk-free rate $\tilde{r} \geq 0$, the time-0 price of this claim can be evaluated using a risk-neutral measure $\mathbb{P}$. In particular, let us denote by $V_B(T)$ the time-0 price of the above claim; then

$$V_B(T) = \mathbb{E}_x(e^{-\tilde{r}\tau_D^+(a)} \cdot \mathbf{1}_{\{S_a < T, X_{g_a} < B\}}), \qquad (3.25)$$

where x is the time-0 price of the underlying.

By Canadizing T, i.e., letting $T = \mathbf{e}_q$ be an exponentially distributed random variable with parameter $q > 0$, which is independent of the underlying price process $X.$, we obtain that

$$\begin{aligned}
\mathbb{E}_x(V_B(\mathbf{e}_q)) &= \mathbb{E}_x(e^{-\tilde{r}\tau_D^+(a)} \mathbf{1}_{\{S_a < \mathbf{e}_q, X_{g_a} < B\}}) \\
&= \mathbb{E}_x(e^{-\tilde{r}\tau_D^+(a)} \mathbf{1}_{\{X_{g_a} < B\}} \mathbb{P}_x(S_a < \mathbf{e}_q | S_a)) \\
&= \mathbb{E}_x(e^{-\tilde{r}\tau_D^+(a) - qS_a} \mathbf{1}_{\{X_{g_a} < B\}}) \\
&= \int_x^B \mathbb{E}_x(e^{-\tilde{r}g_a} | X_{g_a} = m) \mathbb{E}_x(e^{-(\tilde{r}+q)S_a} | X_{g_a} = m) \\
&\quad \times \mathbb{P}_x(X_{g_a} \in dm).
\end{aligned}$$

The price $V_B(T)$ for a pre-specified $T > 0$ is then obtained through Laplace inversion of $\mathbb{E}_x(V_B(\mathbf{e}_q))$:

$$V_B(T) = \mathcal{I}_q\left(\frac{1}{q}\mathbb{E}_x(V_B(\mathbf{e}_q))\right), \qquad (3.26)$$

where $\mathcal{I}_q$ is the Laplace inversion operator in variable q.

In what follows we consider two examples of dynamics for the underlying. In the first example, we consider a Brownian motion with drift as the logarithm of the underlying price process and we are able to provide a closed-form formula for the Canadized price in (3.26). We also consider a CEV model in the second example, a prototypical model for a strict local martingale.

3.4.1. Brownian motion with drift

We consider a Brownian motion with drift $\mu(\cdot) \equiv \mu \in \mathbb{R}$ and diffusion coefficient $\sigma > 0$:

$$dX_t = x + \mu dt + \sigma dW_t, \quad X_0 = x \in I \equiv \mathbb{R}. \qquad (3.27)$$

Here we assume that $\mu = \tilde{r} - \frac{1}{2}\sigma^2$ so that $\{e^{-\tilde{r}t+X_t}\}_{t\geq 0}$ is a martingale under the risk-neutral measure $\mathbb{P}$ (see Figure 3.2). As in Section 2.3.2, let

$$\delta := \frac{\mu}{\sigma^2}, \quad \gamma_q := \sqrt{\delta^2 + \frac{2q}{\sigma^2}};$$

then we can choose the scale function $s(x) = \frac{1}{\delta}(1 - e^{-2\delta x})$ if $\mu \neq 0$ and $s(x) = 2x$ if $\mu = 0$, and

$$W_q(x,y) = 2e^{-\delta(x+y)}\frac{\sinh(\gamma_q(x-y))}{\gamma_q},$$

$$W_{q,1}(x,y) = \gamma_q \coth(\gamma_q(x-y)) - \delta.$$

Applying Proposition 3.2, Proposition 3.4, and Lemma 3.3 we obtain that, $\forall m > x$,

$$\mathbb{E}_x(e^{-qg_a}|X_{g_a} = m) = e^{-[\gamma_q \coth(\gamma_q a) - \delta \coth(\delta a)](m-x)},$$

$$\mathbb{E}_x(e^{-qS}|X_{g_a} = m) = \frac{\gamma_q}{\delta}\frac{\sinh(\delta a)}{\sinh(\gamma_q a)},$$

$$\mathbb{P}_x(X_{g_a} \geq m) = e^{-\frac{2\delta(m-x)}{e^{2\delta a}-1}}.$$

Using (3.26) we have

$$\mathbb{E}_x(V_B(\mathbf{e}_q)) = \frac{\gamma_{\tilde{r}+q}e^{-\delta a}}{\sinh(\gamma_{\tilde{r}+q}a)}\frac{1 - e^{-(\gamma_{\tilde{r}}\coth(\gamma_{\tilde{r}}a)-\delta)(B-x)}}{\gamma_{\tilde{r}}\coth(\gamma_{\tilde{r}}a) - \delta}. \tag{3.28}$$

Notice that we only need to invert the first factor in (3.28) to get the price $V_B(T)$. And the result of this inversion is available in analytical form (see, e.g., Borodin and Salminen (2002, p. 641 and 649)).

3.4.2. The CEV model

In this section we consider a zero drift CEV model with parameter 2. More specifically, we consider a non-negative diffusion with drift coefficient $\mu(\cdot) \equiv 0$ and diffusion coefficient $\sigma(x) = \sigma x^2$ for any $x \in I \equiv \mathbb{R}_{>0}$:

$$dX_t = \sigma X_t^2 dW_t, \quad X_0 = x > a > 0, \tag{3.29}$$

where $\sigma \in \mathbb{R}_{>0}$ is a constant. It is worth pointing out that, the above CEV model can be expressed as the strict local martingale $\{(R_{\sigma^2 t})^{-1}\}_{t\geq 0}$, where $R_. = \{R_t\}_{t\geq 0}$ is a three-dimensional Bessel process starting at $1/x > 0$.

Drawdowns and the Speed of Market Crashes 55

(a) $V_B(T)$ vs. initial position x

(b) Probability density of S_a, various a

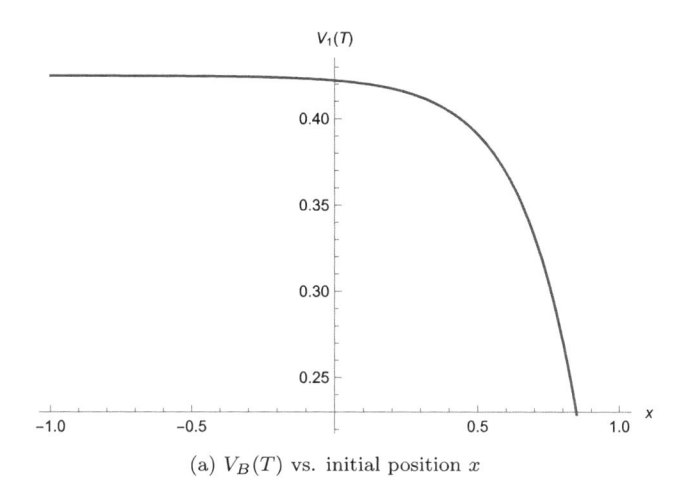

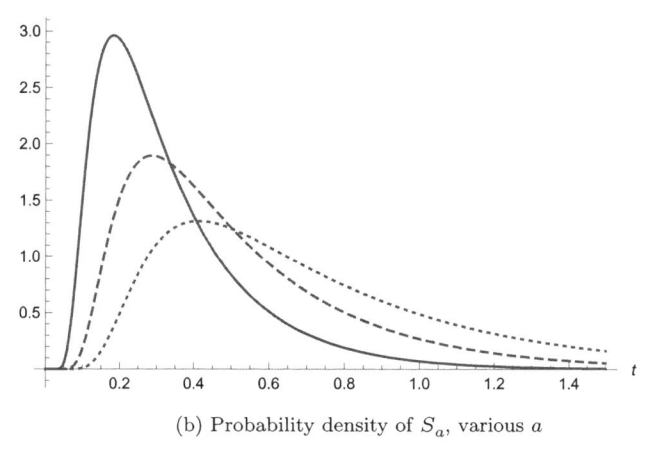

Fig. 3.2. Numerical results under the Brownian motion model (3.27) using the fixed-Talbot method. (a) The value (3.25) as a function of initial position $X_0 = x$. Here we set $T = 0.25$, $B = 1$, $r = 0.02$ and $\sigma = 0.2$. (b) The probability density of S_a for $a = 0.2$ (solid), $a = 0.25$ (dashed), or $a = 0.3$ (dotted).

It is known from Jeanblanc et al. (2009, p. 367) that, $\forall x \in I$, $s(x) = x$ and

$$\phi_q^+(x) = \sqrt{x} K_{\frac{1}{2}}\left(\frac{\sqrt{2q}}{\sigma x}\right) = \sqrt{\frac{\pi}{2} \frac{\sigma}{\sqrt{2q}}} \, x \, e^{-\frac{\sqrt{2q}}{\sigma x}},$$

$$\phi_q^-(x) = \sqrt{x} I_{\frac{1}{2}}\left(\frac{\sqrt{2q}}{\sigma x}\right) = \sqrt{\frac{2}{\pi} \frac{\sigma}{\sqrt{2q}}} \, x \, \sinh\left(\frac{\sqrt{2q}}{\sigma x}\right),$$

where $I_{\frac{1}{2}}(\cdot)$ and $K_{\frac{1}{2}}(\cdot)$ are respectively the modified Bessel functions of the first and second kind of order $\frac{1}{2}$.

Applying Proposition 3.2, Proposition 3.4, and Lemma 3.3, we obtain that, $\forall m > x$,

$$\mathbb{E}_x(e^{-qg_a}|X_{g_a}=m) = \frac{x}{m}e^{\frac{m-x}{a}}\exp\left(-\int_x^m \frac{\sqrt{2q}}{\sigma^2 u^2}\coth\left(\frac{\sqrt{2q}a}{\sigma u(u-a)}\right)du\right),$$

$$\mathbb{E}_x(e^{-q\mathcal{S}_a}|X_{g_a}=m) = \frac{\sqrt{2q}a}{\sigma m(m-a)}\frac{1}{\sinh(\frac{\sqrt{2q}a}{\sigma m(m-a)})},$$

$$\mathbb{P}_x(X_{g_a}>m) = e^{-\frac{m-x}{a}}.$$

Thus, from (3.26) we obtain that

$$\mathbb{E}_x(V_B(\mathbf{e}_q)) = \int_x^B \frac{\sqrt{2(\tilde{r}+q)}}{\sigma \sinh(\frac{\sqrt{2(\tilde{r}+q)}a}{\sigma m(m-a)})} \frac{x\exp(-\int_x^m \frac{\sqrt{2\tilde{r}}}{\sigma^2 u^2}\coth(\frac{\sqrt{2\tilde{r}}a}{\sigma u(u-a)})du)}{m^2(m-a)}dm.$$

3.5. Concluding Remarks

In this chapter, we derive an analytical formula for the joint Laplace transform of the last reset time of the maximum preceding the drawdown, the speed of market crash, and the maximum at the drawdown for a general diffusion process. Using randomizing the strike, we apply this result to price an innovative perpetual claim that can be used as a means of insurance against market crashes. We present formulas of the Canadized claim price in both the Brownian motion with drift model and a CEV model. A possible extension is to consider finite maturity counterpart of the above drawdown insurance. This would require a combination of our results and double Canadization in both the strike and the maturity. The computational cost of the involved Laplace inversion will however be slightly expensive.

3.6. Proof of Lemmas

Proof of Lemma 3.1. We notice that, $\{g_a > t\}$ means that $\{t < \tau_D^+(a)\}$, and the path of X will revisit $\overline{X}_t$ before it reaches $\overline{X}_t - a$. Let $s(\cdot)$ be a scale function of X.; then $\{s(X_u)\}_{u\geq t}$ is a local martingale. By applying the optional sampling theorem to this local martingale upon exiting from an interval, we obtain that

$$Y_t^g = \mathbb{P}_x(g_a > t|\mathcal{F}_t) = \frac{s(X_t) - s(\overline{X}_t - a)}{s(\overline{X}_t) - s(\overline{X}_t - a)} \mathbf{1}_{\{t < \tau_D^+(a)\}}. \quad (3.30)$$

This proves (3.8). We then apply Itô's lemma to process Y^g to obtain that, for any $t < \tau_D^+(a)$,

$$dY_t^g = \frac{d[s(X_t) - s(\overline{X}_t - a)]}{s(\overline{X}_t) - s(\overline{X}_t - a)} - \frac{s(X_t) - s(\overline{X}_t - a)}{[s(\overline{X}_t) - s(\overline{X}_t - a)]^2} d[s(\overline{X}_t) - s(\overline{X}_t - a)].$$

It is easily seen that $ds(X_t) = s'(X_t)\sigma(X_t)dW_t$, and

$$d[s(\overline{X}_t) - s(\overline{X}_t - a)] = [s'(\overline{X}_t) - s'(\overline{X}_t - a)]d\overline{X}_t.$$

Since the measure $d\overline{X}_t$ is supported on $\{t > 0 : X_t = \overline{X}_t\}$, we further have that

$$dY_t^g = \frac{s'(X_t)\sigma(X_t)dW_t}{s(\overline{X}_t) - s(\overline{X}_t - a)} - \frac{s'(\overline{X}_t - a)d\overline{X}_t}{s(\overline{X}_t) - s(\overline{X}_t - a)} - \frac{s'(\overline{X}_t) - s'(\overline{X}_t - a)}{s(\overline{X}_t) - s(\overline{X}_t - a)} d\overline{X}_t$$

$$= \frac{s'(X_t)\sigma(X_t)dW_t}{s(\overline{X}_t) - s(\overline{X}_t - a)} - \frac{s'(\overline{X}_t)d\overline{X}_t}{s(\overline{X}_t) - s(\overline{X}_t - a)}.$$

Equations (3.9) and (3.10) then follow from the fact that $\lim_{t \uparrow \tau_D^+(a)} Y_t^g = 0$.

□

Chapter 4

Frequency of Drawdowns in a Brownian Motion Model

In a filtered probability space $(\Omega, \mathbb{F}, \mathcal{F}, \mathbb{P})$ with filtration $\mathbb{F} = \{\mathcal{F}_t\}_{t \geq 0}$, we consider a drifted Brownian motion $X = \{X_t\}_{t \geq 0}$,

$$X_t = x + \mu t + \sigma W_t, \quad X_0 = x \in \mathbb{R},$$

where $\mu \in \mathbb{R}$, $\sigma > 0$, and $\{W_t\}_{t \geq 0}$ is a standard Brownian motion. The first passage time of the drawdown over level $a > 0$ is denoted by

$$\tau_D^+(a) = \inf\{t > 0 : \overline{X}_t - X_t > a\}, \tag{4.1}$$

where $\overline{x}_t = \sup_{s \in [0,t]} X_t$ is the running maximum process of X..

From a risk management standpoint, large drawdowns should be considered as extreme events of which both the severity and the frequency need to be investigated. Considerable attention has been paid to the severity aspect of the problem by pre-specifying a threshold, namely $a > 0$, of the size of drawdowns, and subsequently studying various properties associated to the first drawdown time $\tau_D^+(a)$. In this chapter, we extend the discussion by investigating the frequency of drawdowns. To this end, we derive the joint distribution of the nth drawdown time, the running maximum, and the value process at the drawdown time for a Brownian motion with drift. Using the general theory on renewal process, we proceed to characterize the behavior of the frequency of drawdown episodes in a long time-horizon. Finally, we introduce some insurance policies which protect against the risk associated with frequent drawdowns. These policies are similar to the sequential barrier options in over-the-counter (OTC) market (see, e.g., Pfeffer (2001)). Through Canadization of maturities, we provide closed-form pricing formulas by making use of the main theoretical results of the chapter.

While sustaining downside risk can be appropriately characterized using the drawdown process and the first drawdown time, economic turmoil and volatile market fluctuations are better described by quantities containing more path-wise information, such as the frequency of drawdowns. The existing knowledge about the first drawdown time $\tau_D^+(a)$ provides only limited and implicit information about the frequency of drawdowns. For the purpose of tackling the problem of frequency directly and systematically, we define in the sequel two types of drawdown time sequences depending on whether the last running maximum needs to be recovered or not.

The first sequence $\{\tilde{\tau}_D^{n,+}(a)\}_{n\geq 1}$ is called the *drawdown times with recovery*, defined recursively as

$$\tilde{\tau}_D^{n,+}(a) := \inf\{t > \tilde{\tau}_D^{n-1,+}(a) : \overline{X}_t - X_t > a, \overline{X}_t > \overline{X}_{\tilde{\tau}_D^{n-1,+}(a)}\}, \quad (4.2)$$

where $\tilde{\tau}_D^{0,+}(a) = 0$. Note that, after each $\tilde{\tau}_D^{n-1,+}(a)$, the corresponding running maximum $\overline{X}_{\tilde{\tau}_D^{n-1,+}(a)}$ must be recovered before the next drawdown time $\tilde{\tau}_D^{n,+}(a)$. In other words, the running maximum is reset and updated only when the previous one is revisited. Since the sample paths of $X_\cdot$ are almost surely continuous, we have that $\overline{X}_{\tilde{\tau}_D^{n,+}(a)} - X_{\tilde{\tau}_D^{n,+}(a)} = a$ a.s. if $\tilde{\tau}_D^{n,+}(a) < \infty$.

The second sequence $\{\tau_D^{n,+}(a)\}_{n\geq 1}$ is called the *drawdown times without recovery*, defined recursively as

$$\tau_D^{n,+}(a) := \inf\{t > \tau_D^{n-1,+}(a) : \overline{X}_{[\tau_D^{n-1,+}(a),t]} - X_t > a\}, \quad (4.3)$$

where $\tau_D^{0,+}(a) := 0$ and $\overline{X}_{[s,t]} := \sup_{u\in[s,t]} X_u$. From definition (4.3), it is implicitly assumed that the running maximum $\overline{X}_{\tau_D^{n,+}(a)}$ is "reset" to $X_{\tau_D^{n,+}(a)}$ at the drawdown time $\tau_D^{n,+}(a)$. In fact, $\tau_D^{n,+}(a)$ is the so-called iterated stopping times associated with $\tau_D^+(a)$ defined as

$$\tau_D^{n,+}(a) = \tau_D^{n-1,+}(a) + \tau_D^+(a) \circ \theta_{\tau_D^{n-1,+}(a)}, \quad (4.4)$$

where $\theta_\cdot$ is the Markov shift operator such that $X_t \circ \theta_s = X_{s+t}$ for $s, t \geq 0$.

Note that both $\tau_D^{n,+}(a)$ and $\tilde{\tau}_D^{n,+}(a)$ are independent of the initial value x for not only the drifted Brownian motion $X_\cdot$, but also a general Lévy process. In view of definitions (4.2) and (4.3), it is clear that the following inclusive relation of the two types of drawdown times holds:

$$\{\tilde{\tau}_D^{n,+}(a)\}_{n\geq 1} \subset \{\tau_D^{n,+}(a)\}_{n\geq 1}.$$

In other words, for each $n \in \mathbb{N}$, there exists a unique positive integer $m \geq n$ such that $\tilde{\tau}_D^{n,+}(a) = \tau_D^{m,+}(a)$ provided that $\tilde{\tau}_D^{n,+}(a) < \infty$.

Our motivations for introducing the two drawdown time sequences are as follows. The drawdown times with recovery $\{\tilde{\tau}_D^{n,+}(a)\}_{n\geq 1}$ are easy to identify from the sample paths of X. by searching the running maximum. Moreover, they are consistent with definition (4.1) of the first drawdown $\tau_D^+(a)$ in the sense that a drawdown can be considered as incomplete if the running maximum has not been revisited. However, there are also some crucial drawbacks of $\{\tilde{\tau}_D^{n,+}(a)\}_{n\geq 1}$ which motivate us to introduce the drawdown times without recovery $\{\tau_D^{n,+}(a)\}_{n\geq 1}$. First, the downside risk during recovering periods is neglected. One or more larger drawdowns may occur in a recovering period. Second, the threshold a needs to be adjusted to gain a more integrated understanding about the severity of drawdowns. In other words, the selection of a becomes tricky. Third, the requirement of recovery is too strong. In real world, a historical high water mark may never be recovered again, as in the case of a financial bubble Jarrow *et al.* (2011).

The rest of the chapter is structured as follows. In Section 4.1, we review some preliminaries on exit times and the first drawdown time $\tau_D^+(a)$ of a Brownian motion with drift. In Section 4.2.1, the frequency rate of drawdowns, and the Laplace transform of $\tilde{\tau}_D^{n,+}(a)$ associated with the distribution of $\overline{X}_{\tilde{\tau}_D^{n,+}(a)}$ and/or $X_{\tilde{\tau}_D^{n,+}(a)}$ are derived. Section 4.2.2 is parallel to Section 4.2.1 but studies the drawdown times without recovery $\{\tau_D^{n,+}(a)\}_{n\geq 1}$. Interesting connections between the two drawdown time sequences are also established. Numerical results based on our analytical formulas are presented in Section 4.3. In Section 4.4, some insurance contracts are introduced to insure against the risk of frequent drawdowns. We conclude this chapter in Section 4.5. Proofs of lemmas can be found in Section 4.6.

4.1. Preliminaries

As usual, we write $\mathbb{E}_x(\cdot) = \mathbb{E}(\cdot \mid X_0 = x)$ for the conditional expectation, $\mathbb{P}_x$ for the corresponding probability. When the random variable inside the expectation is independent of the starting position x, we drop the subscript from the conditional expectation and probability.

For $x \in \mathbb{R}$, consider the first passage times

$$\tau_X^{\pm}(x) = \inf\{t > 0 : X_t \gtrless x\}.$$

For $a < x < b$ and $q > 0$, it is known from (2.22) and the Appendix that

$$\mathbb{E}_x(e^{-q\tau_X^-(a)}) = e^{\beta_q^-(x-a)}, \quad \mathbb{E}_x(e^{-q\tau_X^+(b)}) = e^{\beta_q^+(x-b)}, \qquad (4.5)$$

where

$$\beta_q^{\pm} := -\delta \pm \sqrt{\delta^2 + \frac{2q}{\sigma^2}}, \quad \text{with } \delta := \frac{\mu}{\sigma^2}. \qquad (4.6)$$

By letting $q \downarrow 0$ in (4.5), we have

$$\mathbb{P}_x(\tau_X^+(b) < \infty) = e^{(|\delta|-\delta)(x-b)}, \quad \mathbb{P}_x(\tau_X^-(a) < \infty) = e^{-(\delta+|\delta|)(x-a)}. \qquad (4.7)$$

From Section 3.4.1, one can deduce the following joint Laplace transform of the first drawdown time $\tau_D^+(a)$ and its running maximum $\overline{X}_{\tau_D^+(a)}$.

Lemma 4.1. *For $q, s > 0$, we have*

$$\mathbb{E}(e^{-q\tau_D^+(a) - s\overline{X}_{\tau_D^+(a)}} \mathbf{1}_{\{\tau_D^+(a) < \infty\}}) = \frac{c_q}{b_q + s} \qquad (4.8)$$

where

$$b_q = \frac{\beta_q^+ e^{-\beta_q^- a} - \beta_q^- e^{-\beta_q^+ a}}{e^{-\beta_q^- a} - e^{-\beta_q^+ a}}, \quad c_q = \frac{\beta_q^+ - \beta_q^-}{e^{-\beta_q^- a} - e^{-\beta_q^+ a}}. \qquad (4.9)$$

A Laplace inversion of (4.8) with respect to s results in

$$\mathbb{E}(e^{-q\tau_D^+(a)} \mathbf{1}_{\{\overline{X}_{\tau_D^+(a)} > x\}}) = \frac{c_q}{b_q} e^{-b_q x}, \qquad (4.10)$$

for $x > 0$. Furthermore, letting $x \downarrow 0$ in (4.10), we immediately get

$$\mathbb{E}(e^{-q\tau_D^+(a)} \mathbf{1}_{\{\tau_D^+(a) < \infty\}}) = c_q/b_q. \qquad (4.11)$$

A numerical evaluation of the distribution function of $\tau_D^+(a)$ (and more generally $\tau_D^{n,+}(a)$ and $\tilde{\tau}_D^{n,+}(a)$) by an inverse Laplace transform method will be given in Section 4.3. It is straightforward to check that

$$\lim_{q \downarrow 0} b_q = \lim_{q \downarrow 0} c_q = \frac{2\delta}{e^{2\delta a} - 1}. \qquad (4.12)$$

In particular, when $\mu = 0$, the quantity $\frac{2\delta}{e^{2\delta a}-1}$ is understood as $\lim_{\delta \to 0} \frac{2\delta}{e^{2\delta a}-1} = \frac{1}{a}$. It follows from (4.11) and (4.12) that

$$\mathbb{P}(\tau_D^+(a) < \infty) = \lim_{q \downarrow 0} \mathbb{E}(e^{-q\tau_D^+(a)}) = 1.$$

See also discussions on p. 105 of Bertoin (1996). By taking the derivative of (4.11) with respect to q and letting $q \downarrow 0$, we have

$$\mathbb{E}(\tau_D^+(a)) = \begin{cases} \dfrac{e^{2\delta a} - 1 - 2\delta a}{2\sigma^2 \delta^2} & \text{if } \delta \neq 0, \\ a^2/\sigma^2 & \text{if } \delta = 0. \end{cases} \quad (4.13)$$

Furthermore, from Lemma 3.3 we have

$$\mathbb{P}(\overline{X}_{\tau_D^+(a)} \geq x) = e^{-\frac{2\delta x}{e^{2\delta a}-1}}. \quad (4.14)$$

So the running maximum at the first drawdown time $\overline{X}_{\tau_D^+(a)}$ follows an exponential distribution with mean $(e^{2\delta a} - 1)/(2\delta)$.

4.2. Sequences of Drawdown Times

4.2.1. Drawdown times with recovery

We begin our analysis with the drawdown times with recovery $\{\tilde{\tau}_D^{n,+}(a)\}_{n \geq 1}$ given that their structure leads to a simpler analysis than their counterparts without recovery.

We first consider the asymptotic behavior of the frequency rate of drawdowns with recovery. Let $\tilde{N}_t^a = \sum_{n=1}^{\infty} \mathbf{1}_{\{\tilde{\tau}_D^{n,+}(a) \leq t\}}$ be the number of drawdowns with recovery observed by time $t \geq 0$, and define $\tilde{N}_t^a/t$ to be the frequency rate of drawdowns. It is clear that $\{\tilde{N}_t^a\}_{t \geq 0}$ is a delayed renewal process where the first drawdown time is distributed as $\tau_D^+(a)$, while the subsequent inter-drawdown times are independent and identically distributed as $\tau_X^+(X_{\tau_D^+(a)} + a) \circ \theta_{\tau_D^+(a)}$. From Rolski et al. (1999, Theorem 6.1.1), it follows that, with probability one,

$$\lim_{t \to \infty} \frac{\tilde{N}_t^a}{t} = \begin{cases} \dfrac{1}{\mathbb{E}(\tau_D^+(a)) + \mathbb{E}(\tau_X^+(a))} = \dfrac{2\sigma^2 \delta^2}{e^{2\delta a} - 1} & \text{if } \mu > 0, \\ 0 & \text{if } \mu \leq 0. \end{cases}$$

Moreover, one could easily obtain some central limit theorems for $\tilde{N}_t^a$ by Rolski et al. (1999, Theorem 6.1.2).

Next, we study the joint Laplace transform of $\tilde{\tau}_D^{n,+}(a)$ and $\overline{X}_{\tilde{\tau}_D^{n,+}(a)}$. Note that $X_{\tilde{\tau}_D^{n,+}(a)} = \overline{X}_{\tilde{\tau}_D^{n,+}(a)} - a$ a.s. whenever $\tilde{\tau}_D^{n,+}(a) < \infty$, thus the following theorem is sufficient to characterize the triplet $(\tilde{\tau}_D^{n,+}(a), \overline{X}_{\tilde{\tau}_D^{n,+}(a)}, X_{\tilde{\tau}_D^{n,+}(a)})$.

Theorem 4.1. For $n \in \mathbb{N}$ and $q, x \geq 0$, we have

$$\mathbb{E}(e^{-q\tilde{\tau}_D^{n,+}(a)} 1_{\{\overline{X}_{\tilde{\tau}_D^{n,+}(a)} > x\}}) = \left(\frac{c_q}{b_q}\right)^n e^{-(n-1)\beta_q^+ a} \sum_{m=0}^{n-1} \frac{(b_q x)^m}{m!} e^{-b_q x}. \tag{4.15}$$

Proof. To prove this result, we first condition on the first drawdown time $\tau_D^+(a)$ and subsequently on the time for the process X. to recover its running maximum. Using the strong Markov property of X. and (4.8), it is clear that

$$\mathbb{E}(e^{-q\tilde{\tau}_D^{n,+}(a) - s\overline{X}_{\tilde{\tau}_D^{n,+}(a)}})$$

$$= \mathbb{E}(e^{-q\tilde{\tau}_D^{n,+}(a) - s\overline{X}_{\tilde{\tau}_D^{n,+}(a)}} 1_{\{\tilde{\tau}_D^{n,+}(a) < \infty\}})$$

$$= \mathbb{E}(e^{-q\tau_D^+(a) - s\overline{X}_{\tau_D^+(a)}})\mathbb{E}(e^{-\tau_X^+(a)})\mathbb{E}(e^{-q\tilde{\tau}_D^{n-1,+}(a) - s\overline{X}_{\tilde{\tau}_D^{n-1,+}(a)}})$$

$$= \frac{c_q}{b_q + s} e^{-\beta_q^+ a} \mathbb{E}(e^{-q\tilde{\tau}_D^{n-1,+}(a) - s\overline{X}_{\tilde{\tau}_D^{n-1,+}(a)}})$$

$$= \left(\frac{c_q}{b_q + s}\right)^{n-1} e^{-(n-1)\beta_q^+ a} \mathbb{E}(e^{-q\tau_a - s\overline{X}_{\tau_D^+(a)}})$$

$$= \left(\frac{c_q}{b_q + s}\right)^n e^{-(n-1)\beta_q^+ a}. \tag{4.16}$$

Given that $(b_q/(b_q + s))^n$ is the Laplace transform of an Erlang random variable with mean n/b_q and variance $n/(b_q)^2$, a tail inversion of (4.16) with respect to s yields (4.15). $\square$

In particular, letting $x \downarrow 0$, we have

$$\mathbb{E}(e^{-q\tilde{\tau}_D^{n,+}(a)}) = (c_q/b_q)^n e^{-(n-1)\beta_q^+ a}, \tag{4.17}$$

for $n \in \mathbb{N}$. Furthermore, letting $q \downarrow 0$ in (4.17), together with (4.12) and $\lim_{q \downarrow 0} \beta_q^+ = |\delta| - \delta$, we have

$$\mathbb{P}(\tilde{\tau}_D^{n,+}(a) < \infty) = \begin{cases} 1 & \text{if } \mu \geq 0, \\ e^{2(n-1)\delta a} & \text{if } \mu < 0. \end{cases} \tag{4.18}$$

In other words, a historical running maximum may never be recovered if the drift $\mu < 0$.

Corollary 4.1. *For $n \in \mathbb{N}$ and $x > 0$, we have*

$$\mathbb{P}(\overline{X}_{\tilde{\tau}_D^{n,+}(a)} > x, \tilde{\tau}_D^{n,+}(a) < \infty)$$

$$= \begin{cases} e^{-\frac{2\delta x}{e^{2\delta a}-1}} \sum_{m=0}^{n-1} \frac{1}{m!} \left(\frac{2\delta x}{e^{2\delta a}-1}\right)^m & \text{if } \mu \geq 0, \\ e^{2(n-1)\delta a} e^{-\frac{2\delta x}{e^{2\delta a}-1}} \sum_{m=0}^{n-1} \frac{1}{m!} \left(\frac{2\delta x}{e^{2\delta a}-1}\right)^m & \text{if } \mu < 0. \end{cases} \quad (4.19)$$

Proof. Substituting (4.17) into (4.15) yields

$$\mathbb{E}(e^{-q\tilde{\tau}_D^{n,+}(a)} \mathbf{1}_{\{\overline{X}_{\tilde{\tau}_D^{n,+}(a)} > x\}}) = \mathbb{E}(e^{-q\tilde{\tau}_a^n}) \sum_{m=0}^{n-1} \frac{(b_q x)^m}{m!} e^{-b_q x}. \quad (4.20)$$

Taking the limit when $q \downarrow 0$ in (4.20), and then using (4.12), one arrives at

$$\mathbb{P}(\overline{X}_{\tilde{\tau}_D^{n,+}(a)} > x, \tilde{\tau}_D^{n,+}(a) < \infty) = \mathbb{P}(\tilde{\tau}_D^{n,+}(a) < \infty) \sum_{m=0}^{n-1} \frac{\left(\frac{2\delta x}{e^{2\delta a}-1}\right)^m}{m!} e^{-\frac{2\delta x}{e^{2\delta a}-1}}. \quad (4.21)$$

Substituting (4.18) into (4.21) results in (4.19). □

Note that (4.21) indicates

$$\mathbb{P}(\overline{X}_{\tilde{\tau}_D^{n,+}(a)} > x | \tilde{\tau}_a^n < \infty) = \sum_{m=0}^{n-1} \frac{1}{m!} \left(\frac{2\delta x}{e^{2\delta a}-1}\right)^m e^{-\frac{2\delta x}{e^{2\delta a}-1}}, \quad (4.22)$$

for all $\mu \in \mathbb{R}$. This result can be interpreted probabilistically. Indeed, when $\tilde{\tau}_D^{n,+}(a) < \infty$, $\overline{X}_{\tilde{\tau}_a^m} - \overline{X}_{\tilde{\tau}_a^{m-1}}$ follows an exponential distribution with mean $(e^{2\delta a} - 1)/(2\delta)$ for $m = 1, 2, \ldots, n$. Using the strong Markov property of X., the random variable's $\overline{X}_{\tilde{\tau}_a^m} - \overline{X}_{\tilde{\tau}_a^{m-1}}$ for all $m = 1, 2, \ldots, n$ are all independent, and thus $\overline{X}_{\tilde{\tau}_D^{n,+}(a)} = \sum_{m=1}^{n}(\overline{X}_{\tilde{\tau}_a^m} - \overline{X}_{\tilde{\tau}_a^{m-1}})$ is an Erlang random variable with survival function (4.22).

In particular, as $n \to \infty$, it is easy to check that $\lim_{n \to \infty} \mathbb{P}(\overline{X}_{\tilde{\tau}_D^{n,+}(a)} > x) = \mathbb{P}(\tau_X^+(x) < \infty)$ which agrees with (4.7). For completeness, we conclude this section with a result that is immediate from (4.15) and the fact that $\overline{X}_{\tilde{\tau}_D^{n,+}(a)} - X_{\tilde{\tau}_D^{n,+}(a)} = a$ a.s. whenever $\tilde{\tau}_a^n < \infty$.

Corollary 4.2. *For $n \in \mathbb{N}$ and $x \geq -a$, we have*

$$\mathbb{E}(e^{-q\tilde{\tau}_D^{n,+}(a)} \mathbf{1}_{\{X_{\tilde{\tau}_D^{n,+}(a)} > x\}})$$

$$= \left(\frac{c_q}{b_q}\right)^n e^{-(n-1)\beta_q^+ a} \sum_{m=0}^{n-1} \frac{(b_q(x+a))^m}{m!} e^{-b_q(x+a)}.$$

4.2.2. *Drawdown times without recovery*

In this section, we focus on the drawdown times without recovery which are more challenging to analyze than their counterparts with recovery.

Let $N_t^a = \sum_{n=1}^{\infty} \mathbf{1}_{\{\tau_D^{n,+}(a) \leq t\}}$ be the number of drawdowns without recovery by time $t \geq 0$. Clearly, $\{N_t^a\}_{t \geq 0}$ is a renewal process with independent inter-drawdown times, all distributed as $\tau_D^+(a)$. By Rolski *et al.* (1999, Theorem 6.1.1), it follows that, with probability one,

$$\lim_{t \to \infty} \frac{N_t^a}{t} = \frac{1}{\mathbb{E}(\tau_D^+(a))} = \frac{2\sigma^2 \delta^2}{e^{2\delta a} - 1 - 2\delta a},$$

which is consistent with our intuition based on (4.4). Here again, one can also obtain some central limit theorems for N_t^a by an application of Rolski *et al.* (1999, Theorem 6.1.2).

Next, we characterize the joint distribution of $(\tau_D^{n,+}(a), X_{\tau_D^{n,+}(a)})$ by deriving an explicit expression for $\mathbb{E}(e^{-q\tau_D^{n,+}(a)} \mathbf{1}_{\{X_{\tau_D^{n,+}(a)} > x\}})$.

Theorem 4.2. *For $n \in \mathbb{N}$ and $q, x > 0$, the joint distribution of $(\tau_D^{n,+}(a), X_{\tau_D^{n,+}(a)})$ satisfies*

$$\mathbb{E}(e^{-q\tau_D^{n,+}(a)} \mathbf{1}_{\{X_{\tau_D^{n,+}(a)} > x\}}) = \left(\frac{c_q}{b_q}\right)^n e^{-b_q(x+na)} \sum_{m=0}^{n-1} \frac{(b_q(x+na))^m}{m!}.$$

(4.23)

Proof. Given that $X_{\tau_D^{n,+}(a)} + na$ is a positive random variable (and $X_{\tau_D^{n,+}(a)}$ is not), we prove (4.23) by first deriving an expression for the joint Laplace transform of $(\tau_D^{n,+}(a), X_{\tau_D^{n,+}(a)} + na)$. By conditioning on the first drawdown time and its associated value process, and by making use of the strong Markov property and (4.8), it is clear that for all $s \geq 0$,

$$\mathbb{E}(e^{-q\tau_D^{n,+}(a) - s(X_{\tau_D^{n,+}(a)} + na)})$$

$$= \mathbb{E}(e^{-q\tau_a - s(X_{\tau_D^+(a)} + a)}) \mathbb{E}(e^{-q\tau_D^{n-1,+}(a) - s(X_{\tau_D^{n-1,+}(a)} + (n-1)a)}).$$

$$= \mathbb{E}(e^{-q\tau_D^+(a)-sX_{\tau_D^+(a)}})\mathbb{E}(e^{-q\tau_D^{n-1,+}(a)-s(X_{\tau_a^{n-1}}+(n-1)a)})$$

$$= \frac{c_q}{b_q+s}\mathbb{E}(e^{-q\tau_D^{n-1,+}(a)-s(X_{\tau_D^{n-1,+}(a)}+(n-1)a)})$$

$$= \left(\frac{c_q}{b_q+s}\right)^n. \tag{4.24}$$

The Laplace transform inversion of (4.24) with respect to s results in

$$\mathbb{E}(e^{-q\tau_D^{n,+}(a)}\mathbf{1}_{\{X_{\tau_D^{n,+}(a)}+na\in dy\}}) = (c_q)^n \frac{y^{n-1}e^{-b_q y}}{(n-1)!}dy, \tag{4.25}$$

for $y \geq 0$. Integrating (4.25) over y from $x+na$ to ∞ yields (4.23). □

Letting $s \downarrow 0$ in (4.24), it follows that

$$\mathbb{E}(e^{-q\tau_D^{n,+}(a)}) = (c_q/b_q)^n = (\mathbb{E}(e^{-q\tau_D^+(a)}))^n. \tag{4.26}$$

Note that (4.26) and (4.12) implies that

$$\mathbb{P}(\tau_D^{n,+}(a) < \infty) = 1.$$

It is worth pointing out that the relation $\mathbb{E}(e^{-q\tau_D^{n,+}(a)}) = (\mathbb{E}(e^{-q\tau_D^+(a)}))^n$ holds more generally for X. a general Lévy process or a renewal risk process (also known as the Sparre–Andersen risk model, see, e.g., Andersen (1957)) given that the inter-drawdown times $\tau_D^{1,+}(a)$, and $\{\tau_D^{n,+}(a)-\tau_D^{n-1,+}(a)\}_{n\geq 2}$ form a sequence of i.i.d. random variables.

Similarly, letting $q \downarrow 0$ in (4.23), it follows that

$$\mathbb{P}(X_{\tau_D^{n,+}(a)} \geq x) = e^{-\frac{2\delta(x+na)}{e^{2\delta a}-1}} \sum_{m=0}^{n-1} \frac{1}{m!}\left(\frac{2\delta(x+na)}{e^{2\delta a}-1}\right)^m, \tag{4.27}$$

for $n \in \mathbb{N}$ and $x \geq -na$. As expected, (4.27) is the survival function of an Erlang random variable with mean $n\left(e^{2\delta a}-1\right)/(2\delta)$ and variance $n\left(\left(e^{2\delta a}-1\right)/(2\delta)\right)^2$, later translated by $-na$ units.

Our objective is now to include $\overline{X}_{\tau_D^{n,+}(a)}$ in the analysis of the nth drawdown time. A result particularly useful to do so is provided in Lemma 4.2 which consider a specific constrained Laplace transform of the first passage time to level x.

Lemma 4.2. *For $n \in \mathbb{N}$ and $x > 0$, the constrained Laplace transform of $\tau_X^+(x)$ together with this first passage time occurring before $\tau_D^{n,+}(a)$ is given by*

$$\mathbb{E}(e^{-q\tau_X^+(x)} \mathbf{1}_{\{\tau_X^+(x) < \tau_D^{n,+}(a)\}}) = e^{-b_q x} \sum_{j=0}^{n-1} (c_q e^{-b_q a})^j \frac{x(x+ja)^{j-1}}{j!}. \tag{4.28}$$

In the next theorem, we provide a distributional characterization of the nth drawdown time $\tau_D^{n,+}(a)$ with respect to both $\overline{X}_{\tau_D^{n,+}(a)}$ and $X_{\tau_D^{n,+}(a)}$.

Theorem 4.3. *For $n \in \mathbb{N}$ and $x > 0$, we have*

$$\mathbb{E}(e^{-q\tau_D^{n,+}(a)} \mathbf{1}_{\{\overline{X}_{\tau_D^{n,+}(a)} > x, X_{\tau_D^{n,+}(a)} \in dy\}})$$

$$= (c_q)^n e^{-b_q(y+na)}$$

$$\times \sum_{m=0}^{n-1} \frac{x(x+ma)^{m-1}(y-x+(n-m)a)^{n-1-m} \mathbf{1}_{\{y-x+(n-m)a \geq 0\}}}{m!(n-m-1)!} dy. \tag{4.29}$$

Proof. By conditioning on the drawdown episode during which the drifted Brownian motion process $X.$ reaches level x for the first time and subsequently using the strong Markov property of $X.$, we have

$$\mathbb{E}(e^{-q\tau_D^{n,+}(a)} \mathbf{1}_{\{\overline{X}_{\tau_D^{n,+}(a)} > x, X_{\tau_D^{n,+}(a)} \in dy\}})$$

$$= \sum_{m=0}^{n-1} \mathbb{E}(e^{-q\tau_D^{n,+}(a)} \mathbf{1}_{\{\overline{X}_{\tau_D^{n,+}(a)} > x, X_{\tau_D^{n,+}(a)} \in dy, \tau_D^{m,+}(a) < \tau_X^+(x) < \tau_D^{m+1,+}(a)\}})$$

$$= \sum_{m=0}^{n-1} \mathbb{E}(e^{-q\tau_X^+(x)} \mathbf{1}_{\{\tau_D^{m,+}(a) < \tau_X^+(x) < \tau_D^{m+1,+}(a)\}})$$

$$\times \mathbb{E}_x(e^{-q\tau_D^{n-m,+}(a)} \mathbf{1}_{\{X_{\tau_D^{n-m,+}(a)} \in dy\}}). \tag{4.30}$$

From Lemma 4.2, we know that

$$\mathbb{E}(e^{-q\tau_X^+(x)} \mathbf{1}_{\{\tau_D^{m,+}(a) < \tau_X^+(x) < \tau_D^{m+1,+}(a)\}})$$

$$= \mathbb{E}(e^{-q\tau_X^+(x)} \mathbf{1}_{\{\tau_D^{m,+}(a) < \tau_X^+(x)\}}) - \mathbb{E}(e^{-q\tau_X^+(x)} \mathbf{1}_{\{\tau_D^{m+1,+}(a) < \tau_X^+(x)\}})$$

$$= (c_q)^m \frac{x(x+ma)^{m-1}}{m!} e^{-b_q(x+ma)}. \tag{4.31}$$

By Theorem 4.2, we have

$$\mathbb{E}_x(e^{-q\tau_D^{n-m,+}(a)} \mathbf{1}_{\{X_{\tau_D^{n-m,+}(a)} \in dy\}})$$
$$= (c_q)^{n-m}(y - x + (n-m)a)^{n-m-1} e^{-b_q(y-x+(n-m)a)}$$
$$\times \mathbf{1}_{\{y-x+(n-m)a \geq 0\}}/(n-m-1)! dy. \qquad (4.32)$$

Substituting (4.31) and (4.32) into (4.30) and simplifying, one easily obtains (4.29). □

Recall that $\tau_D^{1,+}(a) = \tilde{\tau}_D^{1,+}(a) = \tau_D^+(a)$ and $X_{\tau_D^+(a)} = \overline{X}_{\tau_D^+(a)} - a$ a.s. Therefore, by letting $q \downarrow 0$ and $x = a$ in (4.31), it follows that, for $m \in \mathbb{N}$,

$$\mathbb{P}(\tilde{\tau}_D^{2,+}(a) = \tau_D^{2+m,+}(a)) = \mathbb{P}(\tau_D^{m,+}(a) < \tau_X^+(a) < \tau_D^{m+1,+}(a))$$
$$= \frac{(m+1)^{m-1}}{m!} \left(\frac{2\delta a}{e^{2\delta a} - 1}\right)^m e^{-\frac{2(m+1)\delta a}{e^{2\delta a} - 1}}, \qquad (4.33)$$

which is the probability mass function of a generalized Poisson random variable (see, e.g., Consul and Famoye (2006, Eq. (9.1)) with $\theta = q = 2\delta a/(e^{2\delta a} - 1)$). For completeness, a random variable Y has a generalized Poisson (θ, q) distribution if its probability mass function $p_Y(\cdot)$ is given by

$$p_Y(m) = \frac{\theta(\theta + qm)^{m-1} e^{-\theta - qm}}{m!}, \quad \forall m \in \mathbb{N}_0,$$

when both $\theta, q > 0$.

Note that a generalization of (4.33) will be proposed in Theorem 4.4.

Remark 4.1. Equation (4.33) can be interpreted as follows: the number of drawdowns *without* recovery between two successive drawdowns with recovery follows a generalized Poisson distribution with $\theta = q = 2\delta a/(e^{2\delta a} - 1)$.

The following result connecting the two drawdown time sequences is provided. It should be noted that the random variable $N^a_{\tilde{\tau}_D^{k,+}(a)} - k$ represents the number of drawdowns without recovery over the first k drawdowns with recovery. When $k = 2$, (4.34) coincides with (4.33).

Theorem 4.4. *For any* $k \in \mathbb{N}$, $N^a_{\tilde{\tau}_D^{k,+}(a)} - k$ *follows a generalized Poisson distribution with parameters* $\theta = 2(k-1)\delta a/(e^{2\delta a} - 1)$ *and*

$q = 2\delta a/(e^{2\delta a} - 1)$, i.e., for $m = 0, 1, 2, \ldots$, we have

$$\mathbb{P}(\tilde{\tau}_D^{k,+}(a) = \tau_D^{k+m,+}(a)) = \mathbb{P}(N_{\tilde{\tau}_D^{k,+}(a)}^a = k+m)$$

$$= \frac{k-1}{m+k-1} \frac{\left(\frac{2(m+k-1)\delta a}{e^{2\delta a}-1}\right)^m}{m!} e^{-\frac{2(m+k-1)\delta a}{e^{2\delta a}-1}}. \quad (4.34)$$

Proof. It is clear that $\{\tilde{\tau}_D^{k,+}(a) = \tau_D^{k+m,+}(a)\}$ corresponds to the event that m drawdowns without recovery will occur over the first k drawdowns with recovery, i.e.

$$\{\tilde{\tau}_D^{k,+}(a) = \tau_D^{k+m,+}(a)\} = \{N_{\tilde{\tau}_a^k}^a = k+m\}.$$

Next we prove $N_{\tilde{\tau}_D^{k,+}(a)}^a - k$ follows a generalized Poisson distribution. By Remark 4.1 and the strong Markov property of X., we know that the numbers of drawdowns without recovery between any two successive drawdowns with recovery are i.i.d. and follow a generalized Poisson distribution with $\theta = q = 2\delta a/(e^{2\delta a} - 1)$. Thus,

$$N_{\tilde{\tau}_D^{k,+}(a)}^a - k = \sum_{i=2}^{k}(N_{\tilde{\tau}_a^i}^a - N_{\tilde{\tau}_a^{i-1}}^a - 1)$$

corresponds to a sum of i.i.d. random variable's with a generalized Poisson distribution $\theta = q = 2\delta a/(e^{2\delta a} - 1)$. Using Consul and Famoye (2006, Theorem 9.1), we have that $N_{\tilde{\tau}_a^k}^a - k$ follows a generalized Poisson distribution with parameters $\theta = 2(k-1)\delta a/(e^{2\delta a} - 1)$ and $q = 2\delta a/(e^{2\delta a} - 1)$. □

Next, we propose the following corollary which can be viewed as an extension to Taylor (1975) and Lehoczky (1977) from the first drawdown case to the nth drawdown without recovery.

Corollary 4.3. For $n \in \mathbb{N}$ and $x > 0$, we have

$$\mathbb{E}(e^{-q\tau_D^{n,+}(a)} 1_{\{\overline{X}_{\tau_D^{n,+}(a)} > x\}}) = \left(\frac{c_q}{b_q}\right)^n \sum_{m=0}^{n-1} \frac{x(x+ma)^{m-1} b_q^m}{m!} e^{-b_q(ma+x)}.$$

Proof. Taking the integral of (4.29) with respect to y in $(-na, \infty)$, we have

$$\mathbb{E}(e^{-q\tau_D^{n,+}(a)} 1_{\{\overline{X}_{\tau_D^{n,+}(a)} > x\}})$$

$$= (c_q)^n \sum_{m=0}^{n-1} \frac{x(x+ma)^{m-1}}{m!(n-m-1)!}$$

$$\times \int_{x-(n-m)a}^{\infty} e^{-b_q(y+na)} (y-x+(n-m)a)^{n-m-1} dy$$

$$= (c_q)^n \sum_{m=0}^{n-1} \frac{x(x+ma)^{m-1}}{m!(n-m-1)!} \int_0^\infty e^{-b_q(z+x+ma)} z^{n-m-1} dz$$

$$= (c_q)^n \sum_{m=0}^{n-1} \frac{x(x+ma)^{m-1}}{m!(n-m-1)!} e^{-b_q(x+ma)} \int_0^\infty e^{-b_q z} z^{n-m-1} dz$$

$$= (c_q)^n \sum_{m=0}^{n-1} \frac{x(x+ma)^{m-1}}{m! b_q^{n-m}} e^{-b_q(x+ma)},$$

which completes the proof. □

The marginal distribution of $\overline{X}_{\tau_D^{n,+}(a)}$ can easily be obtained from Corollary 4.3 by letting $q \downarrow 0$ and subsequently making use of (4.12). Indeed,

$$\mathbb{P}(\overline{X}_{\tau_D^{n,+}(a)} > x) = \sum_{m=0}^{n-1} \frac{x(x+ma)^{m-1} \left(\frac{2\delta}{e^{2\delta a}-1}\right)^m}{m!} e^{-\frac{2\delta(ma+x)}{e^{2\delta a}-1}}. \quad (4.35)$$

Rearrangement of (4.35) yields

$$\mathbb{P}(\overline{X}_{\tau_D^{n,+}(a)} > x) = \sum_{k=0}^{n-1} D_{k,n} \frac{\left(\frac{2\delta x}{e^{2\delta a}-1}\right)^k}{k!} e^{-\frac{2\delta x}{e^{2\delta a}-1}}, \quad (4.36)$$

where $D_{0,n} = 1$, and

$$D_{k,n} = \sum_{m=k}^{n-1} \frac{k \left(\frac{2m\delta a}{e^{2\delta a}-1}\right)^{m-k}}{m(m-k)!} e^{-\frac{2m\delta}{e^{2\delta a}-1} a}$$

$$= \sum_{m=0}^{n-1-k} \frac{k \left(\frac{2(m+k)\delta a}{e^{2\delta a}-1}\right)^m}{(m+k)m!} e^{-\frac{2(m+k)\delta a}{e^{2\delta a}-1}}, \quad (4.37)$$

for $k = 1, 2, \ldots, n-1$. Note that by substituting k by $k+1$ in (4.34), it follows that (4.37) can be rewritten as

$$D_{k,n} = \sum_{m=0}^{n-1-k} \mathbb{P}(\tilde{\tau}_D^{k+1,+}(a) = \tau_D^{k+1+m,+}(a)),$$

which is equivalent to
$$D_{k,n} = \mathbb{P}(\tilde{\tau}_D^{k+1,+}(a) \leq \tau_D^{n,+}(a)) = \mathbb{P}(\tilde{N}^a_{\tau_D^{n,+}(a)} > k).$$

Then,
$$\mathbb{P}(\overline{X}_{\tau_D^{n,+}(a)} \in \mathrm{d}y) = \sum_{k=1}^n d_{k,n} \frac{(\frac{2\delta a}{e^{2\delta a}-1})^k y^{k-1} e^{-\frac{2\delta a}{e^{2\delta a}-1}y}}{(k-1)!}\mathrm{d}y,$$

where $\{d_{k,n}\}_{k=1}^n$ are given by

$$d_{k,n} \equiv D_{k-1,n} - D_{k,n}$$

$$= \sum_{j=k}^n \frac{k-1}{j-1} \frac{\left(\frac{2(j-1)\delta a}{e^{2\delta a}-1}\right)^{j-k}}{(j-k)!} e^{-\frac{2(j-1)\delta a}{e^{2\delta a}-1}}$$

$$\times \left(1 - \sum_{m=0}^{n-j-1} \frac{(m+1)^{m-1}}{m!}\left(\frac{2\delta a}{e^{2\delta a}-1}\right)^m e^{-\frac{2(m+1)\delta a}{e^{2\delta a}-1}}\right).$$

In conclusion, $\overline{X}_{\tau_D^{n,+}(a)}$ follows a mixed-Erlang distribution which is an important class of distribution in risk management (see, e.g., Willmot and Lin (2011) for an extensive review of mixed Erlang distributions).

Remark 4.2. Note that the distribution of $\overline{X}_{\tau_D^{n,+}(a)}$ does not come as a surprise. Indeed, one can obtain the structural form of the distribution of $\overline{X}_{\tau_D^{n,+}(a)}$ by conditioning on $\tilde{N}^a_{\tau_D^{n,+}(a)}$, namely, the number of drawdowns with recovery over the first n drawdowns (without recovery). Using the strong Markov property of the process X and Equation (4.14), it follows that $\overline{X}_{\tau_D^{n,+}(a)}|\tilde{N}^a_{\tau_D^{n,+}(a)} = m$ is an Erlang random variable with mean $m(e^{2\delta a}-1)/(2\delta)$ and variance $m((e^{2\delta a}-1)/(2\delta))^2$ for $m = 1, 2, \ldots, n$. Thus, in (4.36), $D_{k,n}$ can be interpreted as the survival function of $\tilde{N}^a_{\tau_D^{n,+}(a)}$, i.e.,

$$D_{k,n} = \mathbb{P}(\tilde{N}^a_{\tau_D^{n,+}(a)} > k) = \mathbb{P}(\tilde{\tau}_D^{k+1,+}(a) \leq \tau_D^{n,+}(a)).$$

The next corollary investigates the actual drawdown $\overline{X}_t - X_t$ at $t = \tau_D^{n,+}(a)$.

Corollary 4.4. *For $a \leq x \leq na$, we have*

$$\mathbb{E}(e^{-q\tau_D^{n,+}(a)} 1_{\{\overline{X}_{\tau_D^{n,+}(a)} - X_{\tau_D^{n,+}(a)} \leq x\}})$$

$$= (c_q)^n e^{-b_q(na-x)} \sum_{m=0}^{n-1} \left(\frac{(na-x)^m}{b_q^{n-m} m!} \right.$$

$$\left. - \frac{\mathbf{1}_{\{x \leq (n-m)a\}}((n-m)a-x)^{n-m-1} \int_0^\infty e^{-b_q y} y(y+ma)^{m-1} dy}{m!(n-m-1)!} \right).$$

Proof. We have

$$\mathbb{E}(e^{-q\tau_D^{n,+}(a)} \mathbf{1}_{\{\overline{X}_{\tau_D^{n,+}(a)} - X_{\tau_D^{n,+}(a)} > x\}})$$

$$= \int_{-x}^\infty \mathbb{E}(e^{-q\tau_D^{n,+}(a)} \mathbf{1}_{\{\overline{X}_{\tau_D^{n,+}(a)} - X_{\tau_D^{n,+}(a)} > x, X_{\tau_D^{n,+}(a)} \in dy\}})$$

$$+ \mathbb{E}(e^{-q\tau_D^{n,+}(a)} \mathbf{1}_{\{\overline{X}_{\tau_D^{n,+}(a)} - X_{\tau_D^{n,+}(a)} > x, X_{\tau_D^{n,+}(a)} \leq -x\}})$$

$$= \int_{-x}^\infty \mathbb{E}(e^{-q\tau_D^{n,+}(a)} \mathbf{1}_{\{\overline{X}_{\tau_D^{n,+}(a)} > x+y, X_{\tau_D^{n,+}(a)} \in dy\}})$$

$$+ \mathbb{E}(e^{-q\tau_D^{n,+}(a)} \mathbf{1}_{\{X_{\tau_D^{n,+}(a)} \leq -x\}})$$

$$\times \left(1 - e^{-b_q(na-x)} \sum_{m=0}^{n-1} \frac{(b_q(na-x))^m}{m!} \right), \tag{4.38}$$

where the last step is due to (4.23). Moreover, by Theorem 4.3, the first term of (4.38) is given by

$$\int_{-x}^\infty \mathbb{E}(e^{-q\tau_D^{n,+}(a)} \mathbf{1}_{\{\overline{X}_{\tau_D^{n,+}(a)} > x+y, X_{\tau_D^{n,+}(a)} \in dy\}})$$

$$= (c_q)^n \sum_{m=0}^{n-1} \frac{((n-m)a-x)^{n-m-1} \mathbf{1}_{\{-x+(n-m)a \geq 0\}}}{m!(n-m-1)!}$$

$$\times \int_{-x}^\infty e^{-b_q(y+na)}(x+y)(x+y+ma)^{m-1} dy$$

$$= (c_q)^n e^{-b_q(na-x)} \sum_{m=0}^{n-1} \frac{((n-m)a-x)^{n-m-1} \mathbf{1}_{\{x \leq (n-m)a\}}}{m!(n-m-1)!}$$

$$\times \int_0^\infty e^{-b_q z} z(z+ma)^{m-1} dz.$$

Substituting this back into (4.38), we complete the proof. □

4.3. Numerical Results

In this section, we consider a numerical example to compare the distribution of the nth drawdown times $\tilde{\tau}_D^{n,+}(a)$ and $\tau_D^{n,+}(a)$ whose Laplace transforms are given in (4.17) and (4.26), respectively. We implement a numerical inverse Laplace transform approach proposed by Abate and Whitt (2006). For ease of notation, we denote the cumulative distribution functions of $\tau_D^{n,+}(a)$ and $\tilde{\tau}_D^{n,+}(a)$ by $F_n(\cdot)$ and $\tilde{F}_n(\cdot)$, respectively.

Table 4.1 presents the probabilities that at least n drawdowns with or without recovery occur before time 1 for different values of the drift μ. We observe that $F_n(1) > \tilde{F}_n(1)$ for $n \geq 2$ due to the relation between $\tau_D^{n,+}(a)$ and $\tilde{\tau}_D^{n,+}(a)$ given in (4.34). In addition, it shows that $F_n(1)$ increases as μ decreases. However, we observe the opposite trend for $\tilde{F}_n(1)$ when $n \geq 2$. This is because the previous running maximum is less likely to be revisited for a smaller μ. Since the drawdown risk is in principle a type of downside risk, we think smaller μ should lead to higher downside risks. In this sense, we suggest that the drawdown times without recovery are better to capture the essence of drawdown risks.

Table 4.2 is the equivalent of Table 4.1 with a lower volatility $\sigma = 0.12$. We notice that $F_n(1)$ and $\tilde{F}_n(1)$ decrease as σ decreases. We also have an interesting observation that the trend of $\tilde{F}_2(1)$ is not monotone in μ. Again, this is because the occurrence of $\tilde{\tau}_D^{n,+}(a)$ for $n \geq 2$ necessitates a recovery for the previous running maximum. Smaller drift does imply higher drawdown risk, meanwhile the recovery becomes more difficult.

4.4. Insurance of Frequent Relative Drawdowns

In this section, we consider insurance policies protecting against the risk of frequent drawdowns. We denote the price of an underlying asset by

Table 4.1. Distribution of the nth drawdown times when $a = 0.1$ and $\sigma = 0.2$.

	$\mu = 0.1$		$\mu = 0$		$\mu = -0.1$	
	$F_n(1)$	$\tilde{F}_n(1)$	$F_n(1)$	$\tilde{F}_n(1)$	$F_n(1)$	$\tilde{F}_n(1)$
$n = 1$	0.9779	0.9779	0.9908	0.9908	0.9967	0.9967
$n = 2$	0.8759	0.4865	0.9366	0.4406	0.9719	0.3636
$n = 3$	0.6651	0.1024	0.7926	0.0885	0.8874	0.0663
$n = 4$	0.4060	0.0082	0.5652	0.0070	0.7166	0.0050
$n = 5$	0.1942	0.0002	0.3262	0.0002	0.4871	0.0001
$n = 6$	0.0721	0.0000	0.1492	0.0000	0.2696	0.0000

Table 4.2. Distribution of drawdown times when $a = 0.1$ and $\sigma = 0.12$.

	$\mu = 0.1$		$\mu = 0$		$\mu = -0.1$	
	$F_n(1)$	$\tilde{F}_n(1)$	$F_n(1)$	$\tilde{F}_n(1)$	$F_n(1)$	$\tilde{F}_n(1)$
$n=1$	0.5663	0.5663	0.7845	0.7845	0.9257	0.9257
$n=2$	0.1592	0.0339	0.3755	0.0494	0.6509	0.0463
$n=3$	0.0225	0.0002	0.0986	0.0002	0.2891	0.0002
$n=4$	0.0016	0.0000	0.0137	0.0000	0.0730	0.0000
$n=5$	0.0001	0.0000	0.0010	0.0000	0.0099	0.0000
$n=6$	0.0000	0.0000	0.0000	0.0000	0.0007	0.0000

$S_\cdot = \{S_t\}_{t \geq 0}$, with dynamics

$$dS_t = rS_t dt + \sigma S_t dW_t^{\mathbb{Q}}, \qquad S_0 = s_0 \in \mathbb{R}_{>0},$$

where $r \in \mathbb{R}_{>0}$ is the risk-free rate, $\sigma \in \mathbb{R}_{>0}$ and $\{W_t^{\mathbb{Q}}\}_{t \geq 0}$ is a standard Brownian motion under a risk-neutral measure $\mathbb{Q}$. It is well known that

$$S_t = s_0 e^{X_t}, \qquad (4.39)$$

where $X_t = (r - \frac{1}{2}\sigma^2)t + \sigma W_t^{\mathbb{Q}}$.

In practice, drawdowns are often quoted in percentage. For fixed $0 < \alpha < 1$, we denote the time of the first relative drawdown over size α by

$$\varrho_D^+(\alpha) = \inf\{t > 0 : \overline{S}_t - S_t > \alpha \overline{S}_t\},$$

where $\overline{S}_t = \sup_{0 \leq u \leq t} S_u$ represents the running maximum of $S_\cdot$ by time t. By (4.39), it is easy to see that the relative drawdown of the geometric Brownian motion $S_\cdot$ corresponds to the actual drawdown of a drifted Brownian motion $X_\cdot$, namely

$$\varrho_D^+(\alpha) = \inf\{t > 0 : \overline{X}_t - X_t > -\log(1-\alpha)\} = \tau_D^+(\bar{\alpha}),$$

where $\bar{\alpha} = -\log(1-\alpha)$. Similarly, we denote the relative drawdown times with and without recovery by

$$\tilde{\varrho}_D^{n,+}(\alpha) = \inf\{t > \tilde{\varrho}_D^{n-1,+}(\alpha) : \overline{S}_t - S_t \geq \alpha \overline{S}_t, \overline{S}_t > \overline{S}_{\tilde{\varrho}_D^{n-1,+}(\alpha)}\},$$

and

$$\varrho_D^{n,+}(\alpha) = \inf\{t > \varrho_D^{n-1,+}(\alpha) : \overline{S}_{[\varrho_\alpha^{n-1}(S),t]} - S_t > \alpha \overline{S}_{[\varrho_D^{n-1,+}(\alpha),t]}\},$$

respectively. Therefore, we have

$$\tilde{\varrho}_D^{n,+}(\alpha) = \tilde{\tau}_D^{n,+}(\bar{\alpha}) \quad \text{and} \quad \varrho_D^{n,+}(\alpha) = \tau_D^{n,+}(\bar{\alpha}). \qquad (4.40)$$

Next, we consider two types of insurance policies offering a protection against relative drawdowns. For the first one, we assume that the seller pays the buyer $\$k$ at time T if a total of k relative drawdowns over size $0 < \alpha < 1$ occurred prior to time T (for all k). For the relative drawdown times with and without recovery, by (4.40), the risk-neutral prices are given by

$$\tilde{V}_1(T) = e^{-rT} \sum_{k=1}^{\infty} k \mathbb{Q}(\tilde{N}_T^{\bar{\alpha}}(X) = k) = e^{-rT} \mathbb{E}^{\mathbb{Q}}(\tilde{N}_T^{\bar{\alpha}}(X)),$$

and

$$V_1(T) = e^{-rT} \sum_{k=1}^{\infty} k \mathbb{Q}(N_T^{\bar{\alpha}}(X) = k) = e^{-rT} \mathbb{E}^{\mathbb{Q}}(N_T^{\bar{\alpha}}(X)),$$

respectively. For the second type of policies, the seller pays the buyer $\$1$ at the time of each relative drawdown time as long as it occurs before maturity T. Hence, their risk-neutral prices are

$$\tilde{V}_2(T) = \sum_{k=1}^{\infty} \mathbb{E}^{\mathbb{Q}}(e^{-r\tilde{\tau}_{\bar{\alpha}}^k(X)} \mathbf{1}_{\{\tilde{\tau}_D^{k,+}(\bar{\alpha}) \leq T\}}),$$

and

$$V_2(T) = \sum_{k=1}^{\infty} \mathbb{E}^{\mathbb{Q}}(e^{-r\tau_D^{k,+}(\bar{\alpha})} \mathbf{1}_{\{\tau_D^{k,+}(\bar{\alpha}) \leq T\}}),$$

respectively.

Corollary 4.5. *For $q > 0$, we have*

$$\int_0^{\infty} e^{-qT} V_1(T) \mathrm{d}T = \frac{1}{q+r} \frac{\bar{c}_{q+r}/\bar{b}_{q+r}}{1 - \bar{c}_{q+r}/\bar{b}_{q+r}}, \tag{4.41}$$

$$\int_0^{\infty} e^{-qT} \tilde{V}_1(T) \mathrm{d}T = \frac{1}{q+r} \frac{\bar{c}_{q+r}/\bar{b}_{q+r}}{1 - e^{-\bar{\beta}_{q+r}^+ a} \bar{c}_{q+r}/\bar{b}_{q+r}}, \tag{4.42}$$

$$\int_0^{\infty} e^{-qT} V_2(T) \mathrm{d}T = \frac{1}{q} \frac{\bar{c}_{q+r}/\bar{b}_{q+r}}{1 - \bar{c}_{q+r}/\bar{b}_{q+r}}, \tag{4.43}$$

$$\int_0^{\infty} e^{-qT} \tilde{V}_2(T) \mathrm{d}T = \frac{1}{q} \frac{\bar{c}_{q+r}/\bar{b}_{q+r}}{1 - e^{-\bar{\beta}_{q+r}^+ a} \bar{c}_{q+r}/\bar{b}_{q+r}}, \tag{4.44}$$

where $\bar{b}_q = \dfrac{\bar{\beta}_q^+ e^{-\bar{\beta}_q^- \bar{\alpha}} - \bar{\beta}_q^- e^{-\bar{\beta}_q^+ \bar{\alpha}}}{e^{-\bar{\beta}_q^- \bar{\alpha}} - e^{-\bar{\beta}_q^+ \bar{\alpha}}}$, $\bar{c}_q = \dfrac{\bar{\beta}_q^+ - \bar{\beta}_q^-}{e^{-\bar{\beta}_q^- \bar{\alpha}} - e^{-\bar{\beta}_q^+ \bar{\alpha}}}$ *and* $\bar{\beta}_q^{\pm} = \dfrac{-r + \frac{1}{2}\sigma^2 \pm \sqrt{(r - \frac{1}{2}\sigma^2)^2 + 2q\sigma^2}}{\sigma^2}$.

Proof. We provide the proof for $\int_0^\infty V_1(T)e^{-qT}dT$ and $\int_0^\infty V_2(T)e^{-qT}dT$ only. The other two results can be derived in a similar fashion. From the definition of $N_T^{\bar{a}}(X)$, we have the following relation:

$$\mathbb{E}^{\mathbb{Q}}(N_T^{\bar{a}}(X)) = \sum_{k=1}^{\infty} \mathbb{Q}(N_T^{\bar{a}}(X) \geq k) = \sum_{k=1}^{\infty} \mathbb{Q}(\tau_D^{k,+}(\bar{a}) \leq T).$$

By (4.26), it follows that

$$\int_0^\infty V_1(T)e^{-qT}dT = \int_0^\infty e^{-(q+r)T}\mathbb{E}^{\mathbb{Q}}(N_T^{\bar{a}}(X))dT$$

$$= \sum_{k=1}^{\infty} \int_0^\infty e^{-(q+r)T}\mathbb{Q}(\tau_D^{k,+}(\bar{a}) \leq T)dT$$

$$= \frac{1}{q+r}\sum_{k=1}^{\infty} \mathbb{E}^{\mathbb{Q}}(e^{-(q+r)\tau_D^{k,+}(\bar{a})})$$

$$= \frac{1}{q+r}\sum_{k=1}^{\infty} \left(\frac{\bar{c}_{q+r}}{\bar{b}_{q+r}}\right)^n$$

$$= \frac{1}{q+r}\frac{\bar{c}_{q+r}/\bar{b}_{q+r}}{1-\bar{c}_{q+r}/\bar{b}_{q+r}}.$$

For $\int_0^\infty V_2(T)e^{-qT}dT$, by Fubini's theorem and (4.26), we have

$$\int_0^\infty V_2(T)e^{-qT}dT = \sum_{k=1}^{\infty} \int_0^\infty \mathbb{E}^{\mathbb{Q}}(e^{-r\tau_D^{k,+}(\bar{a})}\mathbf{1}_{\{\tau_D^{k,+}(\bar{a})\leq T\}})e^{-qT}dT$$

$$= \sum_{k=1}^{\infty} \int_0^\infty \int_0^T e^{-rt}\mathbb{Q}(\tau_D^{k,+}(\bar{a}) \in dt)e^{-qT}dT$$

$$= \sum_{k=1}^{\infty} \frac{1}{q}\int_0^\infty e^{-(q+r)t}\mathbb{Q}(\tau_{\bar{a}}^n(X) \in dt)$$

$$= \sum_{k=1}^{\infty} \frac{1}{q}\left(\frac{\bar{c}_{q+r}}{\bar{b}_{q+r}}\right)^n$$

$$= \frac{1}{q}\frac{\bar{c}_{q+r}/\bar{b}_{q+r}}{1-\bar{c}_{q+r}/\bar{b}_{q+r}}.$$

This completes the proof. □

Table 4.3. Insurance contracts prices when $\alpha = 0.15$ and $r = 0.05$.

		$V_1(T)$	$\tilde{V}_1(T)$	$V_2(T)$	$\tilde{V}_2(T)$
$T = 1$	$\sigma = 0.1$	0.1102	0.1091	0.1120	0.1108
$T = 2$	$\sigma = 0.1$	0.3011	0.2769	0.3131	0.2885
$T = 3$	$\sigma = 0.1$	0.4743	0.4031	0.5058	0.4318
$T = 1$	$\sigma = 0.2$	1.1777	0.7873	1.2043	0.8081
$T = 2$	$\sigma = 0.2$	2.3815	1.1842	2.4977	1.2550
$T = 3$	$\sigma = 0.2$	3.4651	1.4519	3.7279	1.5890

Remark 4.3. It is worth pointing out that, through expansion of the randomized prices in Corollary 4.5 in terms of exponentials, it is possible to obtain semi-static hedging portfolios as in Chapter 7 (especially, the discussion with GBM following Theorem 7.8). Moreover, capped insurance contracts against frequency of drawdowns can also be formulated and priced using Theorems 4.1, 4.2, and Corollary 4.3.

To conclude, we consider a pricing example for the four types of insurance contracts proposed earlier. The same numerical Laplace transform approach as in the last section is applied.

As expected, Table 4.3 shows that type II contracts have higher prices than type I contracts because of earlier payments (at the moment of each drawdown time instead of the maturity T). It also shows that $\tilde{V}_1(T)$ and $\tilde{V}_2(T)$ are respectively lower than $V_1(T)$ and $V_2(T)$ due to $\tau_D^{n,+}(a) \leq \tilde{\tau}_D^{n,+}(a)$. All the prices increase as T increases or σ increases. Moreover, we can expect that the prices will decrease as α or r increases. The latter is due to a higher discount rate which is the risk-free rate under the risk-neutral measure $\mathbb{Q}$.

4.5. Concluding Remarks

In this chapter, we study the frequency of drawdowns and some of their inherent characteristics. We consider two types of drawdown time sequences depending on whether a historical running maximum is reset or not. For each type, we study the frequency rate of drawdowns, the Laplace transform of the nth drawdown time, the distribution of the running maximum and the value of the underlying process at the nth drawdown time, as well as some other quantities of interest. We establish interesting relationships between these two drawdown time sequences. Finally, insurance policies

Frequency of Drawdowns in a Brownian Motion Model   79

protecting against the risk of frequent drawdowns are proposed and priced using numerical Laplace inversion.

4.6. Proof of Lemmas

Proof of Lemma 4.2. We prove this result by induction on n. For $n = 1$, we have

$$\mathbb{E}(e^{-q\tau_X^+(x)} 1_{\{\tau_X^+(x) < \tau_D^{1,+}(a)\}})$$

$$= \mathbb{E}(e^{-q\tau_X^+(x)}) - \mathbb{E}(e^{-q\tau_X^+(x)} 1_{\{\tau_X^+(x) > \tau_D^{1,+}(a)\}})$$

$$= e^{-\beta_q^+ x} - \int_0^x \mathbb{E}(e^{-q\tau_D^{1,+}(a)} 1_{\{\overline{X}_{\tau_D^{1,+}(a)} \in dy\}}) \mathbb{E}_{y-a}(e^{-q\tau_X^+(x)})$$

$$= e^{-\beta_q^+ x} - \int_0^x c_q e^{-b_q y} e^{-\beta_q^+(x-y+a)} dy$$

$$= e^{-\beta_q^+ x} - c_q e^{-\beta_q^+ a} \frac{e^{-\beta_q^+ x} - e^{-b_q x}}{b_q - \beta_q^+},$$

where we used (4.10) in the third equality.

On the other hand, using the fact that $c_q e^{-\beta_q^+ a} = b_q - \beta_q^+$, we have

$$\mathbb{E}(e^{-q\tau_X^+(x)} 1_{\{\tau_X^+(x) < \tau_D^{1,+}(a)\}}) = e^{-b_q x}.$$

We now assume that (4.28) holds for $n = 1, 2, \ldots, k-1$ and shows that (4.28) also holds for $n = k$. Indeed, by the total probability formula,

$$\mathbb{E}(e^{-q\tau_X^+(x)} 1_{\{\tau_X^+(x) < \tau_D^{k,+}(a)\}})$$

$$= \mathbb{E}(e^{-q\tau_X^+(x)} 1_{\{\tau_X^+(x) < \tau_D^{1,+}(a)\}}) + \mathbb{E}(e^{-q\tau_X^+(x)} 1_{\{\tau_D^{1,+}(a) < \tau_X^+(x) < \tau_D^{k,+}(a)\}})$$

$$= e^{-b_q x} + \int_0^x \mathbb{E}(e^{-q\tau_D^+(a)} 1_{\{\overline{X}_{\tau_D^+(a)} \in dy\}})$$

$$\times \mathbb{E}_{y-a}(e^{-q\tau_X^+(x)} 1_{\{\tau_X^+(x) < \tau_D^{k-1,+}(a)\}}) dy$$

$$= e^{-b_q x} + \int_0^x c_q e^{-b_q y} \mathbb{E}(e^{-q\tau_X^+(x-y+a)} 1_{\{\tau_X^+(x-y+a) < \tau_D^{k-1,+}(a)\}}) dy.$$

Substituting (4.28) at $n = k-1$ into the above yields

$$\mathbb{E}(e^{-q\tau_X^+(x)} \mathbf{1}_{\{\tau_X^+(x) < \tau_D^+(a)^k\}})$$

$$= e^{-b_q x} + c_q e^{-b_q(x+a)}$$

$$\times \sum_{j=0}^{k-2} \int_0^x (c_q e^{-b_q a})^j \frac{(x-y+a)(x-y+(j+1)a)^{j-1}}{j!} dy$$

$$= e^{-b_q x} \left(1 + c_q e^{-b_q a} x + \sum_{j=2}^{k-1} (c_q e^{-b_q a})^j \frac{x(x+ja)^{j-1}}{j!} \right)$$

$$= e^{-b_q x} \sum_{j=0}^{k-1} (c_q e^{-b_q a})^j \frac{x(x+ja)^{j-1}}{j!}.$$

This completes the proof. □

Chapter 5

Occupation Times Related to Drawdowns

In a filtered probability space $(\Omega, \mathbb{F}, \mathcal{F}, \mathbb{P})$ with filtration $\mathbb{F} = \{\mathcal{F}_t\}_{t\geq 0}$, we consider a one-dimensional time-homogenous linear diffusion $X.$ on $I \equiv (l, r) \subset \mathbb{R}$ with natural or entrance-not-exit boundaries. Its evolution is governed by the stochastic differential equation

$$dX_t = \mu(X_t)\,dt + \sigma(X_t)dW_t, \quad X_0 = x \in I, \tag{5.1}$$

where $\{W_t\}_{t\geq 0}$ is a standard Brownian motion with respect to $\mathbb{F}$, and $(\mu(\cdot), \sigma(\cdot))$ is a pair of real-valued functions that satisfy (A.2) and (A.3) in the Appendix.

We introduce the running maximum and minimum processes of $X.$ by

$$\overline{X}_t = \sup_{s \in [0,t]} X_s, \quad \underline{X}_t = \inf_{s \in [0,t]} X_s, \quad \forall t \geq 0.$$

The drawdown process of $X.$, and its dual, the drawup process, are then denoted as $D. = \overline{X}. - X.$ and $U. = X. - \underline{X}.$, respectively. We denote the first passage time of the drawdown and the drawup processes by

$$\tau_D^+(a) = \inf\{t > 0 : D_t > a\},$$
$$\tau_U^+(b) = \inf\{t > 0 : U_t > b\},$$

for any fixed $a, b > 0$. The first passage time of $X.$ is denote by $\tau_X^\pm(x)$:

$$\tau_X^\pm(x) = \inf\{t > 0 : X_t \gtrless x\}, \quad \forall x \in I.$$

The occupation time of a stochastic process is the amount of time the stochastic process stays within a certain range.

In this chapter, we obtain a class of results regarding the law of occupation times of the drawdown process $D.$ or the drawup process $U.$, for the one-dimensional diffusion $X.$. In particular, we derive the Laplace transforms of the occupation times of $X.$ below a fixed level y or below the starting point, until the first exit time or the first passage of drawdown, respectively. Using these results, we proceed to study the law of occupation time of the drawdown process $D.$ above the fixed level y, and of the drawup process $U.$ below y, until the first passage of drawdown, or an exponential time independent of $X.$.

The results obtained can be applied in risk analysis and for option pricing of the drawdown processes. In particular, we consider a time-homogenous linear diffusion with reduced form default model. Using the so-called Omega model (Albrecher *et al.*, 2011; Gerber *et al.*, 2012), we can describe the hazard rate of the default in such a way that it depends on the asset process, its drawdown or drawup processes. Then the probability of default before a large drawdown can be computed. Moreover, our results can be used to price Parisian-like digital call options and α-quantile options of the drawdown process, a non-trivial extension of the option pricing problem for maximum drawdowns (Carr *et al.*, 2011; Pospisil and Večeř, 2008; Večeř, 2006, 2007; Zhang *et al.*, 2013).

As examples of our general result, we present explicit formulas for some of the main results in the cases of Brownian motions with drift and three-dimensional Bessel processes. Moreover, we prove through Laplace transform that, in these two models, the law of the occupation time of the drawdown process above a level is the same as that of the first passage of drawdown at certain threshold.

The rest of the chapter is structured as follows. In Section 5.1, we give definitions of five occupation times related to drawdowns and drawup. In Section 5.2, we derive the Laplace transforms of these occupation times. In Section 5.3, we present explicit formulas for some of the analytical results in the cases of Brownian motion with drift and three-dimensional Bessel process. In Section 5.4, we discuss applications in risk analysis and for option pricing of the results obtained. We conclude this chapter in Section 5.5. Proofs of lemmas can be found in Section 5.6.

For preliminaries on linear diffusion and definitions of the scale function $s(\cdot)$, eigenfunctions $\phi_q^{\pm}(\cdot)$ and other related functions used in this chapter, please refer to the Appendix.

5.1. Definition of Occupation Times

We begin by giving definition of five occupation times that will be studied in this chapter. First, as a preliminary step for drawdown- or drawup-related occupation times, we need to study the occupation time of the underlying process $X.$ below a fixed level. Specifically, fix a $y \in (u,v) \subsetneq I$, we define the occupation time below y before exiting (u,v) by

$$A_y^{u,v} := \int_0^{\tau_X^-(u) \wedge \tau_X^+(v)} \mathbf{1}_{\{X_t < y\}}\, dt. \tag{5.2}$$

By removing the upper barrier in (5.2) and replacing the lower barrier in (5.2) by a moving boundary $\overline{X}. - a$ for some $a > 0$, we obtained the occupation time of $X.$ below y until the first passage of drawdown $\tau_D^+(a)$. In particular, for $x - a, y \in I$, the occupation time below y before the drawdown process $D.$ exceeds a is denoted by

$$B_y^a := \int_0^{\tau_D^+(a)} \mathbf{1}_{\{X_t < y\}}\, dt. \tag{5.3}$$

While the occupation time of $X.$ below y until an exponential random variable independent of $X.$ is well-studied in literature (Li and Zhou, 2013), the new quantity B_y^a defined as above relates the occupation time of $X.$ to its drawdown process $D.$, which can be used to characterize the drawdown risk of $X.$.

To obtain the third occupation time, we replace the indicator in (5.3) by $\mathbf{1}_{\{D_t > y\}}$ for a $y \in (0, a)$. That is,

$$C_y^a := \int_0^{\tau_D^+(a)} \mathbf{1}_{\{D_t > y\}}\, dt. \tag{5.4}$$

The occupation time C_y^a measures the amount of time for the drawdown process $D.$ to finish the "last trip" from y to a. It can be used as a measurement of performance for CUSUM-type stopping rule in change-point detection problems (Poor and Hadjiliadis, 2008). Because of its obvious financial interpretation, C_y^a can also be used as a measure for drawdown risks.

The fourth occupation relates the drawdown to its dual, the drawup process. For any $y \in [a, \infty)$ and $x - a \in I$, we define the occupation time of the drawup process $U.$ below y before the drawdown process $D.$ exceeds a by

$$D_y^a := \int_0^{\tau_D^+(a)} \mathbf{1}_{\{U_t < y\}}\, dt. \tag{5.5}$$

The occupation time D_y^a can be considered as a counterpart of C_y^a defined in (5.4). It measures the amount of time the upward moment stays weak, prior the drawdown reaches a.

The last occupation time is devoted to the occupation time of the drawdown process in an exogenously given finite time-horizon. To that end, we consider the occupation time of the drawdown process $D.$ above y before an independent exponential time $\mathbf{e}_q$ by

$$E_y^q := \int_0^{\mathbf{e}_q} \mathbf{1}_{\{D_t > y\}}\, dt, \tag{5.6}$$

where y is any fixed position number. The occupation time E_y^q can be identified with the Laplace transform of the occupation time in a finite time horizon $T > 0$: $\int_0^T \mathbf{1}_{\{D_t > y\}} dt$, which is closely related to the maximum drawdown $\overline{D}_t$ and other quantiles of $D.$ in the finite time-horizon T.

5.2. Analytical Results

In this section, we begin by computing the Laplace transforms of the occupation time below a level until the first exit time for a linear diffusion process $X.$ defined in (5.1). Although relevant formulas exist for special diffusions, the results for general linear diffusions that we provide here are new. Using this result, we then proceed to study occupation times of $X.$, its drawdown $D.$ and its drawup $U.$ until the first passage of drawdown $\tau_D^+(a)$ or until an exponential time which is independent of $X.$. These new results give several interesting identities and provide means of measuring financial risk and pricing options as we shall in the next section.

5.2.1. *Occupation time below a level until the first exit time*

In this subsection, we derive the law of occupation time $A_y^{u,v}$, which is defined in (5.2).

Lemma 5.1. *For $x, y \in (u, v) \subsetneq I$, $q > 0, p \geq 0$, we have*

$$\mathbb{E}_x \big(e^{-qA_y^{u,v} - p\tau_X^+(v)} \mathbf{1}_{\{\tau_X^+(v) < \tau_X^-(u)\}} \big)$$

$$= \begin{cases} \dfrac{W_{q+p}(x,u)}{W_{q+p}(y,u)} \dfrac{s'(y)/W_p(v,y)}{W_{q+p,1}(y,u) - W_{p,1}(y,v)} & \text{if } x \in (u, y], \\[2ex] \dfrac{W_p(x,y)}{W_p(v,y)} + \dfrac{W_p(v,x)}{W_p(v,y)} \dfrac{s'(y)/W_p(v,y)}{W_{q+p,1}(y,u) - W_{p,1}(y,v)} & \text{if } x \in (y, v), \end{cases}$$

$$\tag{5.7}$$

$$\mathbb{E}_x(e^{-qA_y^{u,v}} \mathbf{1}_{\{\tau_X^+(v) > \tau_X^-(u)\}})$$

$$= \begin{cases} \dfrac{W_q(y,x)}{W_q(y,u)} + \dfrac{W_q(x,u)}{W_q(y,u)} \dfrac{s'(y)/W_q(y,u)}{W_{q,1}(y,u) + \frac{s'(y)}{s(v)-s(y)}} & \text{if } x \in (u,y], \\[2ex] \dfrac{(s(v)-s(x))s'(y)/W_q(y,u)}{(s(v)-s(y))W_{q,1}(y,u) + s'(y)} & \text{if } x \in (y,v), \end{cases}$$

(5.8)

where the scale function of X., $s(\cdot)$, and functions $W_q(\cdot,\cdot)$, $W_{q,1}(\cdot,\cdot)$ are defined as in the Appendix.

Letting $u \downarrow l$ in (5.7) and using Lemma A.2, we obtain the following result.

Corollary 5.1. *For $x \in (y,v) \subsetneq I$, $p > 0, q \geq 0$, we have*

$$\mathbb{E}_x(e^{-q\int_0^{\tau_X^+(v)} \mathbf{1}_{\{X_t < y\}} dt - p\tau_X^+(v)}) = \frac{W_p(x,y)}{W_p(v,y)} + \frac{s'(y)W_p(v,x)/W_p^2(v,y)}{\varphi_{q+p}^{+,'}(y) - W_{p,1}(y,v)},$$

where $\varphi_q^+(x) = (\log \phi_q^+(x))'$.

5.2.2. Occupation time below a level until the first passage of drawdown

In this subsection, we derive the law of the occupation time B_y^a, which is defined in (5.3).

Proposition 5.1. *For $q \geq 0$ and $x \in I$,*

$$\mathbb{E}_x(e^{-qB_x^a}) = \exp\left(-\int_x^{x+a} \frac{s'(u) \cdot W_{q,1}(x, u-a) \, du}{s'(x) + (s(u)-s(x))W_{q,1}(x, u-a)}\right)$$

$$+ \int_x^{x+a} \frac{s'(u)/W_q(x, u-a) \, du}{(1 + (s(u)-s(x))/s'(x) \cdot W_{q,1}(x, u-a))^2}.$$

Proof. We let $\epsilon = \frac{a}{N}$ for a large integer $N > 0$. Using Lebesgue dominated convergence theorem, continuity and strong Markov property of X., we have

$$\log \mathbb{E}_x(e^{-qB_x^a} \mathbf{1}_{\{\overline{X}_{\tau_D^+(a)} \geq x+a\}})$$

$$= \log \mathbb{E}_x(e^{-qB_x^a} \mathbf{1}_{\{\tau_X^+(x+a) < \tau_D^+(a)\}})$$

$$= \log\left(\lim_{N\to\infty} \prod_{i=0}^{N-1} \mathbb{E}_{x+i\epsilon}(\mathrm{e}^{-qA_x^{x+i\epsilon-a,x+(i+1)\epsilon}} \mathbf{1}_{\{\tau_X^+(x+(i+1)\epsilon)<\tau_X^-(x+i\epsilon-a)\}})\right)$$

$$= \lim_{N\to\infty} \sum_{i=0}^{N-1} [\mathbb{E}_{x+i\epsilon}(\mathrm{e}^{-qA_x^{x+i\epsilon-a,x+(i+1)\epsilon}} \mathbf{1}_{\{\tau_X^+(x+(i+1)\epsilon)<\tau_X^-(x+i\epsilon-a)\}}) - 1]$$

$$= -\int_x^{x+a} \frac{s'(u)W_{q,1}(x,u-a)\,\mathrm{d}u}{s'(x)+(s(u)-s(x))W_{q,1}(x,u-a)}.$$

Here we used Lemma 5.1 in the last equality. Moreover, notice that $\mathbb{E}_x(\mathrm{e}^{-qA_x^{u-a,z}} \mathbf{1}_{\{\tau_X^-(u-a)<\tau_X^+(z)\}}) = \mathbb{E}_x(\mathrm{e}^{-qA_x^{u-a,\infty}} \mathbf{1}_{\{\overline{X}_{\tau_X^-(u-a)}<z\}})$. It follows that

$$\mathbb{E}_x(\mathrm{e}^{-qB_x^a} \mathbf{1}_{\{\overline{X}_{\tau_D^+(a)} \in (x,x+a)\}})$$

$$= \int_x^{x+a} \mathbb{E}_x(\mathrm{e}^{-qA_x^{u-a,\infty}} \mathbf{1}_{\{\overline{X}_{\tau_X^-(u-a)} \in \mathrm{d}u\}})$$

$$= \int_x^{x+a} \frac{\partial}{\partial z}\bigg|_{z=u} \mathbb{E}_x(\mathrm{e}^{-qA_x^{u-a,z}} \mathbf{1}_{\{\tau_X^-(u-a)<\tau_X^+(z)\}})\,\mathrm{d}u$$

$$= \int_x^{x+a} \frac{s'(u)/W_q(x,u-a)\,\mathrm{d}u}{(1+(s(u)-s(x))/s'(x) \cdot W_{q,1}(x,u-a))^2},$$

where we used Lemma 5.1 in the last equality. $\square$

5.2.3. Occupation time of the drawdown process until the first passage of drawdown

In this subsection, we derive the law of occupation time C_y^a, which is defined in (5.4). To that end, we first condition on $\overline{X}_{\tau_D^+(a)}$, and then count separately the occupation time before and after the moment when the peak $\overline{X}_{\tau_D^+(a)}$ is realized.

Theorem 5.1. *For $q \geq 0$, $0 < y < a$,*

$$\mathbb{E}_x(\mathrm{e}^{-qC_y^a} \mathbf{1}_{\{\tau_D^+(a)<\infty\}})$$

$$= \int_x^r \frac{s'(m-y)s'(m)/W_q(m-y,m-a)}{s'(m-y)+(s(m)-s(m-y))W_{q,1}(m-y,m-a)}$$

$$\times \exp\left(-\int_x^m \frac{s'(u)W_{q,1}(u-y,u-a)\mathrm{d}u}{s'(u-y)+(s(u)-s(u-y))W_{q,1}(u-y,u-a)}\right)\mathrm{d}m.$$

Proof. Following the conditioning argument in Chapter 3, we consider the last passage time $g_a := \sup\{t \leq \tau_D^+(a) : X_t = \overline{X}_t\}$. It is known that, given X_{g_a}, the path fragments $\{X_t\}_{t \in [0, g_a]}$ and $\{X_t\}_{t \in [g_a, \tau_D^+(a)]}$ are two independent conditional processes. Moreover, by Lemma 3.1, the optional projection of non-increasing process $\mathbf{1}_{\{g_a > t\}}$, $\mathbb{P}_x(g_a > t | \mathcal{F}_t)$ is a supermartingale, with a Doob–Meyer decomposition $\chi_t = M_t - L_t$, where

$$M_t = 1 + \int_0^{t \wedge \tau_D^+(a)} \frac{s'(X_s)\sigma(X_s)\mathrm{d}W_s}{s(\overline{X}_s) - s(\overline{X}_s - a)}, \quad L_t = \int_0^{t \wedge \tau_D^+(a)} \frac{s'(\overline{X}_s)\mathrm{d}\overline{X}_s}{s(\overline{X}_s) - s(\overline{X}_s - a)}.$$

Now introduce a non-negative bounded optional process

$$\Gamma_t = \mathrm{e}^{-q \int_0^t \mathbf{1}_{\{Y_s > y\}} \mathrm{d}s} \mathbf{1}_{\{t < \tau_D^+(a) < \infty\}}, \quad \forall t \geq 0.$$

Using the same argument as in the proof of Theorem 15 on p. 380 of Protter (2003), we have that, for any positive test function $f(\cdot)$ on $[0, \infty)$,

$$\mathbb{E}_x(f(X_{g_a})\Gamma_{g_a}) = \mathbb{E}_x \left(\int_0^\infty f(X_t)\Gamma_t \mathrm{d}L_t \right)$$

$$= \mathbb{E}_x \left(\int_0^\infty \frac{f(X_t)\Gamma_t \cdot s'(\overline{X}_t)\mathrm{d}\overline{X}_t}{s(\overline{X}_t) - s(\overline{X}_t - a)} \right).$$

By using a change of variable, $m = \overline{X}_t$ in the above equation, and also the fact that $X_t = \overline{X}_t$ on the support of measure $\mathrm{d}\overline{X}_t$, we have that

$$\mathbb{E}_x(f(X_{g_a})\Gamma_{g_a})$$

$$= \int_x^r f(m)\mathbb{E}_x(\mathrm{e}^{-q \int_0^{\tau_X^+(m)} \mathbf{1}_{\{D_t > y\}} \mathrm{d}t} \mathbf{1}_{\{\tau_X^+(m) < \tau_D^+(a)\}}) \frac{s'(m)\mathrm{d}m}{s(m) - s(m - a)}. \quad (5.9)$$

On the other hand, using Lemma 3.3 we have that, for all $r > m > x$,

$$\mathbb{P}_x(\tau_X^+(m) < \tau_D^+(a)) = \mathrm{e}^{-\int_x^m \frac{s'(v)}{s(v) - s(v-a)} \mathrm{d}v}, \quad (5.10)$$

$$\mathbb{P}_x(X_{g_a} \in \mathrm{d}m) = \frac{s'(m)}{s(m) - s(m - a)} \mathrm{e}^{-\int_x^m \frac{s'(v)}{s(v) - s(v-a)} \mathrm{d}v}. \quad (5.11)$$

It follows from (5.9) and (5.10) that

$$\mathbb{E}_x(f(X_{g_a})\Gamma_{g_a})$$
$$= \int_x^r f(m) \cdot \mathbb{E}_x(e^{-q\int_0^{\tau_X^+(m)} \mathbf{1}_{\{D_t > y\}} dt} | \tau_X^+(m) < \tau_D^+(a))$$
$$\times \frac{s'(m)}{s(m) - s(m-a)} \exp\left(-\int_x^m \frac{s'(v)}{s(v) - s(v-a)} dv\right) dm$$
$$= \int_x^r f(m) \cdot \mathbb{E}_x(e^{-q\int_0^{\tau_X^+(m)} \mathbf{1}_{\{D_t > y\}} dt} | \tau_X^+(m) < \tau_D^+(a)) \cdot \mathbb{P}_x(X_{g_a} \in dm),$$

where the last line follows from (5.11). It follows that

$$\mathbb{E}_x(e^{-q\int_0^{\tau_X^+(m)} \mathbf{1}_{\{D_t > y\}} dt} | \tau_X^+(m) < \tau_D^+(a)) = \mathbb{E}_x(e^{-q\int_0^{g_a} \mathbf{1}_{\{D_t > y\}} dt} | X_{g_a} = m).$$

To get the conditional expectation on the left-hand side for arbitrary $m > x$, we let $\epsilon = \frac{m-x}{N}$ for a large integer $N > 0$. Using Lebesgue dominated convergence theorem, continuity and strong Markov property of $X.$, we obtain that

$$\mathbb{E}_x(e^{-q\int_0^{\tau_X^+(m)} \mathbf{1}_{\{D_t > y\}} dt} | \tau_D^+(a) > \tau_X^+(m))$$
$$= \lim_{N \to \infty} \prod_{i=0}^{N-1} \mathbb{E}_{x+i\epsilon}(e^{-qA_{x+i\epsilon-y}^{x+i\epsilon-a, x+(i+1)\epsilon}} | \tau_X^+(x+(i+1)\epsilon)$$
$$< \tau_X^-(x+i\epsilon-a))$$
$$= e^{\int_x^m \frac{s'(u)du}{s(u)-s(u-a)}} \exp\left(\int_x^m \frac{\frac{-s'(u)}{s'(u-y)} W_{q,1}(u-y, u-a)}{1 + \frac{s(u)-s(u-y)}{s'(u-y)} W_{q,1}(u-y, u-a)} du\right),$$

where we used Lemma 5.1 in the last equality. Similarly, for the occupation time after the random time g_a, we have that

$$\mathbb{E}_x\left(\exp\left(-q\int_{g_a}^{\tau_D^+(a)} \mathbf{1}_{\{D_t > y\}} dt\right) \bigg| X_{g_a} = m\right)$$
$$= \mathbb{E}_m\left(\exp\left(-q\int_0^{\tau_X^-(m-a)} \mathbf{1}_{\{X_t < m-y\}} dt\right) \bigg| \tau_X^-(m-a) < \tau_X^+(m)\right)$$

$$= \lim_{\epsilon' \downarrow 0} \frac{\mathbb{E}_m(\mathrm{e}^{-qA_{m-y}^{m-a,m+\epsilon'}}; \tau_X^-(m-a) < \tau_X^+(m+\epsilon'))}{\mathbb{P}_m(\tau_X^-(m-a) < \tau_X^+(m+\epsilon'))}$$

$$= \frac{(s(m) - s(m-a))/W_q(m-y, m-a)}{1 + \frac{s(m)-s(m-y)}{s'(m-y)} W_{q,1}(m-y, m-a)}.$$

The result now follows from integration using the density in (5.11). □

5.2.4. Occupation time of the drawup process until the first passage of drawdown

In this subsection, we derive the law of occupation time D_y^a, which is defined in (5.5).

Theorem 5.2. *For all $q > 0$ and $y \geq a$,*

$$\mathbb{E}_x(\mathrm{e}^{-qD_y^a} \mathbf{1}_{\{\tau_D^+(a)<\infty\}})$$

$$= \mathbb{P}_x(\tau_D^+(a) < \tau_U^+(y) \wedge \mathbf{e}_q) + \int_x^{x+a} \frac{s'(u-a) W_q(u,x)}{W_q^2(u, u-a)}$$

$$\times \exp\left(-\int_u^{u+y-a} W_{q,1}(v, v-a)\, \mathrm{d}v\right) \cdot \mathbb{E}_{u+y-a}(\mathrm{e}^{-qB_{u+y-a}^a})\, \mathrm{d}u,$$

where the probability in the first line is given in Theorem 2.4, and the expectation in the last line is given in Proposition 5.1.

Proof. Notice that $D_y^a = \tau_D^+(a)$, $\mathbb{P}_x$-a.s. on the event $\{\tau_D^+(a) < \tau_U^+(y)\}$. On the other hand, on the event $\{\tau_U^+(y) < \tau_D^+(a)\}$, we have $\underline{X}_{\tau_U^+(y)} = X_{\tau_U^+(y)} - y \leq X_{\tau_U^+(y)} - a < \overline{X}_{\tau_D^+(a)} - a$, $\mathbb{P}_x$-a.s. Thus,

$$D_y^a = \tau_U^+(y) + B_{X_{\tau_U^+(y)}}^a \circ \theta_{\tau_U^+(y)},$$

where $\theta_{\cdot}$ is the Markov shift operator.

Using the strong Markov property of $X_{\cdot}$, we have

$$\mathbb{E}_x(\mathrm{e}^{-qD_y^a} \mathbf{1}_{\{\tau_D^+(a)<\infty\}})$$

$$= \mathbb{E}_x(\mathrm{e}^{-q\tau_D^+(a)} \mathbf{1}_{\{\tau_D^+(a)<\tau_U^+(y)\}})$$

$$+ \mathbb{E}_x(\mathrm{e}^{-q\tau_U^+(y)} \mathbf{1}_{\{\tau_U^+(y)<\tau_D^+(a)\}} \mathbb{E}_{X_{\tau_U^+(y)}}(\mathrm{e}^{-qB_{X_{\tau_U^+(y)}}^a}))$$

$$= \mathbb{P}_x(\tau_D^+(a) < \tau_U^+(y) \wedge \mathbf{e}_q)$$
$$+ \int_x^{x+a} \mathbb{P}_x(\tau_U^+(y) < \tau_D^+(a) \wedge \mathbf{e}_q, X_{\tau_U^+(y)} \in y - a + \mathrm{d}u)$$
$$\times \mathbb{E}_{u-a+y}(\mathrm{e}^{-qB_{u-a+y}^a}).$$

The result now follows from Theorem 2.3. □

5.2.5. Occupation time of the drawdown process at an independent exponential time

In this subsection, we derive the law of occupation time E_y^q, which is defined in (5.6).

Theorem 5.3. *For all $q, p > 0$ and $y > 0$,*

$$\mathbb{E}_x(\mathrm{e}^{-pE_y^q})$$
$$= 1 - \exp\left(-\int_x^r \frac{W_{q,1}(u, u-y)\varphi_{q+p}^+(u-y) - W_{q,2}(u-y, u)}{\varphi_{q+p}^+(u-y) - W_{q,1}(u-y, u)} \, \mathrm{d}u\right)$$
$$- \int_x^r \exp\left(-\int_x^m \frac{W_{q,1}(u, u-y)\varphi_{q+p}^+(u-y) - W_{q,2}(u-y, u)}{\varphi_{q+p}^+(u-y) - W_{q,1}(u-y, u)} \, \mathrm{d}u\right)$$
$$\times \frac{p/(q+p) \cdot s'(m)\varphi_{q+p}^+(m-y)/W_q(m, m-y)}{\varphi_{q+p}^+(m-y) - W_{q,1}(m-y, m)} \, \mathrm{d}m,$$

where $\varphi_q^+(x) = (\log \phi_q^+(x))'$.

Proof. Consider the random time $g := \inf\{t \geq 0 : X_t = \overline{X}_{\mathbf{e}_q}\}$. Then we have

$$E_y^q = \int_0^g \mathbf{1}_{\{D_t > y\}} \, \mathrm{d}t + \int_g^{\mathbf{e}_q} \mathbf{1}_{\{D_t > y\}} \, \mathrm{d}t := E_y^{q,1} + E_y^{q,2}.$$

Below we compute the Laplace transforms of $E_y^{q,1}$ and $E_y^{q,2}$ conditioning on $\overline{X}_{\mathbf{e}_q}$. More specifically, for $m > x$, we let $\epsilon = \frac{m-x}{N}$ for a large $N > 0$. Then we have that

$$\frac{\mathbb{E}_x(\mathrm{e}^{-pE_y^{q,1}} ; \overline{X}_{\mathbf{e}_q} \in \mathrm{d}m)}{\mathrm{d}m}$$
$$= -\frac{\partial}{\partial h}\bigg|_{h=0} \mathbb{E}_x(\mathrm{e}^{-p\int_0^{\tau_X^+(m)} \mathbf{1}_{\{D_t > y\}} \, \mathrm{d}t}; \overline{X}_{\mathbf{e}_q} \geq m + h)$$

$$= \exp\left(\lim_{N\to\infty} \sum_{i=0}^{N-1} [\mathbb{E}_{x+i\epsilon}(\mathrm{e}^{-p\int_0^{\tau_X^+(x+(i+1)\epsilon)} 1_{\{X_t<x+i\epsilon-y\}}\,dt - q\tau_X^+(x+(i+1)\epsilon)})$$

$$-1]\right) \varphi_q^+(m)$$

$$= \exp\left(-\int_x^m \frac{W_{q,1}(u, u-y)\varphi_{q+p}^+(u-y) - W_{q,2}(u-y, u)}{\varphi_{q+p}^+(u-y) - W_{q,1}(u-y, u)}\,du\right) \varphi_q^+(m).$$

The third equality follows from Corollary 5.1. On the other hand,

$$\mathbb{E}_x(\mathrm{e}^{-pE_y^{q,2}}|\overline{X}_{\mathbf{e}_q} = m)$$

$$= \lim_{\epsilon'\downarrow 0} \frac{\mathbb{E}_m(\mathrm{e}^{-p\int_0^{\mathbf{e}_q} 1_{\{X_t<m-y\}}\,dt}; \mathbf{e}_q < \tau_X^+(m+\epsilon'))}{\mathbb{P}_m(\mathbf{e}_q < \tau_X^+(m+\epsilon'))}$$

$$= 1 + \lim_{\epsilon'\downarrow 0}\left[\frac{\mathbb{P}_m(\tau_X^-(m-y) < \mathbf{e}_q \wedge \tau_X^+(m+\epsilon'))}{\mathbb{P}_m(\mathbf{e}_q < \tau_X^+(m+\epsilon'))}\right.$$

$$\left.\times \mathbb{E}_{m-y}([\mathrm{e}^{-p\int_0^{\mathbf{e}_q} 1_{\{X_t<m-y\}}\,dt} - 1]; \mathbf{e}_q < \tau_X^+(m+\epsilon'))\right] =: 1 + E_y^{q,3}.$$

To get the limit in the above equation, we use Li and Zhou (2013, Corollary 3.4) to obtain that

$$E_y^{q,3} = -\frac{s'(m)}{\phi_q^{+,\prime}(m)} \frac{\phi_q^{+\prime}(m-y) + \left[\frac{p}{q+p}\phi_q^+(m) - \phi_q^+(m-y)\right]\varphi_{q+p}^+(m-y)}{[\varphi_{q+p}^+(m-y) - W_{q,1}(m-y, m)]W_q(m, m-y)}.$$

It follows that

$$\mathbb{E}_x(\mathrm{e}^{-pE_y^{q,2}}|\overline{X}_{\mathbf{e}_q} = m)$$

$$= \frac{\left[W_{q,1}(m, m-y) - \frac{p}{q+p}\frac{s'(m)}{W_q(m,m-y)}\right]\varphi_{q+p}^+(m-y) - W_{q,2}(m-y, m)}{[\varphi_{q+p}^+(m-y) - W_{q,1}(m-y, m)]\varphi_q^+(m)}.$$

The proof is complete after integration with respect to m. $\square$

5.3. Examples

5.3.1. *Brownian motion with drift*

In this section, we derive a group of explicit formulas for a Brownian motion with drift. In particular, we consider a Brownian motion with drift μ and diffusion coefficient $\sigma > 0$:

$$dX_t = \mu\, dt + \sigma dW_t, \quad X_0 = x \in I \equiv \mathbb{R}.$$

As in Section 2.3.2, let us denote by

$$\delta := \frac{\mu}{\sigma^2}, \quad \gamma := \sqrt{\delta^2 + \frac{2q}{\sigma^2}}.$$

Then we can choose the scale function $s(x) = \frac{1}{\delta}(1 - e^{-2\delta x})$, $w_q = \gamma$, and

$$W_q(x,y) = 2e^{-\delta(x+y)} \frac{\sinh(\gamma(x-y))}{\gamma}, \quad W_{q,1}(x,y) = \gamma \cosh(\gamma(x-y)) - \delta.$$

For occupation time of the drawdown process, using Theorem 5.1 we have the following corollary.

Corollary 5.2. *For any $y \in (0,a)$, the occupation time C_y^a has the same law as the first passage time of the drawdown process $\tau_D^+(a-y)$.*

Proof. Straightforward calculation using Theorem 5.1 yields that, for all $q \geq 0$,

$$\mathbb{E}_0(e^{-qC_y^a}) = \frac{\gamma e^{-\delta(a-y)}}{\gamma \cosh(\gamma(a-y)) - \delta \sinh(\gamma(a-y))} = \mathbb{E}_0(e^{-q\tau_D^+(a-y)}),$$

where the last equality follows from Corollary 2.8 as $b \to \infty$. It follows that the occupation time C_y^a has the same distribution as σ_{a-y} under $\mathbb{P}_0$. □

5.3.2. Three-dimensional Bessel process (BES(3))

In this section we study the case of three-dimensional Bessel process. In particular, we consider

$$dX_t = \frac{1}{X_t}\, dt + dW_t, \quad X_0 = x \in I \equiv \mathbb{R}_{>0}.$$

Then the increasing and the decreasing eigenfunctions of X can be chosen as (see, e.g., Borodin and Salminen (2002, p. 463)):

$$\phi_q^+(x) = \frac{1}{x} \frac{\sinh(\sqrt{2q}x)}{\sinh(\sqrt{2q})}, \quad \phi_q^-(x) = \frac{e^{-\sqrt{2q}(x-1)}}{x}.$$

Fix the scale function $s(x) = -\frac{1}{x}$, we have that $w_q = \frac{\sqrt{2q}e^{\sqrt{2q}}}{\sinh(\sqrt{2q})}$ and

$$W_q(x,y) = \frac{1}{\sqrt{2q}xy}\sinh(\sqrt{2q}(x-y)),$$

$$W_{q,1}(x,y) = -\frac{1}{x} + \sqrt{2q}\coth(\sqrt{2q}(x-y)).$$

Using Theorem 5.1 we have the following corollary.

Corollary 5.3. *For $x > a > y > 0$, the law of the occupation time C_y^a is the same as the first passage time of the drawdown process $\tau_D^+(a-y)$.*

Proof. Straightforward calculation using Theorem 5.1 yields that, for all $q \geq 0$,

$$\mathbb{E}_x(e^{-qC_y^a}) = \frac{1}{\cosh(\sqrt{2q}(a-y))}\left(\frac{x-(a-y)}{x} + \frac{\tanh(\sqrt{2q}(a-y))}{\sqrt{2q}x}\right)$$

$$= \mathbb{E}_x(e^{-q\tau_D^+(a-y)}), \tag{5.12}$$

where the last equality is obtained by substitutions $a \to a-y$ and $y \downarrow 0$ in (5.12). It follows that the law of C_y^a is the same as that of $\tau_D^+(a-y)$. □

Remark 5.1. The results of Corollaries 5.2 and 5.3 show an non-trivial fact: if $X.$ is a drifted Brownian motion or a three-dimensional Bessel process, then for a fixed $y > 0$, the law of $\tau_D^+(y)$ is the same as C_a^{y+a} for any $a > 0$. That is, the amount of time the drawdown process $D.$ spends in $[a, a+y]$ until the stopping time $\tau_D^+(a+y)$ is the same as the first passage of drawdown $\tau_D^+(y)$.

5.4. Applications

5.4.1. *Probabilities regarding drawdowns and defaults*

A realization of a large drawdown is usually considered to be a sign of market recession. In this section, we use a reduced form model for default and compute the probabilities of drawdowns and default. In particular, we consider an asset process $X.$, which is given by a time-homogeneous diffusion process with initial value x and lifetime ζ:

$$dX_t = \mu(X_t)dt + \sigma(X_t)dW_t, \quad t < \zeta. \tag{5.13}$$

Here ζ is an independent positive random variable which models the "default time" of asset process X.. If we assume that the "default time" $\zeta = \mathbf{e}_q$ for a $q > 0$, then the probability that there is a drawdown of a units before a drawup of b units by the default time is given by $\mathbb{P}_x(\tau_D^+(a) < \tau_U^+(b) \wedge \mathbf{e}_q)$, which is readily available from Theorems 2.3 and 2.4.

Moreover, we can consider a more realistic model for the default time ζ, to reflect the fact that a default is usually preceded by realizations of large drawdowns of the asset process. In particular, we adopt the Omega risk model studied in Albrecher et al. (2011), Gerber et al. (2012) and Landriault et al. (2011) to model the hazard rate of ζ at time $t > 0$ as $q\mathbf{1}_{\{D_t > y\}}$:

$$\mathbb{P}_x(\zeta \in t + dt | \zeta > t) = q\mathbf{1}_{\{D_t > y\}} dt. \qquad (5.14)$$

for some fixed $y > 0$. Note that a default is possible only when the drawdown exceeds y. Then the probability distribution of the maximum drawdown at the default is given by

$$\mathbb{P}_x(\overline{D}_\zeta < a) = \mathbb{P}_x(\zeta < \tau_D^+(a)) = 1 - \mathbb{P}_x(\zeta \geq \tau_D^+(a)) = 1 - \mathbb{E}_x(e^{-qC_y^a}).$$

for any $a > y$. The Laplace transform in the above can be found in Theorem 5.1.

Hazard rate of similar form can be considered. For instance, we can model the hazard rate of the default time ζ as $q\mathbf{1}_{\{X_t < x\}}$. Here the initial value x is a critical benchmark level which may trigger a default through default intensity. We can also model the hazard rate of the default time ζ as $q\mathbf{1}_{\{U_t < y\}}$. This is the case in which the default tend to occur when there is not enough upside momentum for the asset process. In both cases, the probability of default before a drawdown of a units can be found using Proposition 5.1 and Theorem 5.2.

5.4.2. *Option pricing for the drawdown process*

Options on maximum drawdown and drawdown processes have drawn lots of attentions in recent years (see, e.g., Carr et al. (2011), Cheridito et al. (2012), Pospisil and Večeř (2008), Večeř (2006), Yamamoto et al. (2010) and Zhang et al. (2013)). In this section, we use a semi-analytic approach to price a large class of options on the drawdown process. In particular, we assume that the market is complete, $\mathbb{P}$ is the risk-neutral measure, and $\tilde{r} \geq 0$ is the risk-free interest rate. We model the underlying process[1] as the time-homogeneous diffusion X. defined in (5.1). Then a Parisian-like (see, e.g., Chesney et al. (1997) for a definition of standard Parisian option) digital call on the drawdown process with barrier $y > 0$, maturity $T > 0$ and strike $K \in (0, T)$ is worth

$$P_0(x, y, K, T) = e^{-\tilde{r}T} \mathbb{P}_x \left(\int_0^T \mathbf{1}_{\{D_t > y\}} \, dt > K \right), \qquad (5.15)$$

at its inception. Using double randomizations: $T = \mathbf{e}_q$ and $K = \mathbf{e}_p$, then the randomized option price is given by

$$\hat{P}_0(x, y, q, p) = e^{-\tilde{r}T} - e^{-\tilde{r}T} \mathbb{E}_x(e^{-p E_y^q}). \qquad (5.16)$$

The Laplace transform in (5.16) is readily available in Theorem 5.3. Hence, the price (5.15) can be computed via double Laplace inversion:

$$P_0(x, y, K, T) = e^{-\tilde{r}T} - e^{-\tilde{r}T} \cdot \mathcal{I}_p \left(\frac{1}{p} \cdot \mathcal{I}_q \left(\frac{1}{q} \mathbb{E}_x(e^{-p E_y^q}) \right) \Big|_T \right) \Big|_K, \qquad (5.17)$$

where $\mathcal{I}_p$ and $\mathcal{I}_q$ are Laplace inversion operators in p and in q, respectively.

Corridor options such as α-quantile option are studied in Miura (1992, 2007). Below we consider pricing of α-quantile options on the drawdown process. To this end, for an $\alpha \in (0, 1]$, we define the α-quantile of the drawdown process during $[0, T]$ by

$$D_T^\alpha := \inf \left\{ y > 0 : \int_0^T \mathbf{1}_{\{D_t > y\}} \, dt \leq (1-\alpha)T \right\}. \qquad (5.18)$$

In particular, $D_T^1 = \overline{D}_T$ is the maximum drawdown at time T. An option on the α-quantile with maturity $T > 0$ and an absolute continuous, bounded payoff function $f(\cdot)$ such that $f(0) = 0$ is worth

$$A_0(x, f, T) = e^{-\tilde{r}T} \mathbb{E}_x(f(D_T^\alpha)), \qquad (5.19)$$

at its inception. We notice that

$$\mathbb{E}_x(f(D_T^\alpha)) = \mathbb{E}_x \left(\int_0^\infty \mathbf{1}_{\{D_T^\alpha \geq u\}} f'(u) \, du \right) = \int_0^\infty f'(u) \cdot \mathbb{P}_x(D_T^\alpha > u) \, du$$

$$= \int_0^\infty f'(u) \cdot \mathbb{P}_x \left(\int_0^T \mathbf{1}_{\{D_t > u\}} dt \geq (1-\alpha)T \right) du.$$

---

[1] Notice that the underlying process is not necessarily an asset price process. It can be, for example, the logarithm of an asset price process.

It follows from (5.15) that

$$A_0(x, f, T) = \int_0^\infty f'(u) \cdot P_0(x, u, (1-\alpha)T, T)\, du. \quad (5.20)$$

Again, by double Laplace inversion and Theorem 5.3 we can compute the price in (5.20).

5.5. Concluding Remarks

In this chapter, we derive analytical formulas for a number of occupation times that are related to the drawdown and the drawup of a linear diffusion process. We present examples with a Brownian motion with drift and a three-dimensional Bessel process, where we prove an identity in law between an occupation time of drawdown and the first passage of drawdown. Finally, these results are applied to address problems in risk analysis of a drawdown Omega model and for pricing of α-quantile options on the drawdown process.

5.6. Proof of Lemmas

Proof of Lemma 5.1. We follow the perturbation method as in Chapter 2. For $\epsilon > 0$ such that $y + \epsilon < b$, we approximate $A_y^{u,v}$ by $A_{y,\epsilon}^{u,v}$:

$$A_{y,\epsilon}^{u,v} := \sum_{n=1}^\infty (\tau_X^{+,n}(y+\epsilon) \wedge \tau_X^-(u) \wedge \tau_X^+(v) - \tau_X^{-,n}(y) \wedge \tau_X^-(u) \wedge \tau_X^+(v)),$$

where $\tau_X^{-,1}(y) := \tau_X^-(y)$, and for $n \geq 1$,

$$\tau_X^{+,n}(y+\epsilon) := \inf\{t \geq \tau_X^{-,n}(y) : X_t \geq y + \epsilon\},$$
$$\tau_X^{-,n+1}(y) := \inf\{t \geq \tau_X^{+,n}(y+\epsilon) : X_t \leq y\}.$$

Using strong Markov property and the continuity of $X_\cdot$, we have that

$$\mathbb{E}_y(e^{-qA_{y,\epsilon}^{u,v} - p\tau_X^+(v)} \mathbf{1}_{\{\tau_X^+(v) < \tau_X^-(u)\}})$$
$$= \mathbb{E}_y(e^{-(q+p)\tau_X^+(y+\epsilon)} \mathbf{1}_{\{\tau_X^+(y+\epsilon) < \tau_X^-(u)\}})$$
$$\times \mathbb{E}_{y+\epsilon}(e^{-qA_{y,\epsilon}^{u,v} - p\tau_X^+(v)} \mathbf{1}_{\{\tau_X^+(v) < \tau_X^-(u)\}})$$
$$= \mathbb{E}_y(e^{-(q+p)\tau_X^+(y+\epsilon)} \mathbf{1}_{\{\tau_X^+(y+\epsilon) < \tau_X^-(u)\}}) \cdot (\mathbb{E}_{y+\epsilon}(e^{-p\tau_X^+(v)} \mathbf{1}_{\{\tau_X^+(v) < \tau_X^-(y)\}})$$
$$+ \mathbb{E}_{y+\epsilon}(e^{-p\tau_X^-(y)} \mathbf{1}_{\{\tau_X^-(y) < \tau_X^+(v)\}}) \mathbb{E}_y(e^{-qA_{y,\epsilon}^{u,v} - p\tau_X^+(v)} \mathbf{1}_{\{\tau_X^+(v) < \tau_X^-(u)\}})),$$

from which we obtain that,

$$\mathbb{E}_y(e^{-qA_{y,\epsilon}^{u,v}-p\tau_X^+(v)}\mathbf{1}_{\{\tau_X^+(v)<\tau_X^-(u)\}})$$

$$= \frac{\mathbb{E}_{y+\epsilon}(e^{-p\tau_X^+(v)}\mathbf{1}_{\{\tau_X^+(v)<\tau_X^-(y)\}})\mathbb{E}_y(e^{-(q+p)\tau_{y+\epsilon}^+}\mathbf{1}_{\{\tau_{y+\epsilon}^+<\tau_X^-(u)\}})}{1-\mathbb{E}_{y+\epsilon}(e^{-p\tau_X^-(y)}\mathbf{1}_{\{\tau_X^-(y)<\tau_X^+(v)\}})\mathbb{E}_y(e^{-(q+p)\tau_{y+\epsilon}^+}\mathbf{1}_{\{\tau_{y+\epsilon}^+<\tau_X^-(u)\}})}$$

$$= \frac{W_p(y+\epsilon,y)}{W_p(v,y)}\frac{W_{q+p}(y,u)/W_{q+p}(y+\epsilon,u)}{1-W_p(v,y+\epsilon)W_{q+p}(y,u)/(W_p(v,y)W_{q+p}(y+\epsilon,u))}. \tag{5.21}$$

The quantity $A_{y,\epsilon}^{u,v}$ measures the time for $X.$ to spend below level y and the time to move from y to $y+\epsilon$, but not from $y+\epsilon$ to y, until $X.$ exits from (u,v). As $\epsilon \downarrow 0$, by continuity of $X.$, we have $A_{y,\epsilon}^{u,v} \to A_y^{u,v}$, $\mathbb{P}_x$-a.s. Using Lebesgue dominated convergence theorem and the continuity of $X.$, letting $\epsilon \downarrow 0$ in (5.21) we have

$$\mathbb{E}_y(e^{-qA_y^{u,v}-p\tau_X^+(v)}\mathbf{1}_{\{\tau_X^+(v)<\tau_X^-(u)\}}) = \frac{s'(y)/W_p(v,y)}{W_{q+p,1}(y,u)-W_{p,1}(y,v)}.$$

It follows that, for $x \in (a,y)$, using strong Markov property of $X.$, we have

$$\mathbb{E}_x(e^{-qA_y^{u,v}-p\tau_X^+(v)}\mathbf{1}_{\{\tau_X^+(v)<\tau_X^-(u)\}})$$

$$= \mathbb{E}_x(e^{-(q+p)\tau_X^+(y)}\mathbf{1}_{\{\tau_X^+(y)<\tau_X^-(u)\}}) \cdot \mathbb{E}_y(e^{-qA_y^{u,v}-p\tau_X^+(v)}\mathbf{1}_{\{\tau_X^+(v)<\tau_X^-(u)\}})$$

$$= \frac{W_{q+p}(x,u)}{W_{q+p}(y,u)}\frac{s'(y)/W_p(v,y)}{W_{q+p,1}(y,u)-W_{p,1}(y,v)}.$$

For $x \in (y,v)$, we can similarly obtain

$$\mathbb{E}_x(e^{-qA_y^{u,v}-p\tau_X^+(v)}\mathbf{1}_{\{\tau_X^+(v)<\tau_X^-(u)\}})$$

$$= \frac{W_p(x,y)}{W_p(v,y)} + \frac{W_p(v,x)}{W_p(v,y)}\frac{s'(y)/W_p(v,y)}{W_{q+p,1}(y,u)-W_{p,1}(y,v)}.$$

Using the similar argument as above, we obtain (5.8). $\square$

Chapter 6

Duration of Drawdowns Under Lévy Models

In this chapter, we consider a one-dimensional Lévy process $X_\cdot = \{X_t\}_{t \geq 0}$ defined on a filtered probability space $(\Omega, \mathbb{F}, \mathcal{F}, \mathbb{P})$ with filtration $\mathbb{F} = \{\mathcal{F}_t\}_{t \geq 0}$. The drawdown process of $X_\cdot$ is defined as

$$D_t = \overline{X}_t - X_t, \quad \forall t \geq 0,$$

where $\overline{X}_t = \sup_{s \in [0,t]} X_s$ is the running maximum of $X_\cdot$ at time t. Let

$$\tau_D^+(a) = \inf\{t > 0 : D_t > a\}$$

be the first passage of drawdown at a pre-specified threshold $a > 0$.

However, from a risk management standpoint, the magnitude itself is not sufficient to provide a comprehensive risk evaluation of extreme drawdown risks. For instance, for extreme risks such as tornado and flooding, it is natural to also investigate the frequency and the duration of drawdowns. In Chapter 4, we studied the frequency of drawdowns for a Brownian motion process by defining two types of drawdown time sequences depending on whether a historical running maximum is reset or not. In this chapter, we will consider the duration of drawdowns, also known as "Time to Recover" (TTR) the historic running maximum in the fund management industry.

Mathematically, the duration of drawdowns of a stochastic process can be considered as the length of excursions from its running maximum. For $t \geq 0$, let $g_t := \sup\{s < t : D_s = 0\}$ be the last time the process $D_\cdot$ is at level 0 (or equivalently $X_\cdot = \overline{X}_\cdot$) before or at time t. The drawdown duration at time t is therefore $t - g_t$. Recall that in Chapter 3, we studied the joint law of $g_{\tau_D^+(a)}$ and the speed of market crash $\tau_D^+(a) - g_{\tau_D^+(a)}$. In this chapter, we are interested in the stopping time

$$\eta_b := \inf\{t \geq b : t - g_t \geq b\}. \tag{6.1}$$

That is, the first time the duration of drawdowns exceeds a pre-specified time threshold $b > 0$. Equivalently, the event $\{\eta_b > t\}$ implies that the maximum duration of drawdowns before time t is shorter than b. Apparently, $\mathbb{P}(\eta_b \geq b) = 1$.

The stopping time η_b is related to the so-called Parisian time, which is the first time the length of excursions from a fixed spatial level (rather than its running maximum) exceeds a pre-specified time threshold (see, e.g., Chesney et al. (1997) and Czarna and Palmowski (2011)). Further, Loeffen et al. (2013) provided an unified proof to derive the probability that the Parisian time occurs in an infinite time-horizon (known as the Parisian ruin probability in actuarial science) for spectrally negative Lévy processes. Notice that, in contrast to the Parisian time, the stopping time η_b is almost surely finite (see, e.g., Bertoin (1996, p. 105)), which motivates us to study the Laplace transform of η_b in this chapter. Another related concept is the so-called red period of the insurance surplus process; see Kyprianou and Palmowski (2007). The red period is measured by the length of time an insurance surplus process shall take to recover its deficit at ruin. But it is different than the distributional study of η_b, especially when $X.$ has no negative jumps.

In this chapter, we begin by developing an approximation technique as in Chapters 2 and 5 to revisit several known Laplace transform results on the magnitude of drawdowns of spectrally negative Lévy processes via basic fluctuation identities.

Second, as the threshold of drawdown magnitude $a \downarrow 0$, we examine the asymptotic behavior of those Laplace transforms for any spectrally negative Lévy process whose scale functions are well-behaved at 0+ (see Assumption 6.1 below). We also show that such asymptotics are robust with respect to the perturbation of arbitrary positive compound Poisson jumps, and hence obtain the asymptotics of drawdown estimates for a class of Lévy models with two-sided jumps.

Finally, we study the duration of drawdowns via the Laplace transform of η_b. First, an approximate scheme for the Laplace transform of η_b is developed. To obtain a well-defined limit, we turn our problem to the behavior of the density of the running maximum process $\overline{X}.$ and the convergence of some potential measure of the drawdown process $D..$ Thanks to the asymptotic results obtained and some recent works on the distribution of the running maxima of Lévy processes (see, e.g., Chaumont (2013), Chaumont and Małecki (2016) and Kwaśnicki et al. (2013)), we obtain the law of η_b in terms of the right tail of the ascending ladder time process for a class of Lévy process with two-sided jumps (a general spectrally negative part plus a positive compound Poisson structure).

The rest of the chapter is structured as follows. In Section 6.1, we review the scale function of spectrally negative Lévy processes and the ascending ladder process of a general Lévy process. In Section 6.2, we revisit some known Laplace transform results on the magnitude of drawdowns of spectrally negative Lévy processes based on an approximation approach. The asymptotic behavior of these Laplace transforms for small threshold is studied in Section 6.3, where we also examine the asymptotic behavior in the presence of positive compound Poisson jumps. In Section 6.4, the Laplace transform of η_b is derived for a large class of Lévy processes with two-sided jumps. Some explicit examples are presented in Section 6.5. We conclude this chapter in Section 6.6. The proofs of lemmas and some results on the extended continuity theorem are presented in Section 6.7.

6.1. Preliminaries

In this section, we briefly introduce some preliminary results for Lévy processes. Readers are referred to Bertoin (1996) and Kyprianou (2006) for a more detailed background.

6.1.1. *Spectrally negative Lévy processes and scale functions*

Consider a spectrally negative Lévy process $X. = \{X_t\}_{t \geq 0}$. The Laplace exponent of $X.$ is given by

$$\psi(s) = \log \mathbb{E}(e^{sX_1}) = -\mu s + \frac{1}{2}\sigma^2 s^2 + \int_{(-\infty,0)} (e^{sx} - 1 - sx\mathbf{1}_{\{x>-1\}})\Pi(\mathrm{d}x), \tag{6.2}$$

for every $s \in \mathbb{H}_{\geq 0} = \{s \in \mathbb{C} : \Re(s) \geq 0\}$. Here, $\sigma \geq 0$ and the Lévy measure $\Pi(\mathrm{d}x)$ is supported on $(-\infty, 0)$ with

$$\int_{(-\infty,0)} (1 \wedge x^2)\Pi(\mathrm{d}x) < \infty.$$

It is known that $X.$ has paths of bounded variation if and only if $\int_{(-1,0)} |x| \Pi(\mathrm{d}x) < \infty$ and $\sigma = 0$. In this case, we can rewrite (6.2) as

$$\psi(s) = sd + \int_{(-\infty,0)} (e^{sx} - 1) \Pi(\mathrm{d}x), \quad \forall s \geq 0, \qquad (6.3)$$

where the drift $d := -\mu + \int_{(-1,0)} |x| \Pi(\mathrm{d}x) > 0$ since otherwise $-X.$ is a subordinator. For any given $q \geq 0$, the equation $\psi(s) = q$ has at least one positive solution, and we denote the largest one by $\Phi(q)$.

Example 6.1. Brownian motion with drift is a Lévy process with no jumps, with Laplace exponent $\psi(s) = \frac{1}{2}\sigma^2 s^2 + \mu s$, where σ is the diffusion coefficient and μ is the drift. In this case, we have $\Phi(q) = -\frac{\mu}{\sigma^2} + \sqrt{(\frac{\mu}{\sigma^2})^2 + \frac{2q}{\sigma^2}}$. Another example of spectrally negative Lévy process is the Cramér–Lundberg process, i.e.,

$$X_t = x + ct - \sum_{i=1}^{N_t} \xi_i,$$

where $c > 0$ is a constant, N_t is a Poisson process with jump intensity $\lambda > 0$, and ξ_i's are i.i.d. random variables with an exponential distribution with mean $1/\nu > 0$. Its Laplace exponent is given by $\psi(s) = cs - \lambda \frac{s}{\nu+s}$, and $\Phi(q) = \frac{q+\lambda-c\nu+\sqrt{(c\nu-q-\lambda)^2 + 4cq\nu}}{2c}$.

It is well known that $\{e^{cX_t - \psi(c)t}\}_{t \geq 0}$ is a martingale for any $c \geq 0$. This gives rise to the change of measure

$$\left.\frac{\mathrm{d}\mathbb{P}^c}{\mathrm{d}\mathbb{P}}\right|_{\mathcal{F}_t} = e^{cX_t - \psi(c)t}, \quad \forall t \geq 0. \qquad (6.4)$$

Under the new measure $\mathbb{P}^c$, $X.$ is still a spectrally negative Lévy process, and its Laplace exponent is given by $\psi_c(s) = \psi(s+c) - \psi(c)$ for all $s \in \mathbb{C}$ such that $s + c \in \mathbb{H}_{\geq 0}$.

For any $q \geq 0$, the q-scale function $W^{(q)} : \mathbb{R} \mapsto \mathbb{R}_{\geq 0}$ is the unique function supported on $\mathbb{R}_{>0}$ with Laplace transform

$$\int_0^\infty e^{-sx} W^{(q)}(x) \mathrm{d}x = \frac{1}{\psi(s) - q}, \quad \forall s > \Phi(q).$$

It is known that $W^{(q)}(\cdot)$ is continuous and increasing on $\mathbb{R}_{>0}$. Henceforth we assume that the jump measure $\Pi(\mathrm{d}x)$ has no atom, then it follows that $W^{(q)}(\cdot) \in C^1(\mathbb{R}_{>0})$ (see, e.g., Kuznetsov et al. (2013, Lemma 2.4)). Moreover, if the Gaussian coefficient $\sigma > 0$ then $W^{(q)}(\cdot) \in C^2(\mathbb{R}_{>0})$ for all $q \geq 0$ (see, e.g., Kuznetsov et al. (2013, Theorem 3.10)). The q-scale function $W^{(q)}(\cdot)$ is closely related to exit problems of the spectrally negative Lévy process X. with respect to first passage times:

$$\tau_X^\pm(x) = \inf\{t > 0 : X_t \gtrless x\}, \quad \forall x \in \mathbb{R}.$$

Two well-known fluctuation identities of spectrally negative Lévy processes are given below (see, e.g., Kyprianou (2006, Theorem 8.1)). For $q \geq 0$ and $0 \leq x \leq a$, we have

$$\mathbb{E}_x(e^{-q\tau_X^+(a)} \mathbf{1}_{\{T_X^+(a) < T_X^-(0)\}}) = \frac{W^{(q)}(x)}{W^{(q)}(a)}, \qquad (6.5)$$

and

$$\mathbb{E}_x(e^{-q\tau_X^-(0)} \mathbf{1}_{\{\tau_X^-(0) < \tau_X^+(a)\}}) = Z^{(q)}(x) - Z^{(q)}(a)\frac{W^{(q)}(x)}{W^{(q)}(a)}, \qquad (6.6)$$

where $Z^{(q)}(x) = 1 + q\int_0^x W^{(q)}(y)\mathrm{d}y$.

The following lemma gives the behavior of scale functions at $0+$ and ∞ (see, e.g., Kuznetsov et al. (2013, Lemmas 3.1, 3.2)). Relation (6.7) is from Egami et al. (2013, Eq. (3.13)).

Lemma 6.1. *For any $q \geq 0$,*

$$W^{(q)}(0+) = \begin{cases} 0 & \text{if } \sigma > 0 \text{ or } \int_{(-1,0)} |x|\Pi(\mathrm{d}x) = \infty \\ & \textit{(unbounded variation)}, \\ \dfrac{1}{d} & \textit{otherwise (bounded variation)}, \end{cases}$$

$$W^{(q),\prime}(0+) = \begin{cases} \dfrac{2}{\sigma^2} & \textit{if } \sigma > 0, \\ \infty & \textit{if } \sigma = 0 \textit{ and } \Pi(-\infty, 0) = \infty, \\ \dfrac{q + \Pi(-\infty, 0)}{d^2} & \textit{if } \sigma = 0 \textit{ and } \Pi(-\infty, 0) < \infty. \end{cases}$$

and

$$\lim_{x \to \infty} \frac{W^{(q),\prime}(x)}{W^{(q)}(x)} = \Phi(q). \qquad (6.7)$$

6.1.2. The ascending ladder process of general Lévy processes

In this subsection, we consider a general Lévy process $X_{\cdot} = \{X_t\}_{t\geq 0}$ characterized by its characteristic exponent

$$\Psi(s) = -\log \mathbb{E}(e^{isX_1}) = i\mu s + \frac{1}{2}\sigma^2 s^2 + \int_{\mathbb{R}\setminus\{0\}} (1 - e^{isx} + isx\mathbf{1}_{\{|x|<1\}})\Pi(dx), \tag{6.8}$$

for all $s \in \mathbb{R}$. If $X_{\cdot}$ has bounded variation, we can rewrite (6.8) as

$$\Psi(s) = -isd + \int_{\mathbb{R}\setminus\{0\}} (1 - e^{isx})\Pi(dx), \tag{6.9}$$

where the drift $d := -\mu - \int_{0<|x|<1} x\Pi(dx)$.

The local time of $X_{\cdot}$ at its running maximum, denoted by $L_{\cdot} = \{L_t\}_{t\geq 0}$, is a continuous, non-decreasing, $[0,\infty)$-valued process. The inverse local time process, also known as the ascending ladder time process, is defined as $L^{-1} = \{L_t^{-1}, t \geq 0\}$ where

$$L_t^{-1} := \begin{cases} \inf\{s > 0 : L_s > t\} & \text{if } t < L_\infty, \\ \infty & \text{otherwise.} \end{cases}$$

The ladder height process $H_{\cdot} = \{H_t\}_{t\geq 0}$ is defined as

$$H_t := \begin{cases} X_{L_t^{-1}} & \text{if } t < L_\infty, \\ \infty & \text{otherwise.} \end{cases}$$

The inverse local time L^{-1} corresponds to the real times at which new maxima are reached, and the ascending ladder height process $H_{\cdot}$ corresponds to the set of new maxima.

The bivariate process $(L_{\cdot}^{-1}, H_{\cdot}) = \{(L_t^{-1}, H_t)\}_{t\geq 0}$, called the ascending ladder process of $X_{\cdot}$, is a two-dimensional (possibly killed) subordinator with joint Laplace transform

$$\mathbb{E}(e^{-\alpha L_t^{-1} - \beta H_t}\mathbf{1}_{\{t<L_\infty\}}) = e^{-\kappa(\alpha,\beta)t}, \quad \alpha, \beta \geq 0.$$

The joint Laplace exponent is given by

$$\kappa(\alpha,\beta) = \kappa(0,0) + \alpha d_L + \beta d_H + \int_{(\mathbb{R}_{>0})^2} (1 - e^{-\alpha x - \beta y})\Lambda(dx, dy), \quad \alpha, \beta \geq 0, \tag{6.10}$$

where $(d_L, d_H) \in \mathbb{R}_{>0}^2$ and Λ is a bivariate intensity measure on $(0, \infty)^2$ satisfying

$$\int_{(\mathbb{R}_{>0})^2} (1 \wedge \sqrt{x^2 + y^2}) \Lambda(\mathrm{d}x, \mathrm{d}y) < \infty.$$

When $L_\cdot^{-1}$ and $H_\cdot$ are independent, Λ takes the form $\Lambda(\mathrm{d}x, \mathrm{d}y) = \Lambda_L(\mathrm{d}x) \delta_0(\mathrm{d}y) + \Lambda_H(\mathrm{d}y) \delta_0(\mathrm{d}x)$ for $x, y \geq 0$. In particular, if X is a spectrally negative Lévy process, one can choose $L_t = \overline{X}_t$, which implies that $L_t^{-1} = \tau_X^+(t)$, $H_t = X_{\tau_X^+(t)} = t$ on $\{t < L_\infty\}$, and further $\kappa(\alpha, \beta) = \Phi(\alpha) + \beta$.

By letting $\beta = 0$ in (6.10), we obtain the Laplace exponent of the ascending ladder time process,

$$-\frac{1}{t} \log \mathbb{E}(\mathrm{e}^{-\alpha L_t^{-1}} \mathbf{1}_{\{t < L_\infty\}}) = \kappa(\alpha, 0)$$
$$= \kappa(0,0) + \alpha d_L + \int_{(0,\infty)} (1 - \mathrm{e}^{-\alpha x}) \nu_L(\mathrm{d}x), \quad \alpha \geq 0,$$

where $\nu_L(\mathrm{d}x) = \Lambda(\mathrm{d}x, (0, \infty))$ is the jump measure of $L_\cdot^{-1}$. It follows from integration by parts that

$$\kappa(\alpha, 0) - \kappa(0, 0) = \alpha(d_L + \int_0^\infty \mathrm{e}^{-\alpha x} \bar{\nu}_L(x) \mathrm{d}x), \quad \alpha \geq 0, \qquad (6.11)$$

where $\bar{\nu}_L(x) := \nu_L(x, \infty)$.

The renewal function $h(\cdot)$ associated with the ladder height process $H_\cdot$ is defined as

$$h(x) := \int_0^\infty \mathbb{P}(H_t \leq x) \mathrm{d}t, \quad x \geq 0. \qquad (6.12)$$

When $X_\cdot$ is a spectrally negative Lévy process, it is easily seen that $h(x) = \int_{(0,x)} \mathrm{e}^{-\Phi(0)t} \mathrm{d}t$ for $x \geq 0$. We recall the follow results (see Bertoin (1996, Theorems III.5 and VI.19)) on the connection between the renewal function and the creeping property. Here we say $X_\cdot$ creeps across x if it enters (x, ∞) continuously.

Lemma 6.2. *The following assertions are equivalent.*

(i) $\mathbb{P}(X_\cdot \text{ creeps across } x) > 0$ for some $x > 0$.
(ii) *The drift coefficient* $d_H > 0$.
(iii) *The renewal function* $h(\cdot)$ *is absolute continuous and* $h'(\cdot)$ *is bounded.*

Moreover, when these assertions hold, there is a version $h'(\cdot)$ *that is continuous and positive on* $(0, \infty)$. *Finally,* $\lim_{x \downarrow 0} h'(x) = \frac{1}{d_H} > 0$ *and* $\mathbb{P}(X_\cdot \text{ creeps across } x) = d_H h'(x)$ *for all* $x > 0$.

6.2. Magnitude of Drawdowns Revisited

In this section, we revisit some known results of the magnitude of drawdowns of spectrally negative Lévy processes via fluctuation identities and an approximation approach introduced by Lehoczky (1977). Such approach is in the spirit of the general Itô's excursion theory.

Lemma 6.3. *For $q \geq 0$ and $x > 0$, we have*

$$\mathbb{E}(e^{-q\tau_X^+(x)} 1_{\{\overline{X}_{\tau_D^+(a)} \geq x\}}) = e^{-\frac{W^{(q),\prime}(a)}{W^{(q)}(a)} x}. \qquad (6.13)$$

By letting $q = 0$ in (6.13), it is easy to see that $\overline{X}_{\tau_D^+(a)}$ follows an exponential distribution with mean $W(a)/W'(a)$. Then it follows from (6.13) that, for $q \geq 0$ and $x \geq 0$,

$$\mathbb{E}(e^{-q\tau_X^+(x)} | \overline{X}_{\tau_D^+(a)} = x) = e^{-(\frac{W^{(q),\prime}(a)}{W^{(q)}(a)} - \frac{W'(a)}{W(a)})x}. \qquad (6.14)$$

Next we consider the following lemma which relates to downward exiting.

Lemma 6.4. *For $q, s \geq 0$, we have*

$$\mathbb{E}_a(e^{-q\tau_X^-(0) - s(a - X_{\tau_X^-(0)})} | \tau_X^-(0) < \tau_X^+(a))$$

$$= \frac{W(a)}{W'(a)} \frac{Z_s^{(p)}(a) W_s^{(p),\prime}(a) - p W_s^{(p)}(a)^2}{W_s^{(p)}(a)}, \qquad (6.15)$$

where $p = q - \psi(s)$, $W_s^{(p)}(\cdot)$ and $Z_s^{(p)}(\cdot)$ are p-scale functions under probability measure $\mathbb{P}^s$.

To obtain the main result of this section, we notice that a sample path of X until $\tau_D^+(a)$ can be split into two parts: the rising part and the subsequent crashing part. Because of the regularity of 0 for $(0, \infty)$, we know that, given $\overline{X}_{\tau_D^+(a)} = x$, the last passage time $g_{\tau_D^+(a)}$ is almost surely the same as $\tau_X^+(x)$ (see also discussions on Kyprianou (2006, p. 158)). Our analysis essentially follows this idea: relations (6.14) and (6.15) correspond to the rising and the crashing part, respectively. The following quadruple Laplace transform is obtained by pasting these two parts at the turning point $g_{\tau_D^+(a)}$.

Theorem 6.1. For $q, r, s, \delta \geq 0$, we have

$$\mathbb{E}(e^{-q\tau_D^+(a) - rg_{\tau_D^+(a)} - sD_{\tau_D^+(a)} - \delta \overline{X}_{\tau_D^+(a)}})$$

$$= \frac{W^{(q+r)}(a)}{\delta W^{(q+r)}(a) + W^{(q+r),\prime}(a)} \frac{Z_s^{(p)}(a) W_s^{(p),\prime}(a) - p W_s^{(p)}(a)^2}{W_s^{(p)}(a)},$$

(6.16)

where $p = q - \psi(s)$.

Proof. By conditioning on the event $\{\overline{X}_{\tau_D^+(a)} = x\}$ for $x > 0$, we have $\tau_D^+(a) = g_{\tau_D^+(a)} + \tau_X^-(x-a) \circ \theta_{g_{\tau_D^+(a)}}$ and $\tau_X^-(x-a) \circ \theta_{g_{\tau_D^+(a)}} < \tau_X^+(x) \circ \theta_{g_{\tau_D^+(a)}}$, $\mathbb{P}$-a.s. where $\theta.$ is the Markov shift operator defined as $X_t \circ \theta_s = X_{t+s}$. Therefore, by (6.14) and (6.15), we obtain

$$\mathbb{E}(e^{-q\tau_D^+(a) - rg_{\tau_D^+(a)} - sD_{\tau_D^+(a)}} | \overline{X}_{\tau_D^+(a)} = x)$$

$$= \mathbb{E}(e^{-(q+r)g_{\tau_D^+(a)} - q(\tau_D^+(a) - g_{\tau_D^+(a)}) - sD_{\tau_D^+(a)}} | \overline{X}_{\tau_D^+(a)} = x)$$

$$= \mathbb{E}(e^{-(q+r)g_{\tau_D^+(a)}} | \overline{X}_{\tau_D^+(a)} = x)$$

$$\times \mathbb{E}_x(e^{-q\tau_X^-(x-a) - s(x - X_{\tau_X^-(x-a)}^-)} | \tau_X^-(x-a) < \tau_X^+(x))$$

$$= e^{-\left(\frac{W^{(q+r),\prime}(a)}{W^{(q+r)}(a)} - \frac{W'(a)}{W(a)}\right)x} \frac{W(a)}{W'(a)} \frac{Z_s^{(p)}(a) W_s^{(p),\prime}(a) - p W_s^{(p)}(a)^2}{W_s^{(p)}(a)}.$$

(6.17)

Multiplying (6.17) by the density of $\overline{X}_{\tau_D^+(a)}$ and then integrating with respect to x, we obtain (6.16). $\square$

Relation (6.16) generalizes (Avram *et al.* (2004, Theorem 1)) by incorporating the joint Laplace transform of $g_{\tau_D^+(a)}$ and $\overline{X}_{\tau_D^+(a)}$. Moreover, by a similar approximation argument, one can solve for the joint distribution of equation (6.16) but with the law of $D_{\tau_D^+(a)}$, which then recovers the sextuple law in Mijatović and Pistorius (2012, Theorem 1) (the running minimum at $\tau_D^+(a)$ can also be easily incorporated).

6.3. Asymptotics of Magnitude of Drawdowns

In this section, we investigate the asymptotics of the Laplace transform (6.16) of the magnitude of drawdowns as $a \downarrow 0$ for spectrally negative Lévy processes. Furthermore, we also show that such asymptotics are robust with respect to the perturbation by positive compound Poisson jumps.

6.3.1. *Spectrally negative Lévy processes*

Henceforth, we make the following assumption on the behavior of the scale function at 0+.

Assumption 6.1.
$$\lim_{x \downarrow 0} xW'(x) = 0.$$

In fact, since $xW'(x) \geq 0$ for all $x > 0$, as long as $W'(\cdot)$ is well-behaved at 0+ in the sense that
$$\lim_{x \downarrow 0} xW'(x) = c, \quad \text{for some } c \in [0, \infty],$$
one deduces from the integrability of $W'(\cdot)$ at 0+ that $c = 0$.

Remark 6.1. From Lemma 6.1, it is clear that Assumption 6.1 holds if the Gaussian component $\sigma > 0$ or $\Pi(-\infty, 0) < \infty$. Moreover, the spectrally negative α-stable process with index $\alpha \in (1, 2)$, whose Laplace exponent $\psi(s) = s^\alpha$ and scale function
$$W(x) = \mathbf{1}_{\{x \geq 0\}} \frac{x^{\alpha-1}}{\Gamma(\alpha)},$$
satisfies Assumption 6.1.

Since scale functions are only known in a few cases, we examine sufficient conditions on the Laplace exponent to identify cases when Assumption 6.1 holds.

Remark 6.2. For a general spectrally negative Lévy process with Laplace exponent $\psi(\cdot)$, by Lemma 6.1, one can choose an arbitrary $s_0 > \Phi(0)$ and define a function $g(x) := \mathbf{1}_{\{x>0\}} e^{-s_0 x} xW'(x)$, which is non-negative and continuous on $\mathbb{R}\setminus\{0\}$. By Kuznetsov et al. (2013, Lemma 3.3) and (6.7), we further know that $g(x) \in L^1(\mathbb{R})$. By integration by parts and analytical continuation, one obtains that
$$\int_{-\infty}^{\infty} e^{isx} g(x)\mathrm{d}x = \varphi(s_0 - is), \quad s \in \mathbb{R},$$
where $\varphi(s) := \frac{s\psi'(s) - \psi(s)}{\psi(s)^2}$ for $\Re(s) \geq 0$. By the Fourier inversion and the dominated convergence theorem, we know that a sufficient condition for

Assumption 6.1 to hold is that $\varphi(s_0 - i\cdot) \in L^1(\mathbb{R})$ as it implies that $g(\cdot)$ is continuous over $\mathbb{R}$.

Lemma 6.5. *Under Assumption 6.1, we have $\lim_{x \downarrow 0} x W^{(q),\prime}(x) = 0$ for every $q \geq 0$.*

Lemma 6.5 is paramount to derive the following asymptotic results.

Theorem 6.2. *Consider a spectrally negative Lévy process $X.$ satisfying Assumption 6.1. For any $q, s \geq 0$, we have*

$$\lim_{\varepsilon \downarrow 0} \frac{W^{(q),\prime}(\varepsilon)}{W^{(q)}(\varepsilon)}[1 - \mathbb{E}(e^{-q\tau_D^+(\varepsilon) - sD_{\tau_D^+(\varepsilon)}^+})]$$

$$= \begin{cases} s & \text{if } X. \text{ has unbounded variation,} \\ s + \dfrac{q - \psi(s)}{d} & \text{if } X. \text{ has bounded variation.} \end{cases}$$

Proof. Using (6.16), one deduces that

$$\frac{W^{(q),\prime}(\varepsilon)}{W^{(q)}(\varepsilon)}[1 - \mathbb{E}(e^{-q\tau_D^+(\varepsilon) - sD_{\tau_D^+(\varepsilon)}^+})]$$

$$= s - (q - \psi(s))\frac{W^{(q),\prime}(\varepsilon)}{W^{(q)}(\varepsilon)} \int_0^\varepsilon e^{-sx} W^{(q)}(x) dx$$

$$+ s(q - \psi(s)) \int_0^\varepsilon e^{-sx} W^{(q)}(x) dx + (q - \psi(s)) e^{-s\varepsilon} W^{(q)}(\varepsilon). \tag{6.18}$$

From the monotonicity of $W^{(q)}(\cdot)$, we have

$$0 \leq \frac{W^{(q),\prime}(\varepsilon)}{W^{(q)}(\varepsilon)} \int_0^\varepsilon e^{-sx} W^{(q)}(x) dx \leq \frac{W^{(q),\prime}(\varepsilon)}{W^{(q)}(\varepsilon)} \varepsilon W^{(q)}(\varepsilon) = \varepsilon W^{(q),\prime}(\varepsilon).$$

It follows from (6.18) and Lemma 6.5 that

$$\lim_{\varepsilon \downarrow 0} \frac{W^{(q),\prime}(\varepsilon)}{W^{(q)}(\varepsilon)} (1 - \mathbb{E}(e^{-q\tau_D^+(\varepsilon) - sD_{\tau_D^+(\varepsilon)}^+})) = s + (q - \psi(s)) W^{(q)}(0+),$$

which ends the proof by Lemma 6.1. □

6.3.2. A class of Lévy models with two-sided jumps

Next we consider a class of Lévy process with two-sided jumps of the form

$$X_t = \widetilde{X}_t + S_t^+, \qquad (6.19)$$

where $\widetilde{X}_\cdot$ a spectrally negative Lévy process satisfying Assumption 6.1, and $S_\cdot^+$ is a compound Poisson process with arrival rate $\lambda^+ = \Pi(\mathbb{R}_{>0}) \in (0,\infty)$ and i.i.d. positive jump size with distribution function $F^+(\cdot)$. The two processes $\widetilde{X}_\cdot$ and $S_\cdot^+$ are assumed to be independent. Since we assume that $|\widetilde{X}_\cdot|$ is not a subordinator and is regular for $(0,\infty)$, it is clear that the same holds for $X_\cdot$.

The characteristic exponent of $X_\cdot$ is given by

$$\Psi(s) = \widetilde{\Psi}(s) + \lambda^+ \int_{\mathbb{R}_{>0}} (1 - e^{isx}) F^+(\mathrm{d}x), \quad s \in \mathbb{R}, \qquad (6.20)$$

where $\widetilde{\Psi}(\cdot)$ is the characteristic exponent of $\widetilde{X}_\cdot$. Henceforth, we add the symbol $\sim$ to all quantities when they relate to the spectrally negative Lévy component $\widetilde{X}_\cdot$ only.

By conditioning on the first positive jump arrival time and the jump size, we have the following representation of the joint Laplace transform of $(\tau_D^+(\varepsilon), D_{\tau_D^+(\varepsilon)})$.

Lemma 6.6. *For $q, s \geq 0$ and $\varepsilon > 0$, we have*

$$\mathbb{E}(e^{-q\tau_D^+(\varepsilon) - s D_{\tau_D^+(\varepsilon)}})$$

$$= \frac{\mathbb{E}(e^{-(q+\lambda^+)\widetilde{\tau}_\varepsilon - s\widetilde{D}_{\widetilde{\tau}_D^+(\varepsilon)}}) + \mathbb{E}(e^{-q\tau_\varepsilon - s D_{\tau_D^+(\varepsilon)}} \mathbf{1}_{\{\tau_D^+(\varepsilon) > \xi_1^+, J_1^+ < D_{\xi_1^+ -}\}})}{1 - \frac{\lambda^+}{q+\lambda^+}(1 - \mathbb{E}(e^{-(q+\lambda^+)\widetilde{\tau}_D^+(\varepsilon)})) + \mathbb{E}(e^{-q\xi_1^+} \mathbf{1}_{\{\widetilde{\tau}_D^+(\varepsilon) > \xi_1^+, J_1^+ < \widetilde{D}_{\xi_1^+ -}\}})},$$

where ξ_1^+ and J_1^+ are the time and size of the first upward jump of $X_\cdot$, respectively.

We present an analogue of Theorem 6.2 for the Lévy process (6.19) with two-sided jumps. Note that by (6.20), the drift of the characteristic exponent d of $\widetilde{X}_\cdot$ and $X_\cdot$ are the same when $\widetilde{X}_\cdot$ has bounded variation.

Theorem 6.3. *Consider the Lévy model* (6.19). *For* $q, s \geq 0$, *we have*

$$\lim_{\varepsilon \downarrow 0} \frac{W^{(q+\lambda^+),\prime}(\varepsilon)}{W^{(q+\lambda^+)}(\varepsilon)}[1 - \mathbb{E}(e^{-q\tau_\varepsilon - sD_{\tau_D^+(\varepsilon)}})]$$

$$= \begin{cases} s & \text{if } \widetilde{X} \text{ has unbounded variation,} \\ s + \dfrac{q - \psi(s)}{d} & \text{if } \widetilde{X} \text{ has bounded variation.} \end{cases} \qquad (6.21)$$

Proof. Since $\widetilde{X}.$ and S^+ are independent and $\{\tau_D^+(\varepsilon) < \xi_1^+\} = \{\widetilde{\tau}_D^+(\varepsilon) < \xi_1^+\}$ a.s., we have

$$\mathbb{P}(\tau_D^+(\varepsilon) > \xi_1^+, J_1^+ < D_{\xi_1^+ -}) = \mathbb{P}(\widetilde{\tau}_D^+(\varepsilon) > \xi_1^+, J_1^+ < \widetilde{D}_{\xi_1^+ -})$$

$$\leq \mathbb{P}(\widetilde{\tau}_D^+(\varepsilon) > \xi_1^+, J_1^+ < \varepsilon)$$

$$= (1 - \mathbb{E}(e^{-\lambda^+ \widetilde{\tau}_D^+(\varepsilon)}))\mathbb{P}(J_1^+ < \varepsilon)$$

$$\leq (1 - \mathbb{E}(e^{-(q+\lambda^+)\widetilde{\tau}_D^+(\varepsilon)}))F^+(\varepsilon). \qquad (6.22)$$

It follows from Theorem 6.2 that

$$\frac{W^{(q+\lambda^+),\prime}(\varepsilon)}{W^{(q+\lambda^+)}(\varepsilon)}\mathbb{P}(\tau_D^+(\varepsilon) > \xi_1^+, J_1^+ < D_{\xi_1^+ -})$$

$$\leq \frac{W^{(q+\lambda^+),\prime}(\varepsilon)}{W^{(q+\lambda^+)}(\varepsilon)}(1 - \mathbb{E}(e^{-(q+\lambda^+)\widetilde{\tau}_D^+(\varepsilon)}))F^+(\varepsilon) = o(1), \qquad (6.23)$$

for small $\varepsilon > 0$. By Lemma 6.6, (6.22) and (6.23), one obtains that

$$\frac{W^{(q+\lambda^+),\prime}(\varepsilon)}{W^{(q+\lambda^+)}(\varepsilon)}(1 - \mathbb{E}(e^{-q\tau_D^+(\varepsilon) - sD_{\tau_D^+(\varepsilon)}}))$$

$$= \frac{\dfrac{W^{(q+\lambda^+),\prime}(\varepsilon)}{W^{(q+\lambda^+)}(\varepsilon)}(1 - \mathbb{E}(e^{-(q+\lambda^+)\widetilde{\tau}_\varepsilon - s\widetilde{D}_{\widetilde{\tau}_D^+(\varepsilon)}})) - \dfrac{\lambda^+}{q+\lambda^+}(1 - \mathbb{E}(e^{-(q+\lambda^+)\widetilde{\tau}_D^+(\varepsilon)}))}{1 - \dfrac{\lambda^+}{q+\lambda^+}(1 - \mathbb{E}(e^{-(q+\lambda^+)\widetilde{\tau}_D^+(\varepsilon)})) + o(1)}$$

$$+ o(1). \qquad (6.24)$$

We first consider $\widetilde{X}.$ has unbounded variation. From Lemma 6.1, we deduce that $\dfrac{W^{(q+\lambda^+),\prime}(\varepsilon)}{W^{(q+\lambda^+)}(\varepsilon)} \to \infty$ as $\varepsilon \downarrow 0$. By Theorem 6.2, this further

implies that
$$1 - \mathbb{E}(e^{-(q+\lambda^+)\widetilde{\tau}_D^+(\varepsilon)}) = o(1). \tag{6.25}$$

One concludes from (6.22) and (6.25) that the denominator on the right-hand side of (6.24) approaches 1 as $\varepsilon \downarrow 0$. Moreover, by Theorem 6.2,

$$\lim_{\varepsilon \downarrow 0} \frac{W^{(q+\lambda^+),\prime}(\varepsilon)}{W^{(q+\lambda^+)}(\varepsilon)} (1 - \mathbb{E}(e^{-q\tau_\varepsilon - sD_{\tau_D^+(\varepsilon)}}))$$

$$= \lim_{\varepsilon \downarrow 0} \frac{W^{(q+\lambda^+),\prime}(\varepsilon)}{W^{(q+\lambda^+)}(\varepsilon)} (1 - \mathbb{E}(e^{-(q+\lambda^+)\widetilde{\tau}_D^+(\varepsilon) - s\widetilde{Y}_{\tau_D^+(\varepsilon)}})) = s.$$

When $\widetilde{X}_\cdot$ has bounded variation but the Lévy measure $\Pi(-\infty, 0) = \infty$, note that (6.25) still holds by Lemma 6.1. Hence, it follows from (6.22) that the denominator on the right-hand side of (6.24) also approaches 1 as $\varepsilon \downarrow 0$. Furthermore, by Theorem 6.2, we obtain

$$\lim_{\varepsilon \downarrow 0} \frac{W^{(q+\lambda^+),\prime}(\varepsilon)}{W^{(q+\lambda^+)}(\varepsilon)} (1 - \mathbb{E}(e^{-q\tau_\varepsilon - sD_{\tau_D^+(\varepsilon)}}))$$

$$= s + \frac{q + \lambda^+ - \widetilde{\psi}(s)}{d} - \frac{\lambda^+}{q+\lambda^+} \frac{q+\lambda^+}{d} = s + \frac{q - \widetilde{\psi}(s)}{d}.$$

Finally, when $\widetilde{X}_\cdot$ has bounded variation and $\Pi(-\infty, 0) < \infty$, by Lemma 6.1 and Theorem 6.2,

$$\lim_{\varepsilon \downarrow 0} (1 - \mathbb{E}(e^{-q\widetilde{\tau}_\varepsilon - s\widetilde{D}_{\widetilde{\tau}_D^+(\varepsilon)}})) = \frac{q + sd - \widetilde{\psi}(s)}{q + \Pi(-\infty, 0)}. \tag{6.26}$$

Then, by (6.24), (6.22) and Theorem 6.2, it is straightforward to verify that

$$\lim_{\varepsilon \downarrow 0} \frac{W^{(q+\lambda^+),\prime}(\varepsilon)}{W^{(q+\lambda^+)}(\varepsilon)} (1 - \mathbb{E}(e^{-q\tau_\varepsilon - sD_{\tau_D^+(\varepsilon)}})) = s + \frac{q - \widetilde{\psi}(s)}{d},$$

which completes the proof. □

6.4. Duration of Drawdowns

In this section, we examine the duration of drawdowns via the Laplace transform of the stopping time η_b defined in (6.1) for the Lévy model with two-sided jumps (6.19).

Duration of Drawdowns Under Lévy Models

To do so, we apply the perturbation approach that has been used in Chapters 2 and 5. To present the main idea, let $\varepsilon > 0$ and define the following sequence of stopping times:

$$\tau_D^{+,1}(\varepsilon) = \tau_D^+(\varepsilon), \quad \vartheta_0^1 = \tau_D^{+,1}(\varepsilon) + \tau_X^+(\overline{X}_{\tau_D^{+,1}(\varepsilon)}) \circ \theta_{\tau_D^{+,1}(\varepsilon)}, \ldots ,$$

$$\tau_D^{+,i}(\varepsilon) = \vartheta_0^i + \tau_D^+(\varepsilon) \circ \theta_{\vartheta_0^i}, \quad \vartheta_0^i = \tau_D^{+,i}(\varepsilon) + \tau_X^+(\overline{X}_{\tau_D^{+,i}(\varepsilon)}) \circ \theta_{\tau_D^{+,i}(\varepsilon)},$$

for $i \in \mathbb{N}$ where we recall θ. stands for the Markov shift operator. An approximation of η_b is given by

$$\eta_b^\varepsilon = \inf\{t \in (\tau_D^{+,i}(\varepsilon), \vartheta_0^i] : t - \tau_D^{+,i}(\varepsilon) \geq b \text{ for some } i \in \mathbb{N}\},$$

for which only excursions of D. with height over ε are considered. By construction, it is clear that η_b^ε is monotonically decreasing as $\varepsilon \downarrow 0$, and $\eta_b = \lim_{\varepsilon \downarrow 0} \eta_b^\varepsilon$, $\mathbb{P}$-a.s.

For fixed $q > 0$, we consider an independent exponential random variable $\mathbf{e}_q$ with mean $1/q$. By the strong Markov property of $X.$,

$$\mathbb{P}(\mathbf{e}_q > \eta_b^\varepsilon) = \mathbb{P}(\mathbf{e}_q > \eta_b^\varepsilon, \vartheta_0^1 > \tau_D^{+,1}(\varepsilon) + b) + \mathbb{P}(\mathbf{e}_q > \eta_b^\varepsilon, \vartheta_0^1 < \tau_D^{+,1}(\varepsilon) + b)$$
$$= \mathbb{P}(\mathbf{e}_q \wedge \vartheta_0^1 > \tau_\varepsilon^1 + b) + \mathbb{P}(\vartheta_0^1 < \mathbf{e}_q \wedge (\tau_D^{+,1}(\varepsilon) + b))\mathbb{P}(\mathbf{e}_q > \eta_b^\varepsilon),$$

which yields

$$\mathbb{P}(\mathbf{e}_q > \eta_b^\varepsilon) = \frac{\mathbb{P}(\mathbf{e}_q \wedge \vartheta_0^1 > \tau_\varepsilon^1 + b)}{1 - \mathbb{P}(\vartheta_0^1 < \mathbf{e}_q \wedge (\tau_D^{+,1}(\varepsilon) + b))}. \qquad (6.27)$$

By conditioning on $D_{\tau_D^{+,1}(\varepsilon)}$ and then using the strong Markov property of $X.$ at time $\tau_D^{+,1}(\varepsilon)$, we find

$$\mathbb{P}(\vartheta_0^1 < \mathbf{e}_q \wedge (\tau_D^{+,1}(\varepsilon) + b))$$
$$= \int_{[\varepsilon,\infty)} \mathbb{E}(e^{-q\tau_D^+(\varepsilon)} \mathbf{1}_{\{D_{\tau_D^+(\varepsilon)} \in dy\}}) \mathbb{P}(\tau_X^+(y) < \mathbf{e}_q \wedge b)$$
$$= \mathbb{E}(e^{-q\tau_D^+(\varepsilon)}) - \int_{[\varepsilon,\infty)} \mathbb{E}(e^{-q\tau_D^+(\varepsilon)} \mathbf{1}_{\{D_{\tau_\varepsilon} \in dy\}}) \mathbb{P}(\tau_X^+(y) > \mathbf{e}_q \wedge b),$$

$$(6.28)$$

and

$$\mathbb{P}(\mathbf{e}_q \wedge \vartheta_0^1 > \tau_\varepsilon^1 + b) = \int_{[\varepsilon,\infty)} \mathbb{E}(e^{-q\tau_D^+(\varepsilon)} \mathbf{1}_{\{D_{\tau_D^+(\varepsilon)} \in dy\}}) \mathbb{P}(\mathbf{e}_q \wedge \tau_X^+(y) > b)$$
$$= e^{-qb} \int_{[\varepsilon,\infty)} \mathbb{E}(e^{-q\tau_\varepsilon} \mathbf{1}_{\{D_{\tau_D^+(\varepsilon)} \in dy\}}) \mathbb{P}(\tau_X^+(y) > b).$$

Substituting the above and (6.28) into (6.27), we obtain

$$\mathbb{E}(e^{-q\eta_b^\varepsilon}) = \mathbb{P}(e_q > \eta_b^\varepsilon)$$
$$= \frac{e^{-qb}\int_{[\varepsilon,\infty)}\mathbb{E}(e^{-q\tau_D^+(\varepsilon)}\mathbf{1}_{\{D_{\tau_D^+(\varepsilon)}\in dy\}})\mathbb{P}(\tau_X^+(y) > b)}{1 - \mathbb{E}(e^{-q\tau_D^+(\varepsilon)}) + \int_{[\varepsilon,\infty)}\mathbb{E}(e^{-q\tau_D^+(\varepsilon)}\mathbf{1}_{\{D_{\tau_\varepsilon}\in dy\}})\mathbb{P}(\tau_X^+(y) > e_q \wedge b)}. \tag{6.29}$$

From the representation (6.29), it seems relevant to define, for $x > 0$ and $p \geq 0$, a bounded auxiliary function

$$f_\varepsilon^{(p)}(t) := \int_{[\varepsilon,\infty)} \mathbb{E}(e^{-q\tau_D^+(\varepsilon)}\mathbf{1}_{\{D_{\tau_D^+(\varepsilon)}\in dy\}})\, \mathbb{P}(\tau_X^+(y) > e_p \wedge t)$$
$$= \int_{[\varepsilon,\infty)} \mathbb{E}(e^{-q\tau_D^+(\varepsilon)}\mathbf{1}_{\{D_{\tau_D^+(\varepsilon)}\in dy\}})\, \mathbb{P}(\overline{X}_{e_p \wedge t} \leq y), \tag{6.30}$$

where the dependence of (6.30) on q is silently assumed. Hence, we rewrite (6.29) as

$$\mathbb{E}(e^{-q(\eta_b^\varepsilon - b)}) = \frac{f_\varepsilon^{(0)}(b)}{1 - \mathbb{E}(e^{-q\tau_D^+(\varepsilon)}) + f_\varepsilon^{(q)}(b)}. \tag{6.31}$$

To obtain a well-defined asymptotics for $f_\varepsilon^{(p)}(b)$ as $\varepsilon \downarrow 0$, the key is to investigate the convergence of the measure $\mathbb{E}(e^{-q\tau_D^+(\varepsilon)}\mathbf{1}_{\{D_{\tau_\varepsilon}\in dy\}})$ as $\varepsilon \downarrow 0$, which is closely related to the asymptotic results of Section 6.3. As we will see below, the convergence of the measure differs according to whether the Lévy process has bounded or unbounded variation.

6.4.1. *Bounded variation case*

We first show that the distribution function of the running maximum of X. is well-behaved.

Proposition 6.1. *Let X. be a Lévy process of bounded variation with a drift $d > 0$ in its characteristic exponent representation (6.9). Then, for any fixed $p \geq 0$ and $t > 0$, the function $F_t^{(p)}(y) := \mathbb{P}(\overline{X}_{e_p \wedge t} \leq y)/y$ is bounded for $y \in (0, \infty)$. Moreover, if we further assume that $\Pi(-\infty, 0) = \infty$ and Π has no atoms on $(-\infty, 0)$, the function $F_t^{(p)}(\cdot)$ is also continuous over $(0, \infty)$.*

Proof. We first consider the case $p = 0$. Using the upper bound in Chaumont and Małecki (2016, Eq. (4.16)) (which holds for a general Lévy process), we know that

$$F_t^{(0)}(y) \leq \frac{e}{e-1} \kappa\left(\frac{1}{t}, 0\right) \frac{h(y)}{y}, \qquad (6.32)$$

where we recall $h(\cdot)$ is the renewal function defined in (6.12). Since $X.$ has bounded variation and $d > 0$, we deduce that $X.$ creeps upwards by Kyprianou (2006, Theorem 7.11). From Lemma 6.2 we know that $h(y)/y$ converges to a finite limit as $y \downarrow 0$. Therefore, we conclude from (6.32) that $F_t^{(0)}(y)$ is bounded for $y \in (0, \infty)$.

Next we consider the case $p > 0$. By the Wiener–Hopf factorization, it is well-known that $\overline{X}_{e_p}$ follows an exponential distribution with mean $1/\widetilde{\Phi}(p) > 0$. Moreover, since $\overline{X}_t \geq \widetilde{X}_t$ a.s. for any $t \geq 0$, one obtains that

$$F_t^{(p)}(y) = \int_0^t p e^{-ps} \frac{\mathbb{P}(\overline{X}_s \leq y)}{y} ds + e^{-pt} \frac{\mathbb{P}(\overline{X}_t \leq y)}{y}$$

$$\leq \int_0^\infty p e^{-ps} \frac{\mathbb{P}(\widetilde{X}_s \leq y)}{y} ds + e^{-pt} F_t^{(0)}(y)$$

$$= \frac{1 - e^{-\widetilde{\Phi}(p)y}}{y} + e^{-pt} F_t^{(0)}(y).$$

By the boundedness of $F_t^{(0)}(\cdot)$, we deduce that $F_t^{(p)}(y)$ is also bounded for $y \in (0, \infty)$.

Finally, suppose that we also have $\Pi(-\infty, 0) = \infty$ and Π has no atoms on $(-\infty, 0)$. For any fixed $t > 0$, by Sato (1999, Theorem 27.7), we know that the law of $\widetilde{X}_t$ is absolute continuous with respect to the Lebesgue measure, so is the law of X_t from the property of convolutions. In addition, by Kyprianou (2006, Theorem 6.5), we know that $X.$ is regular for $(0, \infty)$ as $X.$ has bounded variation and $d > 0$. Therefore, from Chaumont (2013, Theorem 1), we conclude that the law of $\overline{X}_t$ is absolute continuous with respect to the Lebesgue measure. As a consequence, $\mathbb{P}(\overline{X}_{e_p \wedge t} \leq y)/y$ is continuous in $y \in (0, \infty)$. □

Remark 6.3. For the Lévy model (6.19) with $\widetilde{X}.$ has bounded variation and $\Pi(-\infty, 0) = \infty$, it follows that $\mathbb{P}(\overline{X}_{e_p \wedge t} \leq y)/y$ is bounded and continuous for $y \in (0, \infty)$ due to our assumptions that $-\widetilde{X}.$ is not a subordinator, $\widetilde{X}.$ is regular for $(0, \infty)$, and Π has no atom on $(-\infty, 0)$.

We are now ready to present the main result of this subsection.

Theorem 6.4. *Consider the Lévy model (6.19). If $\widetilde{X}.$ has bounded variation and satisfies Assumption 6.1, for any $q > 0$, we have*

$$\mathbb{E}(e^{-q(\eta_b - b)}) = \frac{\int_{\mathbb{R}_{>0}} \mathbb{P}(\overline{X}_b \leq y) \Pi(-dy)}{q + \int_{\mathbb{R}_{>0}} \mathbb{P}(\overline{X}_{e_q \wedge b} \leq y) \Pi(-dy)}.$$

Proof. We first consider the case $\Pi(-\infty, 0) = \infty$. From (6.30) with $p \geq 0$, we have

$$\frac{W^{(q+\lambda^+),\prime}(\varepsilon)}{W^{(q+\lambda^+)}(\varepsilon)} f_\varepsilon^{(p)}(b)$$

$$= \frac{W^{(q+\lambda^+),\prime}(\varepsilon)}{W^{(q+\lambda^+)}(\varepsilon)} \int_{[\varepsilon,\infty)} \mathbb{E}(e^{-q\tau_D^+(\varepsilon)} \mathbf{1}_{\{D_{\tau_D^+(\varepsilon)} \in dy\}}) \mathbb{P}(\overline{X}_{e_p \wedge b} \leq y)$$

$$= \int_{\mathbb{R}_{>0}} \frac{\mathbb{P}(\overline{X}_{e_p \wedge b} \leq y)}{1 - e^{-y}} \frac{W^{(q+\lambda^+),\prime}(\varepsilon)}{W^{(q+\lambda^+)}(\varepsilon)} \mathbf{1}_{\{y \geq \varepsilon\}} (1 - e^{-y})$$

$$\times \mathbb{E}(e^{-q\tau_D^+(\varepsilon)} \mathbf{1}_{\{D_{\tau_D^+(\varepsilon)} \in dy\}})$$

$$= \int_{\mathbb{R}_{>0}} \frac{\mathbb{P}(\overline{X}_{e_p \wedge b} \leq y)}{1 - e^{-y}} \mu_\varepsilon(dy), \qquad (6.33)$$

where $\mu_\varepsilon(dy)$ is a finite measure on $(0, \infty)$ defined as

$$\mu_\varepsilon(dy) = \frac{W^{(q+\lambda^+),\prime}(\varepsilon)}{W^{(q+\lambda^+)}(\varepsilon)} \mathbf{1}_{\{y \geq \varepsilon\}} (1 - e^{-y}) \mathbb{E}(e^{-q\tau_D^+(\varepsilon)} \mathbf{1}_{\{D_{\tau_D^+(\varepsilon)} \subset dy\}}). \qquad (6.34)$$

By Theorem 6.3, we have

$$\lim_{\varepsilon \downarrow 0} \int_{\mathbb{R}_{>0}} e^{-sy} \mu_\varepsilon(dy)$$

$$= \lim_{\varepsilon \downarrow 0} \frac{W^{(q+\lambda^+),\prime}(\varepsilon)}{W^{(q+\lambda^+)}(\varepsilon)} (\mathbb{E}(e^{-q\tau_\varepsilon - sD_{\tau_D^+(\varepsilon)}}) - \mathbb{E}(e^{-q\tau_\varepsilon - (s+1)D_{\tau_D^+(\varepsilon)}}))$$

$$= 1 + \frac{\widetilde{\psi}(s) - \widetilde{\psi}(s+1)}{d},$$

for all $s \geq 0$. On the other hand, we notice from (6.3) that

$$\int_{\mathbb{R}_{>0}} e^{-sy} \frac{1-e^{-y}}{d} \Pi(-dy)$$

$$= \frac{1}{d} \int_{(-\infty,0)} (e^{sy}-1)\Pi(dy) - \frac{1}{d} \int_{(-\infty,0)} (e^{(s+1)y}-1)\Pi(dy)$$

$$= 1 + \frac{\widetilde{\psi}(s) - \widetilde{\psi}(s+1)}{d}.$$

Hence, by Proposition 6.3, one concludes that, as $\varepsilon \downarrow 0$, $\mu_\varepsilon(dy)$ weakly converges to the measure $d^{-1}(1-e^{-y})\Pi(-dy)$, which is a finite measure on $(0,\infty)$ because $\widetilde{X}$. has bounded variation.

From Proposition 6.1 and Remark 6.3, we know that the function $\mathbb{P}(\overline{X}_{\mathbf{e}_p \wedge b} \leq y)/(1-e^{-y})$ is bounded and continuous for $y \in (0,\infty)$. By the definition of weak convergence, it follows from (6.33) that

$$\lim_{\varepsilon \downarrow 0} \frac{W^{(q+\lambda^+),'}(\varepsilon)}{W^{(q+\lambda^+)}(\varepsilon)} f_\varepsilon^{(p)}(b) = \lim_{\varepsilon \downarrow 0} \int_{\mathbb{R}_{>0}} \frac{\mathbb{P}(\overline{X}_{\mathbf{e}_p \wedge b} \leq y)}{1-e^{-y}} \mu_\varepsilon(dy)$$

$$= \int_{\mathbb{R}_{>0}} \frac{\mathbb{P}(\overline{X}_{\mathbf{e}_p \wedge b} \leq y)}{1-e^{-y}} \frac{1}{d}(1-e^{-y})\Pi(-dy)$$

$$= \frac{1}{d} \int_{\mathbb{R}_{>0}} \mathbb{P}(\overline{X}_{\mathbf{e}_p \wedge b} \leq y)\Pi(-dy). \qquad (6.35)$$

Therefore, by (6.31), (6.35) and Theorem 6.3, we have

$$\mathbb{E}(e^{-q\eta_b}) = \frac{e^{-qb} \lim_{\varepsilon \downarrow 0} \frac{W^{(q+\lambda^+),'}(\varepsilon)}{W^{(q+\lambda^+)}(\varepsilon)} f_\varepsilon^{(0)}(b)}{\lim_{\varepsilon \downarrow 0} \frac{W^{(q+\lambda^+),'}(\varepsilon)}{W^{(q+\lambda^+)}(\varepsilon)}(1-\mathbb{E}(e^{-q\tau_D^+(\varepsilon)})) + \lim_{\varepsilon \downarrow 0} \frac{W^{(q+\lambda^+),'}(\varepsilon)}{W^{(q+\lambda^+)}(\varepsilon)} f_\varepsilon^{(q)}(b)}$$

$$= \frac{e^{-qb} \int_{\mathbb{R}_{>0}} \mathbb{P}(\overline{X}_b \leq y)\Pi(-dy)}{q + \int_{\mathbb{R}_{>0}} \mathbb{P}(\overline{X}_{\mathbf{e}_q \wedge b} \leq y)\Pi(-dy)}.$$

Finally, we consider the case that $\Pi(-\infty,0) < \infty$. By (6.26), for any $s \geq 0$, we have

$$\lim_{\varepsilon \downarrow 0} \int_{\mathbb{R}_{>0}} e^{-sy} \mathbb{E}(e^{-q\tau_\varepsilon} \mathbf{1}_{\{D_{\tau_D^+(\varepsilon)} \in dy\}}) = \frac{\widetilde{\psi}(s) - sd + \Pi(-\infty,0)}{q + \Pi(-\infty,0)}$$

$$= \int_{\mathbb{R}_{>0}} e^{-sy} \frac{\Pi(-dy)}{q + \Pi(-\infty,0)}.$$

By Proposition 6.3 we see that the measure $\mathbb{E}(e^{-q\tau_D^+(\varepsilon)}\mathbf{1}_{\{D_{\tau_D^+(\varepsilon)}\in dy\}})$ weakly converges to the measure $\Pi(-dy)/(q+\Pi(-\infty,0))$ as $\varepsilon\downarrow 0$. Since $\mathbb{P}(\overline{X}_{\mathbf{e}_p\wedge b}\leq y)$ is bounded and upper semi-continuous in $y\in(0,\infty)$, it follows from Portemanteau theorem of weak convergence that

$$\limsup_{\varepsilon\downarrow 0} f_\varepsilon^{(p)}(b) = \limsup_{\varepsilon\downarrow 0}\int_{\mathbb{R}_{>0}}\mathbb{P}(\overline{X}_{\mathbf{e}_p\wedge b}\leq y)\mathbb{E}(e^{-q\tau_D^+(\varepsilon)}\mathbf{1}_{\{D_{\tau_D^+(\varepsilon)}\in dy\}})$$

$$\leq \frac{1}{q+\Pi(-\infty,0)}\int_{\mathbb{R}_{>0}}\mathbb{P}(\overline{X}_{\mathbf{e}_p\wedge b}\leq y)\Pi(-dy). \qquad (6.36)$$

On the other hand, since $\mathbb{P}(\overline{X}_{\mathbf{e}_p\wedge b}<y)$ is lower semi-continuous in $y\in(0,\infty)$. By Portemanteau theorem again, we have

$$\liminf_{\varepsilon\downarrow 0} f_\varepsilon^{(p)}(b) \geq \liminf_{\varepsilon\downarrow 0}\int_{\mathbb{R}_{>0}}\mathbb{P}(\overline{X}_{\mathbf{e}_p\wedge b}<y)\mathbb{E}(e^{-q\tau_D^+(\varepsilon)}\mathbf{1}_{\{D_{\tau_D^+(\varepsilon)}\in dy\}})$$

$$\geq \frac{1}{q+\Pi(-\infty,0)}\int_{\mathbb{R}_{>0}}\mathbb{P}(\overline{X}_{\mathbf{e}_p\wedge b}<y)\Pi(-dy)$$

$$= \frac{1}{q+\Pi(-\infty,0)}\int_{\mathbb{R}_{>0}}\mathbb{P}(\overline{X}_{\mathbf{e}_p\wedge b}\leq y)\Pi(-dy), \qquad (6.37)$$

where the last equality holds because Π has no atom on $(-\infty,0)$ and $\mathbb{P}(\overline{X}_{\mathbf{e}_p\wedge b}<y)=\mathbb{P}(\overline{X}_{\mathbf{e}_p\wedge b}\leq y)$ for almost all $y>0$. By letting $\varepsilon\downarrow 0$ in each term of (6.31) and using (6.36), (6.37) and (6.26), this completes the proof of Theorem 6.4. □

6.4.2. Unbounded variation case

We now consider the unbounded variation case for which the following assumption on the density of X_t is made.

Assumption 6.2. *If $X.$ has unbounded variation, we assume that the density of X_t, namely $p_t^X(x)$, is bounded for all $t>0$.*

Remark 6.4. We point out that Assumption 6.2 is identical to Chaumont and Małecki (2016, Assumption (H1)), which is equivalent to the assumption that the characteristic function $e^{-t\Psi(\cdot)}\in L^2(\mathbb{R})$, for all $t>0$. It is also clear that, if $X.$ is a spectrally negative Lévy process with unbounded variation and $Y.$ is an arbitrary Lévy process independent of $X.$, then the sum $X.+Y.$ satisfies Assumption 6.2 as long as $X.$ does. Hence, examples of Levy processes satisfying Assumption 6.2 include processes with $\sigma>0$, or $\sigma = 0$ and with a spectrally negative α-stable jump distribution with $\alpha \in (1, 2)$.

The following proposition shows that, for a Lévy process with unbounded variation satisfying Assumption 6.2, the density of the running maximum at 0+ is well-behaved.

Proposition 6.2. *Let X. be a Lévy process with unbounded variation that creeps upwards and satisfies Assumption 6.2. Then the running maximum $\overline{X}_t$ has a continuous density $p_t^M(\cdot)$ for every $t > 0$ and further,*

$$\lim_{x \downarrow 0} p_t^M(x) = \frac{\bar{\nu}_L(t) + \kappa(0,0)}{d_H} > 0,$$

where $\bar{\nu}_L(\cdot)$ is the tail of the jump measure of the ascending ladder time process (see (6.11)).

Proof. From Lemma 6.2, we know that the renewal density $h'(\cdot)$ can be chosen to be a continuous function with well-defined limit $h'(0) = \frac{1}{d_H} > 0$. Since X. has unbounded variation, Assumption (H2) of Chaumont and Małecki (2016) also holds. By Chaumont and Małecki (2016, Proposition 2, Theorem 1), we know that $\overline{X}_t$ has a continuous density $p_t^M(x)$ for every $t > 0$, and also,

$$\lim_{x \downarrow 0} \frac{p_t^M(x)}{h'(x)} = d_H \lim_{x \downarrow 0} p_t^M(x) = n(\zeta > t),$$

where $n(\zeta > t)$ is the excursion measure of excursions with length over $t > 0$. From (6.11) and (6.14) of Kyprianou (2006) (see also Bertoin (1996), Section IV.4)), we know that

$$n(\zeta > t) = \bar{\nu}_L(t) + \kappa(0,0) > 0,$$

which completes the proof. □

Corollary 6.1. *Under the conditions of Proposition 6.2, for any fixed $p \geq 0$ and $t > 0$, the function $\mathbb{P}(\overline{X}_{e_p \wedge t} \leq y)/y$ is bounded and continuous for $y \in [0, \infty)$, where its value at $y = 0$ is defined as the right limit*

$$\lim_{y \downarrow 0} \frac{\mathbb{P}(\overline{X}_{e_p \wedge t} \leq y)}{y} = \frac{1}{d_H} \left(\int_0^t p e^{-ps} \bar{\nu}_L(s) ds + e^{-pt} \bar{\nu}_L(t) + \kappa(0,0) \right).$$

Proof. From Proposition 6.2, it is only left to justify the limit of $\mathbb{P}(\overline{X}_{\mathbf{e}_p \wedge t} \leq y)/y$ as $y \downarrow 0$. By dominated convergence theorem and Proposition 6.2 again, we have

$$\lim_{y \downarrow 0} \frac{\mathbb{P}(\overline{X}_{\mathbf{e}_p \wedge t} \leq y)}{y} = \int_0^t p \mathrm{e}^{-ps} \lim_{y \downarrow 0} \frac{\mathbb{P}(\overline{X}_s \leq y)}{y} \mathrm{d}s + \mathrm{e}^{-pt} \lim_{y \downarrow 0} \frac{\mathbb{P}(\overline{X}_t \leq y)}{y}$$

$$= \int_0^t p \mathrm{e}^{-ps} \lim_{y \downarrow 0} p_s^M(y) \mathrm{d}s + \mathrm{e}^{-pt} \lim_{y \downarrow 0} p_t^M(y)$$

$$= \frac{1}{d_H} \left(\int_0^t p \mathrm{e}^{-ps} \bar{\nu}_L(s) \mathrm{d}s + \mathrm{e}^{-pt} \bar{\nu}_L(t) + \kappa(0,0) \right),$$

which ends the proof. $\square$

Now we are ready to present the main result of this subsection.

Theorem 6.5. *Consider the Lévy model* (6.19). *If* $\widetilde{X}$. *has unbounded variation and satisfies Assumptions* 6.1 *and* 6.2, *for any* $q > 0$, *we have*

$$\mathbb{E}(\mathrm{e}^{-q(\eta_b - b)}) = \frac{\bar{\nu}_L(b) + \kappa(0,0)}{\int_0^b q \mathrm{e}^{-qt} \bar{\nu}_L(t) \mathrm{d}t + \mathrm{e}^{-qb} \bar{\nu}_L(b) + \kappa(0,0)}.$$

Proof. It is clear that the Lévy model (6.19) creeps upward as its spectrally negative component $\widetilde{X}$. does. Moreover, since $\widetilde{X}$. satisfies Assumption 6.2, by Remark 6.4, we see that all the conditions of Proposition 6.2 are satisfied.

For the finite measure $\mu_\varepsilon(\mathrm{d}y)$ defined in (6.34), it is straightforward to verify from Theorem 6.3 that, for any $s \geq 0$,

$$\lim_{\varepsilon \downarrow 0} \int_{\mathbb{R}_{\geq 0}} \mathrm{e}^{-sy} \mu_\varepsilon(\mathrm{d}y)$$

$$= \lim_{\varepsilon \downarrow 0} \frac{W^{(q+\lambda'),'}(\varepsilon)}{W^{(q+\lambda^+)}(\varepsilon)} (\mathbb{E}(\mathrm{e}^{-q\tau_D^+(\varepsilon) - sD_{\tau_D^+(\varepsilon)}}) - \mathbb{E}(\mathrm{e}^{-q\tau_\varepsilon - (s+1)D_{\tau_D^+(\varepsilon)}}))$$

$$= 1 = \int_{\mathbb{R}_{\geq 0}} \mathrm{e}^{-sy} \delta_0(\mathrm{d}y).$$

It follows from Proposition 6.3 that $\mu_\varepsilon(\mathrm{d}y)$ weakly converges to the Dirac measure $\delta_0(\mathrm{d}y)$ as $\varepsilon \downarrow 0$. Moreover, by Corollary 6.1, we know that the function $\mathbb{P}(\overline{X}_{\mathbf{e}_p \wedge t} \leq y)/(1 - \mathrm{e}^{-y})$ is also bounded and continuous for $y \in [0, \infty)$, where its value at $y = 0$ is defined by the limit as $y \downarrow 0$. From (6.33) and Corollary 6.1, we have

$$\lim_{\varepsilon \downarrow 0} \frac{W^{(q+\lambda^+),\prime}(\varepsilon)}{W^{(q+\lambda^+)}(\varepsilon)} f_\varepsilon^{(p)}(b) = \lim_{\varepsilon \downarrow 0} \int_{\mathbb{R}_{\geq 0}} \frac{\mathbb{P}(\overline{X}_{\mathbf{e}_p \wedge b} \leq y)}{1 - e^{-y}} \mu_\varepsilon(\mathrm{d}y)$$

$$= \lim_{y \downarrow 0} \frac{\mathbb{P}(\overline{X}_{\mathbf{e}_p \wedge b} \leq y)}{1 - e^{-y}}$$

$$= \frac{1}{d_H} \left(\int_0^b p e^{-pt} \bar{\nu}_L(t) \mathrm{d}t + e^{-pb} \bar{\nu}_L(b) + \kappa(0,0) \right).$$

It follows from the above equation, (6.31), and Theorem 6.3 that

$$\mathbb{E}(e^{-q(\eta_b - b)}) = \frac{\lim_{\varepsilon \downarrow 0} \frac{W^{(q+\lambda^+),\prime}(\varepsilon)}{W^{(q+\lambda^+)}(\varepsilon)} f_\varepsilon^{(0)}(b)}{\lim_{\varepsilon \downarrow 0} \frac{W^{(q+\lambda^+),\prime}(\varepsilon)}{W^{(q+\lambda^+)}(\varepsilon)} (1 - \mathbb{E}(e^{-q\tau_D^+(\varepsilon)})) + f_\varepsilon^{(q)}(b)}$$

$$= \frac{\bar{\nu}_L(b) + \kappa(0,0)}{\int_0^b q e^{-qt} \bar{\nu}_L(t) \mathrm{d}t + e^{-qb} \bar{\nu}_L(b) + \kappa(0,0)},$$

which ends the proof. □

In general, the functions $\bar{\nu}_L(\cdot)$ and $\kappa(0,0)$ are only implicitly known via (6.11) and Wiener–Hopf factorization. When X has no positive jumps, we can express $\mathbb{E}(e^{-q\eta_b})$ explicitly in terms of $p_t^X(\cdot)$.

Corollary 6.2. *Let X be a spectrally negative Lévy process with unbounded variation and satisfies Assumptions 6.1 and 6.2. For any $q > 0$, we have*

$$\mathbb{E}(e^{-q(\eta_b - b)}) = \frac{\int_b^\infty \frac{1}{s} p_s^X(0) \mathrm{d}s}{\int_0^b q e^{-qt} \int_t^\infty \frac{1}{s} p_s^X(0) \mathrm{d}s \mathrm{d}t + e^{-qb} \int_b^\infty \frac{1}{s} p_s^X(0) \mathrm{d}s}.$$

Proof. By Kendall's identity, for any fixed $t, y > 0$, we have

$$\frac{1}{y} \mathbb{P}(\overline{X}_t \leq y) = \frac{1}{y} \int_{(t,\infty)} \mathbb{P}(\tau_X^+(y) \in \mathrm{d}s) = \int_t^\infty \frac{1}{s} p_s^X(y) \mathrm{d}s.$$

It follows from Fourier inversion that, for any $y \in \mathbb{R}$ and $s > 0$,

$$0 \leq \frac{1}{s} p_s^X(y) \leq \frac{1}{2\pi s} \int_\mathbb{R} |e^{-s\Psi(u)}| \mathrm{d}u.$$

From the proof of Chaumont and Małecki (2016, Proposition 5), we know that for any fixed $t > 0$,

$$\frac{1}{2\pi}\int_t^\infty \frac{1}{s}\int_{\mathbb{R}} |e^{-s\Psi(u)}|\mathrm{d}u\mathrm{d}s < \infty.$$

By the dominated convergence theorem and Corollary 6.1, we have

$$\frac{\bar{\nu}_L(t) + \kappa(0,0)}{d_H} = \lim_{y\downarrow 0}\frac{\mathbb{P}(\overline{X}_t \le y)}{y} = \int_t^\infty \frac{1}{s}p_s^X(0)\mathrm{d}s,$$

which completes the proof by using Theorem 6.5. □

6.5. Examples

Example 6.2. Consider a Brownian motion with drift model, i.e., $X_t = \mu t + \sigma W_t$ with $\sigma > 0$. For any fixed $t > 0$, we have

$$p_t^X(x) = \frac{1}{\sigma\sqrt{2\pi t}}e^{-\frac{(x-\mu t)^2}{2\sigma^2 t}}.$$

By Remarks 6.1, 6.4 and Corollary 6.2, we have

$$\mathbb{E}(e^{-q(\eta_b - b)}) = \frac{g(b)}{\int_0^b qe^{-qt}g(t)\mathrm{d}t + e^{-qb}g(b)},$$

where $g(t) := \int_t^\infty \frac{1}{s}p_s^X(0)\mathrm{d}s = \frac{2}{\sigma\sqrt{2\pi t}}e^{-\frac{\mu^2 t}{2\sigma^2}} - \frac{2\mu}{\sigma^2}\Phi(-\frac{\mu\sqrt{t}}{\sigma})$ and $\Phi(\cdot)$ is the cumulative distribution function of a standard normal random variable. In Figure 6.1, we implement the fixed-Talbot method to numerically invert the Laplace transform to compute the probability $\mathbb{P}(\eta_b - b \le t)$.

Example 6.3. Consider a spectrally negative α-stable process with Laplace exponent $\psi(s) = s^\alpha$ with $\alpha \in (1,2)$. For fixed $t > 0$, it is well-known (see, e.g., Sato (1999, p. 87–88)) that

$$p_t^X(x) = \frac{1}{\pi}t^{-\frac{1}{\alpha}}\sum_{n=1}^\infty (-1)^{n-1}\frac{\Gamma(1+\frac{n}{\alpha})}{n!}\sin\left(\frac{n\pi}{\alpha}\right)(t^{-\frac{1}{\alpha}}x)^{n-1},$$

where $\Gamma(\cdot)$ is the Gamma function. It follows that

$$\int_t^\infty \frac{1}{s}p_s^X(0)\mathrm{d}s = \frac{\alpha}{\pi}\Gamma\left(\frac{1}{\alpha}\right)\sin\left(\frac{\pi}{\alpha}\right)t^{-\frac{1}{\alpha}}.$$

By Remarks 6.1, 6.4 and Corollary 6.2, we have

$$\mathbb{E}(e^{-q(\eta_b - b)}) = \frac{1}{b^{\frac{1}{\alpha}}\int_0^b qe^{-qt}t^{-\frac{1}{\alpha}}\mathrm{d}t + e^{-qb}}.$$

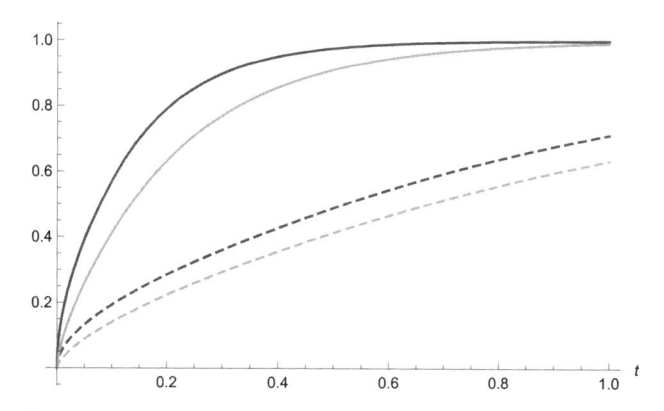

Fig. 6.1. Numerical results for the probability $\mathbb{P}(\eta_b - b \leq t)$ as a function of t, under the Brownian motion model in Example 6.2 with $\mu = 0.1, \sigma = 0.2$ and $b = 0.1$ (black solid) or $b = 0.5$ (black dashed), and under the α-stable process in Example 6.3 with $\alpha = 1.5$ and $b = 0.1$ (gray solid) or $b = 0.5$ (gray dashed).

In Figure 6.1, we implement the fixed-Talbot method to numerically invert the Laplace transform to compute the probability $\mathbb{P}(\eta_b - b \leq t)$.

Example 6.4. Consider a spectrally negative Gamma process with Laplace exponent

$$\psi(s) = sd + \int_{-\infty}^{0} (e^{sx} - 1)\beta|x|^{-1}e^{\alpha x}dx = sd - \beta\log(1 + s/\alpha), \quad s \in \mathbb{H}_{\geq 0},$$

where $\alpha, \beta > 0$ are constants. From Remark 6.2, we define

$$\varphi(s) := \frac{s\psi'(s) - \psi(s)}{\psi(s)^2} = \frac{\beta\log(1 + s/\alpha) - \frac{\beta s}{s+\alpha}}{(sd - \beta\log(1 + s/\alpha))^2}.$$

One can easily verify that, for any fixed $s_0 > \Phi(0)$, we have $\varphi(s_0 + \mathrm{i}\cdot) \in L^1(\mathbb{R})$ which implies Assumption 6.1 holds. Using Kendall's identity and

$$p_t^X(x) = \frac{\alpha^{\beta s}}{\Gamma(\beta t)}(sd - y)^{\beta s - 1}e^{-\alpha(sd-y)}\mathbf{1}_{\{y < sd\}}, \quad x \in \mathbb{R}, \, t > 0,$$

we have for all $y, t > 0$,

$$\mathbb{P}(\tau_X^+(y) > t) = y\int_t^\infty \frac{1}{s}\frac{\alpha^{\beta s}}{\Gamma(\beta s)}\mathbf{1}_{\{y<sd\}}(sd-y)^{\beta s-1}e^{-\alpha(sd-y)}ds.$$

Hence, by Fubini's theorem followed by some calculations, we can show that

$$g(t) := \int_{\mathbb{R}_{>0}} \mathbb{P}(\overline{X}_t \leq y) \Pi(-dy)$$

$$= \int_{\mathbb{R}_{>0}} \mathbb{P}(\tau_X^+(y) > t) \Pi(-dy)$$

$$= \int_{\mathbb{R}_{>0}} y \int_t^\infty \frac{1}{s} \frac{\alpha^{\beta s}}{\Gamma(\beta s)} \mathbf{1}_{\{y < sd\}} (sd-y)^{\beta s - 1} e^{-\alpha(sd-y)} ds \beta \frac{e^{-\alpha y}}{y} dy$$

$$= (d\alpha)^{\beta s} \int_t^\infty \frac{1}{\Gamma(\beta s)} s^{\beta s - 2} e^{-\alpha s d} ds.$$

Using Theorem 6.4, one concludes

$$\mathbb{E}(e^{-q(\eta_b - b)}) = \frac{g(b)}{q + \int_0^b q e^{-qt} g(t) dt + e^{-qb} g(b)}.$$

Example 6.5. Consider Kou's jump-diffusion model given by

$$X_t = \mu t + \sigma W_t + \sum_{i=1}^{N_t^+} J_i^+ - \sum_{j=1}^{N_t^-} J_j^-,$$

where $\mu \in \mathbb{R}$, $\sigma > 0$, $N^\pm$ are two independent Poisson processes with arrival rates $\lambda^\pm > 0$ and $J^\pm$ are a sequence of i.i.d. exponentially distributed random variables with mean $1/\eta^\pm > 0$. Its Laplace exponent is given by

$$\psi(s) = \frac{\sigma^2}{2} s^2 + \mu s - \lambda^- \frac{s}{\eta^- + s} + \lambda^+ \frac{s}{\eta^+ - s}, \quad s \in (-\eta^-, \eta^+).$$

According to Asmussen et al. (2004, Corollary 1) and Kyprianou (2006, Section 6.5.4), it is known that the Laplace exponent of the ascending ladder height is given by

$$\kappa(\alpha, \beta) = \frac{(\beta + \rho_{1,\alpha})(\beta + \rho_{2,\alpha})}{(\beta + \eta^+)}, \quad \alpha, \beta \geq 0,$$

where $\rho_{1,\alpha}$ and $\rho_{2,\alpha}$ are the two largest, distinct non-negative solutions of $\psi(s) = \alpha$ such that $\rho_{1,\alpha} < \eta^+ < \rho_{2,\alpha}$. By Remarks 6.1, 6.4 and Theorem 6.5, one obtains

$$\mathbb{E}(e^{-q(\eta_b - b)}) = \frac{\bar{\nu}_L(b) + \frac{\rho_{1,0} \rho_{2,0}}{\eta^+}}{\int_0^b q e^{-qt} \bar{\nu}_L(t) dt + e^{-qb} \bar{\nu}_L(b) + \frac{\rho_{1,0} \rho_{2,0}}{\eta^+}}.$$

6.6. Concluding Remarks

In this chapter, we study magnitude, asymptotics and duration of drawdowns for some Lévy processes. First, we revisit some useful results on the magnitude of drawdowns for spectrally negative Lévy processes using an approximation approach. For any spectrally negative Lévy process whose scale functions are well-behaved at 0+, we study the asymptotics of drawdown quantities when the threshold of drawdown magnitude approaches zero. We show that such asymptotics is robust to perturbations of additional positive compound Poisson jumps. Finally, using these asymptotic results and some recent advances on the running maximum of Lévy processes, we derive the law of the duration of drawdowns for a large class of Lévy processes. We find that the law of the duration of drawdowns qualitatively depends on the path type of the spectrally negative component of the underlying Lévy process.

6.7. Proof of Lemmas and the Extended Continuity Theorem

The following result is from Kallenberg (2002, Theorem 5.22).

Theorem 6.6 (Extended continuity theorem). *Let $\mu_1, \mu_2, \ldots$ be probability measures on $\mathbb{R}^d$ with characteristic functions $\hat{\mu}_n(t) \to \varphi(t)$ pointwisely for every $t \in \mathbb{R}^d$, where the limit φ is continuous at 0. Then μ_n converges weakly to μ for some probability measure μ in $\mathbb{R}^d$ with $\hat{\mu} = \varphi$. A corresponding statement holds for the Laplace transforms of measures on $(\mathbb{R}_{\geq 0})^d$.*

Proposition 6.3. *Let $\{\mu_n\}_{n \in \mathbb{N}}$ be finite measures on $\mathbb{R}_{\geq 0}$ with Laplace transforms*

$$\hat{\mu}_n(s) = \int_{\mathbb{R}_{\geq 0}} e^{-sy} \mu_n(\mathrm{d}y),$$

for $n \in \mathbb{N}$ and $s \geq 0$. Suppose that $\lim_{n \to \infty} \hat{\mu}_n(s) = \varphi(s)$ for all $s \geq 0$, where $\varphi(\cdot)$ is a positive and continuous function on $[0, \infty)$. Then μ_n weakly converges to μ as $n \to \infty$, for some finite measure μ on $\mathbb{R}_{\geq 0}$, and $\hat{\mu} = \varphi$.

Proof. Since $\lim_{n \to \infty} \hat{\mu}_n(0) = \varphi(0) > 0$, we can consider a sequence of probability measures $\nu_n(\mathrm{d}y) := \mu_n(\mathrm{d}y) \hat{\mu}_n(0)^{-1}$. By our assumptions, it is

easy to see
$$\lim_{n\to\infty} \hat{\nu}_n(s) = \varphi(s)\varphi(0)^{-1},$$
which is a continuous function at 0. By Theorem 6.6, one concludes that $\{\nu_n\}_{n\in\mathbb{N}}$ weakly converges to some probability measure v on $\mathbb{R}_{\geq 0}$ with $\hat{v}(\cdot) = \varphi(\cdot)\varphi(0)^{-1}$. Therefore, by letting $\mu(\cdot) := v(\cdot)\varphi(0)$, we can see that μ_n weakly converges to μ as $n \to \infty$ and $\hat{\mu} = \varphi$. □

Proof of Lemma 6.3. For fixed $x > 0$ and $n \in \mathbb{N}$, let $\{s_{n,i}\}_{i=0}^n$ be a sequence of increasing partitions of the interval $[0, x]$ with $0 = s_{n,0} < s_{n,1} < \cdots < s_{n,n} = x$ and such that $\Delta_n = \max_{1 \leq i \leq n}(s_{n,i} - s_{n,i-1})$ decreases to 0 as $n \to \infty$. Using the strong Markov property of $X.$, we propose to approximate the event $\{\overline{X}_{\tau_D^+(a)} \geq x\}$ by $\bigcap_{m=1}^n \{\tau_X^+(s_{n,i}) < \tau_X^-(s_{n,i-1} - a) | X_0 = s_{n,i-1}\}$, and thus use

$$E_n := \prod_{i=1}^n \mathbb{E}_{s_{n,i-1}}(e^{-q\tau_X^+(s_{n,i})} \mathbf{1}_{\{\tau_X^+(s_{n,i}) < \tau_X^-(s_{n,i-1}-a)\}}),$$

as an approximation of $\mathbb{E}(e^{-q\tau_X^+(x)} \mathbf{1}_{\{\overline{X}_{\tau_D^+(a)} \geq x\}})$. By (6.5), we have

$$E_n = \prod_{i=1}^n \frac{W^{(q)}(a)}{W^{(q)}(a + s_{n,i} - s_{n,i-1})}$$

$$= \exp\left(\sum_{i=1}^n \log\left[1 - \frac{W^{(q)}(a + s_{n,i} - s_{n,i-1}) - W^{(q)}(a)}{W^{(q)}(a + s_{n,i} - s_{n,i-1})}\right]\right).$$

Since $W^{(q)} \in C^1(0, \infty)$ and is increasing on $(0, \infty)$, we have

$$\left(\frac{W^{(q)}(a + s_{n,i} - s_{n,i-1}) - W^{(q)}(a)}{W^{(q)}(a + s_{n,i} - s_{n,i-1})}\right)^2 \leq \left(\frac{W^{(q)}(a + \Delta_n) - W^{(q)}(a)}{W^{(q)}(a)}\right)^2$$

$$\leq K(\Delta_n)^2,$$

for all $1 \leq i \leq n$ and some constant $K > 0$. By the fact that $-\ln(1-\varepsilon) = \varepsilon + o(\varepsilon)$ for small $\varepsilon > 0$, it follows that

$$\mathbb{E}(e^{-q\tau_X^+(x)} \mathbf{1}_{\{\overline{X}_{\tau_D^+(a)} \geq x\}})$$

$$= \lim_{n\to\infty} \exp\left(\sum_{i=1}^n \log\left[1 - \frac{W^{(q)}(a + s_{n,i} - s_{n,i-1}) - W^{(q)}(a)}{W^{(q)}(a + s_{n,i} - s_{n,i-1})}\right]\right)$$

$$= \exp\left(-\lim_{n\to\infty}\sum_{i=1}^{n}\frac{W^{(q)}(a+s_{n,i}-s_{n,i-1})-W^{(q)}(a)}{W^{(q)}(a+s_{n,i}-s_{n,i-1})}\right)$$

$$= e^{-\frac{W^{(q),\prime}(a)}{W^{(q)}(a)}x},$$

which completes the proof. □

Proof of Lemma 6.4. We first consider that $s \leq \Phi(q)$, or equivalently, $q \geq \psi(s)$. For $0 \leq x \leq y$, since $\tau_X^-(0) \wedge \tau_X^+(y)$ is a.s. finite, by change of measure (6.4) and (6.6),

$$\mathbb{E}_x(e^{-q\tau_X^-(0)-s(x-X_{\tau_X^-(0)})}\mathbf{1}_{\{\tau_X^-(0)<\tau_X^+(y)\}}) = \mathbb{E}_x^s(e^{-p\tau_X^-(0)}\mathbf{1}_{\{\tau_X^-(0)<T_X^+(y)\}})$$

$$= Z_s^{(p)}(x) - Z_s^{(p)}(y)\frac{W_s^{(p)}(x)}{W_s^{(p)}(y)}.$$

It follows from (6.5) and the above equation that

$$\mathbb{E}_a(e^{-q\tau_X^-(0)-s(a-X_{\tau_X^-(0)})}|\tau_X^-(0)<\tau_X^+(a))$$

$$= \lim_{\varepsilon\downarrow 0}\mathbb{E}_a(e^{-q\tau_X^-(0)-s(a-X_{\tau_X^-(0)})}|\tau_X^-(0)<\tau_X^+(a+\varepsilon))$$

$$= \lim_{\varepsilon\downarrow 0}\left(Z_s^{(p)}(a) - Z_s^{(p)}(a+\varepsilon)\frac{W_s^{(p)}(a)}{W_s^{(p)}(a+\varepsilon)}\right)\frac{W(a+\varepsilon)}{W(a+\varepsilon)-W(a)}$$

$$= \frac{W(a)}{W'(a)}\frac{Z_s^{(p)}(a)W_s^{(p),\prime}(a)-pW_s^{(p)}(a)^2}{W_s^{(p)}(a)}. \tag{6.38}$$

The other side of the approximation

$$\lim_{\varepsilon\downarrow 0}\mathbb{E}_{a-\varepsilon}(e^{-q\tau_X^-(0)-s(a-X_{\tau_X^-(0)})}|\tau_X^-(0)<\tau_X^+(a))$$

also results in (6.38). The proof is then completed through an analytical extension of (6.15) to $s \geq 0$. □

Proof of Lemma 6.5. Since the scale function $W(\cdot)$ is supported on $(0,\infty)$, for any $k \geq 1$, we have

$$\frac{d}{dx}W^{*(k+1)}(x) = \int_{(0,x)}W'(x-y)W^{*k}(y)dy + W(0+)W^{*k}(x)$$

$$\leq \frac{x^{k-1}}{(k-1)!} W^k(x) \left(\int_{(0,x)} W'(x-y) \mathrm{d}y + W(0+) \right)$$

$$= \frac{x^{k-1}}{(k-1)!} W^{k+1}(x), \tag{6.39}$$

where the inequality above is due to Kyprianou (2006, Eq. (8.23)) and the monotonicity of $W(\cdot)$. By (6.39) and taking derivatives term by term to the well-known identity $W^{(q)}(x) = \sum_{k=0}^{\infty} q^k W^{*(k+1)}(x)$, where $W^{*k}(\cdot)$ is the kth convolution of $W(\cdot)$ with itself, we obtain

$$xW^{(q),\prime}(x) = xW'(x) + x \sum_{k=1}^{\infty} q^k \frac{\mathrm{d}}{\mathrm{d}x} W^{*(k+1)}(x)$$

$$\leq xW'(x) + qxW^2(x) \sum_{k=1}^{\infty} \frac{(qxW(x))^{k-1}}{(k-1)!}$$

$$= xW'(x) + qxW^2(x) e^{qxW(x)}.$$

In view of Assumption 6.1, the proof is complete as $x \downarrow 0$. $\square$

Proof of Lemma 6.6. Recall that ξ_1^+ is exponentially distributed with mean $1/\lambda^+$. By the strong Markov property of X. and the fact that $\{\tau_D^+(\varepsilon) < \xi_1^+\} = \{\tilde{\tau}_D^+(\varepsilon) < \xi_1^+\}$ a.s.,

$$\mathbb{E}(e^{-q\tau_D^+(\varepsilon) - sD_{\tau_D^+(\varepsilon)}})$$

$$= \mathbb{E}(e^{-q\tilde{\tau}_D^+(\varepsilon) - s\tilde{D}_{\tilde{\tau}_\varepsilon}} 1_{\{\tilde{\tau}_D^+(\varepsilon) < \xi_1^+\}})$$

$$+ \mathbb{E}(e^{-q\tau_D^+(\varepsilon) - sD_{\tau_D^+(\varepsilon)}} 1_{\{\tau_D^+(\varepsilon) > \xi_1^+, J_1^+ \geq D_{\xi_1^+ -}\}})$$

$$+ \mathbb{E}(e^{-q\tau_\varepsilon - sD_{\tau_D^+(\varepsilon)}} 1_{\{\tau_D^+(\varepsilon) > \xi_1^+, J_1^+ < D_{\xi_1^+ -}\}})$$

$$= \mathbb{E}(e^{-(q+\lambda^+)\tilde{\tau}_\varepsilon - s\tilde{D}_{\tilde{\tau}_D^+(\varepsilon)}}) + \mathbb{E}(e^{-q\xi_1^+} 1_{\{\tilde{\tau}_D^+(\varepsilon) > \xi_1^+, J_1^+ \geq \tilde{D}_{\xi_1^+ -}\}})$$

$$\times \mathbb{E}(e^{-q\tau_D^+(\varepsilon) - sD_{\tau_D^+(\varepsilon)}}) + \mathbb{E}(e^{-q\tau_D^+(\varepsilon) - sD_{\tau_D^+(\varepsilon)}} 1_{\{\tau_\varepsilon > \xi_1^+, J_1^+ < D_{\xi_1^+ -}\}}),$$

Solving for $\mathbb{E}(e^{-q\tau_D^+(\varepsilon)-sD_{\tau_D^+(\varepsilon)}})$, one obtains

$$\mathbb{E}(e^{-q\tau_D^+(\varepsilon)-sD_{\tau_D^+(\varepsilon)}})$$
$$= \frac{\mathbb{E}(e^{-(q+\lambda^+)\widetilde{\tau}_\varepsilon - s\widetilde{D}_{\widetilde{\tau}_D^+(\varepsilon)}}) + \mathbb{E}(e^{-q\tau_\varepsilon - sD_{\tau_D^+(\varepsilon)}} \mathbf{1}_{\{\tau_D^+(\varepsilon) > \xi_1^+, J_1^+ < D_{\xi_1^+ -}\}})}{1 - \mathbb{E}(e^{-q\xi_1^+} \mathbf{1}_{\{\widetilde{\tau}_\varepsilon > \xi_1^+, J_1^+ \geq \widetilde{D}_{\xi_1^+ -}\}})}.$$
(6.40)

For the denominator on the right-hand side of (6.40), we notice that

$$\mathbb{E}(e^{-q\xi_1^+} \mathbf{1}_{\{\widetilde{\tau}_D^+(\varepsilon) > \xi_1^+, J_1^+ \geq \widetilde{D}_{\xi_1^+ -}\}})$$
$$= \mathbb{E}(e^{-q\xi_1^+}) - \mathbb{E}(e^{-q\xi_1^+} \mathbf{1}_{\{\widetilde{\tau}_D^+(\varepsilon) < \xi_1^+\}}) - \mathbb{E}(e^{-q\xi_1^+} \mathbf{1}_{\{\widetilde{\tau}_D^+(\varepsilon) > \xi_1^+, J_1^+ < \widetilde{D}_{\xi_1^+ -}\}})$$
$$= \lambda^+ (1 - \mathbb{E}(e^{-(q+\lambda^+)\widetilde{\tau}_D^+(\varepsilon)})) - \mathbb{E}(e^{-q\xi_1^+} \mathbf{1}_{\{\widetilde{\tau}_D^+(\varepsilon) > \xi_1^+, J_1^+ < \widetilde{D}_{\xi_1^+ -}\}}) / (q + \lambda^+).$$

The proof of Lemma 6.6 is completed by substituting the above into (6.40). □

Part II
Applications of Drawdown

Chapter 7

Maximum Drawdown Insurance Using Options

In this chapter, we introduce two novel financial products which protect the holder against an asset's price drawing down by a fixed amount by expiry or before it draws up by the same amount. Both claims are issued with a fixed positive strike K and a fixed finite maturity date T. In order to specify their payoff, we let S_t denote the spot price of some asset or portfolio which can be monitored continuously over the fixed time interval $[0,T]$. Let $\overline{S}_t = \sup_{s \in [0,t]} S_s$ and $\underline{S}_t = \inf_{s \in [0,t]} S_s$ be the continuously monitored maximum and minimum of this asset price over $[0,t]$, respectively. Let $D_t = \overline{S}_t - S_t$ be the level of the drawdown process at time $t \in [0,T]$. Similarly, let $U_t = S_t - \underline{S}_t$ be the level of the drawup process at time $t \in [0,T]$. For a fixed $K > 0$, let $\tau_D^+(K)$ and $\tau_U^+(K)$ be the time at which the drawdown process $D.$ and the drawup process $U.$ first reaches K, respectively. The maximum drawdown of an asset or portfolio over a period $[0,T]$ is denoted by $\overline{D}_T = \sup_{t \in [0,T]} D_t$.

The payoff at T of the first claim is $\mathbf{1}_{\{\overline{D}_T \geq K\}}$ for some strike $K > 0$ and that of the second claim is $\mathbf{1}_{\{\tau_D^+(K) \leq \tau_U^+(K) \wedge T\}}$. The premium for both digital calls is analogous to insurance premium. Although insurance on maximum drawdown is not presently underwritten, recent events suggest an interest in synthesizing this insurance. In this chapter, we present model-free static hedges of the second claim using one-touch knockouts, which are a type of double barrier options. Then under symmetry and continuity assumptions, we also derive semi-static hedges of both claims using one-touch knockouts, single barrier one-touches and digital options. The symmetry and continuity assumptions used are separately developed first under arithmetic models and subsequently under geometric and pure jump models. In geometric models, the payoff of the two options introduced is associated with the relative drawdown, maximum drawdown and drawup, which are respectively defined as $D_t^r := \overline{S}_t/S_t$, $\overline{D}_T^r := \sup_{t \in [0,T]} D_t^r$ and $U_t^r := S_t/\underline{S}_t$. Throughout our work, we assume no frictions and no arbitrage.

Since its introduction to finance, the maximum drawdown has been commonly used as a measure of risk of holding an asset over a pre-specified period $[0,T]$. Consequently, a risk averse investor who is concerned that this risk measure realizes to a value larger than expected would presumably be interested in being compensated for large realizations of maximum drawdown. Moreover, the maximum drawdown provides a means to evaluate the risk of holding a hedge fund. An asset manager who knows in advance that her portfolio risk is being evaluated wholly or in part by the portfolio's maximum drawdown is exposed to large realizations of maximum drawdown. In particular, it is not uncommon for managers who experience large maximum drawdowns to see their funds under management rapidly diminish. Since performance fees are typically proportional to funds under management, these fees would diminish accordingly. By purchasing a digital call before any such maximum drawdown is realized, a portfolio manager can insure against the loss of income.

The premium for this digital call can be cheapened if the payoff is lessened. One way to do this is to further introduce dependence of the terminal payoff on the time it takes maximum drawup to reach a level. If the investor holding the digital call is also long the underlying asset, then it seems reasonable that the investor would be willing to give up some of the payoff if a drawup occurs first, in return for reduced premium. Since $\mathbf{1}_{\{\tau_D^+(K) \leq T\}} = \mathbf{1}_{\{\overline{D}_T \geq K\}}$, we have

$$\mathbf{1}_{\{\tau_D^+(K) < \tau_U^+(K) \wedge T\}} = \mathbf{1}_{\{\overline{D}_T \geq K\}} - \mathbf{1}_{\{\tau_U^+(K) < \tau_D^+(K) \leq T\}}.$$

Consider a claim that pays $\mathbf{1}_{\{\tau_D^+(K) < \tau_U^+(K) \wedge T\}}$ dollars at T. In words, the claim pays one dollar at its expiry date T if and only if a drawdown of size K precedes the earlier of a drawup of the same size and the expiry. For brevity, we refer to this claim as a digital call on a K-drawdown preceding a K-drawup. Such a payoff would be of interest to anyone who is more concerned about the downside than the upside, or at least more so than the market is. The payoff from the digital call on the K-drawdown preceding a K-drawup will be smaller than the payoff from a co-terminal digital call on maximum drawdown with strike K because of the possibility that a K-drawup precedes a K-drawdown.

A financial intermediary who provides a digital call on maximum drawdown or K-drawdown preceding a K-drawup to clients, is typically faced with the problem of hedging the exposure and marking the position after the sale. If there exists a hedging strategy which perfectly replicates the payoff of such a digital call under a set of reasonable assumptions, then the mark-to-market value of this replicating portfolio can be used to mark the position of this digital call. A hedging strategy which achieves a perfect replication with the least possible time instances in which trading is involved is undoubtedly more robust than a dynamic hedging strategy which involves continuous trading. Such a replication is also known as static and was introduced in Breeden and Litzenberger (1978). A static replication hedging strategy which involves trading in fairly liquid instruments is a very powerful tool for hedging. An example of such an instrument is a one-touch knockout which is a type of a double barrier option liquidly traded in FX markets.

Although static hedging is not a new concept, the use of double barrier options as hedge instruments in this chapter is one of its main innovations. In particular, in this chapter, we show that there exists a robust static hedge of a digital call on the K-drawdown preceding a K-drawup. The hedge uses positions in one-touch knockouts. We then develop simple sufficient conditions on the underlying asset price dynamics which allow semi-robust replicating strategies to hedge a digital call on maximum drawdown with one-touch knockouts. One-touch knockouts do trade liquidly in the over-the-counter (OTC) currency options market. Our strategy replicates perfectly under a symmetry condition, provided that the running maximum increases only continuously.[1]

One-touch knockouts are not necessarily available for all currency pairs, thus hedging and marking requires the development of additional simple sufficient conditions on the underlying dynamics which allow alternative replicating strategies. In particular, if we enforce symmetry condition and additionally assume the running minimum decreases continuously, then we can develop replicating strategies that use only single barrier one-touches, or even path-independent options. Note that for all above strategies, hedging requires only occasional trading, typically only when maxima or minima change. As path-independent options are not necessarily available for all

---

[1] In general, continuity can be relaxed to skip-free if the state space is discrete. In particular, Section 7.9, we will prove equivalent results when the underlying is a purely jump process with fixed jump size.

currency pairs, one can always impose further dynamical restrictions and resort to classical dynamic hedging. Whenever a model allows the payoff of path-independent options to be dynamically replicated with the underlying asset, it can be used in conjunction with our results to replicate the payoff of calls on maximum drawdown with the same instruments.

The rest of this chapter is structured as follows. In Section 7.1, we formulate the two digital options on drawdowns and introduce all replicating instruments that will be used. In Section 7.2, we develop a model-free static replication of a digital call on the K-drawdown preceding a K-drawup using one-touch knockouts. In Section 7.3, we impose an assumption of continuity and arithmetic symmetry to develop a semi-static replication of a digital call on maximum drawdown with one-touch knockouts. In Section 7.4, we reinforce the arithmetic symmetry assumption in order to develop a semi-static portfolio of one-touches to replicate the payoffs of both target digital calls. While in Section 7.5, we present a semi-static portfolio of binary options on the underlying to replicate the target payoffs under another symmetry assumption. In Sections 7.6 through 7.8, we revisit the replication problems in previous sections under appropriate geometric symmetry assumptions. In Section 7.9, we discuss on how to extend previous results to certain stochastic processes with discrete state space. Finally, we summarize the chapter with some closing remarks in Section 7.10. In Section 7.11, we prove that geometric Brownian motion (GBM) satisfies all assumptions used in Sections 7.7 and 7.8.

7.1. Setup and Replicating Instruments

Suppose that we have some fixed well-defined target payoff of a contingent claim in mind. Although super-replicating strategies are worthy of attention, in this chapter we focus on exact replicating strategies. Hence, we consider a trading strategy in other assets which is replicating, non-anticipating, and self-financing. Such a trading strategy is said to be *robust* if these three properties all hold irrespective of the dynamics of all assets in the economy. The only assumption made is that the market price of all our holdings at expiry is equal to their intrinsic value.

Let $B_t(T)$ be the price of a default-free zero coupon bond paying one dollar with certainty at T. We assume that $B_t(T) > 0$ for all $t \in [0, T]$ and hence no arbitrage implies the existence of a probability measure $\mathbb{Q}^T$ associated with this numéraire. The measure $\mathbb{Q}^T$ is equivalent to the statistical probability measure and hence is usually referred to as an equivalent martingale measure. Under $\mathbb{Q}^T$, the ratios of non-dividend paying asset prices to $\mathrm{B}_t(T)$ are martingales. We will use $\mathbb{Q}^T$ to describe the arbitrage-free values of options in this chapter. The conditional form of this measure on the σ-algebra $\mathcal{F}_t = \sigma\{S_s; s \leq t\}$ generated by the underlying S_t will be denoted by $\mathbb{Q}_t^T$.

Let us denote by $\mathrm{DC}_t^{\overline{D}}(K,T)$ the value at time $t \in [0,T]$ of a digital call on maximum drawdown, and by $\mathrm{DC}_t^{D<U}(K,T)$ the value at time $t \in [0,T]$ of a digital call on the K-drawdown preceding a K-drawup. Their arbitrage-free prices are

$$\mathrm{DC}_t^{\overline{D}}(K,T) := \mathrm{B}_t(T)\mathbb{Q}_t^T(\overline{D}_T \geq K), \tag{7.1}$$

$$\mathrm{DC}_t^{D<U}(K,T) := \mathrm{B}_t(T)\mathbb{Q}_t^T(\tau_D^+(K) \leq \tau_U^+(K) \wedge T). \tag{7.2}$$

In this section, our hedging instruments will be bonds, one-touch knockouts and their spreads.

Before describing the payoff of one-touch knockouts, it will be helpful to introduce terminology that indicates exactly where the spot price is when a barrier option knocks in or knocks out. For fixed barriers $L < S_0 < H$, let $\tau_S^-(L)$ and $\tau_S^+(H)$ be the first passage time of the spot price process S. to the barriers L and H, respectively. That is,[2]

$$\tau_S^-(L) = \inf\{t > 0 : S_t \leq L\},$$

$$\tau_S^+(H) = \inf\{t > 0 : S_t \geq H\}.$$

As usual, we denote $\inf \emptyset = \infty$. Recall that $\underline{S}_t$ is the continuously monitored running minimum of this asset price over $[0,t]$. The payoff $\mathbf{1}_{\{\tau_S^-(K)\leq T\}}$ is the same as the payoff $\mathbf{1}_{\{\underline{S}_T \leq L\}}$. A lower barrier L is said to be skip-free, when it holds that

$$S_{\tau_S^-(L)} = L. \tag{7.3}$$

When we instead have $S_{\tau_S^-(L)} < L$, we say that a barrier has been crossed. While when we have $S_{\tau_S^-(L)} \leq L$, we say that the barrier L has been hit. When we have both $S_{\tau_S^-(L)} = L$ and $\underline{S}_T = L$, we say that the barrier L has been grazed. A one-touch knockout is issued with an in-barrier V, an out-barrier W, and a fixed maturity date T. We assume that the spot

---
[2] Notice that the definition of the first passage time here is slightly different from that in other chapters. This new definition makes it more convenient to implement replication strategies. Moreover, for regular processes such as diffusions, this new definition is actually equivalent to the usual definition we used in other chapters.

stays in between V and W when the one-touch knockout is issued. For concreteness, we will focus on the case in which the out-barrier W is the higher barrier. To describe the payoff of a one-touch knockout formally, let $\tau_S^-(V)$ and $\tau_S^+(W)$ be the first passage times of the spot process S. to V and W respectively. The arbitrage-free value of a one-touch knockout is

$$\text{OTKO}_t(V, W, T) := B_t(T) \mathbb{Q}_t^T (\tau_S^-(V) \leq \tau_S^+(W) \wedge T)$$
$$= B_t(T) \mathbb{Q}_t^T (\tau_S^-(V) \leq T, \overline{S}_{\tau_S^-(V)} < W). \quad (7.4)$$

In words, the one-touch knockout pays one dollar at its maturity date T if and only if the spot price S. hits the in-barrier V before hitting the out-barrier W and this first hitting time to V occurs before the expiry T. Notice that the one-touch knockout also pays one dollar at T if $\tau_S^-(V) \leq \tau_S^+(W) \leq T$. In words, the out-barrier W is extinguished when the in-barrier V is first hit.

Sometimes it is convenient to modify the knockout condition of a one-touch knockout. For example, we consider the following payoff:

$$\text{OTKO}_t(V, W+, T) := B_t(T) \mathbb{Q}_t^T (\tau_S^-(V) \leq T, \overline{S}_{\tau_S^-(V)} \leq W). \quad (7.5)$$

This claim pays out one dollar at expiry if and only if the spot price S. hits the in-barrier V before crossing the out-barrier W and this first hitting time to V occurs before the expiry T.

The last claim which we want to make use of is a sequential double-touch whose payoff is the result of differentiating the payoff of a one-touch knockout in (7.4) with respect to its higher out-barrier W. This claim has a positive payoff if and only if the underlying spot price first touches W and then hits V from above before maturity. We accordingly refer to this claim as a ricochet-upper-first down-and-in:

$$\text{RUFDI}_t(V, W, T) = \lim_{\epsilon \downarrow 0} \frac{\text{OTKO}_t(V, W + \epsilon, T) - \text{OTKO}_t(V, W, T)}{\epsilon}$$
$$= B_t(T) \mathbb{E}_t^{\mathbb{Q}^T} \left(\mathbf{1}_{\{\tau_S(V) \leq T\}} \delta(\overline{S}_{\tau_S(V)} - W) \right). \quad (7.6)$$

Notice that a ricochet-upper-first down-and-in is itself a spread of two one-touch knockouts with slightly different upper out-barriers and identical lower in-barriers set at V.

A one-touch is an option that pays \$1 at its expiry T if and only if a pre-specified threshold has been reached or crossed by the expiry. In particular, the time-t price of a one-touch with barrier B and expiry T is given by

$$\text{OT}_t(B,T) := \begin{cases} B_t(T)\mathbb{Q}_t^T(\tau_S^-(B) \leq T) = B_t(T)\mathbb{Q}_t^T(\underline{S}_T \leq B), & B < S_0, \\ B_t(T)\mathbb{Q}_t^T(\tau_S^+(B) \leq T) = B_t(T)\mathbb{Q}_t^T(\overline{S}_T \geq B), & B > S_0. \end{cases}$$

Let $B \in \mathbb{R}$ be the strike of a digital option on the underlying with expiry T. For $t \in [0, T]$, let $\text{DP}_t(B, T)$ and $\text{DC}_t(B, T)$ denote the prices at time t of a digital put and a digital call on spot, respectively. We define

$$\text{DP}_t(B, T) := B_t(T)\mathbb{Q}_t^T(S_T < B), \tag{7.7}$$

$$\text{DC}_t(B, T) := B_t(T)\mathbb{Q}_t^T(S_T > B). \tag{7.8}$$

Unless in Section 7.9, we assume that, at any time $t \in [0, T]$, each of the random variables $\overline{S}_T$, $\underline{S}_T$, and S_T has a continuous conditional density over $(\overline{S}_t, \infty)$, $(-\infty, \underline{S}_t)$ and $\mathbb{R}$, respectively. So the partial derivatives $\frac{\partial}{\partial B}\text{OT}_t(B, T)$, $\frac{\partial}{\partial B}\text{DP}_t(B, T)$, and $\frac{\partial}{\partial B}\text{DC}_t(B, T)$ are well-defined.

7.2. Static Hedging of the K-drawdown Preceding a K-drawup with One-Touch Knockouts

In what follows, we focus on the payoffs from a digital call written on the K-drawdown preceding a K-drawup. We present a trading strategy in other assets which is replicating, non-anticipating, and self-financing.

Theorem 7.1 (Robust replication: I). *Under frictionless markets, no arbitrage implies that the digital call on the K-drawdown preceding a K-drawup can be valued relative to the prices of bonds, one-touch knockouts and their spreads:*

$$\text{DC}_t^{D<U}(K, T)$$
$$= \text{OTKO}_t(\overline{S}_t - K, \overline{S}_t+, T) + \int_{(\overline{S}_t, \underline{S}_t + K)} \text{RUFDI}_t(H - K, H, T) dH \tag{7.9}$$

for any $t \in [0, \tau_D^+(K) \wedge \tau_U^+(K) \wedge T]$ and $K > 0$.

Proof. Suppose that a digital call on the K-drawdown preceding a K-drawup has been sold at time 0. In order to develop a static hedge, we condition on being at some time t before expiry and before a drawdown or drawup of size K is realized:

$$t \in [0, \tau_D^+(K) \wedge \tau_U^+(K) \wedge T).$$

Then the maximum-to-date $\overline{S}_t$ and the minimum-to-date $\underline{S}_t$ are both known constants that bracket the current spot S_t. The fact that neither a drawdown nor a drawup of size K has yet occurred implies that $\overline{S}_t - \underline{S}_t < K$. As a result, we have

$$\overline{S}_t - K < \underline{S}_t \leq S_t \leq \overline{S}_t < \underline{S}_t + K.$$

Let us focus on the running maximum at time $\tau_D^+(K)$. Since the running maximum is an increasing process, we must have

$$\{\tau_D^+(K) \leq \tau_U^+(K) \wedge T\} = \{\tau_D^+(K) \leq \tau_U^+(K) \wedge T, \overline{S}_{\tau_D^+(K)} \geq \overline{S}_t\}$$
$$= \{\tau_D^+(K) \leq \tau_U^+(K) \wedge T, \overline{S}_{\tau_D^+(K)} \in [\overline{S}_t, \underline{S}_t + K)\}.$$

This is because, if $\overline{S}_{\tau_D^+(K)} = M$ for some $M \geq \underline{S}_t + K$, then either $\tau_S^+(M) < t$ and hence $\tau_D^+(K) \wedge \tau_U^+(K) \leq t$, or else $\tau_S^+(M) \in [t, \tau_D^+(K))$ in which case $\tau_U^+(K) \leq \tau_D^+(K)$. Moreover, by restricting $\overline{S}_{\tau_D^+(K)}$ to the interval $[\overline{S}_t, \underline{S}_t + K)$, we cannot have a K-drawup precedes a K-drawdown, since if $\tau_U^+(K) \leq \tau_D^+(K) \leq T$, then $\overline{S}_{\tau_D^+(K)} > \underline{S}_t + K$. So we can further obtain that

$$\{\tau_D^+(K) \leq \tau_U^+(K) \wedge T\} = \{\tau_D^+(K) \leq \tau_U^+(K) \wedge T, \overline{S}_{\tau_D^+(K)} \in [\overline{S}_t, \underline{S}_t + K)\}$$
$$= \{\tau_D^+(K) \leq T, \overline{S}_{\tau_D^+(K)} \in [\overline{S}_t, \underline{S}_t + K)\}.$$

We now present a key result that allows the digital call to be replicated with one-touch knockouts. Observe that if and when the unit payoff of the digital call is realized, the stock price has to be visiting a new low level:

$$\{\tau_D^+(K) \leq \tau_U^+(K) \wedge T\} = \{\tau_D^+(K) \leq T, \overline{S}_{\tau_D^+(K)} \in [\overline{S}_t, \underline{S}_t + K)\}$$
$$= \{\tau_D^+(K) \leq T, \tau_D^+(K) = \tau_S^-(\overline{S}_{\tau_D^+(K)} - K), \quad (7.10)$$

for any $\overline{S}_{\tau_D^+(K)} \in [\overline{S}_t, \underline{S}_t + K)\}$. The same idea has been used in Chapter 2 to prove Proposition 2.1 and Theorem 2.3.

As a consequence of (7.10), the payoff of a digital call has the following representation:

$$\mathbf{1}_{\{\tau_D^+(K) \leq \tau_U^+(K) \wedge T\}}$$

$$= \mathbf{1}_{\{\tau_D^+(K) \leq T, \tau_D^+(K) = \tau_S^-(\overline{S}_{\tau_D^+(K)} - K), \overline{S}_{\tau_D^+(K)} = \overline{S}_t\}}$$

$$+ \int_{(\overline{S}_t, \underline{S}_t + K)} \mathbf{1}_{\{\tau_D^+(K) \leq T, \tau_D^+(K) = \tau_S^-(H-K)\}} \delta(\overline{S}_{\tau_D^+(K)} - H) \, \mathrm{d}H$$

$$= \mathbf{1}_{\{\tau_S^-(\overline{S}_t - K) \leq T, \overline{S}_{\tau_S^-(\overline{S}_t - K)} = \overline{S}_t\}} + I,$$

where

$$I := \int_{(\overline{S}_t, \underline{S}_t + K)} \mathbf{1}_{\{\tau_S^-(H-K) \leq T\}} \delta(\overline{S}_{\tau_S^-(H-K)} - H) \, \mathrm{d}H.$$

Under no arbitrage assumption, taking expectations of (7.11) under $\mathbb{Q}_t^T$ implies that

$$\mathrm{DC}_t^{D<U}(K,T)$$
$$= \mathrm{OTKO}_t(\overline{S}_t - K, \overline{S}_t+, T) + \int_{(\overline{S}_t, \underline{S}_t + K)} \mathrm{RUFDI}_t(H - K, H, T) \, \mathrm{d}H,$$

for all $t \in [0, \tau_D^+(K) \wedge \tau_U^+(K) \wedge T)$.

If and when $\tau_D^+(K) \wedge \tau_U^+(K) < T$, then at that time, we do not hold any spreads of one-touch knockouts, the one-touch knockout in the portfolio either knocks into a bond if $\tau_D^+(K) \leq \tau_U^+(K)$, or knocks out if $\tau_D^+(K) \geq \tau_U^+(K)$. As a consequence, the digital call can be valued at any $t \in [0,T]$. □

We have shown a robust hedge of the digital call on K-drawdown preceding a K-drawup. This hedge portfolio in Theorem 7.1 can be set up with one-touch knockouts and their spreads, which do trade liquidly in the OTC currency option market. However, to obtain a replicating portfolio of the digital call on maximum drawdown with tradable assets, we need to place structures on the spot price process. We proceed to develop this in the next section.

7.3. Semi-static Hedging of the Maximum Drawdown with One-Touch Knockouts

In this section, we place structures on $S.$, the stochastic process governing the spot price of the underlying asset. In particular, we assume that the running maximum can only increase continuously whenever $\overline{D}_t < K$. Of course, this condition is already met if the process is continuous or only has negative jumps. We also impose a symmetry condition on the process between the first time that a new maximum $\overline{S}_t$ is established and the first exit time of the corridor $(\overline{S}_t - K, \overline{S}_t + K)$. To be more specific, recall that $\tau_S^{\pm}(B)$ denotes the first passage time of the spot price process S. to a upper/lower barrier B. Then $\tau_S^{+}(M+K) \wedge \tau_S^{-}(M-K)$ is the first exit time of a corridor centered at M with lower barrier $M - K$ and higher barrier $M + K$. Then whenever $\overline{S}_t$ increases and $\overline{D}_t < K$, we assume that

$$d\mathbb{Q}_t^T (\tau_S^{-}(\overline{S}_t - K) \wedge \tau_S^{+}(\overline{S}_t + K) \leq T) = 0. \tag{7.11}$$

In words, the risk-neutral probability of exiting before T does not change when moving the barriers along with the running maximum. This condition is met by standard Brownian motion. It is also met by the Ocone martingales (see, e.g., Ocone (1993)).

We will need to impose both of our assumptions in order to replicate a digital call on maximum drawdown using just bonds and one-touch knockouts. The set of stochastic processes that satisfy both assumptions is said to satisfy the following.

Assumption 7.1. *While $\overline{D}_t < K$, the running maximum is continuous. Moreover, let d_M be the differential operator for variable M. Then it holds that*

$$d_M|_{M=\overline{S}_t} \mathbb{Q}_t^T (\tau_S^{-}(M-K) \wedge \tau_S^{+}(M+K) \leq T) = 0,$$

for any t such that $d\overline{S}_t \neq 0$ and $t < \tau_D^{+}(K)$. Here, d_M is the differential operator in variable M.

Suppose that we attempt to replicate the payoff of a digital call on maximum drawdown. At time t when $\overline{D}_t \geq K$, i.e., $t \geq \tau_D^{+}(K)$, we simply hold a bond; but while $\overline{D}_t < K$, we attempt a semi-dynamic strategy by holding a one-touch option with a lower barrier $\overline{S}_t - K$, and rolling up the barrier whenever the running maximum $\overline{S}_t$ increases. No other instruments are held. While this strategy is replicating, it is not yet self-financing as it costs money to move up the lower barrier of a one-touch closer to the spot price. To finance this rollup until $\tau_D^{+}(K) \wedge T$, we assume that Assumption 7.1 holds, i.e., we rely on the continuity of the running maximum and the exit symmetry assumed present when the maximum ticks up. For any $t \in [0, \tau_D^{+}(K) \wedge T)$, suppose that we also hold a one-touch with a barrier set at K dollars above the maximum-to-date. While this augmentation may help finance the rollup of the lower barrier one-touch being held, it no longer replicates the desired payoff, since a path that first experienced a K-drawdown at $\tau_D^{+}(K) < T$ and then hits $\overline{S}_{\tau_D^{+}(K)} + K$ by the expiry T

will trigger payoffs from both one-touches. For $t \in [0, \tau_D^+(K) \wedge T)$, suppose we further alter the strategy by imposing a knockout barrier at the lower level $\overline{S}_t - K$ on the one-touch struck at $\overline{S}_t + K$, and a knockout barrier at the higher level $\overline{S}_t + K$ on the one-touch struck at $\overline{S}_t - K$. Then we are using two one-touch knockouts. It is easily seen that, when the underlying satisfies Assumption 7.1, the latest strategy self-finances and replicates the payoff of a digital call on maximum drawdown. In particular, we have the following theorem.

Theorem 7.2. *Under frictionless markets and Assumption 7.1, no arbitrage implies that the digital call on maximum drawdown can be valued relative to the prices of bonds and one-touch knockouts as*

$$\mathrm{DC}_t^{\overline{D}}(K,T) = \mathrm{OTKO}_t(\overline{S}_t - K, \overline{S}_t + K, T) + \mathrm{OTKO}_t(\overline{S}_t + K, \overline{S}_t - K, T),$$

for $t \in [0, \tau_D^+(K) \wedge T]$ and $K > 0$.

Remark 7.1. If we model $S.$ by a standard Brownian motion starting from 0, then it is well-known that the law of the maximum drawdown $\overline{D}_T$ is identical with the law of $\sup_{t \in [0,T]} |S_t|$. Hence, the probability of the event that $\overline{D}_T \geq K$ is the same as the probability of the event $\{\overline{S}_T \geq K\} \cup \{\underline{S}_T \leq -K\}$, which provides a probabilistic view of the result in Theorem 7.2.

7.4. Semi-static Replication with One-Touches

In the last two sections, we derived static and semi-static hedges of the target digital calls with one-touch knockouts and their spreads. Since one-touch knockouts are relatively illiquid at present, this section presents an alternative semi-static hedge which just uses single-barrier one-touches under symmetry and continuity assumptions.

Suppose that the spot starts inside the corridor between V and W, where V and W are the in-barrier and out-barrier of a one-touch knockout respectively. Let τ be the first exit time of the above corridor, then we impose the following assumption.

Assumption 7.2. *The spot $S.$ cannot exit the corridor between V and W by a jump. If the first exit time $\tau \leq T$, then we have*

$$\mathbb{Q}_\tau^T(\underline{S}_T \leq S_\tau - \Delta) = \mathbb{Q}_\tau^T(\overline{S}_T \geq S_\tau + \Delta), \tag{7.12}$$

for any $\Delta > 0$.

Under the above assumption, we demonstrate that the payoff of a one-touch knockout with in-barrier V and out-barrier W can be semi-statically replicated by a portfolio of one-touches.

Proposition 7.1. *Under frictionless markets and Assumption 7.2, no arbitrage implies that for any $t \in [0, \tau \wedge T]$ with τ being the first exit time to leave the corridor between W and V,*

$$\mathrm{OTKO}_t(V, W, T) = \mathrm{OT}_t(V, T) + \sum_{n=1}^{\infty} [\mathrm{OT}_t(V - 2n\Delta, T) - \mathrm{OT}_t(V + 2n\Delta, T)], \tag{7.13}$$

where $\Delta = |W - V|$. Here we assume that the above infinite sum is absolute convergent.

Proof. Suppose a one-touch knockout with in-barrier V and out-barrier W has been sold at time 0. In order to hedge this position, an investor takes a long position on a series of one-touches with barriers at V, $V - 2\Delta$, $V - 4\Delta, \ldots$ and also takes a short position on a series of one-touches with barriers at $V + 2\Delta$, $V + 4\Delta, \ldots$. If neither barrier is hit by T, then all one-touches expire worthless. If barrier V is hit first, i.e., $S_\tau = V$ then at τ, the one-touch with barrier V becomes a bond, while Assumption 7.2 implies that all of the other one-touches can be costlessly liquidated. The reason is that for each $n = 1, 2, \ldots$, the long position in the one-touch with barrier $V - 2n\Delta$ is canceled by the short position in the one-touch with barrier $V + 2n\Delta$ (see the upper panel of Figure 7.1). On the other hand, if barrier W is hit first, i.e., $S_\tau = W$, then at τ, Assumption 7.2 implies that all of the one-touches can be costlessly liquidated. The reason is that since $V = W - \Delta$, the portfolio can also be considered as long a series of one-touches with barriers at $W - \Delta$, $W - 3\Delta$, $W - 5\Delta, \ldots$, while also being short a series of one-touches with barriers at $W + \Delta$, $W + 3\Delta$, $W + 5\Delta \ldots$ (see the lower panel of Figure 7.1). Hence, for each $n = 1, 2, \ldots$, the long position in the one-touch with barrier $W - (2n - 1)\Delta$ is canceled by the short position in the one-touch with barrier $W + (2n - 1)\Delta$. Since the value of the one-touch portfolio matches the payoff of the one-touch knockout when (S_t, t) exits $(V \wedge W, V \vee W) \times [0, T]$, no arbitrage forces the values prior to exit to be the same. □

Recall that Theorem 7.1 stated that the payoff of a digital call on the K-drawdown preceding a K-drawup can be statically replicated by one-touch knockouts, and Theorem 7.2 stated that under

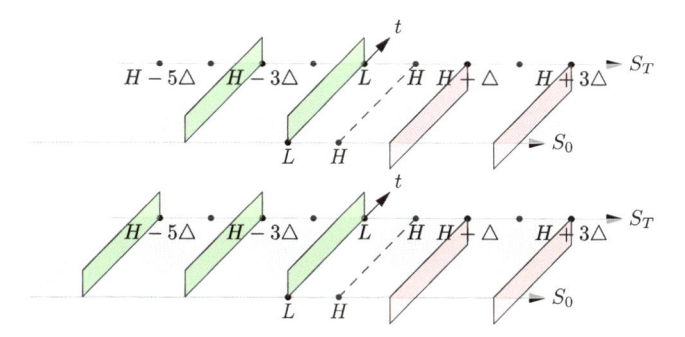

Fig. 7.1. Replication with single barrier one-touches. Long positions are illustrated in green and short positions are illustrated in red. The case that $S_\tau = H$ is depicted in the top penal, where long positions cancel short positions. The case that $S_\tau = L$ is depicted in the bottom penal, where the one-touch struck at L is turned into a bond, and the remaining positions are canceled.

Assumption 7.1, the payoff of a digital call on maximum drawdown can be dynamically replicated by rolling up the barriers of one-touch knockouts. If Assumption 7.2 holds for all barriers of one-touch knockouts being held, then the target digital calls can be replicated just by rolling up the barriers of a portfolio of single barrier one-touches.

In Sections 7.4.1 and 7.4.2, we will separately develop portfolios of one-touches which can be used to replicate the payoff of a digital call on maximum drawdown and the payoff of a digital call on the K-drawdown preceding a K-drawup, respectively.

7.4.1. Hedging the maximum drawdown

In this subsection, we develop a semi-static replication of a digital call on maximum drawdown using one-touches. By Theorem 7.2 and Proposition 7.1, we just need to ensure that Assumption 7.2 holds for all barriers of one-touch knockouts being held. For this purpose, we impose structure on the spot price process.

Assumption 7.3. *While $\overline{D}_t < K$, the running maximum is continuous, and the drawdown cannot jump up by more than $K - D_t$. Moreover, at $t = \tau_D^+(K) \leq T$ or any time t such that $\mathrm{d}\overline{S}_t \neq 0$ and $t < \tau_D^+(K)$, the time-t risk-neutral probability of hitting $\overline{S}_t - \Delta$ before T is the same as the time-t risk-neutral probability of hitting $\overline{S}_t + \Delta$ before T, for any $\Delta > 0$.*

Remark 7.2. Using Proposition 7.1, it can be seen that Assumption 7.3 implies Assumption 7.1. Indeed, under Assumption 7.3, at times t such that

$\mathrm{d}\overline{S}_t \neq 0$, $M = \overline{S}_t$ and $t < \tau_D^+(K)$, evaluating (7.13) at $V = M \mp K$ and $W = M \pm K$ and taking differential with respect to M, we obtain

$$\mathrm{d}_M \mathrm{OTKO}_t(M \mp K, M \pm K, T)$$
$$= \mathrm{OT}'_t(M \mp K, T)\mathrm{d}M$$
$$+ \sum_{n=1}^{\infty} [\mathrm{OT}'_t(M \mp (4n+1)K, T) - \mathrm{OT}'_t(M \pm (4n-1)K, T)]\mathrm{d}M,$$
(7.14)

where $\mathrm{OT}'_t(B, T) = \frac{\partial}{\partial B}\mathrm{OT}_t(B, T)$. On the other hand, Assumption 7.3 indicates that

$$\mathrm{OT}_t(M - \Delta, T) = \mathrm{OT}_t(M + \Delta, T), \quad \forall \Delta > 0.$$

By taking derivative with respect to Δ in the above, we have $\mathrm{OT}'_t(M - \Delta, T) + \mathrm{OT}'_t(M + \Delta, T) = 0$. It follows from (7.14) that

$$0 = \mathrm{d}_M|_{M=\overline{S}_t}[\mathrm{OTKO}_t(\overline{S}_t - K, \overline{S}_t + K, T) + \mathrm{OTKO}_t(\overline{S}_t + K, \overline{S}_t - K, T)]$$
$$= \mathrm{B}_t(T) \cdot \mathrm{d}_M|_{M=\overline{S}_t} \mathbb{Q}_t^T(\tau_S^-(M - K) \wedge \tau_S^+(M + K) \leq T).$$

As a result, we have the following theorem.

Theorem 7.3. *Under frictionless markets and Assumption 7.3, no arbitrage implies that the digital call on maximum drawdown can be valued relative to the prices of bonds and one-touches as*

$$\mathrm{DC}_t^{\overline{D}}(K, T) = \sum_{n=0}^{\infty} (-1)^n [\mathrm{OT}_t(\overline{S}_t - (2n+1)K, T)$$
$$+ \mathrm{OT}_t(\overline{S}_t + (2n+1)K, T)],$$
(7.15)

for any $t \in [0, \tau_D^+(K) \wedge T]$ *and* $K > 0$.

7.4.2. Hedging the K-drawdown preceding a K-drawup

In this subsection, we develop a semi-static replication of a digital call on the K-drawdown preceding a K-drawup using one-touches. By Theorem 7.1 and Proposition 7.1, we just need to ensure Assumption 7.2 holds for all barriers of one-touch knockouts being held. For this purpose we impose structure on the spot price process.

Assumption 7.4. *While $t \leq \tau_D^+(K) \wedge \tau_U^+(K) \wedge T$, the running maximum and the running minimum are continuous. Moreover, at time t such that $d(\overline{S}_t - \underline{S}_t) \neq 0$ and $t \leq \tau_D^+(K) \wedge \tau_U^+(K) \wedge T$, the time-$t$ risk-neutral probability of hitting $S_t - \Delta$ before T is the same as the time-t risk-neutral probability of hitting $S_t + \Delta$ before T, for any $\Delta > 0$.*

Assumption 7.4 is sufficient for applying Proposition 7.1. Evaluating (7.13) at $V = \overline{S}_t - K$ and $W = \overline{S}_t$, we obtain

$$\text{OTKO}_t(\overline{S}_t - K, \overline{S}_t, T)$$

$$= \text{OT}_t(\overline{S}_t - K, T) + \sum_{n=1}^{\infty} [\text{OT}_t(\overline{S}_t - (2n+1)K, T)$$

$$- \text{OT}_t(\overline{S}_t + (2n-1)K, T)], \qquad (7.16)$$

for $K > 0$ and $t \in [0, \tau_S^-(\overline{S}_t - K) \wedge \tau_S^+(\overline{S}_t) \wedge T]$. Differentiating (7.13) with respect to W, and evaluating at $V = H - K$ and $W = H$ implies that for $K > 0$ and $t \in [0, \tau_S^-(H - K) \wedge \tau_S^+(H) \wedge T]$:

$$\text{RUFDI}_t(H - K, H, T) = -2 \sum_{n=1}^{\infty} n \left(\frac{\partial}{\partial H} \text{OT}_t(H - (2n+1)K, T) \right.$$

$$\left. + \frac{\partial}{\partial H} \text{OT}_t(H + (2n-1)K, T) \right), \qquad (7.17)$$

since K is a constant.

Substituting (7.16) and (7.17) in Theorem 7.1, and ignoring the left and right limits, it gives rise to the following theorem.

Theorem 7.4. *Under frictionless markets and Assumption 7.4, no arbitrage implies that the digital call on the K-drawdown preceding a K-drawup can be valued relative to the price of bonds and one-touches as*

$$\text{DC}_t^{D<U}(K, T) = \sum_{n=0}^{\infty} (-1)^{n+1} n [\text{OT}_t(\overline{S}_t - nK, T) + \text{OT}_t(\overline{S}_t + nK, T)],$$

$$(7.18)$$

for any $t \in [0, \tau_D^+(K) \wedge \tau_U^+(K) \wedge T]$ and $K > 0$.

Proof. Suppose that the digital call on the K-drawdown preceding a K-drawup has been sold at time 0. In order to hedge this position, consider a strategy of always holding the replicating portfolio of one-touches on the right-hand side of (7.18). This semi-dynamic trading strategy is followed until the earlier of expiry and the first hitting times of the running drawdown/drawup to the strike K. If the running drawdown increases to K before $\tau_U^+(K)$ and T, then a bond of maturity T is held afterwards.

Since we assume that the running maximum and the running minimum are continuous, the above replicating portfolio never yields a payout due to a hit of barriers outside the corridor $[\underline{S}_t, \overline{S}_t]$. When the running maximum increase or the running minimum decreases continuously with $t < \tau_D^+(K) \wedge \tau_U^+(K) \wedge T$, Assumption 7.4 guarantees that it cost nothing to move the barriers of one-touches in the above portfolio. Hence, the first time to get a cash flow from the above portfolio is when $\overline{S}_t - \underline{S}_t = K$. Let us denote by τ the first time that $\overline{S}_t - \underline{S}_t \geq K$, then clearly $\tau = \tau_D^+(K) \wedge \tau_U^+(K)$. If $\tau > T$, then the one-touches expire worthless, as does the target claim. If $\tau \leq T$, then at τ, $\overline{S}_\tau = \underline{S}_\tau + K$, Proposition 7.1 and Assumption 7.4 imply that the portfolio of one-touches has the same value as the one-touch knockout $\mathrm{OTKO}_\tau(\overline{S}_\tau - K, \overline{S}_\tau, T)$, whose payoff matches the target option, with value zero or the price of a bond. In the former case, $\tau = \tau_U^+(K)$, the one-touches are liquidated for zero; while in the latter case, $\tau = \tau_D^+(K)$, the liquidation proceeds are used to buy the bond. We conclude that in all cases, the payoff of the target digital call is matched by the liquidation value of a non-anticipating self-financing portfolio of bonds and one-touches. Furthermore, the right-hand side of (7.18) is the cost of setting up the replicating strategy at time t. Hence, no arbitrage implies that this cost is also the price of the target claim. □

The hedging strategies in Theorems 7.3 and 7.4 would be easier to implement in practice than the hedges using one-touch knockouts because they do not involve integrating over barriers. If we enforce the symmetry assumption of the underlying spot price process, then it is possible to develop hedging strategies with only digital options on the underlying. We present these results in the next section.

7.5. Semi-static Replication with Path-Independent Options

In the previous section, we developed two semi-static hedges with a series of co-terminal single-barrier one-touches of the target digital calls. Since barrier options are not so liquid for most underlyings, this section presents another semi-static hedge which uses digital options on the underlying. The replication only succeeds under some symmetry and continuity assumptions, which we will make precise.

Consider a spot price process starting inside the corridor between V and W, where V and W are the in-barrier and out-barrier of an OKTO respectively. Let τ be the first exit time of the above corridor, then we impose the following assumption.

Assumption 7.5. *The spot S. cannot exit the corridor between V and W by a jump. If the first exit time $\tau \leq T$, then at time τ, the conditional risk-neutral probability distribution of S_T is symmetric about S_τ.*

The above assumption is met by the standard Brownian motion. The characterization of continuous martingales that satisfy the symmetry in Assumption 7.5 can be found in Tehranchi (2009).

Under Assumption 7.5, we claim that the payoff of a one-touch knockout with skip-free in-barrier V and out-barrier W is replicated by a portfolio of digital options.

Proposition 7.2. *Let τ be the first exit time of the corridor between V and W. Under frictionless markets and Assumption 7.5, no arbitrage implies that for $t \in [0, \tau \wedge T]$,*

(1) *If $V < W$, then*

$$\mathrm{OTKO}_t(V,W,T) = 2\sum_{n=0}^{\infty} \mathrm{DP}_t(V - 2n\triangle, T) - 2\sum_{n=1}^{\infty} \mathrm{DC}_t(V + 2n\triangle, T).$$
(7.19)

(2) *If $V > W$, then*

$$\mathrm{OTKO}_t(V,W,T) = 2\sum_{n=0}^{\infty} \mathrm{DC}_t(V - 2n\triangle, T) - 2\sum_{n=1}^{\infty} \mathrm{DP}_t(V + 2n\triangle, T),$$
(7.20)

where $\triangle = W - V$.

Proof. The idea of the proof is similar as that in Proposition 7.1. We skip the details here. □

In Sections 7.5.1 and 7.5.2, we will separately develop portfolios of digital options which can be used to replicate the payoff of a digital call on maximum drawdown and the payoff of a digital call on the K-drawdown preceding a K-drawup, respectively.

7.5.1. Hedging the maximum drawdown

In this subsection, we develop a semi-static replication of a digital call on maximum drawdown using digital options on the underlying. By Theorem 7.2 and Proposition 7.2, we need to ensure that Assumption 7.5 holds for all barriers of one-touch knockouts being held. For this purpose we impose structure on the spot price process.

Assumption 7.6. *While $\overline{D}_t < K$, the running maximum is continuous, and the drawdown cannot jump up by more than $K - D_t$. Moreover, at $t = \tau_D^+(K) \leq T$ or any time t such that $d\overline{S}_t \neq 0$ and $t < \tau_D^+(K) \wedge T$, the conditional time-t risk-neutral probability distribution of S_T is symmetric about S_t.*

From Proposition 7.2, it is not difficult to see that Assumption 7.6 also implies Assumption 7.1. In fact, under Assumption 7.6, whenever the maximum increases continuously with $\overline{D}_t < K$, evaluating (7.19) and (7.20) at $V = \overline{S}_t \mp K$ and $W = \overline{S}_t \pm K$:

$$\text{OTKO}_t(\overline{S}_t - K, \overline{S}_t + K, T)$$
$$= 2 \sum_{n=0}^{\infty} [\text{DP}_t(\overline{S}_t - (4n+1)K, T) - \text{DC}_t(\overline{S}_t + (4n+3)K, T)],$$
$$\text{OTKO}_t(\overline{S}_t + K, \overline{S}_t - K, T)$$
$$= 2 \sum_{n=0}^{\infty} [\text{DC}_t(\overline{S}_t + (4n+1)K, T) - \text{DP}_t(\overline{S}_t - (4n+3)K, T)].$$

Assumption 7.5 implies that

$$\text{OTKO}_t(\overline{S}_t - K, \overline{S}_t + K, T) = \text{OTKO}_t(\overline{S}_t + K, \overline{S}_t - K, T).$$

As a result, we have the following theorem.

Theorem 7.5. *Under frictionless markets and Assumption 7.6, no arbitrage implies that the digital call on maximum drawdown can be valued relative to the prices of bonds and digital options as*

$$\text{DC}_t^{\overline{D}}(K, T)$$
$$= 2 \sum_{n=0}^{\infty} (-1)^n [\text{DP}_t(\overline{S}_t - (2n+1)K, T) + \text{DC}_t(\overline{S}_t + (2n+1)K, T)],$$

for any $t \in [0, \tau_D^+(K) \wedge T]$ and $K > 0$.

7.5.2. Hedging the K-drawdown preceding a K-drawup

In this subsection, we develop a semi-static replication of a digital call on the K-drawdown preceding a K-drawup using one-touches. By Theorem 7.1 and Proposition 7.2, we need to ensure Assumption 7.5 holds for all barriers of one-touch knockouts being held. For this purpose, we impose structure on the spot price process.

Assumption 7.7. *While $t \leq \tau_D^+(K) \wedge \tau_U^+(K) \wedge T$, the running maximum and the running minimum are continuous. Moreover, at time t such that $d(\overline{S}_t - \underline{S}_t) \neq 0$ and $t \leq \tau_D^+(K) \wedge \tau_U^+(K) \wedge T$, the conditional risk-neutral probability distribution of hitting S_T is symmetric about S_t.*

Assumption 7.7 is sufficient for applying Proposition 7.2. Evaluating (7.19) at $V = \overline{S}_t - K$ and $W = \overline{S}_t$, we obtain

$$\text{OTKO}_t(\overline{S}_t - K, \overline{S}_t, T)$$
$$= 2\sum_{n=0}^{\infty}[\text{DP}_t(\overline{S}_t - (2n+1)K, T) - \text{DC}_t(\overline{S}_t + (2n+1)K, T)], \tag{7.21}$$

for $K > 0$ and $t \in [0, \tau_S^-(\overline{S}_t - K) \wedge \tau_S^+(\overline{S}_t) \wedge T]$. Differentiating (7.19) with respect to W, and evaluating at $V = H - K$ and $W = H$ implies that for $K > 0$ and $t \in [0, \tau_S^-(H - K) \wedge \tau_S^+(H) \wedge T]$:

$$\text{RUFDI}_t(H - K, H, T) = -4\sum_{n=1}^{\infty} n\left[\frac{\partial}{\partial H}\text{DP}_t(H - (2n+1)K, T)\right.$$
$$\left. + \frac{\partial}{\partial H}\text{DC}_t(H + (2n-1)K, T)\right], \tag{7.22}$$

since K is a constant.

Substituting (7.21) and (7.22) in Theorem 7.1, and ignoring the left and right limits, it gives rise to the following theorem.

Theorem 7.6. *Under frictionless markets and Assumption 7.7, no arbitrage implies that the digital call on the K-drawdown preceding a K-drawup can be valued relative to the price of bonds and digital options as*

$$\text{DC}_t^{D<U}(K, T) = 2\sum_{n=0}^{\infty}(-1)^{n+1}n[\text{DP}_t(\overline{S}_t - nK, T) + \text{DC}_t(\overline{S}_t + nK, T)],$$

for $t \in [0, \tau_D^+(K) \wedge \tau_U^+(K) \wedge T]$ and $K > 0$.

7.6. Static Hedging of the K-relative Drawdown Preceding a K-relative Drawup with One-Touch Knockouts

In the previous sections, we developed static and semi-static replications under certain arithmetic symmetry assumptions. However, there are obvious financial limitations of this setup. For example, it requires no carrying cost for the underlying asset; the price of the underlying can be negative with positive probability. In what follows we will consider a more complicated setup, which allows carrying cost and keeps price positive.

As the spot price is always positive, it is much more convenient to consider the percentage drawdown as a measure of risk. Let $D_t^r := \overline{S}_t/S_t$ be the level of the relative drawdown at time $t \in [0,T]$. For a fixed $K > 1$, let $\tau_{D^r}^+(K)$ be the time at which the relative drawdown process D^r first reaches K. As usual, if D^r never reaches K, then we set $\tau_{D^r}^+(K) = \infty$.

Similarly, let $U_t^r := S_t/\underline{S}_t$ be the level of the relative drawup at time $t \in [0,T]$. For a fixed $K > 1$, let $\tau_{U^r}^+(K)$ be the time at which the relative drawup process U^r first reaches K. If U^r never reaches K, then we set $\tau_{U^r}^+(K) = \infty$.

We are interested in digital calls on maximum relative drawdown and digital calls on the K-relative drawdown preceding a K-relative drawup. To describe the payoff of these claims, let $\overline{D}_T^r = \sup_{t \in [0,T]} D_t^r$ be the maximum relative drawdown of the spot price process. A digital call on maximum relative drawdown pays one dollar at expiry if and only if the maximum relative drawdown exceeds K. We denote the price of the option at time t by

$$\mathrm{DC}_t^{\overline{D}^r}(K,T) := \mathrm{B}_t(T)\mathbb{Q}_t^T(\overline{D}_T^r \geq K). \tag{7.23}$$

A digital call on the K-relative drawdown preceding a K-drawup pays one dollar at expiry if and only if the relative drawdown reaches K before the earlier of expiry and the time at which the relative drawup first reaches K. We denote the price of this option at time t by

$$\mathrm{DC}_t^{D^r}(K,T) := \mathrm{B}_t(T)\mathbb{Q}_t^T(\tau_{D^r}^+(K) \leq \tau_{U^r}^+(K) \wedge T). \tag{7.24}$$

Analogous to the absolute drawdown setting in Section 7.2, we can replicate the payoff of the digital call on K-relative drawdown preceding a K-relative drawup with one-touch knockouts and ricochet-upper-first down-and-in claims. The argument is exactly the same as in Theorem 7.1. We present the following result without proof.

Theorem 7.7 (Robust replication: II). *Under frictionless markets, no arbitrage implies that the digital call on the K-relative drawdown preceding a K-relative drawup can be valued relative to the prices of roots, one-touch knockouts and their spreads:*

$$\mathrm{DC}_t^{D^r < U^r}(K,T)$$
$$= \mathrm{OTKO}_t(\overline{S}_t K^{-1}, \overline{S}_t, T) + \int_{(\overline{S}_t, \underline{S}_t K)} \mathrm{RUFDI}_t(HK^{-1}, H, T) \, \mathrm{d}H, \tag{7.25}$$

for any $t \in [0, \tau_{D^r}^+(K) \wedge \tau_{U^r}^+(K) \wedge T]$ and $K > 1$.

In the rest of the chapter, we will develop semi-robust replications of the above two digital options under continuity and certain geometric symmetry assumptions on the dynamics of the spot price process.

7.7. Semi-static Replication with One-Touches in Geometric Models

In the last section we derived a static hedge of one target call with one-touch knockouts and their spreads. Because of illiquidity of one-touch knockouts, this section presents alternative semi-static hedges which just use single-barrier one-touches and lookbacks. The replications only succeed under certain symmetry and continuity assumptions. More specifically, suppose that the spot starts inside the corridor between V and W, where V and W are the in-barrier and out-barrier of a one-touch knockout respectively. Let τ be the first exit time of the above corridor, we assume the following.

Assumption 7.8. *The spot price process S cannot exit the corridor between V and W by a jump. Moreover, there exists a constant q, such that if the first exits time of the above corridor $\tau \leq T$, we have*

$$\mathbb{Q}_\tau^T(\underline{S}_T \leq S_\tau \Delta^{-1}) = \Delta^q \cdot \mathbb{Q}_\tau^T(\overline{S}_T \geq S_\tau \Delta), \tag{7.26}$$

for any $\Delta \geq \frac{V \vee W}{V \wedge W}$.

One of the most important model that satisfy Assumption 7.8 is the geometric Brownian motion. For a proof of this fact, we refer to Remark 7.6 and Section 7.11.

Under the above assumption, a one-touch knockout with in-barrier V and out-barrier W is replicated by a portfolio of one-touches. In particular, we have the following proposition.

Proposition 7.3. *Under frictionless markets and Assumption 7.8, no arbitrage implies that, for any t before the exiting time τ of the corridor between V and W,*

$$\mathrm{OTKO}_t(V,W,T)$$
$$= \mathrm{OT}_t(V,T) + \sum_{n=1}^{\infty} [\triangle^{-nq}\mathrm{OT}_t(V\triangle^{-2n},T) - \triangle^{nq}\mathrm{OT}_t(V\triangle^{2n},T)],$$
(7.27)

where $\triangle = W/V \neq 1$.

Proof. Suppose a one-touch knockout with in-barrier V and out-barrier W has been sold at time 0. In order to hedge this position, consider a strategy of being long a series of one-touches with barriers at V, $V\triangle^{-2}$, $V\triangle^{-4},\ldots$, and also being short a series of one-touches with barriers at $V\triangle^2$, $V\triangle^4,\ldots$. If neither barrier is hit by T, then all one-touches expire worthless. If $\tau \leq T$ and $S_\tau = V$, then at τ, the one-touch with payoff with barrier at V knocks in, while Assumption 7.8 implies that all of the other one-touches can be costlessly liquidated. The reason is that for each $n = 1, 2, \ldots$, the long position in the one-touches with barrier at $V\triangle^{-2n}$, is canceled by the short position in the one-touches with barrier at $V\triangle^{2n}$. Similarly, if $\tau \leq T$ and $S_\tau = W$, then at τ, Assumption 7.8 implies that all of the one-touches can be costlessly liquidated. The reason is that since $V = W\triangle^{-1}$, the portfolio can also be considered as long a series of one-touches with barriers at $W\triangle^{-1}$, $W\triangle^{-3}$, $W\triangle^{-5},\ldots$, while also being short a series of one-touches with barriers at $W\triangle$, $W\triangle^3$, $W\triangle^5 \ldots$:

$$\sum_{n=0}^{\infty} [\triangle^{-nq}\mathrm{OT}_t(W\triangle^{-2n-1},T) - \triangle^{(n+1)q}\mathrm{OT}_t(W\triangle^{2n+1},T)].$$

Hence, for each $n = 0, 1, 2, \ldots$, the long position in the one-touches with barrier at $W\triangle^{-2n-1}$ is canceled by the short position in the one-touch with barrier at $W\triangle^{2n+1}$. Since the value of the one-touch portfolio matches the payoff of the one-touch knockout when (S_t,t) exits $(V \wedge W, V \vee W) \times [0,T]$, no arbitrage forces the values prior to exit to be the same. □

In virtue of Theorem 7.7 and discussion in Section 7.4, Proposition 7.3 plays a crucial role to develop replicating strategies with one-touches for the digital call on K-relative drawdown preceding K-relative drawup. Moreover, we will see that, though not obvious, the digital call on maximum drawdown can also be replicated with one-touches and lookbacks.

7.7.1. Hedging the maximum relative drawdown

In this subsection, we develop a semi-static replication of a digital call on maximum drawdown using one-touches and lookbacks. For this purpose, we impose the following assumption.

Assumption 7.9. *While $MD_t^r < K$, the running maximum is continuous, and the relative drawdown cannot jump up by more than $K - D_t^r$. Moreover, there exists a constant q, so that at $t = \tau_{D^r}^+(K) \leq T$ or any time t such that $d\overline{S}_t \neq 0$ and $t < \tau_{D^r}^+(K)$, the time-t risk-neutral probability of hitting $S_t \Delta^{-1}$ before T is the same as Δ^q times the time-t risk-neutral probability of hitting $S_t \Delta$, for any $\Delta > 0$.*

The above assumption is clearly satisfied by geometric Brownian motion and its independent continuous time-changes. The following result provides a semi-static replication for the digital call on maximum relative drawdown.

Theorem 7.8. *Under frictionless markets and Assumption 7.9, no arbitrage implies that the digital call on relative maximum drawdown can be valued relative to the prices of bonds, one-touches, and lookback options as*

$$\begin{aligned}\mathrm{DC}_t^{\overline{D}^r}(K,T) &= \sum_0^\infty (-1)^n [K^{-nq}\mathrm{OT}_t(\overline{S}_t K^{-2n-1}, T) \\ &\quad + K^{(n+1)q}\mathrm{OT}_t(\overline{S}_t K^{2n+1}, T)] \\ &\quad + q\left[\mathrm{LBP}_t(\overline{S}_t, K, T) - \mathrm{LBC}_t(\overline{S}_t, K, T)\right] \\ &= \mathrm{OTKO}_t(\overline{S}_t K^{-1}, \overline{S}_t K, T) + K^q \cdot \mathrm{OTKO}_t(\overline{S}_t K, \overline{S}_t K^{-1}, T) \\ &\quad + q\left[\mathrm{LBP}_t(\overline{S}_t, K, T) - \mathrm{LBC}_t(\overline{S}_t, K, T)\right],\end{aligned} \quad (7.28)$$

for $t \in [0, \tau_{D^r}^+(K) \wedge T]$ and $K > 1$. Here the prices of the lookback put/call are given by

$$\mathrm{LBP}_t(M, K, T) = \sum_{n=0}^\infty (-1)^n K^{(n+2)q} \int_0^{MK^{-(2n+3)}} \left(\frac{H}{M}\right)^q P_n$$

$$\times \left(q \log \frac{K^{2n+3}}{M/H}\right) \mathrm{OT}_t(H, T) \frac{\mathrm{d}H}{H},$$

$$\mathrm{LBC}_t(M, K, T) = \sum_{n=0}^\infty (-1)^n K^{(n+1)q} \int_{MK^{2n+1}}^\infty P_n$$

$$\times \left(q \log \frac{MK^{2n+1}}{H}\right) \mathrm{OT}_t(H, T) \frac{\mathrm{d}H}{H},$$

where $P_n(x)$ is a polynomial of degree n, satisfying

$$\begin{cases} P_0(x) = 1, \\ P_n(x) + P_{n-1}(x) = \sum_{m=0}^{n}\binom{n}{m}\frac{x^m}{m!} + 2\sum_{m=0}^{n-1}\binom{n}{m+1}\frac{x^m}{m!}, & n = 1, 2, \ldots. \end{cases}$$

Remark 7.3. It is interesting to point out the difference between arithmetic and geometric settings. It is seen from Theorem 7.8 that it is not possible to replicate a digital call on the relative maximum drawdown with just one-touch knockouts, unless $q = 0$, in which case the log price $\log S$ will satisfy the arithmetic symmetry in Assumption 7.3.

To gain some intuition behind the above replicating portfolio, we assume for the moment that the interest rate is a constant, and consider a geometric Brownian motion model $S_t = S_0 e^{\nu t + \sigma W_t}$, where $S_0 > 0$ and $\{W_t\}_{t\geq 0}$ is a standard Brownian motion starting at 0 under the risk-neutral measure $\mathbb{Q}$. From Section 7.11 it is known that Assumption 7.9 holds with $q = -\frac{2\nu}{\sigma^2}$. Notice that $\tau_{Dr}^+(K)$ is the same as the first passage time of the drawdown of the log price $\log S_t$ to level $a = \log K > 0$, which we denote by $\tau_d^+(a)$.

If there is a semi-static portfolio of one-touches for the digital call on maximum drawdown, then their prices must be the same at all time prior $\tau_d^+(a)$. On the other hand, since the maturity T is a free parameter, this price equality must still hold when T is replaced with an independent exponential random variable with mean $1/\lambda > 0$. As a consequence, we obtain an equality between the Laplace transform of $\tau_d^+(a)$, $\mathbb{E}_t^{\mathbb{Q}}(e^{-\lambda \tau_d^+(a)})$, and the "portfolio" of Laplace transforms of first passage times, which holds at all $t < \tau_d^+(a)$. Conversely, for any t prior $\tau_d^+(a)$ such that $S_t = \overline{S}_t$, if we obtain an expansion of the Laplace transform $\mathbb{E}_t^{\mathbb{Q}^T}(e^{-\lambda \tau_d^+(a)})$ in terms of Laplace transforms of first passage times, then we may be able to derive a self-financing replicating portfolio.

We substantiate this idea in the following paragraphs. From (4.11) it is known that, whenever $S_t = \overline{S}_t$

$$\mathbb{E}_t^{\mathbb{Q}}(e^{-\lambda \tau_d^+(a)}) = \frac{e^{-\delta a}}{\cosh(\gamma a) - \frac{\delta}{\gamma}\sinh(\gamma a)} = \frac{e^{-(\gamma+\delta)a}}{\frac{1-\frac{\delta}{\gamma}}{2} + e^{-2\gamma a}\frac{1+\frac{\delta}{\gamma}}{2}},$$

for any fixed $\lambda > 0$, where $\delta = \frac{\nu}{\sigma^2}$ and $\gamma = \sqrt{\delta^2 + 2\lambda/\sigma^2}$. By "expanding" this expression with a power series of $e^{-2\gamma a}$, we obtain

$$\mathbb{E}_t^{\mathbb{Q}}(e^{-\lambda \tau_d^+(a)})$$

$$= \frac{2}{1 - \frac{\delta}{\gamma}} \left[e^{-(\delta+\gamma)a} - \frac{\gamma+\delta}{\gamma-\delta} e^{-(\delta+3\gamma)a} + \left(\frac{\gamma+\delta}{\gamma-\delta}\right)^2 e^{-(\delta+5\gamma)a} + \cdots \right]$$

$$= \sum_{n=0}^{\infty} K^{q(n+1)} \cdot (-1)^n \left(2 - \frac{q}{\gamma-\delta}\right) \left(1 - \frac{q}{\gamma-\delta}\right)^n e^{-(\gamma-\delta)(2n+1)a}.$$

To derive a semi-static portfolio from the above, we have to "hide" the λ-term inside the exponentials, so that we obtain a linear combination of one-touches, which can be used to develop a replicating portfolio. To that end, we let $\eta = \gamma - \delta > 0$ and $\beta = (2n+1)k > 0$, and notice that

$$\left(1 - \frac{q}{\eta}\right)^n e^{-\eta\beta} = \sum_{m=0}^{n} \binom{n}{m} \left(-\frac{q}{\eta}\right)^m e^{-\eta\beta}$$

$$= e^{-\eta\beta} + \sum_{m=1}^{n} \binom{n}{m} (-q)^m \int_{\beta}^{\infty} dx_m \cdots \int_{x_2}^{\infty} e^{-\eta x_1} dx_1$$

$$= e^{-\eta\beta} + \sum_{m=1}^{n} \binom{n}{m} (-q)^m \int_{\beta}^{\infty} e^{-\eta x_1} \frac{(x_1 - \beta)^{m-1}}{(m-1)!} dx_1,$$

where the last equality follows from switching the order of integration. It also follows that

$$\left(2 - \frac{q}{\eta}\right)\left(1 - \frac{q}{\eta}\right)^n e^{-\eta\beta} = 2e^{-\eta\beta} - q \int_{\beta}^{\infty} e^{-\eta x_1} f_n(q(\beta - x_1)) dx_1,$$

where $f_n(\cdot)$ is a degree-n polynomial defined as

$$f_n(x) := \sum_{m=0}^{n} \binom{n}{m} \frac{x^m}{m!} + 2 \sum_{m=0}^{n-1} \binom{n}{m+1} \frac{x^m}{m!}.$$

On the other hand, recall that the Laplace transform of a first passage time is given by (see (4.5))

$$\mathbb{E}_t^{\mathbb{Q}}(e^{-\lambda \tau_{\log S}^+(\log S_t + z)}) = e^{-(\gamma-\delta)z}, \quad \forall z > 0.$$

Hence, we obtain that, whenever $S_t = \overline{S}_t$

$$\mathbb{E}_t^{\mathbb{Q}}(e^{-\lambda \tau_d^+(a)})$$

$$= 2 \sum_{n=0}^{\infty} K^{q(n+1)} (-1)^n \mathbb{E}_t^{\mathbb{Q}}(e^{-\lambda \tau_{\log S}^+(\log(\overline{S}_t K^{2n+1}))})$$

$$-q\sum_{n=0}^{\infty}K^{q(n+1)}(-1)^n$$

$$\times\int_{(2n+1)k}^{\infty}f_n(q((2n+1)k-x))\mathbb{E}_t^Q(e^{-\lambda\tau_{\log S}^+(\log(\overline{S}_t e^x))})dx.$$

By inverting λ, we obtain a time-t price equality: for $t < \tau_{Dr}^+(K)$ such that $S_t = \overline{S}_t$,

$$DC_t^{\overline{D}^r}(K,T)$$

$$= 2\sum_{n=0}^{\infty}K^{q(n+1)}(-1)^n OT_t(\overline{S}_t K^{2n+1}, T)$$

$$- q\sum_{n=0}^{\infty}K^{q(n+1)}(-1)^n$$

$$\times \int_{\overline{S}_t K^{2n+1}}^{\infty} f_n\left(q\log\left(\frac{\overline{S}_t K^{2n+1}}{H}\right)\right) OT_t(H,T)\frac{dH}{H}. \quad (7.29)$$

While the above equality holds as long as price is concerned, the right-hand side of (7.29) does not give a replicating portfolio, because none of the barriers in the one-touches will be reached. We thus use Assumption 7.9 to write: for any $n \geq 0$, whenever $S_t = \overline{S}_t$,

$$2K^{q(n+1)}OT_t(\overline{S}_t K^{2n+1}, T)$$

$$= K^{-nq}OT_t(\overline{S}_t K^{-(2n+1)}, T) + K^{q(n+1)}OT_t(\overline{S}_t K^{2n+1}, T).$$

Then it is easily seen that the one-touch struck at $\overline{S}_t K^{-1}$ will deliver the unit payout at $\tau \equiv \tau_{Dr}^+(K)$, and the rest one-touch has a zero net value at that stopping time. By Proposition 7.3, it is easily seen that the sum in (7.28) has the same value as $OTKO_t(\overline{S}_t K^{-1}, \overline{S}_t K, T) + K^q \cdot OTKO_t(\overline{S}_t K, \overline{S}_t K^{-1}, T)$. To get rid of the integral of one-touches at $\tau \equiv \tau_{Dr}^+(K)$, we "flip" the one-touches about $\overline{S}_\tau K^{-1}$: let us keep the integral for $n = 0$ as is (in order to finance the rollup of the one-touch knock-outs), to cancel this integral at $\tau \leq T$, we need a long position equal to

$$qK^{2q}\int_0^{\overline{S}_t K^{-3}}\left(\frac{H}{\overline{S}_t}\right)^q f_0\left(q\log\left(\frac{\overline{S}_t K^3}{H}\right)\right) OT_t(H,T)\frac{dH}{H},$$

so that, by the identity in Assumption 7.9, the net value is zero at stopping time $\tau_{Dr}^+(K)$. To finance rolling up of this long position with $\overline{S}_t$, we will also need to hold a long position equal to

$$qK^{2q} \int_{\overline{S}_t K^3}^{\infty} f_0\left(q\log\left(\frac{K^3 H}{\overline{S}_t}\right)\right) \text{OT}_t(H,T) \frac{\mathrm{d}H}{H}.$$

However, from (7.29) (the integral term with $n=1$) we know that, to match the price, we will need a net long position equal to

$$qK^{2q} \int_{\overline{S}_t K^3}^{\infty} f_1\left(q\log\left(\frac{\overline{S}_t K^3}{H}\right)\right) \text{OT}_t(H,T) \frac{\mathrm{d}H}{H}.$$

It follows that we need to get rid of the extra long position

$$qK^{2q} \int_{\overline{S}_t K^3}^{\infty} \left[f_1\left(q\log\left(\frac{\overline{S}_t K^3}{H}\right)\right) - f_0\left(q\log\left(\frac{\overline{S}_t K^3}{H}\right)\right)\right] \text{OT}_t(H,T) \frac{\mathrm{d}H}{H}$$

$$= qK^{2q} \int_{\overline{S}_t K^3}^{\infty} P_1\left(q\log\left(\frac{\overline{S}_t K^3}{H}\right)\right) \text{OT}_t(H,T) \frac{\mathrm{d}H}{H}$$

at the stopping time $\tau < T$. To that end, we hold a short position equal to

$$-qK^{3q} \int_0^{\overline{S}_t K^{-5}} \left(\frac{H}{\overline{S}_t}\right)^q P_1\left(q\log\left(\frac{H}{\overline{S}_t K^{-5}}\right)\right) \text{OT}_t(H,T) \frac{\mathrm{d}H}{H},$$

which requires another short position for financing the rollup:

$$-qK^{3q} \int_{\overline{S}_t K^5}^{\infty} P_1\left(q\log\left(\frac{\overline{S}_t K^5}{H}\right)\right) \text{OT}_t(H,T) \frac{\mathrm{d}H}{H}.$$

By using this argument, we can obtain the portfolio stated in Theorem 7.8. It is then straightforward to verify that, independent of the geometric Brownian motion model assumption, self-financing and replicating hold as long as Assumption 7.9 holds.

7.7.2. Hedging the K-relative drawdown preceding a K-relative drawup

In this subsection, we develop a semi-static replication of a digital call on the K-relative drawdown preceding a K-relative drawup using one-touches. The following assumption ensures the validity of the replication.

Assumption 7.10. While $t \leq \tau_{Dr}^+(K) \wedge \tau_{Ur}^+(K) \wedge T$, the running maximum and the running minimum are continuous. Moreover, there exists a constant q, so that at time t such that $d(\overline{S}_t - \underline{S}_t) \neq 0$ and $t \leq \tau_{Dr}^+(K) \wedge \tau_{Ur}^+(K) \wedge T$, we have that

$$\mathrm{OT}_t(S_t \Delta^{-1}, T) = \Delta^q \cdot \mathrm{OT}_t(S_t \Delta, T), \tag{7.30}$$

for any $\Delta > 0$.

Assumption 7.10 is sufficient for applying Proposition 7.3. Evaluating (7.27) at $V = \overline{S}_t/K$ and $W = \overline{S}_t^+$, we obtain

$$\mathrm{OTKO}_t(\overline{S}_t/K, \overline{S}_t^+, T)$$
$$= \sum_{n=0}^{\infty} [K^{-nq}\mathrm{OT}(\overline{S}_t K^{-2n-1}, T) - K^{(n+1)q}\mathrm{OT}_t(\overline{S}_t K^{2n+1}, T)], \tag{7.31}$$

for $K > 0$ and $t \in [0, \tau_S^-(\overline{S}_t/K) \wedge \tau_S^+(\overline{S}_t^+) \wedge T]$. Differentiating (7.27) with respect to W, and evaluating at $V = H/K$ and $W = H$ implies that for $K > 1$ and $t \in [0, \tau_S^-(H/K) \wedge \tau_S^+(H) \wedge T]$:

$$\mathrm{RUFDI}_t(H/K, H, T)$$
$$= -2\sum_{n=1}^{\infty} n[K^{-nq}\frac{\partial}{\partial H}\mathrm{OT}_t(HK^{-2n-1}, T) + K^{nq}\frac{\partial}{\partial H}\mathrm{OT}_t(HK^{2n-1}, T)]$$
$$- \frac{q}{H}\sum_{n=1}^{\infty} n[K^{-nq}\mathrm{OT}_t(HK^{-2n-1}, T) + K^{nq}\mathrm{OT}_t(HK^{2n-1}, T)], \tag{7.32}$$

since K is a constant.

Substituting (7.31) and (7.32) in (7.25), and ignoring the left and right limits, it gives rise to the following theorem.

Theorem 7.9. *Under frictionless markets and Assumption 7.10, no arbitrage implies that the digital call on the K-relative drawdown preceding a K-relative drawup can be valued relative to the prices of bonds and one-touches as*

$$\mathrm{DC}_t^{D^r < U^r}(K, T) = -\sum_{n=1}^{\infty} 2n[K^{-nq}\mathrm{OT}_t(\underline{S}_t K^{-2n}, T)$$
$$+ K^{nq}\mathrm{OT}_t(\underline{S}_t K^{2n}, T)]$$

$$+ \sum_{n=0}^{\infty}(2n+1)[K^{-nq}\mathrm{OT}(\overline{S}_t K^{-2n-1}, T)$$

$$+ K^{(n+1)q}\mathrm{OT}_t(\overline{S}_t K^{2n+1}, T)]$$

$$- q \int_{\overline{S}_t}^{\underline{S}_t K} \sum_{n=1}^{\infty} n[K^{-nq}\,\mathrm{OT}_t(HK^{-2n-1}, T)$$

$$+ K^{nq}\,\mathrm{OT}_t(HK^{2n-1}, T)]\frac{\mathrm{d}H}{H}, \qquad (7.33)$$

for any $t \in [0, \tau_{Dr}^+(K) \wedge \tau_{Ur}^+(K) \wedge T]$ and $K > 1$.

Proof. Suppose a digital call on the K-relative drawdown preceding a K-relative drawup has been sold at time 0. In order to hedge this position, consider a strategy of always holding the replicating portfolio of one-touches on the right-hand side of (7.33). This semi-dynamic trading strategy is followed until the earlier of expiry and the first hitting times of running relative drawdown/drawup to the strike K. If the running relative drawdown increases to K before T, then a bond of maturity T is held afterwards.

Since we assume that the running maximum and the running minimum are continuous, the above replicating portfolio never yields a payout due to a hit of barriers outside the corridor $[\underline{S}_t, \overline{S}_t]$. When the running maximum increases or the running minimum decreases continuously with $t < \tau_{Dr}^+(K) \wedge \tau_{Ur}^+(K) \wedge T$, Assumption 7.10 guarantees that it costs nothing to move the barriers of one-touches in the above portfolio. Hence, the first time to get a cash flow from the above portfolio is when $\overline{S}_t/\underline{S}_t = K$. Let us denote by τ the first time that $\overline{S}_t/\underline{S}_t \geq K$, then clearly $\tau = \tau_{Dr}^+(K) \wedge \tau_{Ur}^+(K)$. If $\tau > T$, then the one-touches expire worthless, as does the target claim. If $\tau \leq T$, then at τ, $\overline{S}_\tau = \underline{S}_\tau K$, by Proposition 7.3 and Assumption 7.10, the portfolio of one-touches has the same value as the one-touch knockout $\mathrm{OTKO}_\tau(\overline{S}_\tau/K, \overline{S}_\tau, T)$, whose value matches the target option, with value either zero or the price of a bond. In the former case, $\tau = \tau_{Ur}^+(K)$, the one-touches are liquidated for zero; while in the latter case, $\tau = \tau_{Dr}^+(K)$, the liquidation proceeds are used to buy the bond. We conclude that in all cases, the payoff of the target digital call is matched by the liquidation value of a non-anticipating self-financing portfolio of bonds and one-touches. Furthermore, the right-hand side of (7.33) is the cost of setting up the replicating strategy at time t. Hence, no arbitrage implies that this cost is also the price of the target claim. □

7.8. Semi-static Replication with Path-Independent Options in Geometric Models

In the previous section, we developed semi-static hedges with a series of co-terminal single-barrier options of the target calls. This section presents another semi-static hedge which uses more liquid path-independent options. The replications only succeed under some symmetry and continuity assumptions, which we will make precise.

Suppose that the spot starts inside the corridor between V and W, where V and W are the in-barrier and the out-barrier of a one-touch knockout respectively. Let τ be the first exit time of this corridor, we impose the following assumption.

Assumption 7.11. *The spot S cannot exit the corridor between V and W by a jump. Moreover, there exists a constant q, such that if the first exit time of the above corridor $\tau \leq T$, we have that*

$$\mathbb{E}_\tau^{Q^T}(f(S_T/S_\tau)) = \mathbb{E}_\tau^{Q^T}((S_T/S_\tau)^q f(S_t/S_T)), \tag{7.34}$$

holds for any bounded non-negative measurable function $f(\cdot)$ on $\mathbb{R}_{>0}$.

Remark 7.4. The symmetry in Assumption 7.11 is often seen in finance literature (Bowie and Carr (1994), Carr and Chou (1997), Carr et al. (1998) and Carr (2011)). In particular, geometric Brownian motions and their independent time-changes all satisfy this assumption. The characterization of continuous martingales that satisfy this symmetry conditions is discussed in Tehranchi (2009).

Remark 7.5. If we alternatively assume that a barrier B is skip-free and (7.34) holds at the first hitting time to B, then a one-touch with barrier at B can be replicated with path-independent options. This is the reflection principle, which we present below for completeness.

Lemma 7.1 (Reflection Principle). *Under frictionless market, a one-touch with skip-free barrier $B > 0$ can be replicated with path-independent options, provided that (7.34) holds at the first hitting time $\tau_S(B)$. In particular, for any $t \in [0, \tau_S(B) \wedge T]$,*

(1) *if $B < \underline{S}_t$,*

$$\mathrm{OT}_t(B,T) = \mathrm{DP}_t(B,T) + B^{-q}\mathrm{P}_{q,t}(B,T), \tag{7.35}$$

(2) if $B > \overline{S}_t$,

$$\mathrm{OT}_t(B,T) = \mathrm{DC}_t(B,T) + B^{-q}\mathrm{C}_{\mathrm{q,t}}(B,T), \qquad (7.36)$$

where the generalized put/call prices $P_{q,t}/C_{q,t}$ are given by

$$\mathrm{P}_{\mathrm{q,t}}(B,T) := B_t(T)\mathbb{E}_t^{\mathbb{Q}^T}(S_T^q \mathbf{1}_{\{S_T < B\}}), \qquad (7.37)$$

$$\mathrm{C}_{\mathrm{q,t}}(B,T) := B_t(T)\mathbb{E}_t^{\mathbb{Q}^T}(S_T^q \mathbf{1}_{\{S_T > B\}}). \qquad (7.38)$$

Remark 7.6. We say a process is skip-free if every element in its state space is skip-free. If the spot price process is skip-free and satisfies Assumption 7.11, it is easily seen that condition (7.26) in Assumption 7.8 is also satisfied. In other words, for a skip-free process, condition (7.34) in Assumption 7.11 is stronger than (7.26) in Assumption 7.8.

It is interesting to point out that, under Assumption 7.11, a one-touch knockout with in-barrier V and out-barrier W can be replicated by a portfolio of path-independent options.

Proposition 7.4. *Let τ be the first exit time of the corridor between V and W. Under frictionless markets and Assumption 7.11, no arbitrage implies that, for $t \in [0, \tau \wedge T]$,*

(1) if $V < W$,

$$\mathrm{OTKO}_t(V, W, T)$$
$$= \sum_{n=0}^{\infty} \left(\frac{1}{\triangle^{nq}} \mathrm{DP}_t(V\triangle^{-2n}, T) + \frac{\triangle^{nq}}{V^q} \mathrm{P}_{\mathrm{q,t}}(V\triangle^{-2n}, T) \right)$$
$$- \sum_{n=1}^{\infty} \left(\triangle^{nq} \mathrm{DC}_t(V\triangle^{2n}, T) + \frac{1}{V^q \triangle^{nq}} \mathrm{C}_{\mathrm{q,t}}(V\triangle^{2n}, T) \right); \qquad (7.39)$$

(2) if $V > W$,

$$\mathrm{OTKO}_t(V, W, T)$$

$$= \sum_{n=0}^{\infty} \left(\frac{1}{\triangle^{nq}} \mathrm{DC}_t(V\triangle^{-2n}, T) + \frac{\triangle^{nq}}{V^q} \mathrm{C}_{\mathrm{q},t}(V\triangle^{-2n}, T) \right)$$

$$- \sum_{n=1}^{\infty} \left(\triangle^{nq} \mathrm{DP}_t(V\triangle^{2n}, T) + \frac{1}{V^q \triangle^{nq}} \mathrm{P}_{\mathrm{q},t}(V\triangle^{2n}, T) \right),$$
(7.40)

where $\triangle = W/V \neq 1$ and $\mathrm{P}_{\mathrm{q},t}/\mathrm{C}_{\mathrm{q},t}$ are defined in (7.37) and (7.38).

Proof. The idea of the proof is similar as that in Proposition 7.3. □

Lemma 7.1 and Proposition 7.4 provide fundamentals of our replication results in this section. In Sections 7.8.1 and 7.8.2, we will separately develop portfolios of path-independent options to replicate the payoff of a digital call on maximum relative drawdown and the payoff of a digital call on the K-relative drawdown preceding a K-relative drawup, respectively.

7.8.1. Hedging the maximum relative drawdown

In this subsection, we develop a semi-static replication of a digital call on maximum relative drawdown using path-independent options. Let us first state the necessary assumptions regarding the dynamics of the spot price process.

Assumption 7.12. *While $MD_t^r < K$, the running maximum is continuous, and the relative drawdown cannot jump up by more than $K - D_t^r$. Moreover, there exists a constant q, so that at $t = \tau_D^+(K) \leq T$ or any time t such that $\mathrm{d}\overline{S}_t \neq 0$ and $t < \tau_{D^r}^+(K)$, we have that*

$$\mathbb{E}_t^{\mathbb{Q}^T}(f(S_T/S_t)) = \mathbb{E}_t^{\mathbb{Q}^T}((S_T/S_t)^q f(S_t/S_T))$$
(7.41)

holds for any bounded non-negative measurable function $f(\cdot)$ on $\mathbb{R}$.

If the spot price process is always continuous, then using Theorem 7.9 and Lemma 7.1, we can develop a replicating portfolio of path-independent options to hedge the digital call on maximum relative drawdown. However, we will show in the next theorem that, under the weaker Assumption 7.12, such a portfolio is also possible.

Theorem 7.10. *Under frictionless markets and Assumption 7.12, no arbitrage implies that the digital call on maximum relative drawdown can* be valued relative to the prices of bonds and path-independent options as

$$\mathrm{DC}_t^{\overline{D}^r}(K,T)$$
$$= \sum_{n=0}^{\infty} (-1)^n K^{-nq} [\mathrm{DP}_t(\overline{S}_t K^{-2n-1}, T) + \overline{S}_t^{-q} \mathrm{C}_{q,t}(\overline{S}_t K^{2n+1}, T)]$$
$$+ \sum_{n=0}^{\infty} (-1)^n K^{(n+1)q} [\mathrm{DC}_t(\overline{S}_t K^{2n+1}, T) + \overline{S}_t^{-q} \mathrm{P}_{q,t}(\overline{S}_t K^{-2n-1}, T)]$$
$$+ q [\mathrm{VP}_t(\overline{S}_t, K, T) - \mathrm{VC}_t(\overline{S}_t, K, T)], \qquad (7.42)$$

for $t \in [0, \tau_{Dr}^+(K) \wedge T]$ and $K > 1$. Here the prices of the vanilla put/call are given by

$$\mathrm{VP}_t(M, K, T) = \sum_{n=0}^{\infty} \frac{(-1)^n}{K^{-(n+2)q}} \int_0^{MK^{-(2n+3)}} \left(\frac{H}{M}\right)^q P_n\left(q \log \frac{K^{2n+3}}{M/H}\right)$$
$$\times [\mathrm{DP}_t(H, T) + H^{-q} P_{q,t}(H, T)] \frac{\mathrm{d}H}{H},$$

$$\mathrm{VC}_t(M, K, T) = \sum_{n=0}^{\infty} (-1)^n K^{(n+1)q} \int_{MK^{2n+1}}^{\infty} P_n\left(q \log \frac{MK^{2n+1}}{H}\right)$$
$$\times [\mathrm{DC}_t(H, T) + H^{-q} C_{q,t}(H, T)] \frac{\mathrm{d}H}{H},$$

where $P_{q,t}/C_{q,t}$ are given in (7.37) and (7.38), and polynomials $\{P_n(x)\}_{n \geq 0}$ are defined in Theorem 7.8.

7.8.2. Hedging the K-relative drawdown preceding a K-relative drawup

In this subsection, we develop a semi-static replication of a digital call on the K-relative drawdown preceding a K-relative drawup using path-independent options. We strengthen Assumption 7.12 in last subsection in order to meet the self-financing requirement of our replication portfolio.

Assumption 7.13. While $t < \tau_{Dr}^+(K) \wedge \tau_{Ur}^+(K) \wedge T$, the running maximum and the running minimum are continuous. Moreover, there exists a constant q, so that at time t such that $\mathrm{d}(\overline{S}_t - \underline{S}_t) \neq 0$ and $t \leq \tau_{Dr}^+(K) \wedge \tau_{Ur}^+(K) \wedge T$, we have that

$$\mathbb{E}_t^{\mathbb{Q}^T}(f(S_T/S_t)) = \mathbb{E}_t^{\mathbb{Q}^T}((S_T/S_t)^q f(S_t/S_T)) \qquad (7.43)$$

holds for any bounded non-negative measurable function $f(\cdot)$ on $\mathbb{R}$.

Assumption 7.13 is sufficient for applying Proposition 7.4. Evaluating (7.39) at $V = \overline{S}_t/K$ and $W = \overline{S}_t$, we obtain

$$\text{OTKO}_t(\overline{S}_t/K, \overline{S}_t, T)$$
$$= \sum_{n=0}^{\infty} \left\{ \frac{1}{K^{nq}} \left[\text{DP}_t(\overline{S}_t K^{-2n-1}, T) - \frac{C_{q,t}(\overline{S}_t K^{2n-1}, T)}{\overline{S}_t^q} \right] \right.$$
$$\left. + K^{(n+1)q} [\overline{S}_t^{-q} P_{q,t}(\overline{S}_t K^{-2n-1}, T) - \text{DC}_t(\overline{S}_t K^{2n+1}, T)] \right\}, \quad (7.44)$$

for $K > 1$.

Differentiating (7.39) with respect to W, and evaluating at $V = H/K$ and $W = H$ implies that for $K > 1$ and $t \in [0, \tau_{H/K}^S \wedge \tau_H^S \wedge T]$:

$$\text{RUFDI}_t(H/K, H, T)$$
$$= -2 \sum_{n=1}^{\infty} n \left(\frac{1}{K^{nq}} \frac{\partial}{\partial H} \text{DP}_t(HK^{-2n-1}, T) \right.$$
$$+ \frac{K^{(n+1)q}}{H^q} \frac{\partial}{\partial H} P_{q,t}(HK^{-2n-1}, T)$$
$$+ K^{nq} \frac{\partial}{\partial H} \text{DC}_t(HK^{2n-1}, T) + \frac{H^{-p}}{K^{(n-1)q}} \frac{\partial}{\partial H} C_{q,t}(HK^{2n-1}, T) \right)$$
$$- \frac{q}{H} \sum_{n=1}^{\infty} n \left(\frac{1}{K^{nq}} \text{DP}_t(HK^{-2n-1}, T) - \frac{K^{(n+1)q}}{H^q} P_{q,t}(HK^{-2n-1}, T) \right.$$
$$\left. + K^{nq} \text{DC}_t(HK^{2n-1}, T) - \frac{H^{-q}}{K^{(n-1)q}} C_{q,t}(HK^{2n-1}, T) \right), \quad (7.45)$$

since K is a constant.

Substituting (7.44) and (7.45) in (7.25), it gives rise to the following theorem.

Theorem 7.11. *Under frictionless markets and Assumption 7.13, no arbitrage implies that the digital call on the K-relative drawdown preceding a K-relative drawup can be valued relative to the prices of bonds and* path-independent options as

$$\begin{aligned}
&\mathrm{DC}_t^{D^r<U^r}(K,T)\\
&= \sum_{n=0}^{\infty} \frac{(2n+1)}{K^{nq}}(\mathrm{DP}_t(\overline{S}_tK^{-2n-1},T) + \overline{S}_t^{-q}\mathrm{C}_{\mathrm{q,t}}(\overline{S}_tK^{2n+1},T))\\
&\quad + \sum_{n=0}^{\infty} \frac{(2n+1)}{K^{-(n+1)q}}(\mathrm{DC}_t(\overline{S}_tK^{2n+1},T) + \overline{S}_t^{-q}\mathrm{P}_{\mathrm{q,t}}(\overline{S}_tK^{-2n-1},T))\\
&\quad - \sum_{n=1}^{\infty} \frac{2n}{K^{nq}}(\mathrm{DP}_t(\underline{S}_tK^{-2n},T) + \underline{S}_t^{-q}\mathrm{C}_{\mathrm{q,t}}(\underline{S}_tK^{2n},T))\\
&\quad - \sum_{n=1}^{\infty} \frac{2n}{K^{-nq}}(\mathrm{DC}_t(\underline{S}_tK^{2n},T) + \underline{S}_t^{-q}\mathrm{P}_{\mathrm{q,t}}(\underline{S}_tK^{-2n},T))\\
&\quad - q\int_{\underline{S}_t}^{\overline{S}_tK} \sum_{n=1}^{\infty} n\left(\frac{\mathrm{DP}_t(HK^{-2n-1},T)}{K^{nq}} + \frac{\mathrm{P}_{\mathrm{q,t}}(HK^{-2n-1},T)}{K^{-(n+1)q}H^q}\right.\\
&\quad \left. + \frac{\mathrm{DC}_t(HK^{2n-1},T)}{K^{-nq}} + \frac{\mathrm{C}_{\mathrm{q,t}}(HK^{2n-1},T)}{K^{(n-1)q}H^q}\right)\frac{\mathrm{d}H}{H}, \quad (7.46)
\end{aligned}$$

for any $t \in [0, \tau_{D^r}^+(K) \wedge \tau_{U^r}^+(K) \wedge T]$ and $K > 1$.

7.9. Poisson Jump Processes

In Sections 7.2–7.8 we developed static and semi-static replications of both digital options under certain continuity and symmetry assumptions. As it is pointed out earlier, the notion of continuity can be extended to skip-freedom so that purely jump models can be considered. In this section, we consider two different skip-free dynamical setups, increasing both complexity and financial realism. The first setup requires no carrying cost for the underlying asset and symmetry in the risk neutral price process. The second setup allows carrying costs and keeps prices positive. We refer to the two setups as the arithmetic case and the geometric case, respectively. In what follows, we will develop replicating portfolio in both cases.

7.9.1. *Arithmetic case*

In this section, we require that the underlying has no carrying cost. This arises if the option we are concerned about is written on a forward price, or is written on a spot price, but only under stringent conditions (see, e.g., Carr (2011)). To cast the results of this section in their most favorable light, we will assume in this section that the barrier option is written on a forward price. The next section allows for non-zero carrying cost on the underlying asset.

Let F_t be the forward price at time $t \in [0,T]$. We assume that F is a continuous-time process. Under the risk-neutral measure $\mathbb{Q}^T$, F has representation

$$F_t = F_0 + a(N_{1,t} - N_{2,t}), \quad t \in [0,T], \qquad (7.47)$$

where $a > 0$ is a constant, N_1 and N_2 are independent identically distributed doubly stochastic processes (Brémaud, 1981), with jump intensity λ_t, which is independent of N_1 and N_2. In words, the forward price F. starts at $F_0 > 0$ and jumps up or down by the amount a according to an independent clock. Clearly, F. will satisfy all arithmetic symmetry conditions of Assumptions 7.1–7.7, if we extend the notion of continuity to skip-freedom. It follows that[3] we can construct replicating portfolios of one-touches or vanilla digital options once we have a replication with one-touch knockouts and their spreads in our hands.

Without loss of generality, let us assume that K is a positive integer multiple of a, so that overshoots are avoided. Since the replicating portfolio in Theorem 7.1 is purely static, one can easily extend the result there to the case in which the underlying is a skip-free process. More specifically, when the underlying process follows (7.47), a ricochet-upper-first down-and-in claim is a real spread of one-touch knockouts

$$\begin{aligned}\text{RUFDI}_t(H-K,H,T) &= B_t(T)\mathbb{Q}_t^T(\underline{S}_T \leq H-K, \overline{S}_{\tau_F^-(H-K)} = H) \\ &= \text{OTKO}_t(H-K, H+a, T) \\ &\quad - \text{OTKO}_t(H-K, H, T),\end{aligned}$$

from which one immediately obtain the following counterpart of Theorem 7.1:

$$\text{DC}_t^{D<U}(K,T) = \text{OTKO}_t(\overline{S}_t - K, \overline{S}_t + a, T) + \sum_{i=1}^{\frac{S_t + K - \overline{S}_t}{a} - 1} \Lambda_t^{(i)},$$

---

[3] This a consequence of Propositions 7.1 and 7.2.

where $\Lambda_t^{(i)}$ are the spreads of one-touch knockouts. That is,

$$\Lambda_t^{(i)} = \mathrm{OTKO}_t(\overline{S}_t + ai - K, \overline{S}_t + a(i+1), T) - \mathrm{OTKO}_t(\overline{S}_t + ai - K, \overline{S}_t + ai, T),$$

for any $t \in [0, \tau_D^+(K) \wedge \tau_U^+(K) \wedge T]$ and $K > 0$.

Similarly, one can modify the result in Theorem 7.2 slightly to obtain a replication of digital call on maximum drawdown:

$$\begin{aligned}\mathrm{DC}_t^{\overline{D}}(K,T) \\ = \mathrm{OTKO}_t(\overline{S}_t - K, \overline{S}_t + K + a, T) + \mathrm{OTKO}_t(\overline{S}_t + K + a, \overline{S}_t - K, T),\end{aligned} \quad (7.48)$$

for $t \in [0, \tau_D^+(K) \wedge T]$ and $K > 0$. The portfolio on the right-hand side of (7.48) obviously replicates the payoff of the digital call on maximum drawdown. Moreover, one can easily check that it is self-financing.

Let us now proceed to treat the complications that arise if we allow carrying costs on the underlying and if we further require that the underlying price process stays positive.

7.9.2. Geometric case

In this section, we will assume that all options are written on the spot price of some underlying asset. Let us consider a filtered risk-neutral probability space $(\Omega, \mathbb{F}, \mathcal{F}, \mathbb{Q}^T)$, $\mathcal{F} = \bigcup_{t \in [0,T]} \mathcal{F}_t$. Let us denote by N_1 and N_2 two independent standard doubly stochastic processes, with positive jump arrival rates $\lambda_{1,t}$ and $\lambda_{2,t}$ under the risk-neutral measure $\mathbb{Q}^T$. We require that the trajectories of the intensities $\lambda_{1,t}$ and $\lambda_{2,t}$ are $\mathcal{F}_0$-measurable, and the ratio $\lambda_{1,t}/\lambda_{2,t}$ is a constant. In particular, for a given positive constant $g > 0$, we assume that

$$\lambda_{1,t}(e^g - 1) + \lambda_{2,t}(e^{-g} - 1) = r_t - q_t, \quad (7.49)$$

where r_t is the riskfree rate and q_t is the dividend rate (see, e.g., Carr and Chou (1997)).

For a given positive constant S_0, we also assume that the stochastic process governing the spot price of the underlying asset is given by

$$S_t = S_0 e^{g(N_{1,t} - N_{2,t})}, \quad t \in [0,T]. \quad (7.50)$$

In words, the spot price $S.$ starts at $S_0 > 0$ and jumps up by the amount $S_{t^-}(e^g - 1) > 0$ or down by the amount $S_{t^-}(e^{-g} - 1) < 0$ at independent exponential times. Note that equation (7.49) implies that the discounted stock price, with discount rate $r_t - q_t$, is a positive martingale.

Before developing any replication portfolio, let us first examine the symmetry properties of the spot price process. Under the risk neutral measure $\mathbb{Q}^T$, the log price is a difference of two independent Poisson processes.

$$\mathrm{d} \log S_t = g(\mathrm{d}N_{1,t} - \mathrm{d}N_{2,t}), \quad t \in [0, T]. \tag{7.51}$$

One could employ Esscher transform (see, e.g., Brémaud (1981) and Shiryaev (1999)) to construct a new probability measure equivalent to $\mathbb{Q}^T$, under which the log price $\log S$ is a symmetric martingale. More specifically, let us define a constant

$$\pi = \frac{1}{2g} \log \frac{\lambda_{2,0}}{\lambda_{1,0}}. \tag{7.52}$$

Then we have a positive martingale

$$Y_t = \exp\left(\pi g(N_{1,t} - N_{2,t}) - \int_0^t (\lambda_{1,s}(e^{\pi g} - 1) + \lambda_{2,s}(e^{-\pi g} - 1))\mathrm{d}s\right)$$

$$=: \left(\frac{S_t}{S_0}\right)^\pi \cdot \phi(t), \quad t \in [0, T], \tag{7.53}$$

Define a new measure $\mathbb{P}^T$ by

$$\mathbb{E}_t^{\mathbb{P}^T}(Z) = \frac{1}{Y_t} \mathbb{E}_t^{\mathbb{Q}^T}(ZY_T), \tag{7.54}$$

for any $\mathcal{F}_T$-measurable random variable Z. Under $\mathbb{P}^T$, the log price $\log S$ is a difference of two independent identically distributed doubly stochastic processes with jump intensity $e^{\pi g}\lambda_1$. Thus, at any time $t \in [0, T]$, for any non-negative measurable function $f(\cdot)$ on $\mathbb{R}_{>0}$, we have

$$\mathbb{E}_t^{\mathbb{P}^T}(f(S_T/S_t)) = \mathbb{E}_t^{\mathbb{P}^T}(f(S_t/S_T)). \tag{7.55}$$

It follows that

$$\mathbb{E}_t^{\mathbb{Q}^T}(f(S_T/S_t)) = \mathbb{E}_t^{\mathbb{P}^T}((S_T/S_t)^{-\pi} \cdot (\phi(t)/\phi(T)) \cdot f(S_t/S_T))$$

$$= \mathbb{E}_t^{\mathbb{P}^T}((S_T/S_t)^\pi \cdot (\phi(t)/\phi(T)) \cdot f(S_t/S_T))$$

$$= \mathbb{E}_t^{\mathbb{Q}^T}((S_T/S_t)^{2\pi} f(S_t/S_T))$$

holds for any bounded non-negative measurable function $f(\cdot)$ on $\mathbb{R}_{>0}$. In other words, the spot price process will satisfy Assumption 7.11, if we extend the notion of continuity to skip-freedom.

By the discussion in Remark 7.6, and the fact that the spot price process is skip-free, it follows that $S.$ will satisfy all geometric symmetry conditions in Assumptions 7.8–7.13. Therefore, it suffices to develop the counterparts of Theorems 7.7 and 7.9 for the model in (7.50).

Without loss of generality, let us assume that $\log K$ is a positive integer multiple of g, so that overshoots are avoided. Since the result in Theorem 7.7 is purely static, it can be easily extended to the model in (7.50). More specifically, a ricochet-upper-first down-and-in claim is a real spread of one-touch knockouts

$$\mathrm{RUFDI}_t(H/K, H, T) = \mathrm{B}_t(T)\mathbb{E}_t^{\mathbb{Q}^T}\left(\mathbf{1}_{\{\underline{S}_T \leq H/K\}}\delta(\overline{S}_{\tau_S^-(H/F)} - H)\right)$$
$$= \mathrm{OTKO}_t(H/K, He^g, T) - \mathrm{OTKO}_t(H/K, H, T), \quad (7.56)$$

from which one immediately obtains

$$\mathrm{DC}_t^{D^r < U^r}(K, T) = \mathrm{OTKO}_t(\overline{S}_t/K, \overline{S}_t e^g, T) + \sum_{i=1}^{\frac{1}{g}\log\frac{S_t K}{\overline{S}_t} - 1} \Gamma_t^{(i)}, \quad (7.57)$$

where $\Gamma_t^{(i)}$ are the spreads of one-touch knockouts. That is,

$$\Gamma_t^{(i)} = \mathrm{OTKO}_t(\overline{S}_t e^{ig}/K, \overline{S}_t e^{(i+1)g}, T) - \mathrm{OTKO}_t(\overline{S}_t e^{ig}/K, \overline{S}_t e^{ig}, T)$$

for any $t \in [0, \tau_{D^r}^+(K) \wedge \tau_{U^r}^+(K) \wedge T]$ and $K > 0$.

Similarly, the result in Theorem 7.9 can be extended. In fact, one can show that a digital call on maximum relative drawdown can be replicated with bonds, one-touch knockouts and lookbacks:

$$\mathrm{DC}_t^{\overline{D}^r}(K, T)$$
$$= \mathrm{OTKO}_t(\overline{S}_t/K, \overline{S}_t Ke^g, T) + K^q \cdot \mathrm{OTKO}_t(\overline{S}_t Ke^g, \overline{S}_t/K, T)$$
$$+ (1 - e^{-qg})[\mathrm{LBP}_t(\overline{S}_t, K, T) - \mathrm{LBC}_t(\overline{S}_t, K, T)],$$

for any $t \in [0, \tau_{D^r}^+(K) \wedge T]$ and $K > 0$. Here the prices of lookback put/call are given by

$$\mathrm{LBP}_t(M, K, T) = \sum_{n=0}^{\infty} \frac{(-1)^n e^{-\lceil \frac{n}{2}\rceil qg}}{K^{(n+1)q}}$$
$$\times \sum_{i \leq \frac{1}{g}\log\frac{M}{K^{2n+3}}} \left(\frac{K^{2n+3}}{Me^{-ig}}\right)^q P_n\left(\log\frac{K^{2n+3}}{Me^{-ig}}\right)$$

$$\times \mathrm{OT}_t(e^{(i-2\lfloor \frac{n+1}{2} \rfloor -1)g}, T),$$

$$\mathrm{LBC}_t(M,K,T) = \sum_{n=0}^{\infty} \frac{(-1)^n}{K^{-(n+1)q}} e^{\lceil \frac{n+1}{2} \rceil qg}$$

$$\times \sum_{i \geq \frac{1}{g} \log(MK^{2n+1})+1} P_n\left(\log \frac{MK^{2n+1}}{e^{(i-1)g}}\right)$$

$$\times \mathrm{OT}_t(e^{(i+2\lfloor \frac{n}{2} \rfloor +1)g}, T),$$

where $\lfloor x \rfloor$ and $\lceil x \rceil$ are the floor and the ceiling functions, and P_n is a function on the lattice $\mathbb{N}_0 \cdot g$, satisfying

$$P_0 = 1, \quad P_n(0) = n+1, \tag{7.58}$$

$$P_{n+1}((i+1) \cdot g) - P_{n+1}(i \cdot g) = e^{qg} P_n((i+1) \cdot g) - P_n(i \cdot g). \tag{7.59}$$

7.10. Concluding Remarks

In this chapter, we develop static replications of a digital call on maximum drawdown and a digital call on the K-drawdown preceding a K-drawup. We then develop semi-static replications of these options using consecutively more liquid instruments under appropriate symmetry and continuity assumptions. We consider two different dynamical setups, increasing in complexity and financial realism. In both cases, our portfolio is self-financing, and only needs occasional trading, typically when the maximum or the minimum changes. Finally, we extend the replication results to the case in which the underlying process is driven by the difference of two independent Poisson processes. We show that the previous semi-static trading strategies continue to replicate the payoffs of these claims with slight modifications.

7.11. Proof for GBM

In this section, we prove that the GBM model satisfies geometric symmetry in (7.34). And because of the continuity of sample paths and discussion in Remark 7.6, we further conclude that the geometric Brownian motion model satisfies Assumptions 7.8–7.13.

Let us begin with a filtered risk-neutral probability space $(\Omega, \mathbb{F}, \mathcal{F}, \mathbb{Q}^T)$ with filtration $\mathbb{F} = \{\mathcal{F}_t\}_{t \geq 0}$. We consider the logarithm of a spot price process given by a drifted Brownian motion

$$\mathrm{d}\log S_t = \nu \mathrm{d}t + \sigma \mathrm{d}W_t, \quad S_0 = 1, t \in [0,T], \tag{7.60}$$

where ν and $\sigma > 0$ are real constants, $\{W_t\}_{t \geq 0}$ is a standard Brownian motion with respect to $\mathbb{F}$. Let us denote by $q = -\frac{2\nu}{\sigma^2}$, then it is easily seen that

$$Y_t = e^{q\sigma W_t - \frac{1}{2}q^2\sigma^2 t} = \left(\frac{S_t}{S_0}\right)^q, \quad t \in [0,T], \tag{7.61}$$

is a positive martingale. Define a new measure $\mathbb{P}^T$ by

$$\mathbb{E}_t^{\mathbb{P}^T}(Z) = \frac{1}{Y_t}\mathbb{E}_t^{\mathbb{Q}^T}(ZY_T), \tag{7.62}$$

for any $\mathcal{F}_T$-measurable random variable Z. Using the Girsanov theorem, we know that, under $\mathbb{P}_t^T$, the log price follows

$$\mathrm{d}\log S_u = -\nu \mathrm{d}u + \sigma \mathrm{d}W_u, \quad u \in [t,T]. \tag{7.63}$$

Thus, at any fixed time $t \in [0,T]$, for any bounded non-negative measurable function $f(\cdot)$ on $\mathbb{R}_{>0}$:

$$\begin{aligned}\mathbb{E}_t^{\mathbb{Q}^T}(f(S_T/S_t)) &= \mathbb{E}_t^{\mathbb{Q}^T}(f(\exp(\log S_T - \log S_t))) \\ &= \mathbb{E}_t^{\mathbb{P}^T}(f(\exp(\log S_t - \log S_T))) \\ &= \mathbb{E}_t^{\mathbb{P}^T}(f(S_t/S_T)) \\ &= \frac{1}{Y_t}\mathbb{E}_t^{\mathbb{Q}^T}(Y_T f(S_t/S_T)) \\ &= \mathbb{E}_t^{\mathbb{Q}^T}((S_T/S_t)^q f(S_t/S_T)). \end{aligned} \tag{7.64}$$

This proves that the GBM model satisfies geometric symmetry in (7.34), and thus satisfies Assumptions 7.8–7.13.

Chapter 8

Fair Premiums of Drawdown Insurances

In this chapter, we discuss the stochastic modeling of drawdowns and study the valuation of a number of insurance contracts against drawdown events. More precisely, the drawdown process is defined as the current relative drop of an asset value from its historical maximum. In its simplest form, the drawdown insurance involves a continuous premium payment by the investor (protection buyer) to insure a drawdown of an underlying asset value to a pre-specified level.

In order to provide the investor with more flexibility in managing the path-dependent drawdown risk, we incorporate the right to terminate the contract early. This early cancellation feature is similar to the surrender right that arises in many common insurance products such as equity-indexed annuities (see, e.g., Cheung and Yang (2005), Moore (2009) and Moore and Young (2005)). Due to the timing flexibility, the investor may stop the premium payment if he/she finds that a drawdown is unlikely to occur (e.g., when the underlying price continues to rise). In our analysis, we rigorously show that the investor's optimal cancellation timing is based on a non-trivial first passage time of the underlying drawdown process. In other words, the investor's cancellation strategy and valuation of the contract will depend not only on current value of the underlying asset, but also its distance from the historical maximum. Applying the theory of optimal stopping as well as analytical properties of drawdown processes, we derive the optimal cancellation threshold and illustrate it through numerical examples.

Moreover, we consider a related insurance contract that protects the investor from a drawdown preceding a drawup. In other words, the insurance contract expires early if a drawup event occurs prior to a drawdown. From the investor's perspective, when a drawup is realized, there is little need to insure against a drawdown. Therefore, this drawup contingency automatically stops the premium payment and is an attractive feature that will potentially reduce the cost of drawdown insurance.

Our model can also be readily extended to incorporate the default risk associated with the underlying asset. To this end, we observe that a drawdown can be triggered by a continuous price movement as well as a jump-to-default event. Among other results, we provide the formulas for the fair premium of the drawdown insurance, and analyze the impact of default risk on the valuation of drawdown insurance.

For our valuation problems, we often work with the joint law of drawdowns and drawups. To this end, some related formulas from Chapter 2 are useful. Compared to the existing literature and our prior work, these chapter's contributions are threefold. First, we derive the fair premium for insuring a number of drawdown events, with both finite and infinite maturities, as well as new provisions like drawup contingency and early termination. In particular, the early termination option leads to the analysis of a new optimal stopping problem (see Section 8.2). We rigorously solve for the optimal termination strategy, which can be expressed in terms of first passage time of a drawdown process. Furthermore, we incorporate the underlying's default risk — a feature absent in other related studies on drawdown — into our analysis, and study its impact on the drawdown insurance premium.

The rest of this chapter is structured as follows. In Section 8.1, we describe a stochastic model for drawdowns and drawups, and formulate the valuation of a vanilla drawdown insurance. In Sections 8.2 and 8.3, we study, respectively, the cancellable drawdown insurance and drawdown insurance with drawup contingency. As extension, we discuss the valuation of drawdown insurance on a defaultable stock in Section 8.4. Section 8.5 concludes the chapter. We include the proofs for a number of lemmas in Section 8.6.

8.1. Model for Drawdown Insurance

We fix a filtered probability space $(\Omega, \mathbb{F}, \mathcal{F}, \mathbb{Q})$ with filtration $\mathbb{F} = \{\mathcal{F}_t\}_{t \geq 0}$. The risk-neutral pricing measure $\mathbb{Q}$ is used for our valuation problems. Under the measure $\mathbb{Q}$, we model a risky asset S by the geometric

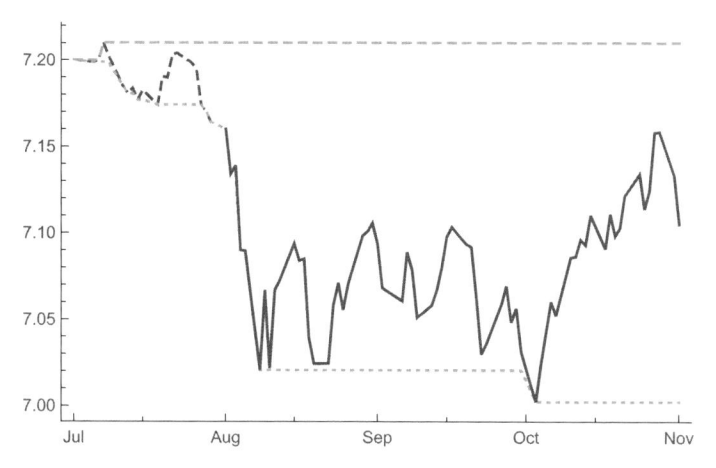

Fig. 8.1. Daily log-price of S&P Index from 07/01/2011 to 11/01/2011. For illustration, July data (shown in black dashed) is used as the reference period to record the historical running maximum (gray dashed) and minimum (gray dotted). At the end of the reference period, the running maximum $\bar{s} = 7.21$ and the log-price $x = 7.16$, so the initial drawdown $y = 0.05$. We remark that the large drawdown in August 2011 due to the downgrade of U.S. debt by S&P.

Brownian motion

$$\frac{dS_t}{S_t} = r dt + \sigma dW_t \qquad (8.1)$$

where $\{W_t\}_{t\geq 0}$ is a standard Brownian motion under $\mathbb{Q}$, and $r > 0$ is the risk-free rate.

We denote by $\overline{S}.$ and $\underline{S}.$, respectively, the processes for the running maximum and running minimum of $S.$. When writing the contract, the insurer may use the historical maximum $\bar{s}$ and minimum $\underline{s}$ recorded from a prior reference period. Consequently, at the time of contract inception, the reference maximum $\bar{s}$, the reference minimum $\underline{s}$ and the stock price need not coincide. This is illustrated in Figure 8.1.

The running maximum and running minimum processes associated with $S.$ are given by

$$\overline{S}_t = \bar{s} \vee \sup_{s \in [0,t]} S_s, \quad \underline{S}_t = \underline{s} \wedge \inf_{s \in [0,t]} S_s. \qquad (8.2)$$

We define the stopping times

$$\varrho_D^+(K) := \inf\{t > 0 : \overline{S}_t/S_t > K\}, \quad \varrho_U^+(K) := \inf\{t > 0 : S_t/\underline{S}_t > K\},$$

respectively as the first times that $S.$ attains a *relative drawdown* of K units and a *relative drawup* of K units. Without loss of generality, we assume that $1 \leq \bar{s}/\underline{s} < K$ so that $\varrho_D^+(K) \wedge \varrho_U^+(K) > 0$, almost surely.

To facilitate our analysis, we shall work with log-prices. Therefore, we define $X_t = \log S_t$ so that

$$X_t = x + \mu t + \sigma W_t, \qquad (8.3)$$

where $x = \log S_0$ and $\mu = r - \frac{\sigma^2}{2}$. We denote by $\overline{X}_t = \log \overline{S}_t$ and $\underline{X}_t = \log \underline{S}_t$, respectively, the running maximum and running minimum of the log price process. Then, the relative drawdown and drawup of $S.$ are equivalent to the absolute drawdown and drawup of the log-price $X.$, namely,

$$\tau_D^+(a) = \inf\{t > 0 : D_t > a\}, \quad \tau_U^+(a) = \inf\{t > 0 : U_t > a\}, \qquad (8.4)$$

where $a = \log K$, $D_t = \overline{X}_t - X_t$ and $U_t = X_t - \underline{X}_t$. Note that under the current model the stopping times $\tau_D^+(a) = \varrho_D^+(K)$ and $\tau_U^+(a) = \varrho_U^+(K)$, and they do not depend on x or equivalently the initial stock price. Throughout the chapter, we denote

$$\delta := \frac{\mu}{\sigma^2}, \quad \gamma := \sqrt{\delta^2 + \frac{2r}{\sigma^2}}. \qquad (8.5)$$

8.1.1. *Drawdown insurance and fair premium*

We now consider an insurance contract based on a drawdown event. Specifically, the protection buyer who seeks insurance on a drawdown event of size a will pay a constant premium payment p continuously over time until the drawdown time $\tau_D^+(a)$. In return, the protection buyer will receive the insured amount α at time $\tau_D^+(a)$. Here, the values p, a and α are pre-specified at the contract inception. The contract value of this drawdown insurance is

$$f(y, p) = \mathbb{E}\left(-\int_0^{\tau_D^+(a)} e^{-rt} p \, dt + \alpha e^{-r\tau_D^+(a)} \bigg| D_0 = y \right) \qquad (8.6)$$

$$= \frac{p}{r} - \left(\alpha + \frac{p}{r}\right) \xi(y), \qquad (8.7)$$

where $\xi(\cdot)$ is the conditional Laplace transform of $\tau_D^+(a)$ defined by

$$\xi(y) := \mathbb{E}(e^{-r\tau_D^+(a)} \mid D_0 = y), \quad 0 \leq y \leq a. \qquad (8.8)$$

This amounts to computing the conditional Laplace transform $\xi(\cdot)$, which admits a closed-form formula as we show next.

Lemma 8.1. *The conditional Laplace transform function $\xi(\cdot)$ is given by*

$$\xi(y) = \frac{e^{\delta y}}{\sinh(\gamma a)}\left(e^{-\delta a}\sinh(\gamma y) + \frac{e^{-\delta a}\gamma\sinh(\gamma(a-y))}{\gamma\cosh(\gamma a) - \delta\sinh(\gamma a)}\right), \quad (8.9)$$

for any $y \in [0,a]$.

Therefore, the contract value $f(y,p)$ in (8.6) is explicit given for any premium rate p. The fair premium $P^\star$ is found from the equation $f(y, P^\star) = 0$, which yields

$$P^\star = \frac{ra\xi(y)}{1-\xi(y)}. \quad (8.10)$$

Remark 8.1. Our formulation can be adapted to the case when the drawdown insurance is paid for upfront. Indeed, we can set $p = 0$ in (8.6), then the price of this contract at time zero is $f(y,0)$. On the other hand, if the insurance premium is paid over a pre-specified period of time T', rather than up to the random drawdown time, then the present value of the premium cash flow $\frac{p}{r}(e^{-rT'} - 1)$ will replace the first term in the expectation of (2.7). In this case, setting the contract value zero at inception, the fair premium is given by $P^\star(T') := \frac{f(y,0)r}{1-e^{-rT'}} > 0$. In Section 8.3, we discuss the case where the holder will stop premium payment if a drawup event occurs prior to drawdown or maturity.

For both the insurer and protection buyer, it is useful to know how long the drawdown is expected to occur. This leads us to compute the expected time to a drawdown of size $a > 0$, under the physical measure $\mathbb{P}$. The measure $\mathbb{P}$ is equivalent to $\mathbb{Q}$, whereby the drift of $S.$ is the annualized growth rate ν, not the risk-free rate r. Under measure $\mathbb{P}$, the log price is

$$X_t = x + \tilde{\mu} t + \sigma W_t^{\mathbb{P}}, \quad \text{with } \tilde{\mu} = \nu - \sigma^2/2,$$

where $\{W_t^{\mathbb{P}}\}_{t\geq 0}$ is a $\mathbb{P}$-Brownian motion.

Proposition 8.1. *The expected time to drawdown of size a is given by*

$$\mathbb{E}^{\mathbb{P}}(\tau_D^+(a)|D_0 = y) = \frac{y\rho(y,a) + (y-a)e^{2\tilde{\delta}(y-a)}\rho(a-y,a)}{\tilde{\mu}}$$
$$+ \rho(y,a)\frac{e^{2\tilde{\delta}a} - 2\tilde{\delta}a - 1}{2\sigma^2\tilde{\delta}^2}, \quad (8.11)$$

where $\rho(y,a) := e^{\tilde{\delta}y}\frac{\sinh(\tilde{\delta}(a-y))}{\sinh(\tilde{\delta}a)}$ and

$$\tilde{\delta} := \tilde{\mu}/\sigma^2. \quad (8.12)$$

Proof. By the Markov property of the process $X.$, we know that $\mathbb{P}$-a.s.

$$\tau_D^+(a) = \tau_X^-(y-a) \wedge \tau_X^+(y) + (\tau_D^+(a) \circ \theta_{\tau_X^+(y)}) \mathbf{1}_{\{\tau_X^+(y) < \tau_X^-(y-a)\}},$$

where $\theta.$ is the standard Markov shift operator. If $\tilde{\mu} \neq 0$, applying the optional sampling theorem to the bounded martingale $\{Y_t\}_{t \in [0, \tau_X^-(y-a) \wedge \tau_X^+(y)]}$ with $Y_t = X_t - \tilde{\mu} t$, we obtain that

$$\mathbb{E}^{\mathbb{P}}(\tau_X^-(y-a) \wedge \tau_X^+(y))$$

$$= \frac{1}{\tilde{\mu}} \mathbb{E}^{\mathbb{P}}(X_{\tau_X^-(y-a) \wedge \tau_X^+(y)})$$

$$= \frac{y \mathbb{P}(\tau_X^+(y) < \tau_X^-(y-a)) + (y-a) \mathbb{P}(\tau_X^-(y-a) < \tau_X^+(y))}{\tilde{\mu}}.$$

Moreover, using Lemma A.1 under the physical measure $\mathbb{P}$ with $q = 0$, we have $\mathbb{P}(\tau_X^+(y) < \tau_X^-(y-a)) = \rho(y,a)$, $\mathbb{P}(\tau_X^-(y-a) < \tau_X^+(y)|X_0 = x) = e^{2\tilde{\delta}(y-a)} \rho(a-y, a)$ and (4.13):

$$\mathbb{E}^{\mathbb{P}}(\tau_D^+(a)|D_0 = 0) = \frac{e^{2\tilde{\delta}a} - 2\tilde{\delta}a - 1}{2\sigma^2 \tilde{\delta}^2};$$

we conclude the proof for $\tilde{\mu} \neq 0$. The case of $\tilde{\mu} = 0$ is obtained by taking the limit $\tilde{\mu} \to 0$. $\square$

8.2. Cancellable Drawdown Insurance

As is common in insurance and derivatives markets, investors may demand the option to voluntarily terminate their contracts early. Typical examples include American options and equity-indexed annuities with surrender rights. In this section, we incorporate a cancellable feature into our drawdown insurance, and investigate the optimal timing to terminate the contract.

With a cancellable drawdown insurance, the protection buyer can terminate the position by paying a constant fee $c > 0$ anytime prior to a pre-specified drawdown of size a. For a notional amount of α with premium rate p, the fair valuation of this contract is found from the optimal stopping problem:

$$V(y,p) = \sup_{\tau \in \mathcal{T}} \mathbb{E}\left(-\int_0^{\tau_D^+(a) \wedge \tau} e^{-rt} p \, dt - c e^{-r\tau} \mathbf{1}_{\{\tau < \tau_D^+(a)\}}\right.$$
$$\left. + \alpha e^{-r\tau_D^+(a)} \mathbf{1}_{\{\tau_D^+(a) \leq \tau < \infty\}} \,\bigg|\, D_0 = y\right), \qquad (8.13)$$

for $y \in [0, a)$. The fair premium $P^\star$ makes the contract value zero at inception, i.e., $V(y, P^\star) = 0$.

We observe that it is never optimal to cancel and pay the fee c at $\tau = \tau_D^+(a)$ since the contract expires and pays at $\tau_D^+(a)$. Hence, it is sufficient to consider a smaller set of stopping times $\mathcal{S} := \{\tau \in \mathbb{F} : 0 < \tau < \tau_D^+(a)\}$, which consists of $\mathbb{F}$-stopping times strictly bounded by $\tau_D^+(a)$. We will show in Section 8.2.2 that the set of *candidate* stopping times is in fact the drawdown stopping times $\tau = \tau_D^-(\theta)$ indexed by their respective thresholds $\theta \in (0, a)$ (see (8.42)).

8.2.1. Contract value decomposition

Next, we show that the cancellable drawdown insurance can be decomposed into an ordinary drawdown insurance and an American-style claim on the drawdown insurance. This provides a key insight for the explicit computation of the contract value as well as the optimal termination strategy.

Proposition 8.2. *The cancellable drawdown insurance value admits the decomposition:*

$$V(y,p) = -f(y,p) + \sup_{\tau \in \mathcal{S}} \mathbb{E}(e^{-r\tau}(f(D_\tau, p) - c) \,|\, D_0 = y), \qquad (8.14)$$

where $f(\cdot, \cdot)$ is defined in (8.6).

Proof. Let us consider a transformation of $V(D_0, p)$. First, by rearranging of the first integral in (8.13) and using $\mathbf{1}_{\{\tau \geq \tau_D^+(a)\}} = 1 - \mathbf{1}_{\{\tau < \tau_D^+(a)\}}$, we obtain

$$V(y,p)$$
$$= \mathbb{E}\left(-\int_0^{\tau_D^+(a)} e^{-rt} p\, dt + \alpha e^{-r\tau_D^+(a)} \,\bigg|\, D_0 = y\right)$$
$$+ \underbrace{\sup_{\tau \in \mathcal{T}} \mathbb{E}\left(\int_{\tau_D^+(a) \wedge \tau}^{\tau_D^+(a)} e^{-rt} p\, dt - (ce^{-r\tau} + \alpha e^{-r\tau_D^+(a)})\mathbf{1}_{\{\tau < \tau_D^+(a)\}} \,\bigg|\, D_0 = y\right)}_{G(\cdot, p)}$$
$$= -f(y,p) + G(y,p). \qquad (8.15)$$

Note that the first term is explicitly given in (8.6) and (8.9), and it does not depend on τ. Since the second term depends on τ only through its truncated counterpart $\tau \wedge \tau_D^+(a) \leq \tau_D^+(a)$, and that $\tau = \tau_D^+(a)$ is suboptimal, we can in fact consider maximizing over the restricted collection of stopping times $\mathcal{S} = \{\tau \in \mathcal{F} : 0 \leq \tau < \tau_D^+(a)\}$. As a result, using the strong Markov property of $X.$, we can write

$$G(y,p) = \sup_{\tau \in \mathcal{S}} \mathbb{E}(e^{-r\tau} \tilde{f}(D_\tau, p) \mathbf{1}_{\{\tau < \infty\}} \,|\, D_0 = y),$$

where for any $y < a$,

$$\tilde{f}(y,p) = \mathbb{E}\left(\int_0^{\tau_D^+(a)} e^{-rt} p\, dt - \alpha e^{-r\tau_D^+(a)} - c \,\bigg|\, D_\tau = y\right). \qquad (8.16)$$

Hence, we complete the proof by simply noting that $\tilde{f}(y,p) = f(y,p) - c$ (cf. (8.16) and (8.6)). □

Using this decomposition, we can determine the optimal cancellation strategy from the optimal stopping problem $G(y)$, which we will solve explicitly in the next subsection.

8.2.2. Optimal cancellation strategy

In order to determine the optimal cancellation strategy for $V(y,p)$ in (8.14), it is sufficient to solve the optimal stopping problem represented by g in

(8.15) for a fixed p. Our method of solution consists of two main steps:

(1) We conjecture a candidate class of stopping times defined by $\tau := \tau_D^-(\theta) \wedge \tau_D^+(a) \in \mathcal{S}$, where

$$\tau_D^-(\theta) = \inf\{t \geq 0 : D_t \leq \theta\}, \quad 0 < \theta < a. \tag{8.17}$$

This leads us to look for a candidate optimal threshold $\theta^\star \in (0, a)$ using the principle of *smooth pasting* (see (8.20)).

(2) We rigorously verify via a martingale argument that the cancellation strategy based on the threshold $\theta^\star$ is indeed optimal.

Step 1. From the properties of Laplace function $\xi(\cdot)$ (see Lemma 8.3 below), we know the reward function $\tilde{f}(\cdot, p) := f(\cdot, p) - c$ in (8.14) is a decreasing concave. Therefore, if $\tilde{f}(0) \leq 0$, then the second term of (8.14) is non-positive, and it is optimal for the protection buyer to never cancel the insurance, i.e., $\tau = \infty$. Hence, in search of non-trivial optimal exercise strategies, it is sufficient to study only the case with $\tilde{f}(0, p) > 0$, which is equivalent to

$$p > \frac{r(c + \alpha \xi(0))}{1 - \xi(0)} \geq 0. \tag{8.18}$$

For each stopping rule conjectured in (8.17), we compute explicitly the second term of (8.14) as

$$g(y, \theta, p) := \mathbb{E}(e^{-r(\tau_D^-(\theta) \wedge \tau_D^+(a))} \tilde{f}(D_{\tau_D^-(\theta) \wedge \tau_D^+(a)}, p) \mid D_0 = y)$$

$$= \begin{cases} e^{\delta(y-\theta)} \dfrac{\sinh(\gamma(a-y))}{\sinh(\gamma(a-\theta))} \tilde{f}(\theta, p) & \text{if } y > \theta, \\ \tilde{f}(y, p) & \text{if } y \leq \theta. \end{cases} \tag{8.19}$$

The *candidate optimal* cancellation threshold $\theta^\star \in (0, a)$ is found from the smooth pasting condition (see, e.g., Peskir and Shiryaev (2006, Section 9.1)):

$$\left.\frac{\partial}{\partial y}\right|_{y=\theta} g(y, \theta, p) = \left.\frac{\partial}{\partial y}\right|_{y=\theta} \tilde{f}(y, p). \tag{8.20}$$

This is equivalent to seeking the root $\theta^\star$ of the equation:

$$F(\theta, p) := [\delta - \gamma \coth(\gamma(a-\theta))]\tilde{f}(\theta, p) - \tilde{f}'(\theta, p) = 0. \tag{8.21}$$

Next, we show that the root $\theta^\star$ exists and is unique.

Lemma 8.2. *There exists a unique $\theta^\star \in (0, a)$ satisfying the smooth pasting condition (8.20).*

Lemma 8.3.

$$\inf_{0<\theta<\theta_0<a} \left\{ \xi''(\theta) + (\gamma \coth(\gamma(a-\theta)) - \delta)\, \xi'(\theta) + \frac{\gamma^2(\xi(\theta) - \xi(\theta_0))}{(\sinh(\gamma(a-\theta)))^2} \right\} \geq 0,$$

and the infimum is attained at $\theta = \theta_0 = a$.

Step 2. With the candidate optimal threshold θ^* from (8.20), we now verify that the candidate value function $g(y, \theta^*, p)$ dominates the reward function $\tilde{f}(y,p) = f(y,p) - c$. Recall that $g(y, \theta^*, p) = \tilde{f}(y,p)$ for $y \in (0, \theta^*)$.

Lemma 8.4. *The value function corresponding to the candidate optimal threshold θ^* satisfies*

$$g(y, \theta^*, p) > \tilde{f}(y, p), \quad \forall y \in (\theta^*, a).$$

By the definition of $g(y, \theta^*, p)$ in (8.19), repeated conditioning yields that the stopped process $\{e^{-r(t \wedge \tau_D^-(\theta^*) \wedge \tau_D^+(a))} g(D_{t \wedge \tau_D^-(\theta^*) \wedge \tau_D^+(a)}, \theta^*, p)\}_{t \geq 0}$ is a martingale. For $y \in [0, \theta^*)$, we have

$$(\mathcal{L} - r)\tilde{f}(y, p) = -\left(\alpha + \frac{p}{r}\right)\left(\frac{1}{2}\sigma^2 \xi''(y) - \mu \xi'(y) - r(\xi(y) - \xi(\theta_0))\right)$$

$$= -\left(\alpha + \frac{p}{r}\right) r\xi(\theta_0) < 0,$$

where $\mathcal{L} = \frac{1}{2}\sigma^2 \frac{\partial^2}{\partial y^2} - \mu \frac{\partial}{\partial y}$ is the infinitesimal generator of drawdown process (acting on $C^1(\mathbb{R}_{\geq 0}) \cap C^2(\mathbb{R}_{>0})$ with vanishing first-order derivative at 0).

As a result, the function $g(\cdot, \theta^*, p) \in C^1([0, a]) \cap C^2((0, \theta^*) \cap (\theta^*, a))$ solves the variational inequality:

$$\max\{\tilde{f}(y, p) - g(y, \theta^*, p), (\mathcal{L} - r)g(y, \theta^*, p)\} = 0, \quad \forall y \in (0, a). \quad (8.22)$$

Hence, the process $\{e^{-rt} g(D_t, \theta^*, p)\}_{t \in [0, \tau_D^+(a)]}$ is a super-martingale that dominates the discounted process $\{e^{-rt} \tilde{f}(D_t, p)\}_{t \in [0, \tau_D^+(a)]}$.

To finalize the proof, we note that for $y \in (\theta^*, a)$ and any stopping time $\tau \in \mathcal{S}$,

$$g(y, \theta^*, p) \geq \mathbb{E}(e^{-r\tau} g(D_\tau, \theta^*, p) \mid D_0 = y)$$
$$\geq \mathbb{E}(e^{-r\tau} \tilde{f}(D_\tau, p) \mid D_0 = y). \quad (8.23)$$

Maximizing over τ, we see that $g(y, \theta^*, p) \geq G(y, p)$. On the other hand, (8.23) becomes an equality when $\tau = \tau_D^-(\theta^*)$, which yields the reverse inequality $g(y, \theta^*, p) \leq G(y, p)$. As a result, the stopping time $\tau_D^-(\theta^*)$ is indeed the solution to the optimal stopping problem (8.16).

In summary, the protection buyer will continue to pay the premium over time until the drawdown process D. either falls to the level $\theta^\star$ in (8.20) or reaches to the level a specified by the contract, whichever comes first. In Figure 8.2(a), we illustrate the optimal cancellation level $\theta^\star$. As shown in our proof, the optimal stopping value function $g(y, \theta^\star, p)$ connects smoothly with the intrinsic value $\tilde{f}(y,p) = f(y,p) - c$ at $y = \theta^\star \equiv \theta^\star(p)$. In Figure 8.2(b), we show that the fair premium $P^\star$ is decreasing with respect to the protection drawdown size a. This is intuitive since the drawdown time $\tau_D^+(a)$ is almost surely longer for a larger drawdown size a and the payment at $\tau_D^+(a)$ is fixed at α. The protection buyer is expected to pay over a longer period of time but at a lower premium rate.

Lastly, with the optimal cancellation strategy, we can also compute the expected time to contract termination, either as a result of a drawdown or voluntary cancellation. Precisely, we have the following proposition.

Proposition 8.3. *For $0 < \theta^\star < y < a$, we have*

$$\mathbb{E}^{\mathbb{P}}(\tau_D^-(\theta^\star) \wedge \tau_D^+(a) | D_0 = y)$$
$$= \frac{(y - \theta^\star)\rho(y - \theta^\star, a - \theta^\star) + (y - a)e^{2\tilde{\delta}(y-a)}\rho(a - y, a - \theta^\star)}{\tilde{\mu}},$$
(8.24)

where $\rho(\cdot, \cdot)$ is defined in Proposition 8.1.

Proof. According to the optimal cancellation strategy, we have

$$\tau_D^-(\theta^\star) \wedge \tau_D^+(a) = \tau_X^+(x + y - \theta^\star) \wedge \tau_X^-(y - a), \quad \mathbb{P}\text{-a.s.}$$

where $\tau_X^-(x) = \inf\{t \geq 0 : X_t < x\}$. Applying the optional sampling theorem to the bounded martingale $\{Y_t\}_{t \in [0, \tau_X^+(x+y-\theta^\star) \wedge \tau_X^-(y-a)]}$ with $Y_t = X_t - \tilde{\mu}t$ if $\tilde{\mu} \neq 0$, or $Y_t = (X_t)^2 - \sigma^2 t$ if $\tilde{\mu} = 0$, we obtain the result in (8.24). □

Remark 8.2. In the finite maturity case, the set of candidate stopping times is changed to $\{\tau \in \mathbb{F} : 0 \leq t \leq T\}$ in (8.13). Similar as in (8.14), the contract value $V_T(y, p)$ at time zero for premium rate p still admits the

Stochastic Drawdowns

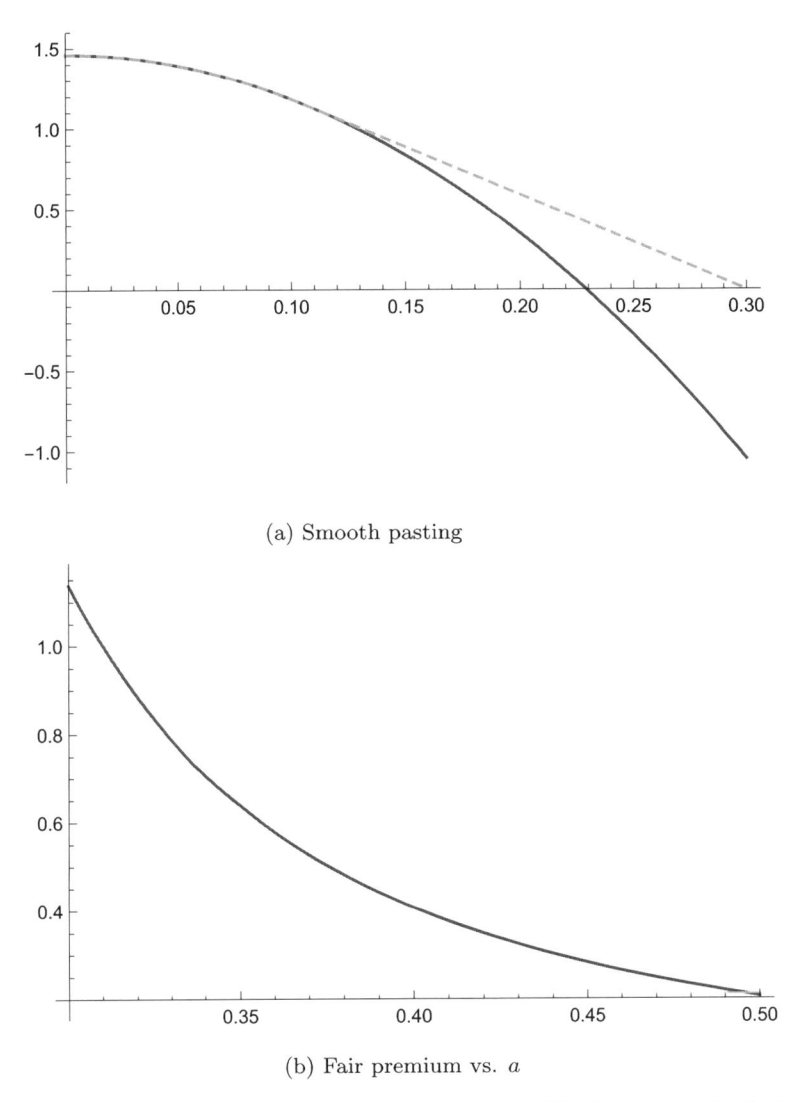

(a) Smooth pasting

(b) Fair premium vs. a

Fig. 8.2. (a) The optimal stopping value function $G(\cdot, p)$ (gray dashed) dominates and pastes smoothly onto the intrinsic value $\tilde{f}(\cdot, p)$ (black solid). It is optimal to cancel the insurance as soon as the drawdown process falls to $\theta^* = 0.1081$ (at which $G(\cdot, p)$ and $\tilde{f}(\cdot, p)$ meet). The parameters are $r = 0.02, \sigma = 0.2, a = 0.3, c = 0.05, \alpha = 1$, and p is taken to be the fair premium value $P^* = 1.1375$ when the initial drawdown $y = 0.15$. That is, at $y = 0.1$, we have $V(y, P^*) = G(y, P^*) - f(y, P^*) = 0$. (b) Given the initial drawdown $y = 0.15$, the fair premium of the cancellable drawdown insurance decreases with respect to the drawdown level a specified for the contract.

decomposition

$$V_T(y,p) = -f_T(0,y,p) + \sup_{0 \leq \tau \leq T} \mathbb{E}(e^{-r\tau}(f_T(\tau, D_\tau, p) - c)\mathbf{1}_{\{\tau < \tau_D^+(a)\}} \mid D_0 = y),$$

where

$$f_T(t,y) = \frac{p}{r} - \left(\alpha + \frac{p}{r}\right)\xi_T(t,y),$$

and $\xi_T(t,y)$ is the conditional Laplace transform of $\tau_D^+(a) \wedge (T-t)$:

$$\xi_T(t,y) = \mathbb{E}(e^{-r(\tau_D^+(a) \wedge (T-t))} \mid D_t = y), \quad 0 \leq t \leq \tau_D^+(a) \wedge T.$$

This problem is no longer time-homogeneous, and the fair premium can be determined by numerically solving the associated optimal stopping problem.

8.3. Incorporating Drawup Contingency

We now consider an insurance contract that provides protection from any specified drawdown with a drawup contingency. This insurance contract may expire early, whereby stopping the premium payment, if a drawup event occurs prior to drawdown or maturity. From the investor's viewpoint, the realization of a drawup implies little need to insure against a drawdown. Therefore, this drawup contingency is an attractive cost-reducing feature to the investor. To facilitate analysis under a general initial condition $D_0 = y, U_0 = z$ with $y, z \geq 0$ and $y + z < a$, we use notation $\mathbb{Q}_{0,y,-z}(\cdot)$ henceforth to denote the law of X. given $(X_0, \overline{X}_0, \underline{X}_0) = (0, y, -z)$. Notice that this probability measure suffices our need since neither the drawdown/drawup event nor the payoff depends on the initial location of the underlying X_0.

8.3.1. *The finite maturity case*

First, we consider the case with a finite maturity T. Specifically, if a a-unit drawdown occurs prior to a drawup of the same size or the expiration date T, then the investor will receive the insured amount α and stop the premium payment thereafter. Hence, the risk-neutral discounted expected payoff to the investor is given by

$$v(y,z,p)$$
$$= \mathbb{E}_{0,y,-z}\left(-\int_0^{\tau_D^+(a)\wedge\tau_U^+(a)\wedge T} e^{-rt}p\,dt + \alpha e^{-r\tau_D^+(a)}\mathbf{1}_{\{\tau_D^+(a)\leq\tau_U^+(a)\wedge T\}}\right). \tag{8.25}$$

The fair premium $P^\star$ is chosen such that the contract has value zero at time zero, that is,

$$v(P^\star) = 0. \tag{8.26}$$

Applying (8.26) to (8.25), we obtain a formula for the fair premium:

$$P^\star = \frac{r\alpha\mathbb{E}_{0,y,-z}(e^{-r\tau_D^+(a)}\mathbf{1}_{\{\tau_D^+(a)\leq\tau_U^+(a)\wedge T\}})}{1 - \mathbb{E}_{0,y,-z}(e^{-r(\tau_D^+(a)\wedge\tau_U^+(a)\wedge T)})}. \tag{8.27}$$

As a result, the fair premium involves computing the expectations $\mathbb{E}_{0,y,-z}(e^{-r\tau_D^+(a)}\mathbf{1}_{\{\tau_D^+(a)\leq\tau_U^+(a)\wedge T\}})$ and $\mathbb{E}_{0,y,-z}(e^{-r(\tau_D^+(a)\wedge\tau_U^+(a)\wedge T)})$. To that end, let us introduce for any $q,y,z,T \geq 0$ such that $y+z < a$ that:

$$L(q,y,z,T) := \mathbb{E}_{0,y,-z}(e^{-q\tau_D^+(a)}\mathbf{1}_{\{\tau_D^+(a)\leq\tau_U^+(a)\wedge T\}})$$
$$= \int_0^T e^{-qt}\,\mathbb{Q}_{0,y,-z}(\tau_D^+(a) \in dt, \tau_U^+(a) > t)\,dt, \tag{8.28}$$

$$R(q,y,z,T) := \mathbb{E}_{0,y,-z}(e^{-q\tau_U^+(a)}\mathbf{1}_{\{\tau_U^+(a)\leq\tau_D^+(a)\wedge T\}})$$
$$= \int_0^T e^{-rt}\,\mathbb{Q}_{0,y,-z}(\tau_U^+(u) \in dt, \tau_D^+(a) > t)\,dt. \tag{8.29}$$

Then we can rewrite (8.27) as

$$P^\star = \frac{r\alpha L(r,y,z,T)}{1 - L(r,y,z,T) - R(r,y,z,T) - e^{-rT}(1 - L(0,y,z,T) - R(0,y,z,T))}.$$

In the special case that $y = z = 0$, an infinite series expression of $L(r,0,0,T)$ is available in Theorem 2.2. In general, one can compute $L(r,y,z,T)$ by using numerical integration in (8.28), with the density given in the next lemma.

Lemma 8.5. *In the model* (8.3), *for* $y, z \geq 0$ *such that* $y + z < a$, *we have*

$$\frac{\mathbb{Q}_{0,y,-z}(\tau_D^+(a) \in dt, \tau_U^+(a) > t)}{dt} = q(t, y - a, y) + \int_{y-a}^{-z} g(t, u) du, \quad (8.30)$$

where functions $g(\cdot, \cdot)$ *and* $q(\cdot, \cdot, \cdot)$ *are respectively defined in Proposition 2.1 and* (2.12).

As discussed in the proof of Corollary 2.5, the density appeared in (8.29) has the following property:

$$\frac{1}{dt}\mathbb{Q}_{0,y,-z}(\tau_U^+(a) \in dt, \tau_D^+(a) > t) = \frac{1}{dt}\tilde{\mathbb{Q}}_{0,z,-y}(\tau_D^+(a) \in dt, \tau_U^+(a) > t),$$

where $\tilde{\mathbb{Q}}$ is a probability measure under which X. has the same law as $-X$. under $\mathbb{Q}$. Hence, by replacing μ by $-\mu$ and switching the roles of y and z in (8.30), we obtain density $\tilde{\mathbb{Q}}_{0,z,-y}(\tau_D^+(a) \in dt, \tau_U^+(a) > t)/dt$, so $R(r, y, z, T)$ can also be computed via numerical integration in (8.29).

Remark 8.3. If the protection buyer pays a periodic premium at times $t_i = i\Delta t$, $i = 0, \ldots, n - 1$, with $\Delta t = T/n$, then the fair premium is

$$p^{(n)*} = \frac{\alpha \mathbb{E}_{0,y,-z}\left(e^{-r\tau_D^+(a)} 1_{\{\tau_D^+(a) \leq \tau_U^+(a) \wedge T\}}\right)}{\sum_{i=0}^{n-1} e^{-rt_i}\mathbb{Q}_{0,y,-z}(\tau_D^+(a) \wedge \tau_U^+(a) > t_i)}. \quad (8.31)$$

Compared to the continuous premium case, the fair premium $p^{(n)*}$ here involves a sum of the probabilities: $\mathbb{Q}_{0,y,-z}(\tau_D^+(a) \wedge \tau_U^+(a) > t_i)$, each can be computed using $1 - L(r, y, z, t_i) - R(r, y, z, t_i)$.

8.3.2. *Perpetual case*

Now, we consider the drawdown insurance contract that will expire not at a fixed finite time T but as soon as a drawdown/drawup of size a occurs. To study this perpetual case, we take $T = \infty$ in (8.25). As the next proposition shows, we have a simple closed-form solution for the fair premium P^*, allowing for instant computation of the fair premium and amenable for sensitivity analysis.

Proposition 8.4. *The perpetual drawdown insurance fair premium* $P^\star$ *is given by*

$$P^\star = \frac{r\alpha L^\infty(r,y,z)}{1 - L^\infty(r,y,z) - R^\infty(r,y,z)}, \qquad (8.32)$$

where for any $q, y, z \geq 0$ *such that* $y + z < a$,

$$L^\infty(q,y,z) := \mathbb{E}_{0,y,-z}(e^{-q\tau_D^+(a)} \mathbf{1}_{\{\tau_D^+(a) < \tau_U^+(a)\}})$$
$$= F(q,y,\delta) - G(q,z,\delta) + G(q,a-y,\delta), \qquad (8.33)$$

$$R^\infty(q,y,z) := \mathbb{E}_{0,y,-z}(e^{-q\tau_U^+(a)} \mathbf{1}_{\{\tau_U^+(a) < \tau_D^+(a)\}})$$
$$= F(q,z,-\delta) - G(q,y,-\delta) + G(q,a-z,-\delta), \qquad (8.34)$$

with

$$F(q,y,\delta) := e^{\delta(y-a)} \frac{\sinh(y\sqrt{\delta^2 + 2q/\sigma^2})}{\sinh(a\sqrt{\delta^2 + 2q/\sigma^2})},$$

$$G(q,z,\delta) := \sigma^2 \frac{\sqrt{\delta^2 + 2q/\sigma^2}}{2q} e^{-\delta z}$$
$$\times \frac{\delta \sinh(a\sqrt{\delta^2 + 2q/\sigma^2}) + \sqrt{\delta^2 + 2q/\sigma^2} \cosh(z\sqrt{\delta^2 + 2q/\sigma^2})}{\sinh^2(a\sqrt{\delta^2 + 2q/\sigma^2})}.$$

Proof. In the perpetual case, the fair premium is clearly given by (8.32). Thus, we only need to prove the second line in (8.33) and (8.34). To that end, we multiply both sides of (8.53) by e^{-qt} and integrate t over $(0, \infty)$. Then we obtain that

$$L^\infty(q,y,z) = \mathbb{E}(e^{-q\tau_X^-(y-a)} \mathbf{1}_{\{\tau_X^-(y-a) < \tau_X^+(y)\}})$$
$$+ \int_{y-a}^{z} \frac{\partial}{\partial a} \mathbb{E}(e^{-q\tau_X^-(u)} \mathbf{1}_{\{\tau_X^-(u) < \tau_X^+(u+a)\}}) du. \qquad (8.35)$$

By Lemma A.1, we have that for $u \in [y-a, -z]$ that,

$$\mathbb{E}(e^{-q\tau_X^-(u)} \mathbf{1}_{\{\tau_X^-(u) < \tau_X^+(u+a)\}}) = e^{\delta u} \frac{\sinh((u+a)\sqrt{\delta^2 + 2q/\sigma^2})}{\sinh(a\sqrt{\delta^2 + 2q/\sigma^2})},$$

$$\frac{\partial}{\partial a} \mathbb{E}(e^{-q\tau_X^-(u)} \mathbf{1}_{\{\tau_X^-(u) < \tau_X^+(u+a)\}}) = \sqrt{\delta^2 + 2q/\sigma^2} e^{\delta u} \frac{\sinh(-u\sqrt{\delta^2 + 2q/\sigma^2})}{\sinh^2(a\sqrt{\delta^2 + 2q/\sigma^2})}.$$

Plugging the above into (8.35) yields $L^\infty(q,y,z)$. Using the reflection argument as before, we know that the expression for $R^\infty(q,y,z)$ follows from replacing δ by $-\delta$ and switching y with z in (8.33). This completes the proof of the proposition. □

Finally, the probability that a drawdown is realized prior to a drawup, meaning that the protection amount will be paid to the buyer before the contract expires upon drawup, is given by the following proposition.

Proposition 8.5. *Let $y, z \geq 0$ such that $y + z < a$. Then*

$$\mathbb{P}_{0,y,-z}(\tau_D^+(a) < \tau_U^+(a))$$

$$= e^{2\tilde{\delta}(y-a)}\rho(a-y,a) + \frac{e^{-\frac{2\tilde{\mu}}{\sigma^2}(a-y) + 2\tilde{\delta}(a-y-z)} - e^{-2\tilde{\delta}z}}{4\sinh^2(\tilde{\delta}a)}, \quad (8.36)$$

where $\rho(\cdot,\cdot)$ is defined in Proposition 8.1.

Proof. From the proof of Proposition 8.4, we obtain that

$$\mathbb{P}_{0,y,-z}(\tau_D^+(a) < \tau_U^+(a))$$
$$= \lim_{q \downarrow 0}(F(q,y,\tilde{\delta}) - G(q,z,\tilde{\delta}) + G(q,a-y,\tilde{\delta}))$$
$$= e^{2\tilde{\delta}(y-a)}\rho(a-y,a) + \lim_{q \downarrow 0}(G(q,a-y,\tilde{\delta}) - G(q,z,\tilde{\delta})).$$

Finally, l'Hôpital's rule yields the last limit and (8.36). □

In Figure 8.3(a), we see that the fair premium increases with the maturity T, which is due to the higher likelihood of the drawdown event at or before expiration. For the perpetual case, we illustrate in Figure 8.3(b) that higher volatility leads to higher fair premium. From this observation, it is expected that in a volatile market drawdown insurance would become more costly.

8.4. Drawdown Insurance on a Defaultable Stock

In contrast to a market index, an individual stock may experience a large drawdown through continuous downward movement or a sudden default event. Therefore, in order to insure against the drawdown of the stock, it is useful to incorporate the default risk into the stock price dynamics. To this end, we extend our analysis to a stock with reduced-form (intensity based) default risk.

(a) Fair premium P^* vs. maturity T

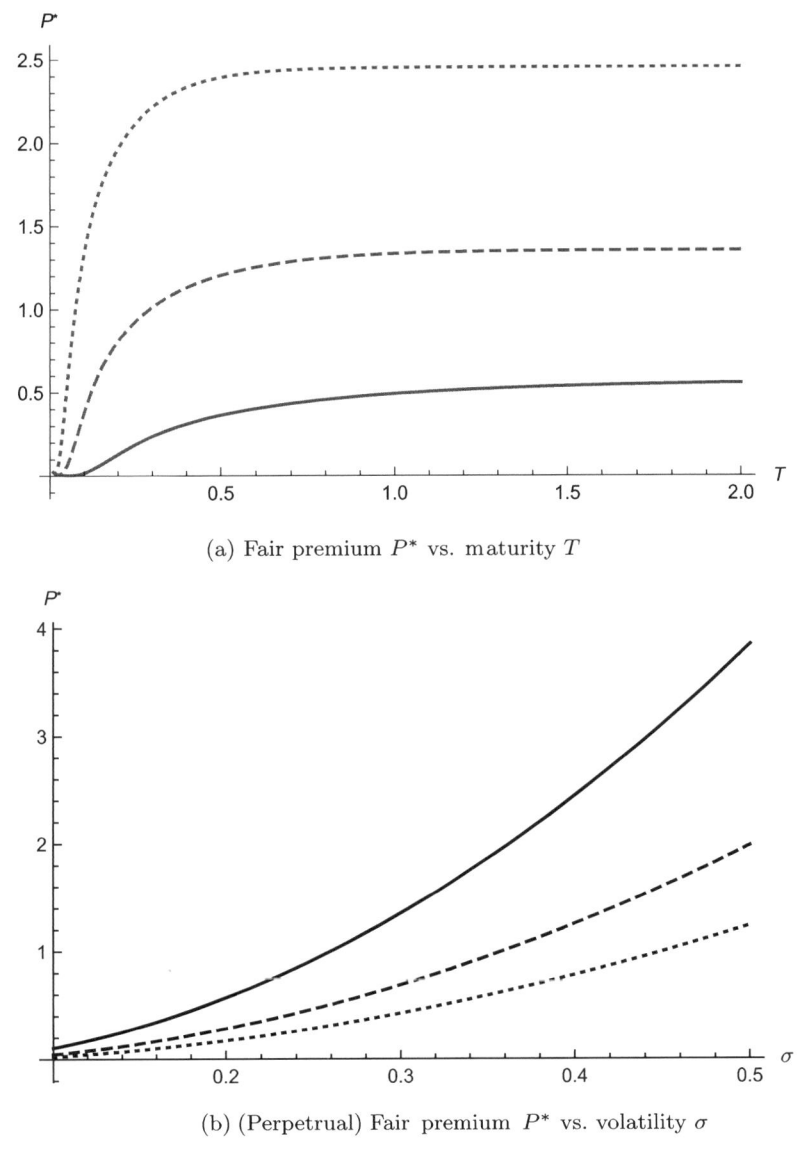

(b) (Perpetrual) Fair premium P^* vs. volatility σ

Fig. 8.3. (a) The fair premium of a drawdown insurance is increasing with the maturity T and the volatility σ. Here we fix $a = 0.3$, and plotted $\sigma = 0.2$ (solid), $\sigma = 0.3$ (dashed) or $\sigma = 0.4$ (dotted). (b) The fair premium of a perpetual drawdown insurance also increases with volatility σ, with $a = 0.3$ (solid), $a = 0.4$ (dashed), or $a = 0.5$ (dotted). Parameters used: $r = 0.02$, initial drawdown and drawup $y = z = 0.1$ and $\alpha = 1$.

Under the risk-neutral measure $\mathbb{Q}$, the defaultable stock price $\tilde{S}$. evolves according to

$$d\tilde{S}_t = (r+\lambda)\tilde{S}_t\,dt + \sigma\tilde{S}_t\,dW_t - \tilde{S}_{t-}\,dN_t, \quad \tilde{S}_0 = \tilde{s} > 0, \qquad (8.37)$$

where λ is the constant default intensity for the single jump process $N_t = 1_{\{t \geq \zeta\}}$, with $\zeta \sim \exp(\lambda)$ independent of the Brownian motion W. under $\mathbb{Q}$. At ζ, the stock price immediately drops to zero and remains there permanently, i.e., for a.e. $\omega \in \Omega$, $\tilde{S}_t(\omega) = 0, \forall t \geq \zeta(\omega)$. Similar equity models have been considered, e.g., in Merton (1976) and more recently in Kovalov and Linetsky (2006), among others.

The drawdown events are defined similarly as in (8.4) where the log-price is now given by

$$\tilde{X}_t = \begin{cases} \log \tilde{S}_0 + (r + \lambda - \frac{1}{2}\sigma^2)t + \sigma W_t, & t < \zeta, \\ -\infty, & t \geq \zeta. \end{cases}$$

We follow a similar definition of the drawdown insurance contract from Section 8.1. One major effect of a default event is that it causes drawdown and the contract will expire immediately. In the perpetual case, the premium payment is paid until $\tau_D^+(a) \wedge \tau_U^+(a)$ if it happens before both the default time ζ and the maturity T, or until the default time ζ if $T \geq \tau_D^+(a) \wedge \tau_U^+(a) \geq \zeta$. Notice that, if neither drawup nor drawdown of size a happens before ζ, then the drawdown time $\tau_D^+(a)$ will coincide with the default time, i.e., $\tau_D^+(a) = \zeta$. The expected value to the buyer is given by

$$v(y,z,p)$$
$$= \mathbb{E}_{0,y,-z}\left(-\int_0^{\tau_D^+(a) \wedge \tau_U^+(a) \wedge \zeta \wedge T} e^{-rt}p\,dt + \alpha e^{-r\tau_D^+(a)}1_{\{\tau_D^+(a) \leq \tau_U^+(a) \wedge \zeta \wedge T\}}\right).$$

Again, the stopping times $\tau_D^+(a)$ and $\tau_U^+(a)$ based on $\tilde{X}$ do not depend on x, and therefore, the contract value $v(\cdot,\cdot,\cdot)$ is a function of the initial drawdown y and drawup z.

Under this defaultable stock model, we obtain the following useful formula for the fair premium.

Proposition 8.6. *Let $L_\lambda(q,T) \equiv L(q,y,z,T)$ and $R_\lambda(q,T) \equiv R(q,y,z,T)$ as in (8.28) and (8.29) respectively but with $\mu = r + \lambda - \frac{1}{2}\sigma^2$. Then the fair* premium for a drawdown insurance maturing at T, written on the defaultable stock in (8.37) is given by

$$P^\star = \alpha \frac{rL_\lambda(r+\lambda,T) + \lambda - \lambda R_\lambda(r+\lambda,T) - \lambda e^{-(r+\lambda)T}C_\lambda(T)}{1 - L_\lambda(r+\lambda,T) - R_\lambda(r+\lambda,T) - e^{-(r+\lambda)T}C_\lambda(T)}, \quad (8.38)$$

where $C_\lambda(T) = 1 - L_\lambda(0,T) - R_\lambda(0,T)$.

Proof. Similar as in (8.27), the fair premium $P^\star$ satisfies

$$P^\star = \frac{r\alpha \mathbb{E}_{0,y,-z}(e^{-r\tau_D^+(a)} \mathbf{1}_{\{\tau_D^+(a) < \tau_U^+(a) \wedge \zeta \wedge T\}})}{1 - \mathbb{E}_{0,y,-z}(e^{-r(\tau_D^+(a) \wedge \tau_U^+(a) \wedge \zeta \wedge T)})}. \quad (8.39)$$

We first derive the expectation in the numerator. By conditioning on the value of ζ, we have the following possibilities: {for some $t \in [0,T], \tau_D^+(a) < \tau_U^+(a) \wedge t, t < \zeta < T\}$, $\{\tau_D^+(a) < \tau_U^+(a) \wedge T, \zeta \geq T\}$, and $\{\tau_D^+(a) \wedge \tau_U^+(a) \wedge T \geq \zeta\}$, where the drawdowns in first two cases are caused by diffusion movement of the Brownian motion since the default is only realized after the event $\{\tau_D^+(a) < \tau_U^+(a) \wedge T\}$ occurs, and the drawdown in the last case is due to the default. Hence, we obtain that

$$\mathbb{E}_{0,y,-z}(e^{-r\tau_D^+(a)} \mathbf{1}_{\{\tau_D^+(a) < \tau_U^+(a) \wedge \zeta \wedge T\}})$$

$$= \int_0^T \lambda e^{-\lambda t} \mathbb{E}_{0,y,-z}(e^{-r\tau_D^+(a)} \mathbf{1}_{\{\tau_D^+(a) \leq \tau_U^+(a) \wedge t\}}) dt$$

$$+ e^{-\lambda T} \mathbb{E}_{0,y,-z}(e^{-r\tau_D^+(a)} \mathbf{1}_{\{\tau_D^+(a) \leq \tau_U^+(a) \wedge T\}})$$

$$+ \mathbb{E}_{0,y,-z}(e^{-r\zeta} \mathbf{1}_{\{\tau_D^+(a) \wedge \tau_U^+(a) \wedge T \geq \zeta\}})$$

$$= \int_0^T e^{-(r+\lambda)s} \mathbb{Q}_{0,y,-z}(\tau_D^+(a) \in ds, \tau_U^+(a) > s) ds$$

$$+ \int_0^T \lambda e^{-(r+\lambda)t} \mathbb{Q}_{0,y,-z}(\tau_D^+(a) \wedge \tau_U^+(a) \geq t) dt.$$

By applying integration by parts to the integral in the last line, we obtain that

$$\mathbb{E}_{0,y,-z}(e^{-r\tau_D^+(a)} \mathbf{1}_{\{\tau_D^+(a) < \tau_U^+(a) \wedge \zeta \wedge T\}})$$

$$= L_\lambda(r+\lambda,T) + \frac{\lambda}{r+\lambda}\left(1 - e^{-(r+\lambda)T}\mathbb{Q}_{0,y,-z}(\tau_D^+(a) \wedge \tau_U^+(a) \geq T)\right.$$

$$+ \int_0^T e^{-(r+\lambda)t} \frac{\partial}{\partial t} \mathbb{Q}_{0,y,-z}(\tau_D^+(a) \wedge \tau_U^+(a) \geq t) dt \Bigg)$$

$$= L_\lambda(r+\lambda, T) + \frac{\lambda}{r+\lambda}[1 - e^{-(r+\lambda)T}\mathbb{Q}_{0,y,-z}(\tau_D^+(a) \wedge \tau_U^+(a) \geq T)$$

$$- L_\lambda(r+\lambda, T) - R_\lambda(r+\lambda, T)].$$

Moreover, we notice that $\mathbb{Q}_{0,y,-z}(\tau_D^+(a) \wedge \tau_U^+(a) \geq T) = 1 - \mathbb{Q}_{0,y,-z}(\tau_D^+(a) < \tau_U^+(a) \geq T) - \mathbb{Q}_{0,y,-z}(\tau_U^+(a) < \tau_D^+(a) \geq T) = 1 - L_\lambda(0,T) - R_\lambda(0,T) = C_\lambda(T)$. So the numerator of (8.39) is given by

$$\frac{rL_\lambda(r+\lambda, T) + \lambda - \lambda R_\lambda(r+\lambda, T) - \lambda e^{-(r+\lambda)T} C_\lambda(T)}{r+\lambda}.$$

Similarly, the Laplace transform of $\tau_D^+(a) \wedge \tau_U^+(a) \wedge \zeta \wedge T$ in the denominator of (8.39) is given by

$$\mathbb{E}_{0,y,-z}\big(e^{-r(\tau_D^+(a) \wedge \tau_U^+(a) \wedge \zeta \wedge T)}\big)$$

$$= \mathbb{E}_{0,y,-z}\big(e^{-r(\tau_D^+(a) \wedge \tau_U^+(a))} \mathbf{1}_{\{\tau_D^+(a) \wedge \tau_U^+(a) < \zeta \wedge T\}}\big)$$

$$+ e^{-rT}\mathbb{Q}_{0,y,-z}(\tau_D^+(a) \wedge \tau_U^+(a) > T, \zeta > T)$$

$$+ \mathbb{E}_{0,y,-z}\big(e^{-r\zeta} \mathbf{1}_{\{\tau_D^+(a) \wedge \tau_U^+(a) \wedge T \geq \zeta\}}\big)$$

$$= \int_0^T e^{-(r+\lambda)s} \mathbb{Q}_{0,y,-z}(\tau_D^+(a) \wedge \tau_U^+(a) \in ds)$$

$$+ e^{-(r+\lambda)T}\mathbb{Q}_{0,y,-z}(\tau_D^+(a) \wedge \tau_U^+(a) > T)$$

$$+ \frac{\lambda}{r+\lambda}[1 - e^{-(r+\lambda)T}\mathbb{Q}_{0,y,-z}(\tau_D^+(a) \wedge \tau_U^+(a) \geq T) - L_\lambda(r+\lambda, T)$$

$$- R_\lambda(r+\lambda, T)]$$

$$= L_\lambda(r+\lambda, T) + R_\lambda(r+\lambda, T)$$

$$+ \frac{\lambda}{r+\lambda}[1 - L_\lambda(r+\lambda, T) - R_\lambda(r+\lambda, T)]$$

$$+ e^{-(r+\lambda)T} \frac{r}{r+\lambda} \mathbb{Q}_{0,y,-z}(\tau_D^+(a) \wedge \tau_U^+(a) \geq T)$$

$$= \frac{\lambda}{r+\lambda} + \frac{r}{r+\lambda}[L_\lambda(r+\lambda, T) + R_\lambda(r+\lambda, T) + e^{-(r+\lambda)T} C_\lambda(T)],$$

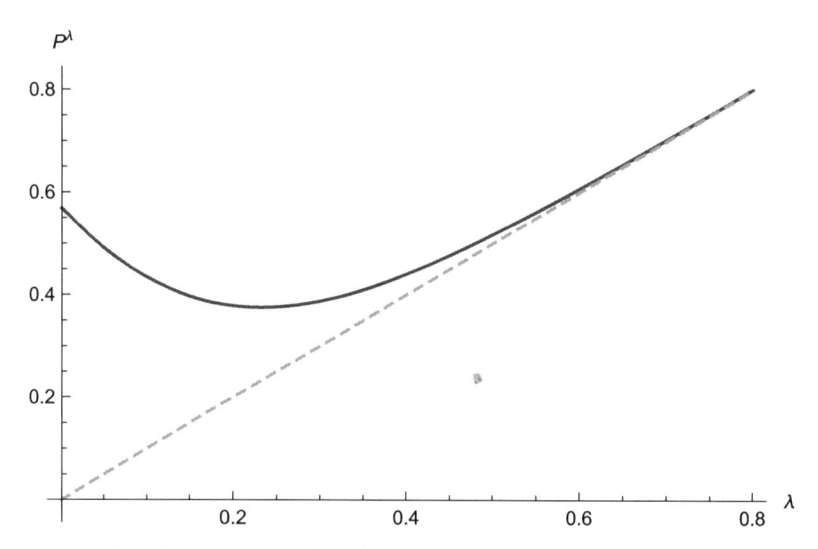

Fig. 8.4. The fair premium (solid) P^* in (8.40) as a function of the default intensity λ dominates the straight dashed line $\alpha\lambda$. As $\lambda \to \infty$, the fair premium $P^* \to \alpha\lambda$. Parameters: $r = 0.02, \sigma = 0.2$, initial drawdown and drawup $y = z = 0.1, \alpha = 1$ and $a = 0.3$.

where in the second equality we used our previous derivation for expectation $\mathbb{E}_{0,y,-z}(e^{-r\zeta}1_{\{\tau_D^+(a)\wedge\tau_U^+(a)\wedge T\geq\zeta\}})$. Plugging the above into (8.39) yields (8.38). □

By taking $T \to \infty$ in (8.38), we obtain the fair premium for the perpetual drawdown insurance in closed form.

Proposition 8.7. Let $L_\lambda(q) \equiv L(q,y,z)$ and $R_\lambda(q) \equiv R(q,y,z)$ as in (8.33) and (8.34) but with $\mu = r + \lambda - \frac{1}{2}\sigma^2$. Then the fair premium for the perpetual drawdown insurance written on the defaultable stock in (8.37) is given by

$$P^* = \frac{\alpha\left(rL_\lambda(r+\lambda) + \lambda - \lambda R_\lambda(r+\lambda)\right)}{1 - L_\lambda(r+\lambda) - R_\lambda(r+\lambda)}. \tag{8.40}$$

In Figure 8.4, we illustrate for the perpetual case that the fair premium is increasing with the default intensity λ and approaches $\alpha\lambda$ for high default risk. This observation, which can be formally shown by taking the limit in (8.40), is intuitive since high default risk implies that a drawdown will more likely happen and that it is most likely triggered by a default.

8.5. Concluding Remarks

In this chapter, we study the practicality of insuring against market crashes and propose a number of tractable ways to value drawdown protection. Under the geometric Brownian motion dynamics, we provide the formulas for the fair premium for a number of insurance contracts, and examine its behavior with respect to key model parameters. In the cancellable drawdown insurance, we show that the protection buyer would monitor the drawdown process and optimally stop the premium payment as the drawdown risk diminished. Also, we investigate the impact of default risk on drawdown and derived analytical formulas for the fair premium.

8.6. Proof of Lemmas

In order to prepare for our proofs on the cancellable drawdown insurance in Section 8.2, we summarize a number of properties for the conditional Laplace transform of $\tau_D^+(a)$ (see (8.8)).

Proposition 8.8. *The conditional Laplace transform function $\xi(\cdot)$ has the following properties:*

(1) $\xi(\cdot)$ *is positive and increasing on* $(0, a)$.
(2) $\xi(\cdot)$ *satisfies differential equation*

$$\frac{1}{2}\sigma^2 \xi''(y) - \mu \xi'(y) = r\xi(y), \qquad (8.41)$$

with the Neumann condition

$$\xi'(0) = 0.$$

(3) $\xi(\cdot)$ *is strictly convex, i.e., $\xi''(y) > 0$ for $y \in (0, a)$.*

Proof. Property (i) follows directly from the definition of $\xi(y)$ and strong Markov property. Property (ii) follows directly from differentiation of (8.9). For property (iii), the proof is as follows. If $\mu \geq 0$, then (8.41) implies that

$$\xi''(y) = 2\delta \xi'(y) + \frac{2r}{\sigma^2}\xi(y) > 0, \quad y \in (0, a).$$

If $\mu < 0$, then (8.43) and (8.41) imply that for $y \in (0, a)$,

$$\xi'(y) = (\gamma + \delta)[\xi(y) - e^{(\delta-\gamma)y}\xi(0)],$$

$$\xi''(y) = 2\delta\xi'(y) + \frac{2r}{\sigma^2}\xi(y)$$

$$= (\gamma + \delta)^2 \xi(y) - 2\delta(\gamma + \delta)e^{(\delta-\gamma)y}\xi(0) > 0.$$

The last inequality follows from the fact that $\mu < 0$ and $\gamma + \delta > 0$. Hence, strict convexity follows. □

Proof of Lemma 8.1. Define the first time that the drawdown process $\{D_t\}_{t \geq 0}$ decreases to a level $\theta \geq 0$ by

$$\tau_D^-(\theta) := \inf\{t \geq 0 : D_t \leq \theta\}. \tag{8.42}$$

By the strong Markov property of process $D_\cdot$ at $\tau_D^-(0)$, we have that for $t \leq \tau_D^+(a)$,

$$\xi(D_t) = \mathbb{E}(e^{-r\tau_D^+(a)} \mid D_t)$$

$$= \mathbb{E}(e^{-r\tau_D^+(a)} \mathbf{1}_{\{\tau_D^+(a) < \tau_D^-(0)\}} \mid D_t) + \mathbb{E}(e^{-r\tau_D^-(0)} \mathbf{1}_{\{\tau_D^+(a) > \tau_D^-(0)\}} \mid D_t)\xi(0)$$

$$= e^{\delta(D_t - a)} \frac{\sinh(\gamma D_t)}{\sinh(\gamma a)} + e^{\delta D_t} \frac{\sinh(\gamma(a - D_t))}{\sinh(\gamma a)} \xi(0). \tag{8.43}$$

Therefore, the problem is reduced to finding $\xi(0)$, which is given in (4.11):

$$\xi(0) = \frac{e^{-\delta a}\gamma}{\gamma \cosh(\gamma a) - \delta \sinh(\gamma a)}.$$

Substituting this to (8.43) yields (8.9). □

Proof of Lemma 8.2. In view of (8.20), we seek the root θ^* of the equation:

$$F(\theta) := [\delta - \gamma \coth(\gamma(a - \theta))]\tilde{f}(\theta) - \tilde{f}'(\theta) = 0. \tag{8.44}$$

To this end, we compute

$$F'(\theta) = \frac{-\gamma^2 \tilde{f}(\theta)}{(\sinh(\gamma(a-\theta)))^2} - [\gamma \coth(\gamma(a-\theta)) - \delta]\tilde{f}'(\theta) - \tilde{f}''(\theta). \tag{8.45}$$

Since $\tilde{f}(\cdot)$ is monotonically decreasing from $\tilde{f}(0) > 0$ to $\tilde{f}(a) = -\alpha - c < 0$, there exists a unique $\theta_0 \in (0, a)$ such that $\tilde{f}(\theta_0) = 0$. We have

$F(\theta_0) = -\tilde{f}'(\theta_0) > 0$ by (8.44) and $F(0) = (\frac{\mu}{\sigma} - \gamma \coth(\gamma a))\tilde{f}(0) < 0$, which implies that $F(\theta) = 0$ has at least one solution $\theta^\star \in (0, \theta_0)$. Moreover, for $\theta \in (\theta_0, a)$, $\tilde{f}(\theta) < 0$ and hence $F(\theta) > 0$ by (8.44), there is no root in (θ_0, a).

Next, we show the root is unique by proving that $F'(\theta) > 0$ for all $\theta \in (0, \theta_0)$. To this end, we first observe from (8.6) that $\tilde{f}$ can be expressed as $\tilde{f}(\theta) = C(\xi(\theta_0) - \xi(\theta))$, for $\theta, \theta_0 \in (0, a)$, where $C = (\alpha + \frac{p}{r}) > 0$ and $C\xi(\theta_0) = \frac{p}{r} - c$. Putting these into (8.45), we express $F'(\theta)$ in terms ξ instead of $\tilde{f}$. In turn, verifying $F'(\theta) > 0$ is reduced to the following lemma. $\square$

Proof of Lemma 8.3. We begin by using (8.41) to rewrite the statement in the lemma as

$$\inf_{0 < \theta < \theta_0 < a} \left\{ (\gamma \coth(\gamma(a - \theta)) + \delta) \, \xi'(\theta) \right.$$
$$\left. + \left(\gamma^2 \coth^2(\gamma(a - \theta)) - \delta^2 \right) \xi(\theta) - \frac{\gamma^2 \xi(\theta_0)}{\sinh^2(\gamma(a - \theta))} \right\} \geq 0.$$

By the strong Markov property of process $D_\cdot$, the function $\xi(\cdot)$ satisfies a more general version of (8.43). Specifically, for $0 \leq y_1, y_2 < a$,

$$\xi(y_2) = e^{\delta(y_2 - a)} \frac{\sinh(\gamma(y_2 - y_1))}{\sinh(\gamma(a - y_1))} + e^{\delta(y_2 - y_1)} \frac{\sinh(\gamma(a - y_2))}{\sinh(\gamma(a - y_1))} \xi(y_1). \tag{8.46}$$

Define for $y \in [0, a)$,

$$\Lambda(y) = \frac{e^{-\delta y} \xi(y)}{\sinh(\gamma(a - y))}. \tag{8.47}$$

Then function $\Lambda(\cdot)$ satisfies (see (8.46))

$$\Lambda(y_2) - \Lambda(y_1) = \frac{e^{-\delta a} \sinh(\gamma(y_2 - y_1))}{\sinh(\gamma(a - y_1)) \cdot \sinh(\gamma(a - y_2))}, \quad \forall y_1, y_2 \in [0, a),$$

from which we can easily obtain that

$$\Lambda'(y) = \frac{\gamma e^{-\delta a}}{\sinh^2(\gamma(a - y))} > 0, \quad \forall y \in [0, a). \tag{8.48}$$

Straightforward computation shows that

$$\Lambda'(y) = e^{-\delta y} \frac{(\gamma \coth(\gamma(a - y)) - \delta)\xi(y) + \xi'(y)}{\sinh(\gamma(a - y))} > 0, \quad \forall y \in [0, a).$$

Thus,

$$\xi'(y) = \Lambda'(y)e^{\delta y}\sinh(\gamma(a-y)) - (\gamma\coth(\gamma(a-y)) - \delta)\xi(y). \quad (8.49)$$

Using (8.49), the above inequality is equivalent to

$$\inf_{0<\theta<\theta_0<a}\{\Lambda'(\theta)[e^{\delta\theta}(\gamma\cosh(\gamma(a-\theta)) + \delta\sinh(\gamma(a-\theta))) - \gamma e^{\delta a}\xi(\theta_0)]\} \geq 0.$$

Let us denote by

$$H(\theta,\theta_0) = e^{\delta\theta}\left(\gamma\cosh(\gamma(a-\theta)) + \delta\sinh(\gamma(a-\theta))\right) - \gamma e^{\delta a}\xi(\theta_0).$$

We will show that

$$\inf_{0<\theta<\theta_0<a} H(\theta,\theta_0) \geq 0.$$

Notice that for $\theta \in [0,\theta_0]$,

$$\frac{\partial H}{\partial \theta} = -\frac{2r}{\sigma^2}e^{\delta\theta}\sinh(\gamma(a-\theta)) < 0,$$

therefore

$$\inf_{0\leq\theta\leq\theta_0} H(\theta,\theta_0) = H(\theta_0,\theta_0).$$

Moreover,

$$\frac{\partial}{\partial \theta_0} H(\theta_0,\theta_0) = -\frac{2r}{\sigma^2}e^{\delta\theta_0}\sinh(\gamma(a-\theta_0)) - \gamma e^{\delta a}\xi'(\theta_0) < 0.$$

As a result,

$$\inf_{0\leq\theta\leq\theta_0<a} H(\theta,\theta_0) = H(k,a) = 0.$$

This completes the proof of Lemma 8.3. $\square$

Proof of Lemma 8.4. Let us define for any $y \in [\theta^*, a)$ that

$$J(y) := g(y,\theta^*,p) - \tilde{f}(y,p) = C\left(\beta(y)(\xi(\theta_0) - \xi(\theta^*)) + \xi(y) - \xi(\theta_0)\right),$$

where $C = \alpha + \frac{p}{r} > 0$. We check its derivatives with respect to x:
$$J'(y) = C\left(\beta'(y)(\xi(\theta_0) - \xi(\theta^\star)) + \xi'(y)\right), \qquad (8.50)$$
$$J''(y) = C\left(\beta''(y)(\xi(\theta_0) - \xi(\theta^\star)) + \xi''(y)\right), \qquad (8.51)$$

where
$$\beta(y) = \frac{g(y, \theta^\star, p)}{f(\theta^\star, p)} = e^{\delta(y-\theta^\star)} \frac{\sinh(\gamma(a-y))}{\sinh(\gamma(a-\theta^\star))}, \quad y \in (\theta^\star, a). \qquad (8.52)$$

Using probabilistic nature of function $\beta(\cdot)$ we know that it is positive and decreasing. Therefore, if $\mu \leq 0$, we have
$$\beta''(y) = 2\delta\beta'(y) + \frac{2r}{\sigma^2}\beta(y) > 0 \;\Rightarrow\; J''(y) \geq C\xi''(y) > 0.$$

On the other hand, if $\mu > 0$, from (8.52) we have
$$\beta'(y) = (\delta - \gamma)\beta(y) + \frac{\gamma e^{\delta(y-\theta^\star) - \gamma(a-y)}}{\sinh(\gamma(a-\theta^\star))},$$
$$\beta''(y) = 2\delta\beta'(y) + \frac{2r}{\sigma^2}\beta(y) = (\gamma - \delta)^2 \beta(y) + 2\delta \frac{\gamma e^{\delta(y-\theta^\star) - \gamma(a-y)}}{\sinh(\gamma(a-\theta^\star))} > 0,$$
$$\Rightarrow J''(y) \geq C\xi''(y) > 0.$$

So in either case ($\mu \leq 0$ or $\mu > 0$), $J'(\cdot)$ is an increasing function, and
$$J'(y) > J'(\theta^\star) = 0, \quad \forall y \in (\theta^\star, a),$$
which implies that
$$J(y) > J(\theta^\star) = 0, \quad \forall y \in (\theta^\star, a).$$
This completes the proof. □

Proof of Lemma 8.5. We begin by differentiating both sides of (7.9) under the Brownian motion model X. with respect to maturity t to obtain that
$$\mathbb{Q}_{0,y,-z}(\tau_D^+(a) \in dt, \tau_U^+(a) > t)$$
$$= q(t, y-a, y)dt + \left(\int_{y-a}^{-z} \frac{\partial}{\partial a} q(t, u, u+a) du\right) dt$$
$$= q(t, y-a, y)dt + \left(\int_{y-a}^{-z} g(t, u) du\right) dt, \qquad (8.53)$$
where $q(t, u, u+a) = \mathbb{Q}(\tau_X^-(u) \in dt, \tau_X^+(u+a) > t) = \mathbb{Q}(\tau_X^-(u) \in dt, \overline{X}_t < u+a)$, which was derived in Proposition 2.1. This completes the proof. □

Chapter 9

Optimal Trading with a Trailing Stop

Trailing stops are a popular trade order widely used by proprietary traders and retail investors to provide downside protection for an existing position. In contrast to a fixed stop-loss exit, a trailing stop is characterized by a stochastic floor that moves in parallel to the running maximum of the asset price. A trailing stop is triggered when the prevailing price of an asset falls below the stochastic floor. In essence, it allows an investor to specify a limit on the maximum possible loss while not limiting the maximum possible gain. The downside protection is also dynamic as the stochastic floor is raised whenever the asset price moves upward.

In addition to setting a trailing stop order, the investor can also use a limit order to sell at certain price target. Indeed, if the price is sufficiently high, the investor may prefer to sell immediately as opposed to waiting to set off the trailing stop. The investor's position will be liquidated by either order. In this chapter, we investigate the optimal timing to liquidate a position subject to a trailing stop. Mathematically, we recognize the trailing stop as a timing constraint in the sense that it installs a path-dependent random maturity into the liquidation problem, rendering the problem significantly more difficult to solve. Furthermore, the investor can also decide when to establish the position. This leads us to analyze the optimal timing to enter the market. In sum, we study an optimal double stopping problem subject to a trailing stop. By using excursion theory of linear diffusion, we derive the value functions using the smallest concave majorant characterization, and discuss the effect of trailing stopping on the optimal trading strategies analytically and numerically. Among our results, we reduce the problem of finding the optimal timing strategies to solving an ODE problem, which forms the basis of our numerical scheme in determining the optimal asset acquisition and liquidation regions.

In general, a trailing stop can be defined as the first time when the asset price $X.$ drops below $f(\overline{X}.)$, where $\overline{X}.$ is the running maximum process of $X.$, and f is an increasing function such that $f(x) < x$ for all x in the support of $X..$ In applied probability literature, such a stopping time is related to the drawdown process and its first passage time. We refer to Lehoczky (1977), Zhang (2015) and Zhang and Hadjiliadis (2012a), for a partial list of studies on drawdowns under linear diffusions. Moreover, the optimality of trailing stops in exercising Russian options and detecting abrupt changes can be found in Shepp and Shiryaev (1993) and Zhang et al. (2015), respectively.

The incorporation of a trailing stop can be viewed as introducing a random maturity or stopping time constraint to the optimal stopping problem, in the sense that any admissible stopping time must come before triggering the trailing stop. Related studies by the authors include optimal stopping problems with maturities determined by an occupation time (Rodosthenous and Zhang, 2017) or by a default time (Leung and Yamazaki, 2013), and optimal mean reversion trading with a fixed stop-loss exit (Leung and Li, 2015). In particular, part of our study (Section 9.2) generalizes the analytical framework of Leung and Li (2015) to general linear diffusions, and the results from optimal stopping subject to a fixed stop-loss exit will prove to be directly useful for solving the analogous problem with a trailing stop.

The remaining of the chapter is structured as follows. Section 9.1 presents stochastic framework for our trading problem. In Section 9.2, we study an optimal trading problem with a fixed stop-loss. Then, in Section 9.3, we study the optimal stopping problems for trading with a trailing stop. To illustrate our analytical results, we consider trading under the exponential Ornstein–Uhlenbeck (OU) model, and numerically compute the optimal acquisition and liquidation regions in Section 9.4. We also provide a sensitivity analysis on the optimal trading strategies with respect to model parameters. We conclude this chapter in Section 9.5. Proofs omitted can be found in Leung and Zhang (2017).

9.1. Model Formulation

Let us consider a risky asset value process $X. = \{X_t\}_{t \geq 0}$ modeled by a time-homogeneous linear diffusion on $I \equiv (l, r) \subset \mathbb{R}$ with natural boundaries, and the infinitesimal generator:

$$\mathcal{L} = \frac{1}{2}\sigma^2(x)\frac{\partial^2}{\partial x^2} + \mu(x)\frac{\partial}{\partial x}, \quad \forall x \in I, \tag{9.1}$$

where $(\mu(\cdot), \sigma(\cdot))$ is a pair of real-valued functions on I that satisfy (A.2) and (A.3) in the Appendix. For any $\bar{x} \in I$, the running maximum of $X.$ is denoted by

$$\overline{X}_t = \bar{x} \vee \sup_{s \in [0,t]} X_s, \quad \forall t \geq 0.$$

The first passage time of $X.$ is denoted by $\tau_X^{\pm}(x)$:

$$\tau_X^{\pm}(x) = \inf\{t > 0 : X_t \gtreqless x\}, \quad \forall x \in I.$$

We consider an investor who holds long one unit of the risky asset $X..$ Our objective is to investigate the optimal trading strategy with a trailing stop. To this end, we consider the problem of optimal early liquidation of this risky asset, given a pre-specified trailing stop mandatory liquidation order. Specifically, we will model liquidation time by a stopping time τ of the underlying process $X.$, and the reward to be realized upon liquidation by $h(X_\tau)$, where $h(\cdot)$ is a real-valued increasing function on I, such that $\{x \in I : h(x) > 0\} \neq \emptyset$. Fix a function $f(\cdot)$ on I, such that

$$\begin{array}{c} f(\cdot) \text{ is continuous, strictly increasing on } I, \\ \text{for all } x \in I, f(x) \in I, f(x) < x. \end{array} \tag{9.2}$$

Then, we define the *stochastic floor* by $f(\overline{X}.)$, where $\overline{X}.$ is the running maximum of $X..$ The trailing stop, denoted by ρ_f, is defined as the first time the asset value $X.$ reaches the stochastic floor $f(\overline{X}.)$ from above. That is,

$$\rho_f := \inf\{t > 0 : X_t < f(\overline{X}_t)\}. \tag{9.3}$$

Remark 9.1. We give two standard choices of the floor function $f(\cdot)$ here. For example, if $I = \mathbb{R}$, setting $f(x) = x - a$ for some $a > 0$ gives the absolute drawdown floor, and ρ_f is the first time $X.$ falls from its maximum $\overline{X}.$ by a units. Another specification when $I = \mathbb{R}_{>0}$, $f(x) = (1 - \alpha)x$ for some $\alpha \in (0, 1)$, gives the percentage drawdown, and ρ_f is the first time $X.$ falls from its maximum $\overline{X}$ by $(100 \times \alpha)\%$, as depicted in Figure 9.1 with $\alpha = 0.3$.

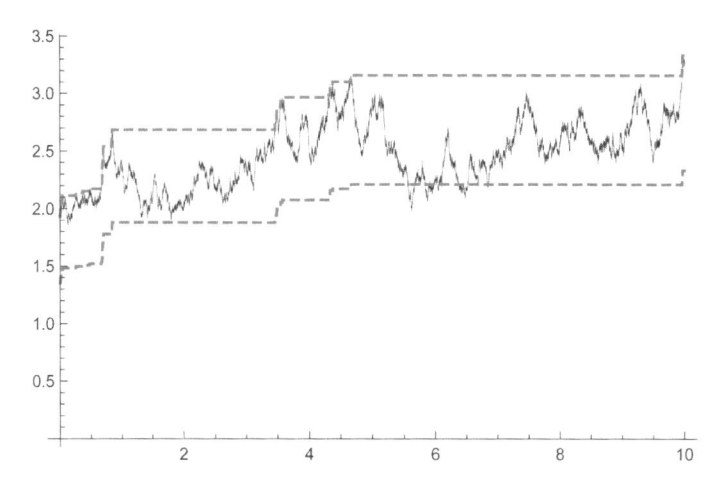

Fig. 9.1. Sample paths of the asset price (black solid), its running maximum (gray dashed), and the 30%-drawdown floor representing the trailing stop (red dashed).

The investor faces the following optimal stopping problem:

$$v_f(x, \bar{x}) := \sup_{\tau \in \mathcal{T}_f^\mathsf{T}} \mathbb{E}_{x,\bar{x}}(e^{-q\tau} h(X_\tau) \mathbf{1}_{\{\tau < \infty\}}), \qquad (9.4)$$

where $q > 0$ is a subjective discounting rate, and $\mathcal{T}_f^\mathsf{T}$ is the set of all stopping times of X that stop no later than the trailing stop ρ_f. Notice that ρ_f puts a mandatory selling order of the risky asset, pre-specified by the investor.

To quantify the gain in terms of expected discounted reward from liquidating earlier than the trailing stop time ρ_f, we define the *early liquidation premium* by the difference

$$p_f(x, \bar{x}) := v_f(x, \bar{x}) - g_f(x, \bar{x}), \qquad (9.5)$$

where the second term represents the expected discounted reward from waiting to sell at the trailing stop, that is,

$$g_f(x, \bar{x}) := \mathbb{E}_{x,\bar{x}}(e^{-q\rho_f} h(X_{\rho_f}) \mathbf{1}_{\{\rho_f < \infty\}}). \qquad (9.6)$$

As a convention, we define $\infty - \infty = \infty$ if both terms on the right-hand side of (9.5) are infinity. Clearly, we have $p_f(x, \bar{x}) \geq 0$ for all $x, \bar{x} \in I$ with $x \leq \bar{x}$. For our study, the early liquidation premium turns out to be amenable to analysis and give intuitive interpretations. The related concepts of early/delayed exercise/purchase premium have been analyzed in pricing American options (see, e.g., Carr et al. (1992)) and derivatives trading (see, e.g., Leung and Ludkovski (2011)), among other applications.

Remark 9.2. If floor functions $f_1(\cdot), f_2(\cdot)$ both satisfy (9.2), and $f_1(x) \leq f_2(x)$ for all $x \in I$, then for every fixed $x \in I$, we have the inequalities:

$$h(x) \leq v_{f_2}(x, \bar{x}) \leq v_{f_1}(x, \bar{x}) \leq \sup_{\tau \in \mathcal{T}} \mathbb{E}_x(e^{-r\tau} h(X_\tau) \mathbf{1}_{\{\tau < \infty\}}), \qquad (9.7)$$

where $\mathcal{T}$ is the set of all stopping times of $X.$.

Given the optimal value $v_f(x, \bar{x})$, another related problem is

$$v_f^{(1)}(x) = \sup_{\tau \in \mathcal{T}} \mathbb{E}_x(e^{-q\tau}(v_f(X_\tau, X_\tau) - h_b(X_\tau)) \mathbf{1}_{\{\tau < \infty\}}), \qquad (9.8)$$

where $h_b(\cdot)$ is an increasing function on I such that $h_b(x) \geq h(x)$ for all $x \in I$,[1] and $\sup_{x \in I}(v_f(x,x) - h_b(x)) > 0$, $\mathcal{T}$ is the set of all stopping times with respect to the filtration generated by $X.$. The problem arises, for example, in optimal acquisition of the asset $X.$ when $h_b(x) = x + c_b$, where $c_b \geq 0$ is a transaction fee. In general, if we assume that $h_b(X)$ is the price the investor need to pay to acquire one unit of the risky asset, then (9.8) represents the problem of finding the optimal time to purchase this risk asset. Note that the investor will select the optimal time to sell but subject to a trailing stop exit. For this reason, we will call the problem in (9.8) the optimal acquisition problem with a trailing stop, even for a general reward $h_b(\cdot)$.

Remark 9.3. Note that in (9.8), we apply the value function $v_f(x, \bar{x})$ only with $x = \bar{x}$. From a practical point of view, this is the most relevant case since a trailing stop should be placed based on the price at which the asset was purchased, rather than an arbitrary reference price.

In summary, the solutions to (9.8) and (9.4) yield the optimal trading strategy that involves buying a risky asset and selling it later while being protected by a trailing stop.

9.1.1. *Standing assumption*

We now discuss the following standing assumption on the reward function $h(\cdot)$.

---
[1]If there is an $x \in I$ such that $h_b(x) < h(x)$, then immediate selling after purchasing when the asset price is at x yields a strictly positive profit with certainty, hence an arbitrage.

Assumption 9.1. *The reward function $h(\cdot)$ is increasing, twice differentiable on I, and there is an x_0 in the interior of I such that*

$$(\mathcal{L} - q)h(x) \geq 0 \text{ if and only if } x \leq x_0. \tag{9.9}$$

Moreover, we have

$$\lim_{x \to r} \frac{h(x)}{\phi_q^+(x)} < \sup_{x > x_0} \frac{h(x)}{\phi_q^+(x)} < \infty, \tag{9.10}$$

Remark 9.4. By Dayanik and Karatzas (2003, Proposition 5.10), it is easily seen that Assumption 9.1 ensures the finiteness of the upper bound in (9.7) for all $x \in I$. Moreover, the assumption implies that the optimal stopping time for the upper bound is of threshold type, as proved in the following lemma.

Lemma 9.1. *Under Assumption 9.1, there is an $x^\star \in [x_0, r)$ such that*

$$\sup_{\tau \in \mathcal{T}} \mathbb{E}_x(e^{-r\tau} h(X_\tau) \mathbf{1}_{\{\tau < \infty\}}) = \mathbb{E}_x(e^{-r\tau_X^+(x^\star)} h(X_{\tau_X^+(x^\star)}) \mathbf{1}_{\{\tau_X^+(x^\star) < \infty\}}).$$

Lemma 9.1 shows that Assumption 9.1 is sufficient for the optimality of up-crossing strategy $\tau_X^+(x^\star)$ in optimal stopping problem $\sup_{\tau \in \mathcal{T}} \mathbb{E}_x(e^{-r\tau} h(X_\tau) \mathbf{1}_{\{\tau < \infty\}})$, where $x^\star$ is a constant in (x_0, r). Since we interpreted $h(X_\tau)$ as the proceeds from selling the risky asset, the economic insight of this result is that, under no constraint (i.e., no trailing stops), it is optimal to sell the asset when its price is sufficiently high. Thus, apart from analytical tractability considerations, Assumption 9.1 is also economically reasonable for our trading problem.

Remark 9.5. We give a few examples in which Assumption 9.1 holds. First, let $h(x) = x - K$ for some constant $K > 0$, and X. be the Black–Scholes model, i.e., $\mu(x) = \mu x, \sigma(x) = \sigma x$ for all $x \in I = \mathbb{R}_{>0}$, with constants $\mu < q, \sigma > 0.$[2] Second, we can let $h(x) = x$ and X. be the Ornstein–Uhlenbeck process, i.e., $\mu(x) = \lambda(\theta - x)$ and $\sigma(x) = \sigma$ for $x \in I = \mathbb{R}$, with constants $\lambda, \sigma > 0$ and $\theta \in \mathbb{R}$.

9.2. Optimal Trading with a Fixed Stop-Loss

To gain some intuition for our solution method for the problem in (9.4) with a trailing stop, we first consider the optimal stopping problems

---

[2] It is well-known that if $\mu \geq q$, then the optimal stopping region is the empty set.

when the investor uses a fixed stop-loss exit instead of a trailing stop. Precisely, arbitrarily fix a $y \in I$, we consider the following class of problems indexed by y:

$$V_y(x) := \sup_{\tau \in \mathcal{T}_y^{\mathsf{S}}} \mathbb{E}_x(e^{-q\tau} h(X_\tau) \mathbf{1}_{\{\tau < \infty\}}), \qquad (9.11)$$

where $\mathcal{T}_y^{\mathsf{S}}$ is the set of all stopping times of X. that stops no later than the first passage time to level y, $\tau_X^-(y)$. The problem in (9.11) puts a *mandatory liquidation* constraint upon hitting the fixed stop-loss level y from above.

The special cases of the problem in (9.11) with the reward function $h(x) = x - c$ driven by the OU and CIR processes have been studied in Cartea *et al.* (2015), Leung and Li (2015) and Leung *et al.* (2014, 2015). In this section, we present the analysis of problem (9.11) driven by a general linear diffusion.

9.2.1. *Optimal liquidation subject to a stop-loss exit*

We now study the optimal liquidation problem (9.11) where X. follows a general linear diffusion (see (A.1)). To facilitate our analysis, we also consider the extended case of (9.11) for $y = l$, in which case we have

$$V_l(x) = \sup_{\tau \in \mathcal{T}} \mathbb{E}_x(e^{-q\tau} h(X_\tau) \mathbf{1}_{\{\tau < \infty\}}). \qquad (9.12)$$

Notice that the value function $V_l(\cdot)$ has already been derived in Lemma 9.1.

Remark 9.6. For each fixed $x \in I$, the mapping $y \mapsto V_y(x)$ is obviously non-increasing over $[l, r)$.

Remark 9.7. The connection between (9.4) and (9.11) can be seen as follows. For any $x, \bar{x} \in I$ such that $x \in (f(\bar{x}), \bar{x}]$, by the $\mathbb{P}_{x,\bar{x}}$-a.s. inequality that $\rho_f \leq \tau_X^-(f(\bar{x}))$, we know that $\mathcal{T}_f^{\mathsf{T}} \subset \mathcal{T}_{f(\bar{x})}^{\mathsf{S}}$. Hence, $v_f(x, \bar{x}) \leq V_{f(\bar{x})}(x)$. As a consequence, if we define the optimal liquidation regions

$$\mathcal{S}_f^{\mathsf{T,L}}(\bar{x}) := \{x \in (l, \bar{x}] : v_f(x, \bar{x}) = h(x)\}, \quad \forall \bar{x} \in I, \qquad (9.13)$$

$$\mathcal{S}_y^{\mathsf{S,L}} := \{x \in I : V_y(x) = h(x)\}, \qquad \forall y \in I, \qquad (9.14)$$

then we have

$$(\mathcal{S}_{f(\bar{x})}^{\mathsf{S,L}} \cap (l, \bar{x}]) \subset \mathcal{S}_f^{\mathsf{T,L}}(\bar{x}), \qquad \forall \bar{x} > 0.$$

Additionally, if $\bar{x} \in \mathcal{S}_{f(\bar{x})}^{\mathsf{S,L}}$ then we have $(\mathcal{S}_{f(\bar{x})}^{\mathsf{S,L}} \cap (l, \bar{x}]) = \mathcal{S}_f^{\mathsf{T,L}}(\bar{x})$, since in this case it is optimal to liquidate before X. reaching a new maximum.

Proposition 9.1. *Under Assumption 9.1, for any fixed $y \in (l, x_0)$, there is a finite threshold $b(y) \in (x_0, r)$ such that*[3]

$$V_y(x) = \mathbb{E}_x(e^{-q(\tau_X^+(b(y)) \wedge \tau_X^-(y))} h(X_{\tau_X^+(b(y)) \wedge \tau_X^-(y)})), \quad \forall x \in I. \quad (9.15)$$

Here $b(y)$ can be identified as the smallest solution over (x_0, r) to

$$h'(b) - h(b)\frac{\phi_q^{-\prime}(b)}{\phi_q^-(b)} = \frac{\phi_q^-(b)\psi_q'(b)}{\psi_q(b) - \psi_q(y)}\left(\frac{h(b)}{\phi_q^-(b)} - \frac{h(y)}{\phi_q^-(y)}\right). \quad (9.16)$$

Moreover, the mapping $y \mapsto b(y)$ is strictly decreasing and differentiable over (l, x_0), with limits $b(x_0-) = x_0$, and $b(l+) \leq x^\star < r$, where $x^\star$ is defined in Lemma 9.1.

Corollary 9.1. *If $y \in [x_0, r)$, then the stopping region $\mathcal{S}_y^{S,L} = I$, i.e., there is no continuation region.*

9.3. Optimal Trading with a Trailing Stop

In this section, we apply the results we obtained to study the optimal liquidation problem (9.4) and the optimal acquisition problem (9.8).

9.3.1. *Optimal liquidation*

Returning to the problem in (9.4), we will first use results in Proposition 9.1 to construct a candidate threshold type strategy for liquidation before the trailing stop ρ_f.

Corollary 9.2. *There is a unique $b_f^\star \geq x_0$ such that $b(f(\bar{x})) > \bar{x}$ if and only if $\bar{x} < b_f^\star$. Moreover, $b_f^\star$ is the unique solution over $(x_0, f^{-1}(x_0))$ to $\Gamma(\bar{x}) = 0$, where*

$$\Gamma(\bar{x}) := \frac{1}{\psi_q'(\bar{x})}\left(\frac{h'(\bar{x})}{\phi_q^-(\bar{x})} - \frac{h(\bar{x})\phi_q^{-\prime}(\bar{x})}{(\phi_q^-(\bar{x}))^2}\right) - \frac{\frac{h(\bar{x})}{\phi_q^-(\bar{x})} - \frac{h(f(\bar{x}))}{\phi_q^-(f(\bar{x}))}}{\psi_q(\bar{x}) - \psi_q(f(\bar{x}))}. \quad (9.17)$$

Moreover, $\Gamma(\bar{x}) > 0$ if $l < \bar{x} < b_f^\star$, and $\Gamma(\bar{x}) < 0$ if $f^{-1}(x_0) > \bar{x} > b_f^\star$.

---

[3]Notice that in the expectation (9.15) we do not have the indicator $\mathbf{1}_{\{\tau_X^+(b(y)) \wedge \tau_X^-(y) < \infty\}}$, as it is equal to 1 almost surely.

Let us suppose for now that $\bar{x} \geq b_f^\star$.

(1) If we still have $f(\bar{x}) < x_0$, then by the definition of $b_f^\star$ given in Corollary 9.2, we have $b(f(\bar{x})) \leq \bar{x}$. Thus, by Remark 9.7,
$$h(x) \leq v_f(x, \bar{x}) \leq V_{f(\bar{x})}(x), \quad \forall x, \bar{x} \in I \text{ with } x \leq \bar{x},$$
$$((l, f(\bar{x})] \cap [b(f(\bar{x})), \bar{x}]) \equiv (\mathcal{S}_{f(\bar{x})}^{\mathsf{S,L}} \cup (l, \bar{x}]) = \mathcal{S}_f^{\mathsf{T,L}}(\bar{x}).$$

(2) If $f(\bar{x}) \geq x_0$, then by Corollary 9.1, we can use the same argument as above to conclude that $(l, \bar{x}] \equiv (\mathcal{S}_{f(\bar{x})}^{\mathsf{S,L}} \cap (l, \bar{x}]) = \mathcal{S}_f^{\mathsf{T,L}}(\bar{x})$.

As a consequence we obtain the following theorem.

Theorem 9.1. *Under Assumption 9.1, for $x, \bar{x} \in I$ with $x \leq \bar{x}$ and $\bar{x} \geq b_f^\star$, we have*
$$v_f(x, \bar{x}) \equiv V_{f(\bar{x})}(x).$$
So the optimal stopping time is $\rho_f \wedge \tau_X^+(b(f(\bar{x})))$.

In what follows, we consider the remaining case $l < x \leq \bar{x} < b_f^\star$ and we shall establish the optimality of the stopping rule $\tau_X^+(b_f^\star) \wedge \rho_f$. To this end, we first calculate the associated value of this strategy, denoted by $u_f(x, \bar{x})$. In particular, by the strong Markov property of $X.$, applying Lemma A.1 we have for any $x \in (f(\bar{x}), \bar{x})$ with $\bar{x} < b_f^\star$,

$$\begin{aligned}u_f(x, \bar{x}) &:= \mathbb{E}_{x,\bar{x}}(e^{-r(\rho_f \wedge \tau_X^+(b_f^\star))} h(X_{\rho_f \wedge \tau_X^+(b_f^\star)})) \\ &= h(f(\bar{x})) \mathbb{E}_x(e^{-q\tau_X^-(f(\bar{x}))} \mathbf{1}_{\{\tau_X^-(f(\bar{x})) < \tau_X^+(\bar{x})\}}) \\ &\quad + u_f(\bar{x}, \bar{x}) \mathbb{E}_x(e^{-q\tau_X^+(\bar{x})} \mathbf{1}_{\{\tau_X^+(\bar{x}) < \tau_X^-(f(\bar{x}))\}}) \\ &= \phi_q^-(x) \left(\frac{h(f(\bar{x}))}{\phi_q^-(f(\bar{x}))} \frac{\psi_q(\bar{x}) - \psi_q(x)}{\psi_q(\bar{x}) - \psi_q(f(\bar{x}))} \right. \\ &\quad \left. + \frac{u_f(\bar{x}, \bar{x})}{\phi_q^-(\bar{x})} \frac{\psi_q(x) - \psi_q(f(\bar{x}))}{\psi_q(\bar{x}) - \psi_q(f(\bar{x}))} \right), \end{aligned} \quad (9.18)$$

where for $\bar{x} < b_f^\star$, we have
$$\begin{aligned}u_f(\bar{x}, \bar{x}) &= h(b_f^\star) \mathbb{E}_{\bar{x},\bar{x}}(e^{-q\tau_X^+(b_f^\star)} \mathbf{1}_{\{\tau_X^+(b_f^\star) < \rho_f\}}) \\ &\quad + \mathbb{E}_{\bar{x},\bar{x}}(e^{-q\rho_f} h(X_{\rho_f}) \mathbf{1}_{\{\rho_f < \tau_X^+(b_f^\star)\}}). \end{aligned} \quad (9.19)$$

The two expectations in (9.19) can be computed using standard calculation using excursion theory.

Lemma 9.2. *For any* $b > \bar{x}$, *we have*

$$\mathbb{E}_{\bar{x},\bar{x}}(e^{-q\rho_f} h(X_{\rho_f}) \mathbf{1}_{\{\rho_f < \tau_X^+(b)\}})$$
$$= \int_{\bar{x}}^{b} \frac{h(f(v))}{\phi_q^-(f(v))} \frac{\phi_q^-(\bar{x})\psi_q'(v)}{\psi_q(v) - \psi_q(f(v))} \exp\left(-\int_{\bar{x}}^{v} \frac{\psi_q'(u)\,du}{\psi_q(u) - \psi_q(f(u))}\right) dv,$$

and

$$\mathbb{E}_{\bar{x},\bar{x}}(e^{-q\tau_X^+(b)} \mathbf{1}_{\{\tau_X^+(b) < \rho_f\}}) = \frac{\phi_q^-(\bar{x})}{\phi_q^-(b)} \exp\left(-\int_{\bar{x}}^{b} \frac{\psi_q'(u)\,du}{\psi_q(u) - \psi_q(f(u))}\right).$$

In particular, as $b \to r$ *we obtain the value of the plain trailing stop (defined in* (9.6))

$$g_f(\bar{x},\bar{x}) = \int_{\bar{x}}^{r} \frac{h(f(v))}{\phi_q^-(f(v))} \frac{\phi_q^-(\bar{x})\psi_q'(v)}{\psi_q(v) - \psi_q(f(v))} \exp\left(-\int_{\bar{x}}^{v} \frac{\psi_q'(u)\,du}{\psi_q(u) - \psi_q(f(u))}\right) dv,$$

and for $f(\bar{x}) < x \leq \bar{x}$,

$$g_f(x,\bar{x}) = \phi_q^-(x) \left(\frac{(hf(\bar{x}))}{\phi_q^-(f(\bar{x}))} \frac{\psi_q(\bar{x}) - \psi_q(x)}{\psi_q(\bar{x}) - \psi_q(f(\bar{x}))} \right.$$
$$\left. + \frac{g_f(\bar{x},\bar{x})}{\phi_q^-(\bar{x})} \frac{\psi_q(x) - \psi_q(f(\bar{x}))}{\psi_q(\bar{x}) - \psi_q(f(\bar{x}))} \right).$$

To establish the optimality of $\tau_X^+(b_f^*) \wedge \rho_f$ when $0 < x \leq \bar{x} < b_f^*$, we need to show that the value of the rule $u_f(x,\bar{x})$ dominates the reward function $h(x)$. This claim can be proved by using (9.18) and the optimality of b_f^* (see Corollary 9.2).

Lemma 9.3. *For all* $\bar{x} \in (l, b_f^*)$ *and* $x \in (f(\bar{x}), \bar{x}]$, *we have* $u_f(x, \bar{x}) > h(\bar{x})$.

Lemma 9.3 says that waiting until $\tau_X^+(b_f^*) \wedge \rho_f$ yields positive "time value" $u_f(x,\bar{x}) - h(x) > 0$ for all $f(\bar{x}) < x \leq \bar{x} < b_f^*$, so this region should be part of the optimal continuation region. On the one hand, before hitting b_f^*, this region is obviously the maximum possible continuation region. Furthermore, upon hitting b_f^* we have $\bar{x} = b_f^*$, and the case has already been treated in Theorem 9.1, which suggest immediate stopping at $\tau_X^+(b_f^*)$. So we know that the stopping time $\tau_X^+(b_f^*) \wedge \rho_f$ is optimal for problem (9.4) if $\bar{x} < b_f^*$.

Theorem 9.2. *Under Assumption 9.1, we have for all $l < x \leq \bar{x} < b_f^\star$ that*

$$v_f(x,\bar{x}) \equiv u_f(x,\bar{x}) = \mathbb{E}_{x,\bar{x}}(e^{-q(\tau_X^+(b_f^\star) \wedge \rho_f)}) h(X_{\tau_X^+(b_f^\star) \wedge \rho_f}),$$

where $b_f^\star$ is defined in Corollary 9.2. Moreover, the mapping $f \mapsto b_f^\star$ is non-increasing over all functions satisfying (9.2).

Proof. The only claim that needs a proof is the monotonicity of $f \mapsto b_f^\star$. But that is due to Remark 9.2 and the structure of the optimal stopping region. □

Corollary 9.3. *The value of the plain trailing stop $g_f(x,\bar{x})$ given in Lemma 9.2 is finite. Moreover, for any $f(\bar{x}) < x \leq \bar{x} < b_f^\star$, the early liquidation premium before the trailing stop ρ_f is*

$$p_f(x,\bar{x}) = \frac{\phi_q^-(x)}{\phi_q^-(b_f^\star)} \frac{\psi_q(x) - \psi_q(f(\bar{x}))}{\psi_q(\bar{x}) - \psi_q(f(\bar{x}))}$$

$$\times \exp\left(\int_{\bar{x}}^{b_f^\star} \frac{-\psi_q'(u)du}{\psi_q(u) - \psi_q(f(u))}\right) (h(b_f^\star) - g_f(b_f^\star, b_f^\star)),$$

where $g_f(b_f^\star, b_f^\star)$ is given in Lemma 9.2. If $f(\bar{x}) < x_0$, $\bar{x} \geq b_f^\star$ and $f(\bar{x}) < x < b(f(\bar{x}))$ (see Proposition 9.1 for the existence of $b(y)$), then the early liquidation premium given by the trailing stop ρ_f is

$$p_f(x,\bar{x}) = \frac{\phi_q^-(x)}{\phi_q^-(b(f(\bar{x})))} \frac{\psi_q(x) - \psi_q(f(\bar{x}))}{\psi(b(f(\bar{x}))) - \psi_q(f(\bar{x}))} (h(b(f(\bar{x}))) - g_f(b(f(\bar{x})), \bar{x})).$$

Finally, if $f(\bar{x}) < x_0$, $\bar{x} \geq b_f^\star$ and $b(f(\bar{x})) \leq x \leq \bar{x}$, or $f(\bar{x}) \geq x_0$ and $f(\bar{x}) < x \leq \bar{x}$, then the early liquidation premium given by the trailing stop ρ_f is

$$p_f(x,\bar{x}) = h(x) - g_f(x,\bar{x}).$$

Remark 9.8. If the first inequality in (9.10) is an equality, then the optimal threshold $b_f^\star$ may be at the boundary r, in which case, it will be optimal not to liquidate before the trailing stop. That is, $p_f(x,\bar{x}) = 0$ for all $x, \bar{x} \in I$ such that $x \in (f(\bar{x}), \bar{x}]$.

9.3.2. *Optimal acquisition with a trailing stop*

In this section, we consider the optimal stopping problem related to acquisition with a trailing stop, which we recall as follows:

$$v_f^{(1)}(x) = \sup_{\tau \in \mathcal{T}} \mathbb{E}_x(e^{-q\tau}(v_f(X_\tau, X_\tau) - h_b(X_\tau))\mathbf{1}_{\{\tau < \infty\}}), \quad (9.20)$$

where $\mathcal{T}$ is the set of all stopping times of X., and $\sup_{x \in I}(v_f(x,x) - h_b(x)) > 0$.

Let us define the optimal acquisition region with a trailing stop as

$$\mathcal{S}_f^{\mathsf{T,A}} := \{x \in I : v_f^{(1)}(x) = v_f(x,x) - h_b(x)\}.$$

Following Dayanik and Karatzas (2003, Proposition 5.10) and (9.19), to determine $\mathcal{S}_f^{\mathsf{T,A}}$, it suffices to obtain the smallest concave majorant of

$$H^{(1)}(z) := \frac{v_f(x,x) - h_b(x)}{\phi_q^-(x)}, \quad \text{where } z = \psi_q(x) \in \mathbb{R}_{>0}, x \in I. \quad (9.21)$$

In light of Theorem 9.1, we know that for $x \geq b_f^\star$, we have $v_f(x,x) - h_b(x) = h(x) - h_b(x) \leq 0$, so we must have $\mathcal{S}_f^{\mathsf{T,A}} \subset I \setminus [b_f^\star, r) = (l, b_f^\star)$. Therefore, if we denote by

$$\overline{z}_f^\star := \sup \arg \max_{z \in \mathbb{R}_{>0}} H^{(1)}(z), \quad (9.22)$$

then we have $H^{(1)}(\overline{z}_f^\star) > 0$ (since $\sup_{x > 0}(v_f(x,x) - h_b(x)) > 0$), and $\overline{z}_f^\star \in [0, \psi_q(b_f^\star))$, and the smallest concave majorant of $H^{(1)}(\cdot)$ over $[\overline{z}_f^\star, \infty)$ must be given by the constant function $H^{(1)}(\overline{z}_f^\star)$, so we can deduce that $\mathcal{S}_f^{\mathsf{T,A}} \subset (l, \psi_q^{-1}(\overline{z}_f^\star)]$. However, no further information about $\mathcal{S}_f^{\mathsf{T,A}}$ is available under general diffusions, mainly due to lack of information about the concavity of $H^{(1)}(\cdot)$. In fact, as seen in Lemma 9.4 below, even in the special case $h_b(\cdot) \equiv h(\cdot)$, function $H^{(1)}(\cdot)$ over $(0, \psi_q(b_f^\star))$ is the difference between a convex function $H_f(\cdot)$ over $(0, \psi_q(b_f^\star))$ and a function $H(\cdot)$ that is convex over $(0, \psi_q(x_0))$ and is strictly concave over $(\psi_q(x_0), \psi_q(b_f^\star))$, so we only know that $H^{(1)}(\cdot)$ is convex on $(\psi_q(x_0), \psi_q(b_f^\star))$, but the concavity of this function over $(0, \psi_q(x_0))$ is not available to us.

Lemma 9.4. *Consider function*

$$H_f(z) := \frac{v_f(x,x)}{\phi_q^-(x)}, \quad H(z) := \frac{h(x)}{\phi_q^-(x)}, \quad \text{where } z = \psi_q(x) \in \mathbb{R}_{>0}. \quad (9.23)$$

Then $H_f(\cdot)$ is convex on $(0, \psi_q(b_f^\star))$, and $H(\cdot)$ is strictly concave on $(\psi_q(x_0), \infty)$ and is convex on $(0, \psi_q(x_0))$.

Remark 9.9. If X. follows a Black–Scholes model with drift $\mu < q$, and volatility $\sigma > 0$, then it will never be optimal to acquire the stock in the narrow sense: i.e., if $h(x) = x - c_s$ and $h_b(x) = x + c_b$ for $c_s > 0$ and $c_b \geq 0$, the transaction fee at liquidation is equal to $c_s > 0$, and the transaction fee at purchase is equal to c_b. To see this, we recall that $v_f(x,x) < V_0(x) = \mathbf{1}_{\{x<b\}}(\frac{x}{b})^{\beta^+}(b-c_s) + \mathbf{1}_{\{x\geq b\}}(x-c_s)$, where $\beta^+ = \delta + \sqrt{\delta^2 + 2q/\sigma^2} > 1$ with $\delta = \frac{\mu}{\sigma^2} - \frac{1}{2}$, and $b = \frac{\beta c_s}{\beta - 1}$. By convexity of $V_0(\cdot)$ we know that $V_0(x) - h(x) < c_s$ for all $x \in \mathbb{R}_{>0}$, so $v_f(x,x) - h(x) < c_s$ for all $x \in \mathbb{R}_{>0}$, for any floor function $f(\cdot)$ that satisfies (9.2). Thus, we have $v_f(x,x) - h_b(x) = v_f(x,x) - h(x) - (c_b + c_s) < -c_b \leq 0$, so the payoff function for problem (9.20) to be negative throughout $\mathbb{R}_{>0}$, which means that the optimal stopping region is empty. To get a non-empty stopping region for problem (9.20), one needs to replace $h(\cdot)$ with a different function. We present a case study in the next example.

Example 9.1. Assuming that $\mu(x) = \mu x, \sigma(x) = \sigma x, h(x) = h_b(x) = x - Kx^{-\epsilon}$ for all $x \in I \equiv \mathbb{R}_{>0}$, where $\mu \in \mathbb{R}$ such that $\mu < q$, and $\sigma, K > 0$ and $\epsilon \geq 0$ such that $\frac{1}{2}\sigma^2\epsilon(\epsilon+1) - \mu\epsilon - q < 0$. Let $f(x) = (1-\alpha)x$ for some $\alpha \in (0,1)$. Then we have $\mathcal{S}_f^{\mathrm{T,A}} = (0, \underline{b}_f^\star]$, where $\underline{b}_f^\star := \psi_q^{-1}(\overline{z}_f^\star)$ with $\overline{z}_f^\star$ given in (9.22). That is, for all $x \in I$

$$v_f^{(1)}(x) = \mathbb{E}_x(e^{-q\tau_X^-(\underline{b}_f^\star)}(v_f(X_{\tau_X^-(\underline{b}_f^\star)}, X_{\tau_X^-(\underline{b}_f^\star)}) - h_b(X_{\tau_X^-(\underline{b}_f^\star)}))\mathbf{1}_{\{\tau_X^-(\underline{b}_f^\star) < \infty\}}).$$

In general, one can analyze the concavity of $H^{(1)}(\cdot)$ (and hence the optimal stopping region) on a case-by-case basis with possibly helps of numerical computation. To demonstrate the idea, let us define

$$z_f^\star := \psi_q(\underline{b}_f^\star), \quad \varphi(z) := \psi_q(f(\psi_q^{-1}(z))), \quad \forall z \in \mathbb{R}_{>0}. \tag{9.24}$$

It is clear that $\varphi(\cdot)$ is an increasing function such that $0 < \varphi(z) < z$. From Lemma 9.2 we have for all $z \in (0, z_f^\star)$

$$H_f(z) = \exp\left(-\int_z^{z_f^\star} \frac{d\nu}{\nu - \varphi(\nu)}\right) H(z_f^\star)$$
$$+ \int_z^{z_f^\star} H(\varphi(\nu)) \exp\left(-\int_z^\nu \frac{dw}{w - \varphi(w)}\right) \frac{d\nu}{\nu - \varphi(\nu)}, \tag{9.25}$$

where $H_f(\cdot)$ is defined in (9.23).

To obtain the smallest concave majorant of $H^{(1)}(\cdot)$, we need to numerically evaluate $H_f(\cdot)$. To that end, it will be more convenient to rewrite

(9.25) into an equivalent first-order linear ODE form:

$$\begin{cases} H'_f(z) = \dfrac{H_f(z) - H(\varphi(z))}{z - \varphi(z)}, & \forall z \in (0, z_f^\star), \\ \text{subject to } H_f(z_f^\star) = H(z_f^\star). \end{cases} \quad (9.26)$$

Then we can use Mathematica's NDSolve command to efficiently compute the values of $H^{(1)}(\cdot)$ and its derivatives.[4]

9.4. Case Study: Trading with a Trailing Stop under the Exponential OU Model

In this section, we apply the results in Section 9.3 to an exponential OU model:

$$dX_t = X_t\left(\lambda(\theta - \log X_t) + \frac{1}{2}\sigma^2\right)dt + \sigma X_t dW_t, \quad X_0 = x \in I \equiv \mathbb{R}_{>0}, \quad (9.27)$$

where $\{W_t\}_{t>0}$ is a standard Brownian motion, $\lambda, \sigma > 0$ are positive constants, and $\theta \in \mathbb{R}$ is the long term average for the log-price $\log X$:

$$d(\log X_t) = \lambda(\theta - \log X_t)dt + \sigma dW_t.$$

With reference to functions $\phi_q^\pm(\cdot)$, it is well-known (see, e.g., Borodin and Salminen (2002, p. 542)) that

$$\phi_q^!(x) = e^{\frac{\lambda}{2\sigma^2}(y-\theta)^2} D_{-\frac{q}{\lambda}}\left(\frac{\sqrt{2\lambda}}{\sigma}(y - \theta)\right),$$

$$\phi_q^-(x) = e^{\frac{\lambda}{2\sigma^2}(y-\theta)^2} D_{-\frac{q}{\lambda}}\left(\frac{\sqrt{2\lambda}}{\sigma}(\theta - y)\right),$$

where $y = \log x$, and $D_\nu(\cdot)$ is the parabolic cylinder function with parameter ν. We are interested in optimal liquidation and acquisition of

---

[4]The procedure can be conveniently generalized to allow for distinct discounting rates for the acquisition and liquidation problems.

one unit of an risky asset whose price is modeled by $X.$. To that end, we let

$$h(x) = x - c_0, \quad h_b(x) = x + c_0, \quad \forall x \in I,$$

where $c_0 \geq 0$ is a transaction cost to buy or sell. Then it follows that, for any $q > 0$

$$(\mathcal{L} - q)h(x) = \left(\lambda(\theta - \log x) + \frac{1}{2}\sigma^2 - q\right)x + qc_0, \quad \forall x \in I,$$

which is a strictly decreasing function with range equal to $\mathbb{R}$. Moreover, by the asymptotic behavior of $D_\nu(\cdot)$ (see, e.g., Temme (2000, Eq. (1.8))), we know that the reward function $h(\cdot)$ satisfies Assumption 9.1.

9.4.1. Value function and optimal strategy

Upon purchasing of the asset, we set a percentage drawdown trailing stop, i.e., $f(x) = (1-\alpha)x$, where $\alpha \in (0,1)$ is a constant.

In this study, we select the following parameter values:

$$\lambda = 0.6, \theta = 1, \sigma = 0.2, q = 0.05, c_0 = 0.02, \alpha = 0.3. \tag{9.28}$$

This means that we will liquidate the asset whenever its price drops from its running maximum since the acquisition by more than 30%.

In Figure 9.2(a), we plot the function $H(\cdot)$ defined as in (9.23). We also have plotted the function $H_f(\cdot)$ defined as in (9.19) (see also (9.25)), which is obtained by first solving equation (9.17) with $f(x) = (1-\alpha)x$ for $b_f^\star(=2.8845)$, and then using ODE (9.25) to numerically obtain $H_f(\cdot)$. We notice that, in contrast to the value function for a fixed stop-loss level (Proposition 9.1, see also Leung and Li (2015)), the function $H_f(\cdot)$ is not concave over $(0, \psi_q(b_f^\star))$. This is because, although $\phi_q^-(x)H_f(\psi_q(x)) = v_f(x, x)$ is the value function for the optimal stopping problem (9.4) when $x = \bar{x}$, it does not yield a martingale of $(X_t, \overline{X}_t)$, which requires using the function $v_f(x, \bar{x})$, not $v_f(x, x)$.

In Figure 9.2(b), we plot the reward function $h(x)$ and the value function $v_f(x, x)$ for the optimal liquidation problem (9.4) with $x = \bar{x}$.

In Figure 9.2(c), we plot the function $H^{(1)}(z)$ defined in (9.21) under the current exponential OU model. By checking the function's derivative numerically, we conclude that it is concave to the left of its maximum point.

(a) $H_f(z)$ vs. $H(z)$

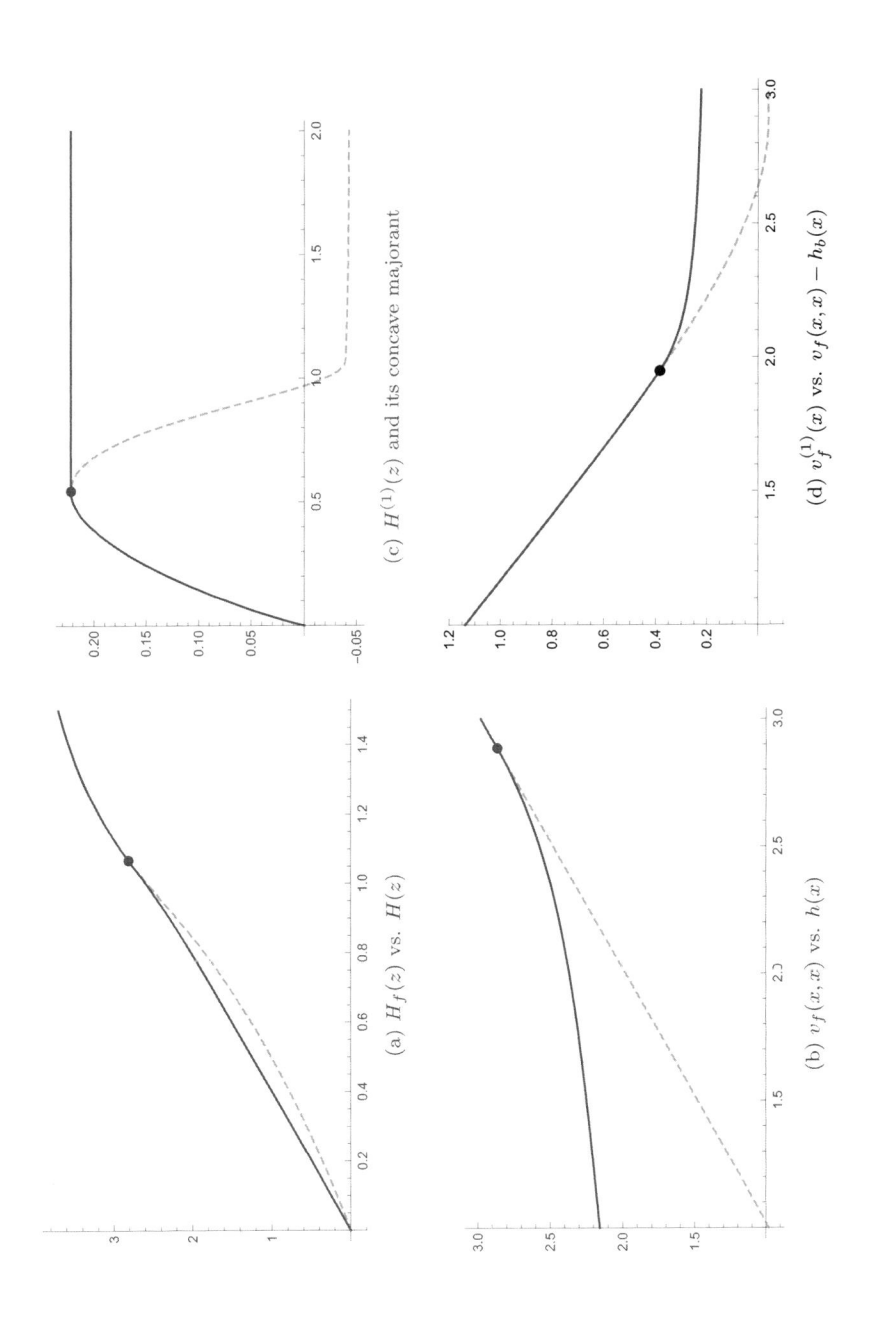

(b) $v_f(x,x)$ vs. $h(x)$

(c) $H^{(1)}(z)$ and its concave majorant

(d) $v_f^{(1)}(x)$ vs. $v_f(x,x) - h_b(x)$

Hence, the smallest concave majorant is given by

$$\hat{H}^{(1)}_{f,q}(z) = H^{(1)}(z \wedge \bar{z}^\star_f), \quad \forall z \in \mathbb{R}_{>0}.$$

Therefore, in this case, the optimal acquisition strategy is to purchase the asset once the price is lower than $\underline{b}^\star_f = 1.9488$.

In Figure 9.2(d), we plot the function $v_f(x,x) - h_b(x)$ and the value function $v_f^{(1)}(x)$ for the optimal acquisition problem (9.8), and the "pasting point" is at $\psi_q^{-1}(\bar{z}^\star_f) = 1.9488$.

In summary, for the exponential OU model (9.27) with parameters as given in (9.28), the optimal trading strategy is to purchase the asset when price is lower than $\psi_q^{-1}(\bar{z}^\star_f) = 1.9488$, and setup the 30% trailing stop order as an exit plan, and then wait until either the trailing stop is being activated or the price reaches target $b^\star_f = 2.8845$.

Lastly, in Figure 9.3 we plot the early liquidation premium of $\rho_f \wedge \tau_X^+(b^\star_f)$ over the plain trailing stop ρ_f when $x = \bar{x}$. This measure the "value" of our result in problem (9.4). By Corollary 9.3, we know that, for each $x \in I$,

$$p_f(x,x) = \exp\left(\int_x^{b^\star_f \vee x} \frac{-\psi'_q(u)du}{\psi_q(u) - \psi_q(f(u))}\right)\left(h(b^\star_f \vee x) - g_f(b^\star_f \vee x, b^\star_f \vee x)\right). \quad (9.29)$$

To numerically evaluate (9.29), we use the fusion of a "limiting order" $\tau_X^+(b)$ and the trailing stop ρ_f, with b chosen sufficiently large so that both $\mathbb{E}_x(e^{-q(\tau_X^+(b) \wedge \rho_f)}\mathbf{1}_{\{\tau_X^+(b)<\rho_f\}})$ and $h(b)\mathbb{E}_x(e^{-q(\tau_X^+(b) \wedge \rho_f)}\mathbf{1}_{\{\tau_X^+(b)<\rho_f\}})$ are sufficiently small for all x in the plotting region of Figure 9.3. Then $g_f(x,x)$ is approximated by the value of this strategy, which is subsequently solved using an ODE similar as (9.26).

In Figure 9.3, we compare the early liquidation premium $p_f(x,x)$ with the function $x - f(x) = \alpha x$ ($\alpha = 0.3$), which is the maximum loss of the trailing stop order if the price X. reaches the trailing floor immediately

---

Fig. 9.2. Numerical results under the exponential OU model (9.27): (a) Plots of function $H(z)$ (dashed gray) and $H_f(z)$ (solid black). The "pasting point" $\psi_q(b^\star_f) = 1.0674$ is indicated by the black dot. (b) Plots of the reward function $h(x)$ (dashed gray) and the value function $v_f(x,x)$ (solid black). The "pasting point" is $b^\star_f = 2.8845$ (black dot). (c) Plots of the reward function $H^{(1)}(z)$ (dashed gray) and its smallest concave majorant (solid black), along with the "pasting point" $\bar{z}^\star_f = 0.5441$ (black dot). (d) Plots of the reward function $v_f(x,x) - h_b(x)$ (dashed gray) and the value function $v_f^{(1)}(x)$ (solid black), and the "pasting point" $\underline{b}^\star_f = 1.9488$ (black dot).

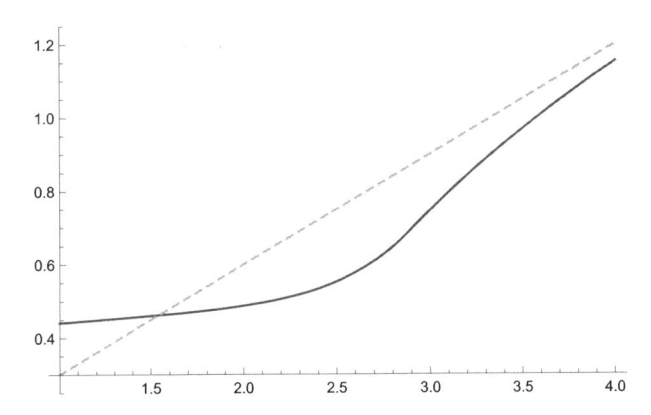

Fig. 9.3. Earlier liquidation premium (black) $p_f(x,x)$ and function $x-f(x) = \alpha x$ (gray dashed) under the exponential OU model (9.27).

(but without an overshoot). We notice that, for large x, the gain from our strategy over the plain trailing stop approaches 30% of the price level. Take into account of discounting and transaction costs, this example suggests that setting a trailing stop when the asset price is high will almost always incur a 30% loss at exit.

9.4.2. Sensitivity analysis

The following illustrative numerical examples will shed light on the sensitivity of the optimal acquisition and liquidation thresholds, $\underline{b}_f^\star$ and $b_f^\star$, with respect to the trailing stop level α, and transaction cost c_0. This involve numerical computation of the thresholds, as well as the critical level where function $(\mathcal{L} - q)h(x)$ vanishes. In Figure 9.4(a), we plot $(b_f^\star, x_0, \underline{b}_f^\star)$ as a function of the trailing stop level α, with x_0 (the dashed line) defined in Assumption 9.1. The optimal liquidation level $b_f^\star$ is increasing in α, confirming our result in Theorem 9.2. Moreover, the optimal acquisition level $\underline{b}_f^\star$ is also increasing in α. Recalling that a higher α means a lower trailing stop trigger, this means that a larger downside protection induces the investor to enter the market earlier. As seen in Figure 9.4(a), the investor with a higher α will acquire the asset at a price level closer to the critical level x_0. Our numerical results also suggest that, for small α, it may not be optimal to initiate the position at all, because the gain to be realized at the sell order at $b_f^\star$ or at the trailing stop will be too low compared to the transaction cost c_0. In such cases, we observe that $\sup_{x \in \mathbb{R}}(v_f(x,x) - h(x)) < c_0 = 0.02$.

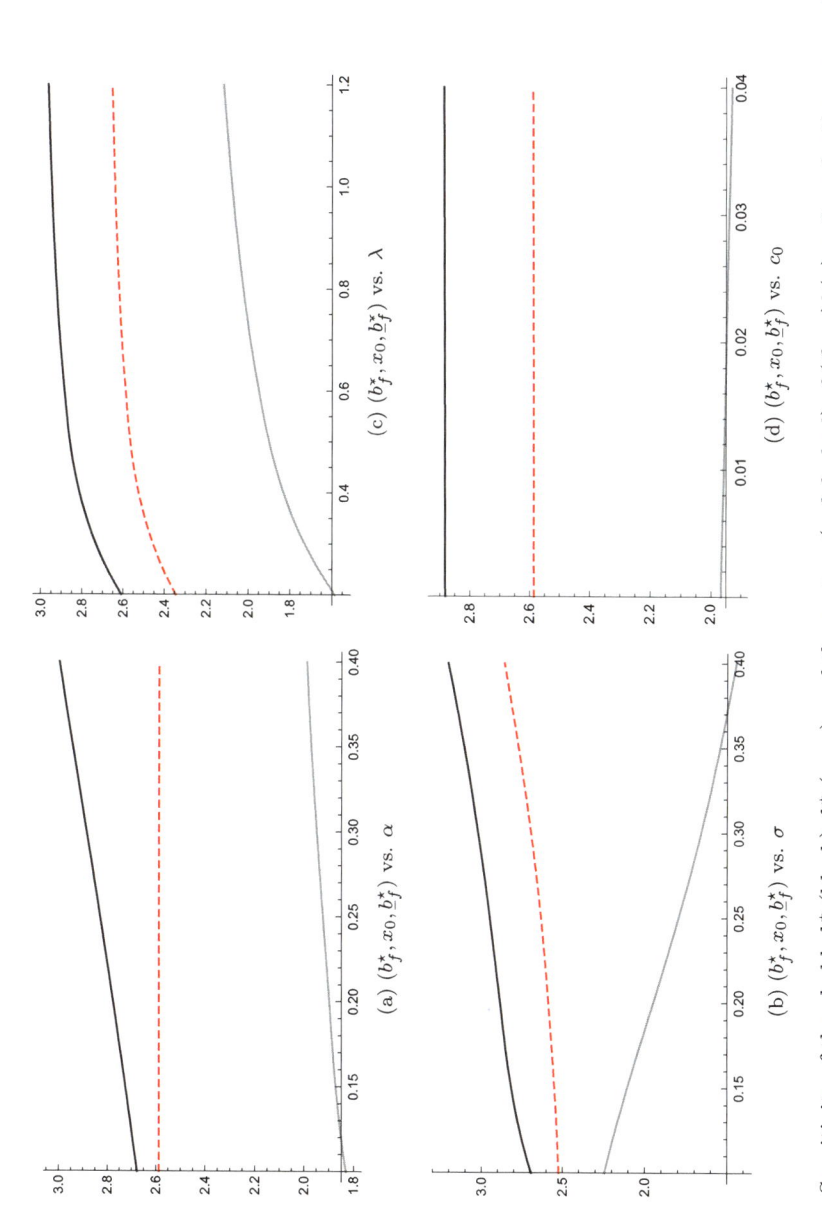

Fig. 9.4. Sensitivity of thresholds $b_f^\star$ (black), $\underline{b}_f^\star$ (gray), and the root x_0 (red dashed) of $(\mathcal{L}-q)h(x)=0$, under the exponential OU model (9.27): (a) dependence on $\alpha \in [0.1, 0.4]$; (b) dependence on $\sigma \in [0.1, 0.4]$; (c) dependence on $\lambda \in [0.2, 1.2]$; and (d) dependence on $c_0 \in [0, 0.04]$. In all figures, other parameters are set as in (9.28).

In Figure 9.4(b), we plot $(b_f^\star, x_0, \underline{b}_f^\star)$ as a function of the asset's volatility parameter σ. We see that, as σ increases, the optimal liquidation level increases, thanks to stronger force from the Brownian motion. However, the acquisition price level is lower for higher σ, which means that the investor is willing to establish a position at a lower price. However, higher volatility will increase the likelihood for the asset price to reach low levels earlier, so the actual entry time by the investor may be earlier or later. The decreasing pattern of $\underline{b}_f^\star$ with respect to σ suggests that the investor voluntarily lowers the take-profit level to mitigate the risk of realizing a reduced profit or a loss at the trailing stop in a more volatile market.

Figure 9.4(c) illustrates the effect of the asset's rate of mean reversion λ. A higher λ means that the log-price will move around its long-term mean θ faster. As a response, the investor enters the market earlier at a higher entry level and exit at a lower level, resulting in a quick roundtrip, as reflected in the plot by the increasing trends of $b_f^\star$ and $\underline{b}_f^\star$ with respect to λ. Moreover, their distance is shrinking as λ continues to increase. Intuitively, since the asset price tends to rapidly revert to the mean, it does not make sense to select entry and exit price levels that are far apart and away from the mean as the chance of execution is too low.

The effect of transaction cost c_0 is shown in Figure 9.4(d), where we plot $(b_f^\star, x_0, \underline{b}_f^\star)$ as a function of c_0. The optimal liquidation (respectively, acquisition) level $b_f^\star$ (respectively, $\underline{b}_f^\star$) increases (respectively, decreases) slightly with respect to c_0. To interpret, higher transaction costs discourage both acquisition and liquidation, though the effect is not significant. Nevertheless, as pointed out in our analysis above, while there is always a finite optimal liquidation price $b_f^\star$ given any transaction cost, a high transaction cost may make the trade unprofitable and thus exclude market entry.

9.5. Concluding Remarks

In this chapter, we study the problem of timing buy and then sell an asset subject to a trailing stop. Under a general linear diffusion framework, we study an optimal double stopping problem with a random path-dependent maturity. Specifically, we first derive the optimal liquidation strategy prior to a given trailing stop, and prove the optimality of using a sell limit order in conjunction with the trailing stop. Our analytic results for the liquidation problem is then used to solve for the optimal strategy to acquire the asset and simultaneously initiate the trailing stop. The method of solution also lends itself to an efficient numerical method for computing the optimal acquisition and liquidation regions. For illustration, we implement an example and conduct a sensitivity analysis under an exponential OU model.

Appendix

Briefly on One-Dimensional Linear Diffusions

We review some useful facts about one-dimensional linear diffusion below. Consider a linear diffusion process $X. = \{X_t\}_{t \geq 0}$ on $I \equiv (l, r) \subset \mathbb{R}$ with the infinitesimal generator:

$$\mathcal{L} = \frac{1}{2}\sigma^2(x)\frac{\partial^2}{\partial x^2} + \mu(x)\frac{\partial}{\partial x}, \quad \forall x \in I, \tag{A.1}$$

where $(\mu(\cdot), \sigma(\cdot))$ is a pair of real-valued functions on I such that

$$\sigma^2(x) > 0, \quad \forall x \in I, \tag{A.2}$$

$$\forall x \in I, \exists \epsilon > 0 \quad \text{such that} \quad \int_{x-\epsilon}^{x+\epsilon} \frac{1+|\mu(y)|}{\sigma^2(y)} dy < \infty. \tag{A.3}$$

Notice that this guarantees that the stochastic differential equation that governs the evolution of $X.$ has a unique weak solution (see, e.g., Karatzas and Shreve (1991, p. 329–353)). We assume that the boundaries of I are natural or entrance-not-exit (see, e.g., Itô and McKean (1965, p. 108)), hence inaccessible after time 0.

A scale function of $X.$, $s(\cdot)$, is an increasing function from I to $\mathbb{R}$, such that $(\mathcal{L}_X s)(x) = 0$ for all $x \in I$. That is, a scale function $s(\cdot)$ is an increasing function on I such that the process $\{s(X_t)\}_{t \geq 0}$ is a local martingale. In particular, one can choose $s'(x) = \exp(-\int_{\kappa'}^{x} 2\mu(y)/\sigma^2(y) dy)$ for some fixed $\kappa' \in I$. For any scale function of $X.$, the process $\{s(X_t)\}_{t \geq 0}$ is a local martingale.

Denoting by the first passage times of X.

$$\tau_X^{\pm}(y) = \inf\{t > 0 : X_t \gtreqless y\}, \quad \forall y \in I. \tag{A.4}$$

It is well-known that, for any $q > 0$, the Laplace transforms of the first passage times $\tau_X^{\pm}(y)$ give two independent solutions to the Sturm–Liouville equation $\mathcal{L}f(x) = qf(x)$. Specifically, for $x, \kappa \in I$, let us define

$$\phi_q^+(x) := \begin{cases} \mathbb{E}_x(e^{-q\tau_X^+(\kappa)}) & \text{if } x \leq \kappa, \\ \dfrac{1}{\mathbb{E}_\kappa(e^{-q\tau_X^+(x)})} & \text{if } x > \kappa, \end{cases} \qquad \phi_q^-(x) := \begin{cases} \dfrac{1}{\mathbb{E}_\kappa(e^{-q\tau_X^-(x)})} & \text{if } x \leq \kappa, \\ \mathbb{E}_x(e^{-q\tau_X^-(\kappa)}) & \text{if } x > \kappa. \end{cases}$$

Then the function $\phi_q^+(\cdot)$ (respectively, $\phi_q^-(\cdot)$) is a increasing (respectively, decreasing) positive solution of $\mathcal{L}f(x) = qf(x)$. Moreover, if boundary l (respectively, r) is inaccessible, then $\phi_q^-(l+) = \infty$ (respectively, $\phi_q^+(r-) = \infty$).

Fix a scale function $s(\cdot)$, there exists a constant $w_q > 0$ such that (see, e.g., Borodin and Salminen (2002, p. 19))

$$w_q \cdot s'(x) = \phi_q^{+,\prime}(x)\phi_q^-(x) - \phi_q^{-,\prime}(x)\phi_q^+(x). \tag{A.5}$$

Furthermore, we define function

$$W_q(x, y) := w_q^{-1} \cdot \det \begin{bmatrix} \phi_q^+(x) & \phi_q^+(y) \\ \phi_q^-(x) & \phi_q^-(y) \end{bmatrix}$$

$$= w_q^{-1} \phi_q^-(x)\phi_q^-(y)(\psi_q(x) - \psi_q(y)), \quad \forall x, y \in I, \tag{A.6}$$

where

$$\psi_q(x) := \frac{\phi_q^+(x)}{\phi_q^-(x)}, \quad \forall x \in I. \tag{A.7}$$

By the boundary behavior of X., we have $\phi_q^-(l+) = \phi_q^+(r-) = \infty$, hence $\psi_q(\cdot)$ is a strictly increasing function that maps I onto $\mathbb{R}_+$.

Regarding the first exit time of X. from a finite interval, we recall the following result regarding the first exit of X. from Lehoczky (1977, p. 603).

Lemma A.1. *Suppose that $x, y, z \in I$ such that $y < x < z$, for $q \geq 0$, we have*

$$\mathbb{E}_x(e^{-q\tau_X^-(y)} \mathbf{1}_{\{\tau_X^-(y) < \tau_X^+(z)\}}) = \mathbb{P}_x(\tau_X^-(y) < \tau_X^+(z) \wedge \mathbf{e}_q) = \frac{W_q(x,z)}{W_q(y,z)},$$

$$\mathbb{E}_x(e^{-q\tau_X^+(z)} \mathbf{1}_{\{\tau_X^+(z) < \tau_X^-(y)\}}) = \mathbb{P}_x(\tau_X^+(z) < \tau_X^-(y) \wedge \mathbf{e}_q) = \frac{W_q(y,x)}{W_q(y,z)},$$

where $\mathbf{e}_q$ is an (independent of X.) exponential random variable with mean $1/q$.

When $q = 0$, we extend the definition of $W_q(\cdot, \cdot)$ using

$$W_0(x,y) := s(x) - s(y). \tag{A.8}$$

Then the function $W_q(\cdot, \cdot)$ has the following properties.

Lemma A.2. *For any $x, y, z \in I$ with $x \neq y$, $q > 0$*

$$W_q(x,y) = -W_q(y,x), \quad \frac{\partial}{\partial x}\frac{W_q(x,y)}{W_q(x,z)} = \frac{W_q(y,z)}{W_q^2(x,z)} s'(x),$$

$$\lim_{q \downarrow 0} W_q(x,y) = W_0(x,y), \quad \lim_{q \downarrow 0} W_{q,1}(x,y) = s'(x)/(s(x) - s(y)),$$

where we have defined functions

$$W_{q,1}(x,y) := \frac{\frac{\partial}{\partial x} W_q(x,y)}{W_q(x,y)}, \quad W_{q,2}(x,y) := \frac{\frac{\partial^2}{\partial x \partial y} W_{q,1}(x,y)}{W_q(x,y)}. \tag{A.9}$$

Proof. Most formulas are straightforward and we omit the proofs for them. In the sequel we only prove

$$\lim_{q \downarrow 0} W_q(x,y) = W_0(x,y), \quad \forall x, y \in I.$$

To that end, we use (A.5) to obtain that, for $x \geq y$, $x, y \in I$,

$$\frac{\partial}{\partial x}\left(\frac{\phi_q^-(x)}{\phi_q^+(x)}\right) = -w_q \frac{s'(x)}{(\phi_q^+)^2(x)} \Rightarrow W_q(x,y) = \phi_q^+(x)\phi_q^+(y) \int_y^x \frac{s'(u)}{(\phi_q^+)^2(u)} du.$$

We observe from the regularity of X. that, $\phi_q^+(u)$, $u \in [y,x]$ is uniformly bounded (away from 0) for all $q \in [0, q_0]$ for any fixed $q_0 > 0$:

$$0 < \mathbb{E}_y(e^{-q_0 \tau_X^+(\kappa)}) \leq \phi_q^+(u) \leq \frac{1}{\mathbb{E}_\kappa(e^{-q_0 \tau_X^+(x)})} < \infty, \quad \forall u \in [y,x].$$

Moreover, for $u \in [y, x] \subsetneq I$.

$$\lim_{q \to 0+} \phi_q^+(u) = \begin{cases} \mathbb{P}_u(\tau_X^+(\kappa) < \infty) & \text{if } u \leq \kappa \\ \dfrac{1}{\mathbb{P}_\kappa(\tau_X^+(u) < \infty)} & \text{if } u > \kappa \end{cases} = \lim_{y \downarrow l} \frac{s(u) - s(y)}{s(\kappa) - s(y)}$$

$$= \beta_1 s(u) + \beta_2,$$

for some constant β_1, β_2 depending on the behavior of limit $\lim_{y \downarrow l} s(y)$. By dominated convergence theorem, as $q \downarrow 0$,

(1) if $\beta_1 \neq 0$,

$$W_q(x, y) \to (\beta_1 s(x) + \beta_2)(\beta_1 s(y) + \beta_2) \int_y^x \frac{s'(u) du}{(\beta_1 s(u) + \beta_2)^2}$$

$$= \frac{1}{\beta_1}[(\beta_1 s(x) + \beta_2) - (\beta_1 s(y) + \beta_2)]$$

$$= s(x) - s(y) = W_0(x, y);$$

(2) if $\beta_1 = 0$, then $\beta_2 \geq \mathbb{E}_y(e^{-q_0 \tau_X^+(\kappa)}) > 0$, and

$$W_q(x, y) \to \beta_2^2 \int_y^x \frac{s'(u) du}{\beta_2^2} = s(x) - s(y) = W_0(x, y). \tag{A.10}$$

This completes the proof. □

Bibliography

Abate, J. and Valkó, P. (2004). Multi-precision Laplace transform inversion, *International Journal for Numerical Methods in Engineering* **60**, 5, pp. 979–993.

Abate, J. and Whitt, W. (2006). A unified framework for numerically inverting Laplace transforms, *INFORMS Journal on Computing* **18**, pp. 408–421.

Albrecher, H., Gerber, H. and Shiu, E. (2011). The optimal dividend barrier in the Gamma–Omega model, *European Actuarial Journal* **1**, 1, pp. 43–55.

Andersen, S. (1957). On the collective theory of risk in case of contagion between claims, *Transactions of the XVth International Congress of Actuaries* **2**, pp. 104–125.

Anderson, T. (1960). A modification of the sequential probability ratio test to reduce the sample size, *Annals of Mathematical Statistics* **31**, 1, pp. 165–197.

Angoshtari, B., Bayraktar, E. and Young, V. (2015). Minimizing the expected lifetime spend in drawdown under proportional consumption, *Finance Research Letters* **15**, pp. 106–114.

Angoshtari, B., Bayraktar, E. and Young, V. (2016a). Minimizing the probability of lifetime drawdown under constant consumption, *Insurance: Mathematics and Economics* **69**, pp. 210–223.

Angoshtari, B., Bayraktar, E. and Young, V. (2016b). Optimal investment to minimize the probability of drawdown, *Stochastics: An International Journal of Probability and Stochastic Processes* **88**, 6, pp. 946–958.

Asmussen, S., Avram, F. and Pistorius, M. R. (2004). Russian and American put options under exponential phase-type Lévy models, *Stochastic Processes and their Applications* **109**, 1, pp. 79–111, doi:10.1016/j.spa.2003.07.005.

Avram, F., Kyprianou, A. E. and Pistorius, M. R. (2004). Exit problems for spectrally negative Lévy processes and applications to (Canadized) Russian options, *Annals of Applied Probability* **14**, pp. 215–235.

Avram, F., Vu, N. L. and Zhou, X. (2017). On taxed spectrally negative Lévy processes with draw-down stopping, *Insurance: Mathematics and Economics* **76**, pp. 69–74.

Baurdoux, E., Palmowski, Z. and Pistorius, M. (2017). On future drawdown of lévy processes, *Stochastic Processes and their Applications* **127**, 8, pp. 2679–2698.

Ben-Salah, Z., Guérin, H., Morales, M. and Firouzi, H. O. (2015). On the depletion problem for an insurance risk process: new non-ruin quantities in collective risk theory, *European Actuarial Journal* **5**, 2, pp. 381–425.

Bertoin, J. (1996). *Lévy Processes*, Cambridge Tracts in Mathematics, Vol. 121 (Cambridge University Press, Cambridge).

Borodin, A. and Salminen, P. (2002). *Handbook of Brownian Motion: Facts and Formulae*, 2nd edn. (Birkhäuser).

Bowie, J. and Carr, P. (1994). Static simplicity, *Risk* **7**, pp. 45–49.

Breeden, D. and Litzenberger, R. (1978). Price of state contingent claims implicit in option prices, *Journal of Business* **51**, pp. 621–651.

Brémaud, P. (1981). *Point Processes and Queues, Martingale Dynamics* (Springer, New York).

Burghardt, G., Duncan, R. and Liu, L. (2003). Deciphering drawdown, *Risk* **5**, pp. S16–S20.

Cai, N., Chen, N. and Wan, X. (2010). Occupation times of jump-diffusion processes with double exponential jumps and the pricing of options, *Mathematics of Operations Research* **35**, 2, pp. 412–437.

Carr, P. (2011). Semi-static hedging of barrier options under Poisson jumps, *International Journal of Theoretical and Applied Finance* **14**, 7, pp. 1091–1111.

Carr, P. and Chou, A. (1997). Breaking barriers, *Risk* **10**, pp. 139–146.

Carr, P., Ellis, K. and Gupta, V. (1998). Static hedging of exotic options, *Journal of Finance* **53**, 3, pp. 1165–1190.

Carr, P., Jarrow, R. and Myneni, R. (1992). Alternative characterizations of American put options, *Mathematical Finance* **2**, pp. 87–105.

Carr, P. and Madan, D. (1999). Option valuation using the fast Fourier transform, *Journal of Computational Finance* **2**, 4, pp. 61–73.

Carr, P. and Madan, D. (2001). Optimal positioning in derivative securities, *Quantitative Finance* **1**, pp. 19–37.

Carr, P., Zhang, H. and Hadjiliadis, O. (2011). Maximum drawdown insurance, *International Journal of Theoretical and Applied Finance* **14**, 8, pp. 1195–1230.

Carraro, L., El Karoui, N. and Obłój, J. (2012). On Azéma–Yor processes, their optimal properties and the Bachelier-drawdown equation, *The Annals of Probability* **40**, 1, pp. 372–400.

Cartea, A., Jaimungal, S. and Penalva, J. (2015). *Algorithmic and High-Frequency Trading* (Cambridge University Press, Cambridge).

Chaumont, L. (2013). On the law of the supremum of Lévy processes, *Annals of Probability* **41**, 3A, pp. 1191–1217.

Chaumont, L. and Małecki, J. (2016). The asymptotic behavior of the density of the supremum of Lévy processes, *Annales de l'Institut Henri Poincaré (B) Probabilités et Statistiques* **52**, 3, pp. 1178–1195.

Chekhlov, A., Uryasev, S. and Zabarankin, M. (2005). Drawdown measure in portfolio optimization, *International Journal of Theoretical and Applied Finance* **8**, 1, pp. 13–58.

Chen, X., Landriault, D., Li, B. and Li, D. (2015). On minimizing drawdown risks of lifetime investments, *Insurance: Mathematics and Economics* **65**, pp. 46–54.

Cheridito, P., Nikeghbali, A. and Platen, E. (2012). Processes of class Sigma, last passage times, and drawdowns, *SIAM Journal on Financial Mathematics* **3**, 1, pp. 280–303.

Cherny, V. and Obłój, J. (2013). Portfolio optimisation under non-linear drawdown constraint in a semi-martingale financial model, *Finance and Stochastics* **17**, 4, pp. 771–800.

Chesney, M. and Gauthier, L. (2006). American Parisian options, *Finance and Stochastics* **10**, 4, pp. 475–506.

Chesney, M., Jeanblanc, M. and Yor, M. (1997). Brownian excursions and Parisian barrier options, *Advances in Applied Probability* **29**, 1, pp. 165–184.

Chesney, M., Jeanblanc-Picque, M. and Yor, M. (1995). Parisian options and excursions theory, in *The 5th Annual Derivative Conference* (Cornell).

Cheung, K. and Yang, H. (2005). Optimal stopping behavior of equity-linked investment products with regime switching, *Insurance: Mathematics and Economics* **37**, 3, pp. 599–614.

Consul, P. and Famoye, F. (2006). *Lagrangian Probability Distributions* (Birkhäuser, Boston).

Cui, Z. and Nguyen, D. (2017). Magnitude and speed of consecutive market crashes in a diffusion model, *Methodology and Computing in Applied Probability*, pp. 1–19.

Cvitanić, J. and Karatzas, I. (1995). On portfolio optimization under drawdown constraints, *IMA Lecture Notes in Mathematical Applications* **65**, pp. 77–78.

Czarna, I. and Palmowski, Z. (2011). Ruin probability with Parisian delay for a spectrally negative Lévy risk process, *Journal of Applied Probability* **48**, 4, pp. 984–1002.

Dassios, A. and Wu, S. (2010). Perturbed Brownian motion and its application to Parisian option pricing, *Finance and Stochastics* **14**, pp. 473–494.

Dayanik, S. and Karatzas, I. (2003). On the optimal stopping problem for one-dimensional diffusions, *Stochastic Processes and their Applications Appl.* **107** (**2**), pp. 173–212.

Derman, E., Ergener, D. and Kani, I. (1994). Forever hedged, *Risk* **7**, pp. 139–145.

Douady, R., Shiryaev, A. and Yor, M. (2000). On probability characteristics of "downfalls" in a standard Brownian motion, *Theory of Probability and Its Applications* **44**, pp. 29–38.

Egami, E., Leung, T. and Yamazaki, K. (2013). Default swap games driven by spectrally negative Lévy processes, *Stochastic Processes and their Applications* **123**, 2, pp. 347–384.

Egami, M. and Oryu, T. (2015). An excursion-theoretic approach to regulator's bank reorganization problem, *Operations Research* **63**, 3, pp. 527–539.

Egami, M. and Oryu, T. (2017). A direct solution method for pricing options involving the maximum process, *Finance and Stochastics*, **21**, 4, pp. 967–993.

Elie, R. and Touzi, N. (2008). Optimal lifetime consumption and investment under drawdown constraint, *Finance and Stochastics* **12**, pp. 299–330.

Forde, M., Pogudin, A. and Zhang, H. (2013). Hitting times, occupation times, trivariate laws and the forward Kolmogorov equation for a one-dimensional diffusion with memory, *Advances in Applied Probability* **45**, 3, pp. 860–875.

Gapeev, P. and Rodosthenous, N. (2014). Optimal stopping problems in diffusion-type models with running maxima and drawdowns, *Journal of Applied Probability* **51**, 3, pp. 799–817.

Gapeev, P. and Rodosthenous, N. (2016a). On the drawdowns and drawups in diffusion-type models with running maxima and minima, *Journal of Mathematical Analysis and Applications* **434**, pp. 413–431.

Gapeev, P. and Rodosthenous, N. (2016b). Perpetual American options in diffusion-type models with running maxima and drawdowns, *Stochastic Processes and their Applications* **126**, 7, pp. 2038–2061.

Gerber, H., Shiu, E. and Yang, H. (2012). The Omega model: from bankruptcy to occupation times in the red, *European Actuarial Journal* **2**, 2, pp. 259–272.

Glynn, P. and Iglehart, D. (1995). Trading securities using trailing stops, *Management Science* **41**, pp. 1096–1106.

Goldberg, L. and Mahmoud, O. (2017). Drawdown: from practice to theory and back again, *Mathematics and Financial Economics* **11**, 3, pp. 275–297.

Graversen, S. and Shiryaev, A. (2000). An extension of P. Lévy's distributional properties to the case of a Brownian motion with drift, *Bernoulli* **6**, 4, pp. 615–620.

Grossman, S. J. and Zhou, Z. (1993). Optimal investment strategies for controlling drawdowns, *Mathematical Finance* **3**, 3, pp. 241–276.

Hadjiliadis, O. (2005). *Change-point detection of two-sided alternative in a Brownian motion model and its connection to the gambler's ruin problem with relative wealth perception*, Ph.D. thesis, Columbia University.

Hadjiliadis, O. and Večeř, J. (2006). Drawdowns preceding rallies in a Brownian motion model, *Quantitative Finance* **5**, 5, pp. 403–409.

Hadjiliadis, O., Zhang, H. and Poor, H. V. (2009). One-shot schemes for decentralized quickest detection, *IEEE Transactions on Information Theory* **55**, 7, pp. 3346–3359.

Hu, Y., Shi, Z. and Yor, M. (2015). The maximal drawdown of the Brownian meander, *Electronic Communications in Probability* **20**, 39, pp. 1–6.

Imkeller, N. and Rogers, L. (2014). Trading to stops, *SIAM Journal on Financial Mathematics* **5**, 1, pp. 753–781.

Itô, K. and McKean, H. (1965). *Diffusion Processes and Their Sample Paths* (Springer).

Jarrow, R., Kchia, Y. and Protter, P. (2011). How to detect an asset bubble, *SIAM Journal on Financial Mathematics* **2**, pp. 839–865.

Jeanblanc, M., Yor, M. and Chesney, M. (2009). *Mathematical Methods for Financial Markets* (Springer Finance).

Jeulin, T. (1980). Semi-martingale et grossissement d'une filtration, in *Lecture Notes in Mathematics* 833 (Springer, Berlin), pp. 61–72.

Jeulin, T. and Yor, M. (1978). Grossissement d'une filtration et semi-martingales: formules explicites, in *Lecture Notes in Mathematics* 649 (Springer, Berlin), pp. 78–97.

Johansen, A. (2003). Characterization of large price variations in financial markets, *Physica A: Statistical Mechanics and its Applications* **324**, 1–2, pp. 157–166.

Kallenberg, O. (2002). *Foundations of Modern Probability*, 2nd edn., Probability and its Applications (Springer, New York).

Karatzas, I. and Shreve, S. (1991). *Brownian motion and Stochastic Calculus* (Springer).

Kardaras, C. (2015). On the stochastic behavior of optional processes up to random times, *The Annals of Applied Probability* **25**, 2, pp. 429–464.

Kovalov, P. and Linetsky, V. (2006). Pricing convertible bonds with stock price, interest rate and credit risks, Working Paper, Northwestern University.

Kuznetsov, A., Kyprianou, A. E. and Rivero, V. (2013). The theory of scale functions for spectrally negative Lévy processes, *Springer Lecture Notes in Mathematics* **2061**, pp. 97–186.

Kwaśnicki, M., Małecki, J. and Ryznar, M. (2013). Suprema of Lévy processes, *Annals of Probability* **41**, pp. 2047–2065.

Kyprianou, A. E. (2006). *Introductory Lectures on Fluctuations of Lévy Processes with Applications*, Universitext (Springer, Berlin).

Kyprianou, A. E. and Palmowski, Z. (2007). Distributional study of de Finetti's dividend problem for a general Lévy insurance risk process, *Journal of Applied Probability* **44**, 2, pp. 428–448.

Kyprianou, A. E., Pardo, J. C. and Pérez, J. L. (2014). Occupation times of refracted Lévy processes, *Journal of Theoretical Probability* **27**, 4, pp. 1292–1315.

Landriault, D., Li, B. and Li, S. (2015a). Analysis of a drawdown-based regime-switching Lévy insurance model, *Insurance: Mathematics and Economics* **60**, pp. 98–107.

Landriault, D., Li, B. and Zhang, H. (2015b). On the frequency of drawdowns for Brownian motion processes, *Journal of Applied Probability* **52**, 1, pp. 191–208.

Landriault, D., Li, B. and Zhang, H. (2017a). On magnitude, asymptotics and duration of drawdowns for Lévy models, *Bernoulli* **23**, 1, pp. 432–458.

Landriault, D., Li, B. and Zhang, H. (2017b). A unified approach for drawdown (drawup) of time-homogeneous Markov processes, *Journal of Applied Probability* **54**, 2, pp. 603–636.

Landriault, D., Renaud, J.-F. and Zhou, X. (2011). Occupation times of spectrally negative Lévy processes with applications, *Stochastic Processes and Their Applications* **121**, 11, pp. 2629–2641.

Leal, P. C. and Mendes, B. (2005). Maximum drawdown: models and applications, *Journal of Alternative Investments* **7**, 4, pp. 83–91.

Lehoczky, J. (1977). Formulas for stopped diffusion processes with stopping times based on the maximum, *Annals of Probability* **5**, 4, pp. 601–607.

Leung, T. and Li, X. (2015). Optimal mean reversion trading with transaction costs and stop-loss exit, *International Journal of Theoretical and Applied Finance* **18**, 3, p. 1550020.

Leung, T., Li, X. and Wang, Z. (2014). Optimal starting–stopping and switching of a CIR process with fixed costs, *Risk and Decision Analysis* **5**, 2, pp. 149–161.

Leung, T., Li, X. and Wang, Z. (2015). Optimal multiple trading times under the exponential OU model with transaction costs, *Stochastic Models* **31**, 4, pp. 554–587.

Leung, T. and Ludkovski, M. (2011). Optimal timing to purchase options, *SIAM Journal on Financial Mathematics* **2**, 1, pp. 768–793.

Leung, T. and Yamazaki, K. (2013). American step-up and step-down credit default swaps under Lévy models, *Quantitative Finance* **13**, 1, pp. 137–157.

Leung, T. and Zhang, H. (2017). Optimal trading with a trailing stop, Available at https://ssrn.com/abstract=2895437.

Li, B. and Zhou, X. (2013). The joint Laplace transforms for diffusion occupation times, *Advances in Applied Probability* **45**, pp. 1049–1067.

Loeffen, R., Czarna, I. and Palmowski, Z. (2013). Parisian ruin probability for spectrally negative Lévy processes, *Bernoulli* **19**, 2, pp. 599–609.

Loeffen, R., Renaud, J.-F. and Zhou, X. (2014). Occupation times of intervals until first passage times for spectrally negative Lévy processes, *Stochastic Processes and their Applications* **124**, 3, pp. 1408–1435.

Magdon-Ismail, M. and Atiya, A. (2004). Maximum drawdown, *Risk* **17**, 10, pp. 99–102.

Magdon-Ismail, M., Atiya, A., Pratap, A. and Abu-Mostafa, Y. (2004). On the maximum drawdown of a Brownian motion, *Journal of Applied Probability* **41**, 1, pp. 147–161.

Mahmoud, O. (2017). The temporal dimension of risk, *Journal of Risk* **19**, 3, pp. 57–93.

Meilijson, I. (2003). The time to a given drawdown in Brownian motion, *Seminaire de Probabilités XXXVII*, pp. 94–108.

Merton, R. (1976). Option pricing when underlying stock returns are discontinuous, *Journal of Financial Economics* **3**, pp. 125–144.

Mijatović, A. and Pistorius, M. (2012). On the drawdown of completely asymmetric Lévy processes, *Stochastic Processes and their Applications* **122**, 11, pp. 3812–3836.

Miura, R. (1992). A note on look-back options based on order statistics, *Hitotsubashi Journal of Commerce and Management* **27**, 1, pp. 15–28.

Miura, R. (2007). Rank process, stochastic corridor and applications to finance, in *Advances in Statistical Modeling and Inference, Essays in Honor of Kjell A Doksum*, Chapter 26, pp. 529–542.

Moore, K. (2009). Optimal surrender strategies for equity-indexed annuity investors, *Insurance: Mathematics and Economics* **44**, 1, pp. 1–18.

Moore, K. and Young, V. (2005). Optimal design of a perpetual equity-indexed annuity, *North American Actuarial Journal* **9**, 1, pp. 57–72.

Nikeghbali, A. (2006). A class of remarkable submartingales, *Stochastic Processes and Their Applications* **116**, 6, pp. 917–938.

Ocone, D. (1993). A symmetry characterization of conditionally independent increment martingales, in *Barcelona Seminar on Stochastic Analysis*, Vol. 32 (Birkhäuser, Basel), pp. 147–167.

Ott, C. (2013). Optimal stopping problems for the maximum process with upper and lower caps, *The Annals of Applied Probability* **23**, 6, pp. 2327–2356.

Peskir, G. (1998). Optimal stopping of the maximum process: the maximality principle, *Annals of Probability* **26**, 4, pp. 1614–1640.

Peskir, G. and Shiryaev, A. N. (2006). *Optimal Stopping and Free-Boundary Problems*, Lectures in Mathematics (Birkhäuser, ETH Zurich).

Pfeffer, D. (2001). Sequential barrier options, *Algo Research Quarterly* **4**, pp. 65–74.

Pitman, J. and Yor, M. (1999). Laplace transforms related to excursions of a one-dimensional diffusion, *Bernoulli* **5**, 2, pp. 249–255.

Pitman, J. and Yor, M. (2003). Hitting, occupation and inverse local times of one-dimensional diffusions: martingale and excursion approaches, *Bernoulli* **9**, 1, pp. 1–24.

Poor, H. and Hadjiliadis, O. (2008). *Quickest Detection* (Cambridge University Press).

Pospisil, L. and Večeř, J. (2008). PDE methods for the maximum drawdown, *Journal of Computational Finance* **12**, pp. 59–76.

Pospisil, L. and Večeř, J. (2010). Portfolio sensitivities to the changes in the maximum and the maximum drawdown, *Quantitative Finance* **10**, 6, pp. 617–627.

Pospisil, L., Večeř, J. and Hadjiliadis, O. (2009). Formulas for stopped diffusion processes with stopping times based on drawdowns and drawups, *Stochastic Processes and its Applications* **119**, 8, pp. 2563–2578.

Protter, P. (2003). *Stochastic Integration and Differential Equations* (Springer).

Rebonato, R. and Gaspari, V. (2006). Analysis of drawdowns and drawups in the US$ interest-rate market, *Quantitative Finance* **6**, 4, pp. 297–326.

Revuz, D. and Yor, M. (1999). *Continuous Martingale and Brownian Motions*, 3rd edn. (Springer).

Rodosthenous, N. and Zervos, M. (2017). Watermark options, *Finance and Stochastics* **21**, 1, pp. 157–186.

Rodosthenous, N. and Zhang, H. (2017). Beating the Omega clock: an optimal stopping problem with random time-horizon under spectrally negative Lévy models, *The Annals of Applied Probability*, forthcoming.

Rolski, T., Schmidli, H., Schmidt, V. and Teugels, J. (1999). *Stochastic Processes for Insurance and Finance* (Wiley, New York).

Ross, S. (2008). *A First Course in Probability* (Prentice-Hall).

Salkuyeh, K. (2006). Positive integer powers of the tridiagonal Toeplitz matrix, *International Mathematical Forum* **1**, 22, pp. 1061–1065.

Salminen, P. and Vallois, P. (2007). On maximum increase and decrease of Brownian motion, *Annales de l'Institut Henri Poincaré (B) Probabilités et Statistiques* **43**, 6, pp. 655–676.

Sato, K. (1999). *Lévy Processes and Infinitely Divisible Distributions* (Cambridge University Press, Cambridge).

Sbuelz, A. (2005). Hedging double barriers with singles, *International Journal of Theoretical and Applied Finance* **8**, pp. 393–406.

Schuhmacher, F. and Eling, M. (2011). Sufficient conditions for expected utility to imply drawdown-based performance rankings, *Journal of Bank and Finance* **35**, 9, pp. 2311–2318.

Sekine, J. (2013). Long-term optimal investment with a generalized drawdown constraint, *SIAM Journal on Financial Mathematics* **4**, 1, pp. 452–473.

Shepp, L. and Shiryaev, A. N. (1993). The Russian option: reduced regret, *Annals of Applied Probability* **3**, 3, pp. 603–631.

Shiryaev, A. N. (1996). Minmax optimality of the method of cumulative sums (CUSUM) in the continuous time, *Russian Mathematical Surveys* **51**, 4, pp. 750–751.

Shiryaev, A. N. (1999). *Essentials of Stochastic Finance* (World Scientific).

Sornette, D. (2003). *Why Stock Markets Crash: Critical Events in Complex Financial Systems* (Princeton University Press).

Tanré, E. and Vallois, P. (2007). Range of Brownian motion with drift, *Journal of Theoretical Probability* **19**, 1, pp. 46–69.

Taylor, H. (1975). A stopped Brownian motion formula, *Annals of Probability* **3**, 2, pp. 234–246.

Tehranchi, M. (2009). Symmetric martingales and symmetric smiles, *Stochastic Processes and Their Applications* **119**, pp. 3785–3797.

Temme, N. (2000). Numerical and asymptotic aspects of parabolic cylinder functions, *Journal of Computational and Applied Mathematics* **121**, 1–2, pp. 221–246.

Večeř, J. (2006). Maximum drawdown and directional trading, *Risk* **19**, 12, pp. 88–92.

Večeř, J. (2007). Preventing portfolio losses by hedging maximum drawdown, *Wilmott* **5**, 4, pp. 1–8.

Warburton, A. and Zhang, Z. (2006). A simple computational model for analyzing the properties of stop-loss, take profit, and price breakout trading strategies, *Computers and Operations Research* **33**, 1, pp. 32–42.

Willmot, G. and Lin, X. (2011). Risk modeling with the mixed Erlang distribution, *Applied Stochastic Models in Business and Industry* **27**, pp. 2–16.

Yamamoto, K., Sato, S. and Takahashi, A. (2010). Probability distribution and option pricing for drawdown in a stochastic volatility environment, *International Journal of Theoretical and Applied Finance* **13**, 2, pp. 335–354.

Yin, G., Zhang, Q. and Zhuang, C. (2010). Recursive algorithms for trailing stop: stochastic approximation approach, *Journal of Optimization Theory and Applications* **146**, 1, pp. 209–231.

Zhang, H. (2015). Occupation time, drawdowns, and drawups for one-dimensional regular diffusion, *Advances in Applied Probability* **47**, 1, pp. 210–230.

Zhang, H. and Hadjiliadis, O. (2010). Drawdowns and rallies in a finite time-horizon, *Methodology and Computing in Applied Probability* **12**, 2, pp. 293–308.

Zhang, H. and Hadjiliadis, O. (2012a). Drawdowns and the speed of market crash, *Methodology and Computing in Applied Probability* **14**, pp. 739–752.

Zhang, H. and Hadjiliadis, O. (2012b). Quickest detection in a system with correlated noise, *Proceedings of the 51st IEEE Conference on Decision and Control*, pp. 4757–4763.

Zhang, H., Hadjiliadis, O., Schäfer, T. and Poor, H. V. (2014). Quickest detection in coupled systems, *SIAM Journal on Control and Optimization* **52**, 3, pp. 1567–1596.

Zhang, H., Leung, T. and Hadjiliadis, O. (2013). Stochastic modeling and fair valuation of drawdown insurance, *Insurance, Mathematics and Economics* **53**, pp. 840–850.

Zhang, H., Rodosthenous, N. and Hadjiliadis, O. (2015). Robustness of the N-CUSUM stopping rule in a Wiener disorder problem, *The Annals of Applied Probability* **25**, 6, pp. 3405–3433.

Index

A

α-quantile option, 95
Ascending ladder
    height, 104
    time, 104

B

Binary option, 139
Brownian motion with drift, 24, 53, 59, 91
Brownian motion with drift model, 122

C

CEV model, 54
Characteristic exponent of a Lévy process, 104

D

Digital call
    on maximum drawdown, 137
    on the K-drawdown preceding a K-drawup, 137
Doob–Meyer decomposition, 45
Drawdown, 1
Drawdown insurance, 178
    cancellable, 180
    on a defaultable stock, 191

Drawdown insurance with drawup contingency
    finite maturity, 187
    perpetual, 189
Drawdown times
    with recovery, 60
    without recovery, 60
Drawup, 4
Duration of drawdown, 99

E

Early liquidation premium, 206, 213, 220
Exponential OU model, 216

G

Geometric Brownian motion, 35, 156, 172, 177

K

Kou's model, 124

L

Lévy process, 99
    spectrally negative, 101
Laplace exponent of a spectrally negative Lévy process, 101
Linear diffusion, 28, 43, 81, 205, 225